# Christopher Okigbo
## 1930–67
*Thirsting for Sunlight*

# Christopher Okigbo

## 1930–67

*Thirsting for Sunlight*

OBI NWAKANMA

 JAMES CURREY

James Currey
www.jamescurrey.com
is an imprint of Boydell & Brewer Ltd
PO Box 9, Woodbridge, Suffolk IP12 3DF, UK
and of Boydell & Brewer Inc.
668 Mt Hope Avenue, Rochester, NY 14620–2731, USA
www.boydellandbrewer.com

First published in hardback 2010
First published in paperback in Nigeria by HEBN 2010
First published in paperback in the rest of the world by James Currey 2017

The publisher has no responsibility for the continued existence or accuracy of URLs for
external or third-party internet websites referred to in this book, and does not guarantee
that any content on such websites is, or will remain, accurate or appropriate.

This publication is printed on acid-free paper

British Library Cataloguing in Publication Data is available on request

ISBN 978-1-84701-013-1 (James Currey cloth)
ISBN 978-1-84701-179-4 (James Currey paperback)
ISBN 978-978-081-371-0 (HEBN paperback)

Typeset in 10/11 pt Monotype Garamond
by Long House Publishing Services, Cumbria, UK

Printed and bound in Great Britain by
TJ International Ltd, Padstow, Cornwall

*For Pius Okigbo*

1924–2000

---

*Matthew Oparaocha Nwakanma*

1933–2009

# Published Work of Christopher Okigbo

*Heavensgate* first published © Mbari 1962
*Distances* first published in *Transition No. 16* 1964
*Silences* first published:
Part 1 *Lament of the Silent Sisters* in *Transition No. 8* 1963
and Part II *Lament of the Drums* © Mbari 1965
*Path of Thunder* first published in *Black Orpheus*, February 1968
*Limits* © Christopher Okigbo 1964
*Labyrinths with Path of Thunder* (London, Ibadan, Nairobi: Heinemann 1971. Published in association with Mbari Publishers, Ibadan; reprinted by Africa World Press: Trenton, NJ, 2008)

$\qquad$ *Heavensgate*
I $\quad$ 'The Passage' (1961)
II $\quad$ 'Initiations' (1960/1)
III $\quad$ 'Watermaid' (1961)
IV $\quad$ 'Lustra' (1960/1)
V $\quad$ 'Newcomer' (1961)

$\qquad$ *Limits*
I–IV $\quad$ 'Siren Limits' (1961)
V–XII $\quad$ 'Fragments out of the Deluge (1961/2)

$\qquad$ *Silences*
I $\quad$ 'Lament of the Silent Sisters' (1962)
II $\quad$ 'Lament of the Drums' (1964)

$\qquad$ *Distances* [1964]

$\qquad$ *Path of Thunder*

'Dance of the Painted Maidens', in Maja-Pearce, Adewale (ed.) *Collected Poems of Christopher Okigbo* (London: William Heinemann 1986)
'Debtor's Lane' (1958) *The Horn*, 3:2 (1959-60)
*Four Canzones* (1956-61) *Black Orpheus* 2 (1962)
'Lament of the Flutes' (Ojoto, 1960), in Langston Hughes (ed.) *Poems from Black Africa* (Bloomington, IN: Indiana University Press, 1963)
'Moonglow' in Frances Ademola (ed.) *Reflections: Nigerian Prose and Verse* (Lagos: African Universities Press, 1962)

# Contents

# Preface

I first stumbled across the name Christopher Okigbo in the scorebooks and cricket records at the Government College, Umuahia – the English-style public boarding school at which Okigbo preceded me by what seemed like light years. He gained my admiration originally for his abilities in cricket. Then in 1984, one year after leaving the Government College, Umuahia, I read a memorial piece written on Okigbo by the journalist Mike Awoyinfa, which appeared in the *National Concord*.[1] My curiosity was reinforced by a birthday gift of *Labyrinths* from my father.

After my first encounter with Christopher Okigbo's poetry, love grew like a mustard seed. I was challenged to make a full discovery of Okigbo's human essence, a prospect, which I thought, would unveil the enigma of the poetry. That first encounter was an initiation: it was the first time of experiencing total submission to the lure of poetry – the haunting lyricism of Okigbo's poetry – at the end of which there was, in fact, no end. There was only that purge of the emotions described by the critic Sunday Anozie as so characteristic of Okigbo's poetry.[2]

Works by Sunday Anozie and Professor D.I Nwoga offered me only brief, though useful, biographical insights into the life of the poet. I felt that more needed to be done to give flesh to Okigbo's bones. I wanted to recover him fully as an individual who lived intensely, and who wrote poetry that was volcanic and enchanting. In setting about this task, however, there was the immediate problem of a generational gap. In my case, I never met Christopher Okigbo. I was but an infant during the Biafra War which brought Okigbo's life to a sudden halt.

In 1988 the idea for this book actually germinated. I was on the final lap of undergraduate work in the English department of the University of Jos, where Okigbo's friend the critic Professor Gerald Moore, had laid a firm foundation in literary studies. I did however make an important leap: I visited Nsukka and spoke with the renowned critic D. I. Nwoga, Professor of English at the University of Nigeria, who suggested a general layout for the book. Donatus Nwoga, one of the foremost scholars of Okigbo's poetry, communicated on and off with me about the biography until his untimely death in 1992.

The meeting with Professor Nwoga was fortunate. He exposed me to materials which kindled my interest, and I was furnished with zeal to work, even if I would not have sufficient time until later. Nduka Otiono's essay on Okigbo in the *Guardian*[3] of August 1990, spurred me further on my path, especially as it contained assertions which I felt could be further clarified and placed in broader terms around the life of the poet. Each time I read Okigbo, something seemed not quite finished. It was a feeling as mystical as the moment of apprehending the irresolute testament of Coleridge's 'Kubla Khan'. By placing Okigbo in time and clothing him with spirit, I hoped to close a crucial gap in modern African literature.

Literary biographies are necessarily difficult. Any attempt to evaluate the true worth of the writer and the true worth of the written word is subjective. Furthermore, there is not much of a tradition of literary biographies in Africa. Most of the writers who have emerged in the middle of the twentieth century still dominate the discourse of modern African literature and retain a contemporaneity which denies, I think, such biographical evaluation. Happily there are exceptions, such as the biography of the poet Léopold Senghor by the French biographer Armand Guibert and, more recently, Ezenwa Ohaeto's biography of the novelist Chinua Achebe.

There have also been some attempts to investigate and present the impact of Christopher Okigbo's poetry in post-colonial society – the domain of which he traverses magnificently. Several scholarly works have been dedicated to the study of this poetry, but they have tended only to dwell briefly, quite marginally in fact, on the complete life of Christopher Okigbo. The effect is that we do get a glimpse of the poet, but always in fragments. Most important among these are Sunday Anozie's *Christopher Okigbo: Creative Rhetoric,* D. I. Nwoga's *Perspectives on Okigbo,* and, more recently, Dubem Okafor's *Dance of Death: Nigerian Nation and Christopher Okigbo's Poetry.* Ali Mazrui's novel *The Trial of Christopher Okigbo* is also worthy of mention here. It puts Okigbo up for judgment, accused of sacrificing an artistic life for the cause of Biafra. The true value of such a work is in its fictional power to invent an overdetermined, figural presence and utilize this image of the poet to investigate and scrutinize the grey area between artistic commitment and martyrdom.

*Christopher Okigbo: Thirsting for Sunlight* does not attempt to raise critical or philo-sophic questions about the value of the literary text; rather, it aims at tracing Okigbo's path of growth and the influences that conspired to shape his life and poetry. It brings in an organic, sometimes interpretive tension, the various aspects of Okigbo's short but dramatic life – those 'dissonant airs' that he mentions in his own introduction to his poetry, which merge into the fullness of his personality. *Thirsting for Sunlight* also seeks to do for Okigbo in part, and only in part, what he set out himself to do in his now possibly permanently lost book, *Pointed Arches,* of which he wrote in a letter to his friend Sunday Anozie on 5 May 1966:

> *Pointed Arches* is neither fiction nor criticism nor autobiography. It is an attempt to describe the growth of the poetic impulse in me, an account of certain significant facts in my experience of life and letters that conspired to sharpen my imagination. It throws some light on certain apparently irreconcilable features in my work and life and places them in a new perspective.[4]

Because of the generational gap between Okigbo and myself, I have tried to 're-assemble' Christopher Okigbo from the points of view of his contemporaries with whom he shared his life intimately. Although Chinua Achebe, John Pepper Clark, Wole Soyinka, M.J.C. Echeruo or Ben Obumselu – indeed, any of Okigbo's numerous friends and contemporaries – would have been best suited to write a full account of his life, the simple fact is that they had not and, it seemed, were hardly likely to, is enough reason for this book to emerge. Perhaps members of that generation were hampered by events too personal and too painful to recall, especially Okigbo's early death under tragic circumstances. They may have been too scarred by memory and wished to put themselves at an emotional distance from the events of the Biafran war.

It is in any case the duty of a new generation of writers and literary historians to do the job of recovering for posterity the lives of those who have given vitality and illumination to our collective cultural experience and social history. Already, the generation born after independence is more familiar with the other icons of modern Nigerian literature: Chinua Achebe, Wole Soyinka, J.P. Clark and Gabriel Okara than they are with Christopher Okigbo. It is in that sense also, that this book is written largely for this anteceding generation so as to point to them on the map of time one of the twentieth century's most inspired voices.

In whatever way an explanation is offered, it always was difficult not to feel significant grief in remembering Christopher Okigbo. This has been my experience in encounters with his numerous friends and associates while researching his life: their recollections of Okigbo were frequently tinged with resigned regret and deeply felt tenderness to his memory. Occasions demand that certain deeply personal aspects of this account remain private. Therefore, out of respect for many of my informants, I have allowed no full mention of certain names, especially of some the women who at one point or another shared in Okigbo's complicated love life. This is deliberate. When this book began to take shape, many of these women had their own lives, and Okigbo's memory had become a mere aspect of a romantic past. I have taken time through extensive interviews and responses to weigh and cross check information, so I feel confident that I have done a work considerably devoid of the fancies, which time sometimes imposes on memory.

Okigbo's poetry is an elaborate ritual which reveals the complex dimensions of his experience of life. The poetry he wrote between 1958 and 1967 represents the period of his personal soul-search, his self-recovery, his imaginative awakening, and his creative homecoming or triumph, or coming to terms over 'a cruel past.'[5] However, for various reasons it has been difficult for scholars of Christopher Okigbo's poetry to arrive at a complete explanation of his agonistic impulse. In many cases, they merely associate his poetry with the abstract mythic forms of his modernist imagination, rather than the deeply personal meanings of his autobiographical quest, his cries of anguish that emerge out of a life tortured by profound self-doubts, complicated desires and the deep need for love – and to entertain. This is because in the seeming difficulty of Okigbo's poetry there was always a mask that hid him, and thus the failure to fully comprehend the man and the story of his life buried in his poetry. Mercifully, Okigbo's poetry actually offers an autobiographical statement. It is a *tour de force*; taking the trajectory of history to pursue the intimate process of his life; its failures, its pains and its triumphs. It accounts for the various phases of these events – like his own 'stations of the cross.'

Christopher Okigbo is entirely in the frame of the Whitmanian artist who encapsulates everything. Okigbo, this supremely kinetic and complex individual, has become perhaps not only one of the most celebrated figures of modern African literature but also one of the most significant figures among late modern twentieth-century poets. He retains a heroic, enigmatic dimension to his personality. Although he died young, his poetry encodes the essence of his uncommon life. It is rare that seventy-two pages of poetry shape the canon in any tradition.

Okigbo has made a deep impact on the character of modern Nigerian and African poetry – so much so that his strains abound in many of the works of serious poets coming out of Africa in the postcolonial period. Since his collected work, *Labyrinths* appeared in 1972 Okigbo has inspired a cult following far more than any writer of his generation in Africa. Ordinary readers of his poetry are however fed the constant fare about the difficulty or impenetrability of Okigbo's poetry. Yet, subsequent generations have invoked him as an emblem of the cult of rebellion, of the poet as a man of action, as an individual whose final statement was one of sacrifice and martyrdom. A phenomenon truly has been spawned which could be called 'Okigbolatry.' His influence among the new poets in Africa is so pervasive that his stature is ensured as one of the greatest poets to have emerged out of Africa writing in the English language.

Okigbo in poetry, Chinua Achebe in the fiction and Wole Soyinka in drama, are emblems of the best of modern Nigerian writing in English in the twentieth century. Yet, as a result of his untimely death, he is not as well known in academic circles outside Africa as his two compatriots. It is my hope that this biography will introduce Okigbo to a wider English-speaking international audience, who would find his poetry one of the most important and refreshing of African modernist poetic voices. For a poet of the stature of Christopher Okigbo, who is possibly the single most influential and most anthologized poet of his generation in Africa, there is an unfortunate narrowness among academics in determining how he is taught or read.

Okigbo's voice is charged, historical and importunate. It speaks to the depths of the events of his colonial and post-colonial encounters, and it reflects the conjunction of both history and the power of the poetic emotion. His voice is as valid today. It is a voice which provides insight into the dilemma of Africa and of the anguish of the individual poet who feels called upon by the times to bear its burden of memory and witness. It is also the burden of collective memory intertwined with the deeply private or personal. From Okigbo's poetry, we in fact, glimpse his anguish reconciled to the complex events, from the disruptions suffered out of colonialism to the elation of freedom associated with political independence, from the deep private scars of failed love to the anomie of postcolonial society. This poetry, more than any other written at this time in Africa, deals with man in his social and spiritual cosmos. It is this interaction of the material nature of the public voice with the tortured spiritual quest, that makes Okigbo unique as the poet of his generation.

This biography may therefore go beyond the simple account of a poet's life. As it gathers unto itself, I hope that it may well portray the period, the historical milieu that fashioned his sensibility and the deepest moments of his personal experience. I hope that it captures the lives of those individuals with whom he experienced the period. It may paint the picture of that entire generation between the colonial and postcolonial eras which was so utterly imbued with an idea of its own place in history yet, by some unfortunate fate, failed to realize it.[6] The life of the poet Christopher Okigbo is thus important in the sense that it harbours a reflection of the significant moments of Nigerian political history and of an important phase in the emergence of modern African literature of the twentieth century.

Man trudges along the corridors of time in quest for experience, seeking the timeless meanings of events which define or inscribe individual experience: Okigbo's experience explains a collective history and this book, in recounting his life, offers memory collectively shared. For, somehow through the poetry he wrote, Okigbo became a chronicler of Nigeria's national quest, the turbulence of his time, and the invocation of the soul of the entire black world in the era. The meaning, and the essential resolution of that historic quest individuated in Okigbo's poetry becomes etherized in the deeper fulfillment of his prophecy, and the ultimate pain of his anguished cry:

O mother mother Earth, unbind me; let this be
my last testament; let this be
The ram's hidden wish to the sword the sword's
secret prayer to the scabbard – ....

Earth, unbind me; let me be the prodigal; let this be
    the ram's ultimate prayer to the tether…

An old star departs, leaves us here on the shore
Gazing heavenward for a new star approaching;
The new star appears, foreshadows its going
Before a going and coming that goes on forever…[7]

Had Christopher Okigbo's star remained but a little longer among us, what more would he have left us? Somewhere in 1967 his story ends, prematurely. But he leaves us the enduring image of that sapling in the forest, still thirsting for sunlight.

The poet Okigbo lived a life so filled with the tumult of human spirit that his sister-in-law Georgette said several years after his death: 'Chris couldn't have lived long on earth.'[8] His was a life measured in the vast possibilities of his genius and its tragic, unnecessary end at the valley of death around Opi. Okigbo lived with dramatic intensity and enchantment – whether as a child at Ekwulobia, or at Fiditi as a teacher, or in Biafra as a combatant. He lived greedily, pursuing the sensuous life with the gusto of the prodigal: he had a mind that was explosive, so in need of experience and so very passionate. In his pursuit of the liberated pleasures he was constantly ahead of his time – and it was the time of the flower children. Poet, soldier, and lover, classical scholar, gun-runner, and civil servant, teacher, librarian, father, and even the water goddess Idoto's 'prodigal' – Christopher Okigbo was all of these rolled into one.

Obi Nwakanma
Lagos

## NOTES

1 Awoyinfa's essay appeared on the National Concord.
2 Sunday Anozie, *Christopher Okigbo: Creative Rhetoric* (New York: Africana Publishers, 1971).
3 Nduka Otiono, 'Christopher Okigbo: The Judgment of Time', *Guardian*, 25 August 1990.
4 Sunday Anozie, *Christopher Okigbo: Creative Rhetoric.*
5 Ben Obumselu, 'Christopher Okigbo: Poetic Portrait'. Essay delivered at 'Song for Idoto': A Celebration of Christopher Okigbo, National Museum, Enugu, 2 November 1996.
6 Wole Soyinka described this generation as 'the wasted generation' in his Agip Lectures, 1985.
7 Christopher Okigbo, from 'Elegy for Alto', *Labyrinths with Path of Thunder* (London: Heinemann, 1971), pp. 71–2.
8 Interview with Georgette Okigbo, Ilupeju, Lagos, 1992.

# Acknowledgements

In the course of this work I have relied on individuals too numerous to mention here to reconstruct the life and times of the poet Christopher Okigbo. Some, however, deserve special acknowledgement. The famous critic and Okigbo scholar Prof. Donatus Ibe Nwoga was the first person with whom I had discussions on the Okigbo biography when I visited him at Nsukka and I remained in occasional but lively correspondence with him on the subject of Okigbo until his untimely death in 1991. The solitude in me remembers him. I would like particularly to acknowledge the following, who sadly have also passed on, but without whose generosity and insight this work would certainly be poorer: Ambassador Leslie Harriman with whom I spent many evenings at the Apapa Boat club, with his wife Clara Edewor-Harriman, on the subject of his best friend, the poet; Prof. Eugene Femi Odunjo, Eno Namsey, Sam Okudu, Olu Akaraogun, Caleb Olaniyan, Rajat Neogy, Peter Chigbo, Rex Akpofure, Prof. Chike Obi, Ikpehare Aig-Imokhuede, G.I.C Eneli, Gaius Anoka, Gamaliel Onosode, Ralph Opara, Kalada Hart, Bola Ige, Nkem Nwankwo, Moses Udebiuwa, Ignatius Atigbi and Brigadier George Kurubo who both fed me numerous times at the Island club, Lagos, while recounting the life and times of Okigbo to me; Sunday Anozie, Banjo Solarun, Ben Enwonwu, Eme Awa, Okigbo's former boss, the minister, Kola Balogun , his former teachers at Umuahia, Prof. Saburi Biobaku, Wilberforce Alagoa, Isaac Dagogo Erekosima, Mr. W. Wareham; Dr. Kenneth Mellanby, first principal of the University College, Ibadan who generously agreed to a long chat with me in his Sheraton room in Lagos with his wife Gene, when he came to deliver the *Guardian* lecture; and the Welsh poet and Okigbo's friend, Peter Thomas who not only corresponded but also sent me manuscripts of his unpublished writings on Okigbo. I am also greatly indebted to Chinua Achebe with whom I first spoke about Okigbo in his country home in Ogidi during his visit to Nigeria in 1998; Wole Soyinka in spite of his busy schedule agreed to speak with me in his Abeokuta office, and even during his exile in the heat of events in 1994 managed also to correspond with me about Okigbo. I have at various times spoken with novelist V. C. Ike; the poet Gabriel Okara hosted me to a long conversation at his home at the Elekahia Estate in Port Harcourt, C.C. Momah who also generously provided me pictures; Ali Mazrui who first pointed me most auspiciously to Rajat Neogy, Alex Olu Ajayi, Dr. Patrick Amenechi, Bode Olajumoke, Ola Ladipo, Godwin Adokpaye. J.P. Clark who pointed me towards his poems *Casualties* during my visit to his home at the Ikeja GRA; Phillip Asiodu, Ulli Beier who gave me invaluable insights on Okigbo at a party hosted for him and his wife Georgina by the late Renarte Albertsen in Victoria Island, Lagos; Col. Ben Gbulie,

Femi Osofisan, James Ezeilo, Col. Tony Eze, Don Egbue, Lawrence Amu, Etim J. Ekong, Dr. Ebong Etuk, the Okali brothers: O.U. Okali and Prof. David O. Okali, Mmaju Kazie, Johnson C. Obi, Prof. Wilfred Chukudebelu, the critic Gerald Moore, Laz Ekwueme, Mabel Segun, Lewis Nkosi, Dubem Okafor, Helen Chukwuma, Augustine Onyeneke, publisher of the *Vanguard,* Sam Amuka, former University of Nigeria librarian, Sam Nwoye, Lalage Bown, Keith Sambrook, Obiorah Udechukwu, M.J.C. Echeruo, Isidore Okpewho, Obiwu who first pointed me to Okigbo's letter to V.C. Ike, and Kayode Jibowu, who spoke to me through a round of Golf at the Ikeja club. My numerous conversations and correspondences with these individuals enriched my perspectives on Okigbo. Various members of the Okigbo family also deserve special acknowledgement. The poet's brothers Lawrence Okigbo and Pius Okigbo were very supportive of my explorations. I spent a number of invigorating evenings with Dr. Pius Okigbo especially at his Sanusi Fafunwa home on Victoria Island talking about the poet. I am also grateful for the very useful insights of Okigbo's sisters Susan Anakwenze and Victoria Okuzu, and to Prof. Bede Okigbo, Dr. Charles Okigbo, and the younger Patrick Okigbo. The poet's wife, Ms Judith Safinat Attah, Nigeria's former minister for Women affairs and Ambassador to Spain and the Holy See most generously agreed to sit down with me to talk about her husband on the very eve of her departure to Rome to assume her new posting as Nigeria's Ambassador. I thank Ossie Enekwe, former Director of the Hansberry Institute of African Studies, University of Nigeria, Nsukka, who made it possible for me to spend some time there in 2000. Two men have been most generous and supportive of this work: Torch O. Taire, who not only has made available his time and library to me, but has always encouraged me in moments of self doubt. Prof. Ben Obumselu has been my guide through this work, steering towards that for which the poet himself depended so much on him: clarity. There are numerous individuals who saw me through emotionally difficult moments in the evolution of this work: my uncle Eugene and his family who gave me shelter and love in Lagos; my friends, but especially Maik and Angela Nwosu, Amanze Ibe, David Nosike, Ndubisi Obiorah, and of course, Elizabeth Nwaizu, whose love and friendship I am incapable of repaying. I would love to also acknowledge James Currey and Lynn Taylor, my editors at James Currey press, for all their work in the making of this book. Finally, my wife Mira, without whose judicious insight and valuable comments this work, again, would have been most impoverished deserves my highest gratitude. Needless to say, all shortcomings in this work can only be of my making.

# Chronology

|  |  |  |
|---|---|---|
| 16 August | 1930 | Christopher Okigbo is born in Ojoto. |
|  | 1935 | Anna Okigbo, the poet's mother dies in Amawbia. |
|  | 1936 | Okigbo family moves to Adazi. Okigbo enters the infant classes where he is first taught nursery ryhmes by the Irish nuns. |
|  | 1937 | James Okigbo marries Elizabeth, Okigbo's step-mother. |
|  | 1940 | The Okigbo family moves to Ekwulobia where the poet's father becomes headmaster of St. Joseph's School. |
|  | 1942 | Christopher Okigbo's father is transferred to St. Joseph's School, Asaba where Christopher enrolls in Standard IV. |
| June/December | 1944 | Okigbo passes Standard VI and takes the Government College, Umuahia entrance exam. |
| January | 1945 | Christopher Okigbo is admitted into the elite Government College, Umuahia. Among his contemporaries are the novelists Chinua Achebe (1944), V. C. Ike (1945) and Elechi Amadi (1948). |
|  | 1950 | Okigbo is admitted to University College, Ibadan to study Classics |
|  | 1951 | He meets and falls in love with Judith Safi Attah, princess and daughter of the powerful Attah of Igbirah who was a student at the St. Theresa's Girls School, Ibadan. |
|  | 1955 | He fails his degree examination, and leaves briefly to work for the Nigerian Tobacco Company (NTC). |
|  | 1956 | He returns to the University College Ibadan to repeat his degree examination, and graduates in June with Third Class honors. He returns to his job at the NTC as Sales Manager. |
|  | 1957 | Okigbo is employed as Trainee Manager at UAC with Leslie Harriman, Peter Chigbo, George Nwanze, and Michael Ibru. That same year he resigned from the UAC, and was recruited into the Administrative Service of the colonial civil service as Assistant Secretary and posted to be Private Secretary to the new Nigerian Minister for Information and Research, Kola Balogun. |
|  | 1958 | Okigbo embarks on his first international trip in the entourage of the Minister for Information and Research to |

the United States, Canada, and England. He proposes to Safi in Oxford. Late that year Okigbo was sacked from his civil service job.

December 1958    Alex Olu Ajayi offers him a job as Vice-Principal at the Fiditi Grammar School where he moves to teach Latin, Greek and English literature. He begins work on the *Four Canzones*.

1959    Meets John Pepper Clark who had also abandoned his studies that year at the University College, Ibadan following an emotional breakdown. Okigbo and Clark begin a life-long friendship. 'Debtors Lane' appears in *The Horn* magazine, the student journal edited by J.P. Clark.

1 October 1960    Nigeria becomes independent.

6 October 1960    Okigbo moves to the newly established University of Nigeria, Nsukka as the Acting University Librarian and begins work on *Heavensgate*.

1961    Okigbo completes *Heavensgate* and *Limits*. He is moved to the Library of the Enugu Campus of the University of Nigeria. Okigbo resigns late in 1961 and joins the Cambridge University Press as West African Regional Manager. Okigbo becomes part of the founding of the Mbari club in Ibadan and one of the editors of the *Black Orpheus* magazine.

1962    *Heavensgate* appears in *Black Orpheus*. Okigbo attends the Kampala Conference on African Writers in Makerere where he first reads *Limits*. He meets Rajat Neogy, editor and publisher of *Transition* magazine in Kampala. *Limits* appears in *Transition*. Okigbo becomes West African editor of the *Transition* magazine. *Limits* is published in Frances Ademola's *Reflections*. Okigbo completes 'Lament of the Silent Sisters.'

1963    Okigbo resigns as one of the editors of the *Black Orpheus* magazine. 'Lament of the Silent Sisters' appears in *Transition*. Okigbo had sent 'Lament of the Silent Sisters' to Henry Rago editor of *Poetry* magazine Chicago on May 23. His poem 'Lament of the Flutes' (with two flutes) also appear in Langston Hughes' *Poems from Black Africa*. Okigbo marries Safi Attah in a private ceremony in Ibadan.

1964    Okigbo's daughter, Ibrahimat Obiageli is born at the University College Hospital, Ibadan. Okigbo writes his poem 'Dance of the Painted Maidens' in celebration of the birth of his daughter. He completes work on 'Lament of the Drums,' the second part of the *Silences*. He writes the elegiac 'Lament of the Mask' a commemorative poem for W.B. Yeats published by Maxwell and Bushrui that year. Okigbo becomes increasingly politically disillusioned following the 1964 national census.

1965    He participates in the Commonwealth Festival of Arts in London, where 'Lament of the Drums' and 'Dance of the Painted Maidens' are first performed. Okigbo begins work on *Path of Thunder*.

| | | |
|---|---|---|
| 15 January | 1966 | Christopher Okigbo's close friend, Major Emmanuel A Ifeajuna leads the first military coup in Nigeria in Lagos. The coup fails. |
| 17 January | 1966 | Ifeajuna arrives at Okigbo's home, Cambridge House, from where Okigbo smuggles him out to Ghana through the Dahomey border. |
| February | 1966 | Okigbo brings back Ifeajuna from Ghana, along with the poet J. P. Clark, on the request of the military Head of State, Major General Aguiyi-Ironsi. |
| 29 July | 1966 | General Ironsi is assassinated in Ibadan. An ethnic cleansing of the Igbo commences. Okigbo escapes assassination both at his home in Cambridge House and at the road to the Ikeja airport in Lagos. |
| August | 1966 | Okigbo settles in Enugu and begins Citadel Press, a publishing house he sets up with his friends, the novelists Chinua Achebe and V.C. Ike. |
| September | 1966 | Okigbo begins to run arms into Biafra on behalf of the Eastern regional government. |
| 6 July | 1967 | The Nigerian civil war begins. Okigbo volunteers for the Biafran forces and goes to fight to defend Nsukka. |
| 20 September | 1967 | Okigbo is killed in action at Opi junction. |

For he was a shrub among the poplars.
Needing more roots
More sap to grow to sunlight,
Thirsting for sunlight ...

(from 'Siren Limits', *Limits* I–IV 1961)


Death lay in ambush that evening in that island;
voice sought its echo that evening in that island.

And the eye lost its light,
the light lost its shadow.

For the wind, eternal suitor of dead leaves,
unrolled his bandages to the finest swimmer ...

(from *Distances* 1964)

1. 1945 School House photo, Government College, Umuahia. The boys sitting on the grass (or lowest step of the Admin Block) were mostly freshers: Sitting from the left Bassey Inyang, V.C. Ike, Celestine Egbuchulam, boy name unknown. Okigbo sits third from the right followed by Okoye, and Onuorah. C.C. Momah stands third from left directly behind the seated row; J.O. Onwuka stands sixth from left (same row). Godwin Momah, stands in the back row, second from left, next to the boy over whose head is scribbled R.I.P. The House Master Alagoa sits fourth from the left on the second row.
(Reproduced by kind permission of C.C. Momah)

2. 1947 School House cricket team at Government College, Umuahia. Standing left to right: Godwin Egbuna, C.C. Momah, Christopher Okigbo, Francis Egbuonu, Jack and Furo. Sitting: Nsolo, Donatus Oparah, Ajegbo, Alagoa (House Master), another Master (name unknown), Oranu and Osamor. (Reproduced by kind permission of C.C. Momah)

3. University College, Ibadan, cricket team, 1950. Okigbo stands in the back row, fourth from left, with C.C. Momah sixth from left, followed by Leslie Harriman. This picture was taken during the cricket trials in Lagos at the Race Course, opposite King's College.
(Reproduced by kind permission of C.C. Momah)

4. Reunion of Government College, Umuahia students (date unknown). Okigbo stands second from the left, between Peter Chigbo and Emmanuel Ojinma, followed by Aguocha, Ralph Opara (younger brother of Do. Opara), O.O. Uguru, Chike Momah, Izuorah and Fidelis Udeh. Squatting: Igwilo, two people (names unknown), E.J Ekong and Wilfred Chukwude-belu. (Reproduced by kind permission of C.C. Momah)

5. Fiditi Grammar School football team, 1959/60. Okigbo the football master stands with cap on in the back row. Sitting centre is Alex Olu Ajayi, Principal of the Fiditi Grammar School
(Reproduced by kind permission of Sarah Ladipo-Manyika)

6. Christopher Okigbo, Chinua Achebe and Alex Olu Ajayi. This picture was taken when Okigbo and Ajayi visited Achebe in Enugu in 1960.

7. Makerere conference, 1962. Left to right: Gabriel Okara, Christopher Okigbo, Segun
Olusola and Saunders Redding (American Society of African Culture).
(This photograph first appeared in *West Africa* magazine, 1962)

8. Okigbo's marriage to Judith Safinat Attah in
Enugu, 1962. The bridesmaid, standing behind
the couple, is Georgette, Pius Okigbo's wife to
whom he dedicated the poem 'Newcomer'.
(Reproduced by kind permission of Obiageli Ibrahimat
Okigbo)

9. Okigbo as best man at his friend Torch Taire's wedding in Ibadan, 1965.
(Reproduced by kind permission of Torch Taire)

10. Okigbo at Cambridge House with his nephew John (Lawrence Okigbo's son)
(Reproduced by kind permission of Obiageli Ibrahimat Okigbo)

11. Okigbo plays on his
guitar at Cambridge
House, Ibadan
(Reproduced by kind permission
of Obiageli Ibrahimat Okigbo)

12. Okigbo lights
his pipe
(Reproduced by kind permission
of Obiageli Ibrahimat Okigbo)

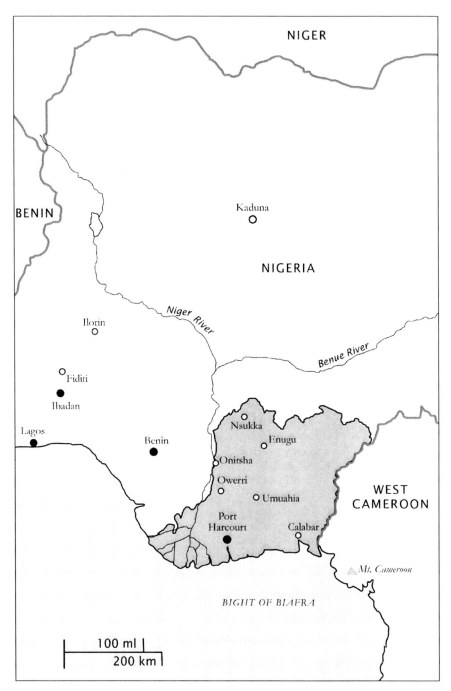

NIGER

BENIN

Kaduna
O

NIGERIA

Ilorin
O

Niger River

Benue River

O Fiditi
● Ibadan

Lagos
●

Benin
●

Nsukka
O

Enugu
O

O Onitsha

O Owerri

O Umuahia

Port
Harcourt
●

Calabar
O

WEST
CAMEROON

▲ Mt. Cameroon

BIGHT OF BIAFRA

| 100 ml |
| 200 km |

Map 1  Nigeria. The shaded area is the old Eastern Region, which was declared to be the Republic of Biafra.

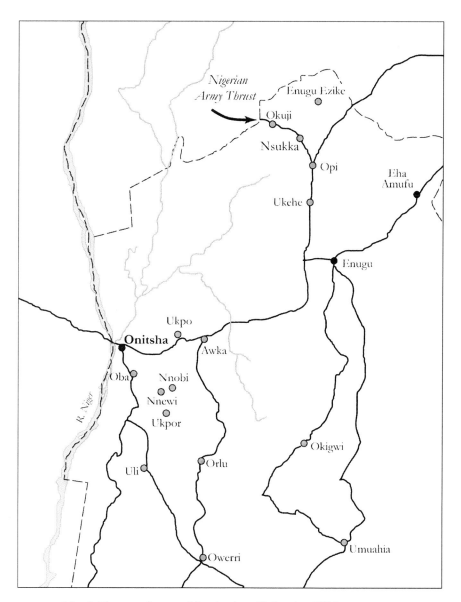

Map 2  The part of eastern Nigeria where Christopher Okigbo grew up near
Onitsha and the area to the north where he fought to liberate the University
of Nigeria, Nsukka

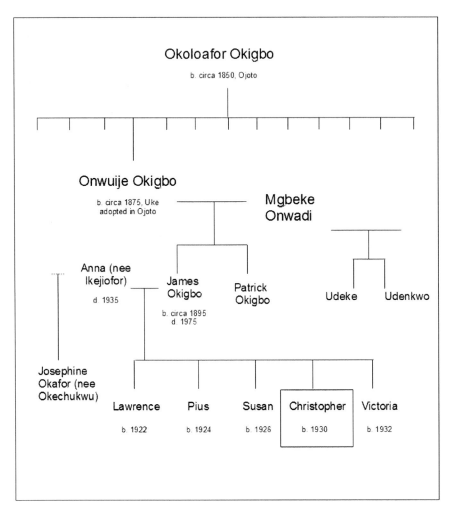

Okigbo family tree

# 1

## *A river goddess, his mother's death & a headmaster father*

OJOTO 1930–45

---

Before you, mother Idoto,
    naked I stand;
before your watery presence,
    a prodigal

leaning on an oilbean,
lost in your legend.

('The Passage')

Ojoto, Christopher Okigbo's birthplace, nestles deeply in what was once the tropical forest, east of Onitsha, the trading city near the river Niger. The hills rise and taper into a valley; the landscape falls into a rolling pattern which ends in Ojoto about fifteen miles away. The dusty red earth is roused in the dry seasons. The old dirt road forms into mysterious pathways from Nnewi to Onitsha, through Obosi and Nkpor, and through Umuoji to Oba. These are the neighbouring towns. Ojoto indeed lies between Oba and Nnewi. It is a densely populated part of the Igbo world. In Igbo communities, life throbs around a system of filial linkages – the kinship system in which all experience is collectively shared. Ojoto was no different. People have lived for thousands of years in this deep forest enclave in the heart of Igboland.

Ojoto men and women, like most Igbo people of Eastern Nigeria, are known for being restless and adventurous. Contact with European 'civilization' late in the nineteenth century gave impetus to that restless mobility. Before the turn of the twentieth century, people in Ojoto were mostly farmers and merchants, who traded across the somewhat dangerous terrain of Obosi and Nkpor to Onitsha, and even across the River Niger to Aboh and Asaba and far beyond. There are palm beaches. A deep green canvas of foliage envelops the landscape when the rains come. There are the eternal rivalries between clans, at the root of which is the fierce independence for which the Igbo are noted. Communal histories had been preserved through the oral process; the mythologies woven around the communal lore and enterprise indicate a shared memory of place and time, but also of distinct movements, displacements, diversity, and the hybrid of people weaving in and out of time. This movement of people gave Ojoto its own dynamism.

Eight clans make up Ojoto – Ire, where the Ajani shrine that harbors the goddess Idoto is located – Ezeke, Umuechem, Ezema, and Ojo, which is the clan from which Christopher Okigbo's forebears come. There are also Enugo, Ndiabo and Umuezema.

Some of the clans lie at the lower banks of the Idoto River, while others inhabit the upper escarpment where the forest snuggles into the upland. These clans constitute what is known as '*Ojoto enu*' – the upland Ojoto – the ones living down the hill in close clusters are '*Ojoto uno*'. The Idoto River carves its path through these kindred communities. It also runs its serpentine course beyond the sacred groves, holding mysteries in its depths, especially for the active imagination of a child like Christopher. The river then flows beyond in widening gestures, washing into the bowels of the great river – the Omambala (Anambra) River, down in the floodplains. The Ajani shrine of 'mother Idoto' is located in Ojoto, by one of the groves leading to the Idoto River.

Okigbo's maternal uncle, Nweze, was the priest of the Ajani shrine when Christopher Okigbo was growing up, and before that Nweze, Okigbo's maternal grandfather, Ikejiofor, held the title. In Christopher Okigbo's childhood, oilbean trees still lined much of the undulating waterfront leading to the Ajani shrine. These trees were part of the cult of the water goddess of Oto, the deity that owned the river. Idoto, in other words, was consecrated as the spirit of all life with her twin-consort – Ukpaka Oto – the male archetype and alter ego to the feminine. The river itself, Idoto's habitation, is the sacred source, the site of communal ritual and worship. Like most river-dwelling communities among the Igbo, it is apparent that generations of Ojoto people depended on their powerful water deity for all ritual meaning. During Okigbo's childhood in the 1930s, even at the height of the influence of the Christian missionaries and the European 'civilizing mission', most of Idoto's awesome presence could still be felt, and its worship remained intact. With the guardianship of the deity in the trust of his family, Okigbo always felt himself part of the lineage of the priesthood of the goddess.

As a child, Christopher Okigbo experienced the mystery of Idoto's worship. Growing among the customs of this community he could, sense the profound power of the goddess of Ojoto. In any case the Idoto River was also the place of entertainment, and like many children, Christopher Okigbo frolicked in the river purely for sport. He wrote later in the introduction to *Labyrinths* of the Idoto River with touching nostalgia, an acknowledgement of the significance of the river as '... the village stream of which I drank, in which I washed, as a child...'[1]

Onitsha was close which ensured that the powerful influences of 'the new world' of Europe penetrated Ojoto earlier than other more outlying Igbo communities. By the the first quarter of the nineteenth century, Onitsha had become an important center of commerce from which the Christian missions began to evangelize most of the Igbo heartland. The result was the disruption of the social structure of the traditional societies. The Igbo formed an organic, decentralized chain of communities – a federation of autonomous clans and people who thrived on an egalitarian, republican spirit. European anthropologists later described the Igbo as acephalous. From the borders of southeastern Nigeria, the Igbo groups spread to the fringes of Agbor on the western side of the River Niger. The Igbo speak the same language, with sometimes overt, dialectal variations, from the heartland to the lands across the great River Niger. From the Island of Bonny to Ikwerre, Oguta, Ukwuani, and to most of the riverine Igbo communities, this dialectal difference becomes more complex. The mostly republican pattern of their social organization ensured that no central authority could weld them together into a political purpose. Power resided in kin groups – the *umunna* – each pursuing its own commerce and diplomacy without intervention.

The typical Igbo social system is organized around the family with a head, the age grade, the cult of titled men. The hamlets, the villages and the town with a market place, are usually where most commercial and diplomatic relationships are conducted. Here is also where the central assembly of the people meets regularly and sometimes the shrines of the various deities – chief of which is Ala, the earth goddess – are located. The Igbo system was of such sophistication that individual participation was supreme. Each decision was based on consensus. Being autonomous, every community addressed its peculiar concerns and imposed its own sanctions based on the compact with the earth goddess. Social conduct thrived on the sovereignty of these independent communities on the principles of egalitarianism, freedom, individualism and a certain distrust of supreme authority. There were no absolute monarchs. Each man worshipped his own gods and followed the path carved for him by his *chi*. C.L. Innes and Bernth Lindfors capture the effects of British colonialism on the Igbo world in their introduction to *Critical Perspectives on Chinua Achebe*:

> When the British assumed control of Nigeria in the late nineteenth century they assumed, as other powers have conveniently assumed, that they brought 'history' and enlightenment and progress to a people which had no social, political and religious traditions of its own. Those religious beliefs, which differed from their own they called superstition or fetishism, the differences in political and social structure they called chaos. In 1900, the British imposed a system of direct rule over Ibos by dividing their territory into areas ruled by District Commissioners and appointing Ibos to act as warrant chiefs, clerks and messengers to assist them, a system resented by the Ibos not only because it was an alien imposition violating their democratic structure, but also because those who accepted the appointments were men without status, and without allegiance to their own communities. In modern terms they were collaborators. In 1918 (sic), Lord Lugard introduced 'indirect rule' as a policy for the whole of Nigeria, the District Commissioners were removed, and the warrant chiefs were given greater power, often resulting in great abuse of power.[2]

This violation of the cultural and moral ethos of the Igbos resulted in the initial resistance, which is imaginatively retold in the writings of Chinua Achebe, especially in *Things Fall Apart* and *Arrow of God*. This destructive conflict imaginatively replayed in the tragic persona of Okonkwo and Ezeulu in those novels. When he began writing, Okigbo himself vividly described this conflict, the disruption of the spiritual foundation (he called it 'the profanation of the mysteries'), which bound the Igbo people to their moral and mystical universe. In the place of resistance came slow acquiescence and the rise of the moral and ethical order of this 'new world' shaped by European mores under which Christopher Okigbo and his generation grew. Like that great bird described in Okigbo's poem, 'Fragments out of the Deluge', British colonialism spread her wings over the soul of the traditional Igbo society, accompanied by its own new mysteries and power. The Roman Catholics were to become the most influential mission in this part of Igboland.

One of the men who initially led a resistance against this intrusion of colonial power was Okoloafor Okigbo, patriarch of the Okigbo family. Oral accounts indicate that he was born early in the fifth decade of the nineteenth century, possibly around 1850. A description of him indicates that he was one of the most outstanding men of his generation in Ojoto.[3] Even before the advent of the white man, he had achieved some renown in the surrounding cluster of clans in what later became known as the Idemili area of Anambra state. As a warrior, he led Ojoto in many of those inter communal wars which marked much of nineteenth-century Igbo history. He was above all, a farmer of note. Okoloafor Okigbo was reputed to have participated in the lucrative trade in produce and, possibly, slaves beyond the great river at Aboh. He was imbued with a stoutness of heart and the spirit of adventure. The proof of his talent and distinction could be gleaned from the fact that he belonged to that aristocracy of titled men, the ozo, in Ojoto.[4]

Okigbo's ancestral tree seems however to have taken its roots beyond Ojoto. There are accounts that his grandfather Onwuije, came originally from the Ubulu-Enu kindred in Uke, another town also in the Idemili area of present Anambra state of Nigeria.[5] There are various accounts of how he naturalized in Ojoto following the dramatic circumstances that forced his migration from Uke. The implication of this family history is important: it means that in the strict patrilineal conventions of most of Igboland, the Okigbo family does not essentially belong to Ojoto. The Okigbo family history and oral testimony obtained from Ojoto testify two possible accounts for Onwuije's emigration. Onwuije was the only son of Eze Okigbo's sister married in Uke. As a result of the early demise of his father, Onwuije became the subject of an intricate family plot about the succession to a traditional estate. Although he was still very young, Onwuije was considered a natural claimant to the inheritance of his dead father and, therefore, an impediment to the ambitions of his uncles. Life in Uke soon became precarious and intolerable for both Onwuije and his widowed mother. As a result, Onwuije's mother took her son away to her own family at Ojoto-Uno, seeking refuge in Ojoto. His maternal uncle, the prominent Eze Okigbo in Ojoto, adopted him.

There is also another version of the story of Onwuije. It is suggested that he fled from Uke and sought refuge with his uncle Okigbo because he had a killed a man in his youth. To kill another human in traditional Igbo society was viewed as an abominable act. The law of reprisal in Igboland at the time was unambiguous: whoever shed another fellow's blood would pay with his blood, or at the least be banished. Onwuije was to suffer the same fate. He was held in manacles waiting for the oracle at Ogbunike to sanction his death. Before the oracle spoke however, Eze Okigbo organized his nephew's dramatic escape to Ojoto where he adopted him into his own household. This account in fact insists that Onwuije arrived in Ojoto in chains. There are suggestions also that it was Okoloafor Okigbo's family's feud that led to a plot being hatched to kill Okigbo. Okoloafor Okigbo was very young, it was said, when his father died. His mother had taken him to his maternal home in Ojoto Obo-Ofia where he grew up. The time came when he was to inherit his father's portion of the family estate, but his uncles plotted to usurp him, claiming that he was nowhere to be found. Elders of the clan, unwilling to do an injustice, gave his uncles seven weeks to think about it; they also secretly sent a message to the young Okoloafor who returned in time from Obo-Ofia to Ojoto-Uno to assume his estate. But apprehensive of the circumstances of his return to Ojoto-Uno, Okoloafor's elder sister sent her son Onwuije from Uke to Ojoto, to stay and protect the life of her brother.

Thus Onwuije grew up in Ojoto and found his own family. He met and fell in love with an Ojoto woman, Mgbeke Onwadi by whom he had only two children – James Okoyeodu and Patrick Nnajiofor. But Onwuije also died young, leaving a young widow and the two children. Unable to withstand the troop of suitors, Mgbeke Onwadi remarried in Umuoji, where she gave birth to two daughters – Udenkwo and Udeke – Christopher Okigbo's paternal aunts. She left behind in Ojoto her two children by Onwuije, who were adopted by their great uncle Eze Okigbo – already quite prominent and significant in the clan. He had grown to such prominence by the latter part of the nineteenth century that he had risen to the highest titles that anyone could aspire to in Ojoto, becoming head of the *ndi ichie* – that council or conclave of titled elders of the community, whose authority was widely respected in Igbo communities. This fact is faithfully recorded on the wall of the clan's *Obi* behind Ichie Ububa's house in Ojoto. Indeed by the time of his death around 1921 Eze Okigbo was reckoned to be one of the most influential men of his generation in Ojoto.

The advent of British colonialism saw the introduction by 1900 of warrant chiefs in Igboland. Ojoto people were one of the people who decided to choose from among themselves someone who would represent them before the British colonial authority. Their choice was Okoloafor Okigbo. He was a man known for his boldness , which was an advantage in representing Ojoto before the white men at Onitsha and Awka. Okoloafor Okigbo thus became one of the earliest people in Igboland to interact at close official range with British colonial officers. His peers in Igboland included the legendary Onyeama in Eke, father of the judge Charles Daddy Onyeama, who served as the first African at the World Court in The Hague; and Kodilinye in Obosi, whose son Professor H. Kodilinye became one of Nigeria's notable scholars of modern medicine. These men came to make tyrannical claims to power in republican Igbo, as glimpsed in the historian Adiele Afigbo's account, *Warrant Chiefs in Igbo Land*.

Okoloafor Okigbo's authority sprang first from his physical endowments. He had an awe-inspiring presence, a clear intellect and a visionary reading of his time. He did what most men at the time refused to do: he chose to educate all but his eldest son by sending them to the new schools established by the white men. He apprehended the imperative of social change and understood that a new elite would emerge among the younger generation who must understand the ways of the white men. He did not send his female children to school, possibly because women's education came much later to Igboland.

While his other sons went off to Onitsha to the white man's school, Okoloafor Okigbo set up his first son Nnaebue, as heir to his colonial warrant. He took Nnaebue around with him so that he could learn first-hand the intricacies of dealing with the colonial authority and master the art of diplomacy. He exposed Nnaebue to the rudiments of colonial judicial processes by taking him to the courts at Onitsha and Awka. This was important because the warrant chief also acted as local magistrate and jury. Nnaebue was also initiated into the highest Ozo titles and went through the painful rites of the *ichi*, the rituals of scarification, which were accompanied by expensive ceremonies. This was Okoloafor Okigbo's way of establishing a stake in both worlds: the old, passing Igbo world and the new powerful, modern European world with all its complexities. (Nnaebue was father to Professor Bede Okigbo.)

Okoloafor Okigbo's actions had remarkable vision in this period at the height of the Igbo resistance against the European intrusion. The really enterprising young men in the communities engaged themselves with farming, trading or other enterprises. People who were sent off to the white man's schools were those who were deemed to be social misfits – the weaklings – or those who needed to be punished or disciplined. But Okoloafor Okigbo saw it differently. His decision to send his younger boys to the new school sprang partly from a a shrewd instinct. In the murky, cut-throat business of colonialism he needed people around him he could trust. Since he could not read or write the English language, he often depended on interpreters in his dealings with the colonial authority. He felt that if he sent his own children to school, they would understand the white man's strange language and appreciate his mysterious ways; they would then become his interpreters before the white man.

It was said that Okoloafor Okigbo even negotiated and convinced the Catholic mission at Onitsha to start a school in Ojoto. He then implored every Ojoto man to send his sons to the school. But Ojoto men, like most Igbo people, were stubborn.

They were suspicious, even amused, at the ways of the white men and refused to send their children to the new Catholic school. The school had to close down because of under-enrollment.

Okoloafor Okigbo was thus compelled to send his own sons farther away to Onitsha, where there were well-established schools. He insisted that every one of his sons be accompanied by a minder and many of those escorts also got an education. Okoloafor also insisted that each of his sons who went away to school should also own farms and cultivate them by hired labor. This ensured that his children retained an abiding interest in the land and in the values of their people even as they learned the new ways of the white man. In his mind was a bridging of the old and the new world in his mind.

Among Okoloafor Okigbo's children was James Okoyeodu Okigbo. He was also one of the earliest converts to the Catholic Church through the missionary works of the charismatic Irish priest, Joseph Shanahan. James Okigbo went on to train as a teacher, and became one of the pioneers of Catholic mission education. The result of the activities of their pioneering spirit could certainly be measured in the surge of Igbo education in the 1920s and 1930s; it was the moment of intellectual ferment among the Igbo. One beneficiary was the novelist Chinua Achebe who described that era as '... one burst of energy'[6] that saw the Igbo close the gap between themselves and those who had been ahead of them in pursuit of a western education. James Okigbo, born in 1895 when English colonial power was newly arrived in this part of Africa, grew up schooled in the dominant tradition of his people. His later conversion to Christianity and his deep faith in the Roman Catholic Church, came to shape his life profoundly. He pursued his calling with the fanatical fervour of the new convert.

The Roman Catholic Mission at this time was evangelising from Onitsha to Owerri, expanding and building schools. A new energy had gripped the Igbo, who were cautious, but now receptive to change. Many more people began to sense the advantages of subscribing to the new western ethos in a world in rapid transition. The 1920s would prove to be a challenging time for James Okigbo to begin his work as a mission school teacher in Igboland. After elementary school in Onitsha and teacher training at the Catholic Teachers' Training School in Igbariam, he joined the mission school system, starting as a pupil teacher and ending as a headmaster. Those like James Okigbo, with their English education, who came to work in the mission school system, became the new elite.

Schoolmasters were especially well regarded in that era of rapid transition. They were seen as figures of modernity – the most knowledgeable people in the new ways of that unfolding world. They were highly visible in their communities. They were people of style. The pioneer teachers in the Igbo world were placed in a social hierarchy next only to the colonial District Officers. They became the bridge between the British colonial officers and the local population which was still in awe, because of the tyrannical power that they exerted. Many of those pioneer teachers became the subject of local mythology and legend. There was an abundance of stories regarding the life of James Okigbo. For instance, he was described by a family in Ekwulobia as 'an affable, fashionable, and very cultivated man of his time.'[7] He was also by all accounts a generous man. 'My grandmother told me that but for Mr. Okigbo, my father would never have gone to school.'[8]

James Okoyeodu Okigbo helped to establish and also taught in many new Catholic mission schools in various parts of the old Eastern region. He helped to shape the generation of children born between 1920 and 1945 into the colonial culture. Mr. Okigbo's work took him as far south in Igboland as Owerri and westwards, across the great Niger, to Asaba. At the root of his engagement was a commitment to his faith in the Roman Catholic Church, which he professed to the end of his life. However, he was like the typical early Christian converts – essentially hybrid. Although his practice of Catholicism was zealous and doctrinaire, he nevertheless retained contact with important aspects of the traditional Igbo moral view of the world. But he brought the zeal of the convert to his work in his various teaching assignments at Adazi, Owerri, Ugwuoba, Onitsha, Nnobi, Amawbia, Ekwulobia, Asaba and several other locations in Igboland where he taught until he retired from the Catholic school system as a headmaster in 1955. Onitsha had a fairly well established school system, but in the other places James Okigbo's job was to mould from scratch every new school to which he was sent by the Catholic mission. It was arduous work in those early years. The pay was poor. Life was itinerant.

In 1920, James Okigbo married Anna Onugwalobi, daughter of Ikejiofor, priest of the Ajani shrine of Ire, Ojoto. James and Anna moved to the various duty posts to which his job as a Catholic schoolteacher took him. Anna was expected to share this life of the peripatetic schoolteacher. Accounts indicate that she adapted well to her role; they tell the story of a typical pioneer teacher's wife who, considering the circumstances of her time, was enlightened, fashionable, outgoing and was said to have read the bible in Igbo. She had become quite wealthy from her trade in clothes and jewelry, and was said to be one of the very few Igbo women of her time to dress in the expensive fashion of the elegant Saro women in Onitsha.[9] She was a remarkable and independent woman.

Anna had been in an earlier marriage with Okechukwu, who at the time held the Ogene title in Onitsha and with whom she had a daughter, Josephine. But the marriage did not last. It is said that Anna abandoned her matrimonial home, rejecting all entreaties to return made by Ogene Okechukwu. Her first husband, the story goes, sent many emissaries to her father, Ikejiofor, and is said to have actually refused the dowry which he paid for her when it was returned because he was still deeply in love with Anna. But Anna would not return. She had fallen in love with the teacher, James, and she had become a Christian convert. The marriage was formally dissolved only when Anna's father took the final step of returning the dowry through the native authority courts at Onitsha.

Anna and James Okigbo had six children between them. Lawrence, the first child, was born in 1922 at Isu. Pius, who came two years later in 1924, was born at Ogbunike. Susan, the first daughter of the marriage, was born in 1926 at Nnobi. Early in 1928, while at Onitsha, they had a girl, but she died early in unfortunate circumstances. The infant accidentally fell into a fire and died from serious burns.[10] Victoria came later, born at Amawbia in 1932.

Christopher Okigbo, the fifth child, was born late in the morning of 16 August 1930 at Ojoto. No record exists in any official district documents, but the schoolmaster kept a faithful record of the birth of his children. Christopher Okigbo was said to have been a strong little baby. He proved to be a rather difficult child who kept Anna awake through endless crying. As Pius indeed recollected in his memorial tribute to his brother in 1995, Christopher 'showed his guts early by learning to cry even without provocation (or better still shriek) even more so when provoked.'[11] It was an early sign of a stubborn will.

Anna Okigbo was especially attached to Christopher. She felt a keen and immediate bonding with her last son, because she recognized that he was special in many ways. He had an entertaining and lively spirit even as a child. However, it was also a love borne out of her close and affectionate relationship to her own father, Ikejiofor. Christopher was generally believed to have re-incarnated Anna's father. She fondly called the young Christopher '*nna m*' ('my father'). The Igbo took for granted the notion that an individual may return in human form after death through a cycle of rebirth. This metaphysical view of existence was still strong among the Igbo of Anna Okigbo's generation, although new Christian converts were taught to disregard such pagan views. But even as the Christian missions struggled to dissuade belief in the traditional world – with its rituals, its myths and its world of spirits – Anna, like many Igbo Christian converts of her generation was deeply aware of the cosmology of the Igbo world. Much of the affection for her fifth child doubtlessly sprang from this connection to her past. There were signs that offered proof to her conviction. According to Okigbo family legend, Christopher was born with birthmarks that convinced everybody that he was Ikejiofor returned. It was said that little Christopher, restless and temperamental even as a child, possessed a remarkable physical and emotional resemblance with his illustrious maternal grandfather.

In his lifetime, Ikejiofor – priest of the Ajani shrine – was considered one of the leading figures of his community. Accounts of him are of an intrepid, stubborn and mercurial man. A man of violence, he led several clan wars for Ojoto. It was in one of such skirmishes that he died. His death came, it was said, from gunshot wounds to his neck in a bloody, inter clan clash. Christopher was born with birthmarks that very closely resembled the same marks of injury from which Ikejiofor is said to have died. Everybody who knew Ikejiofor agreed that his grandson resembled him in remarkable ways.

Christopher Okigbo's adoption of Idoto, the family deity, as a poetic symbolism rests on this notion of a cyclic return and renewal. Okigbo's maternal family in Ire, Ojoto, is a traditional priestly aristocracy with a long history of tending the ancient shrine of two of the most powerful deities in Ojoto. This sacred function apparently made the family quite prominent in the community, for the priesthood of the Ajani shrine which harbored Idoto, the water goddess, the principal deity of all Ojoto people was an important ritual position. It was a traditional position of privilege, which gave the priest of the Ajani shrine the authority to proclaim Ojoto's sacred sanctions, as well as regulate the balance of her spiritual life. Okigbo's family was thus central to the carrying out of some of the most important religious rites of the Ojoto people; it endowed its family with ritual authority.

Ukpaka-Oto was the chief deity – the male consort of the goddess. But Idoto was the deity who symbolized the river and its mysterious depth. She was sacred as the mother of the entire community. The symbols of the cult veneration for these communal deities are by the python and the tortoise which, Christopher Okigbo would years later explain to Marjory Whitelaw in his home in Ibadan in 1965, represented 'the penis' and 'the female clitoris.'[12] The phallic symbolism denotes the sexual union of the deities and their place within the myth of regeneration. Christopher Okigbo was apparently deeply influenced by this notion of his own re-incarnation in Ikejiofor. He took that association with the water goddess very seriously. But for the conversion of his parents to Christianity, and Okigbo's early induction to the Christian faith and education, he was the rightful successor to the traditional priestly functions of the Ajani shrine.

When Ikejiofor died from those gunshot wounds sustained in battle, the priesthood went to his son Nweze Ikejiofor, Okigbo's maternal uncle and Anna Okigbo's immediate younger brother. It is noteworthy that throughout his life, and as a poet, Christopher Okigbo regarded his uncle only as a regent to the priesthood. Okigbo found poetry as an important means of fulfilling the ritual obligations of this priesthood to Idoto, whose cult of worship he celebrated at the very beginning of his imaginative odyssey. But this would be many years later.

Christopher Okigbo's birth in 1930 coincided with a significant shift in the Igbo world: the Igbo people began to embrace fully this new age more rapidly after years of resistance. One dramatic event occurred in that very year with consequence for the Igbo ritual world – the desacralisation of Eze Nri Obalike, the symbol of Igbo spiritual and political autonomy. He was publicly humiliated, brought forcibly to the district courts in Awka by colonial officials. Igbo resistance crumbled after thirty years and six major British expeditionary campaigns. This act was part of the 'profanation of the mysteries' which Okigbo later writes about in his poetry, with the image of the eagles conquering the bombax tree in *Limits*.[13]

An age was passing. A new world had come with values that would transform the nature of traditional society and shift allegiances from the deities of Igboland to the new Christian god. Colonialism was displacing the cultural and economic rights of the indigenous Africans. Evelyn Waugh traveling through Kenya encountered a lovely American called Kiki, to whom a rich British settler at Lake Naivasha in the white Highlands had given 'two or three miles of lake-front as a Christmas present.'[14] At another point in the vast empire, a young British police officer was having a twinge of conscience. He had been called to execute an elephant publicly, in order to impress 'the natives' on the apparent might of the British. That young officer in Her Majesty's service was George Orwell, and he wrote:

> ...it was at that moment that I first grasped the hollowness, the futility of the white man's dominion in the East. Here was I, the white man with his gun, standing in front of the unarmed native crowd - seemingly the leading actor in the piece. But in reality I was an absurd puppet pushed to and fro by the will of those yellow faces behind.[15]

Orwell's disillusion not withstanding, the powerful symbol of the empire as all-conquering was forcefully demonstrated to the natives.

Christopher Okigbo was thus born straight into that world of imperial domination. Events in his life, and in the life of his generation, would construct the unique context through which he evolved emotionally and intellectually to apprehend a world in spiritual conflict. In Europe, the feeling may have persisted in that period that the British Empire had suffered a crisis of self-confidence as a result of the Great War, and that its hands were slipping from the reins; in the colonies, however, the feeling and the reality were different. The decades of the 1930s and the 1940s saw the sudden surge of intellectual activity among Igbo people, the triumph of the phenomenon of mass education.[16] Okigbo belonged to this triumphant generation empowered by its own heady expectations among the Igbo.

The decade of the 1930s saw the emergence of the first generation of university-educated Igbo men. Igbo society was slowly surfacing from the disruption of its world by European penetration. Igbo men who had traveled overseas for their education began to return home. In 1932, within two years of the birth of Christopher Okigbo, the first Igbo medical doctor, Dr. Simon E. Onwu, returned from his studies overseas to a lavish reception organized by the newly formed Igbo State Union in Port Harcourt. Dr. Akanu Ibiam, who graduated from St. Andrew's in Scotland in 1933, followed him shortly after. He quickly established his reputation as a missionary doctor. The first Igbo lawyer, Louis Mbanefo, arrived from Cambridge also not too long after in 1935.

The accomplishments of a remarkable young Igbo man who had studied in America, Nnamdi Azikiwe, were celebrated in the popular song 'Zik, *nwa jelu oyibo*' (translated as 'Zik, great traveler to the land of white folk'). Dr. Nnamdi Azikiwe arrived home from the United States through Gold Coast in 1935. He had been renowned as the editor of the *African Morning Post* in Accra; his journalism had raised the hackles of the British colonial government, leading to sedition charges after publication of his article 'Does the African Have a God?' By 1937 he returned to Nigeria and established the *West African Pilot* in Lagos. His momentum lent color to the nationalist struggle. He had a great message of hope and liberty to Africans: to free themselves from the shackles of ignorance, through education. 'Each one train one' became the rallying cry of the Igbo modernizing movement in that decade.

From accounts of their lives together, Okigbo's parents had a very intimate marriage. Anna Okigbo was also a typical, traditional Igbo housewife, who organized the home and took care of other existential details while her husband was immersed in his work. Life as the spouse of a schoolmaster was demanding. She bore the strain, with the studied grace of most of the traditional women of her generation. She shared her husband's fervent Christian faith, which became the fulcrum of their lives. Pius Okigbo recalled this aspect of the Okigbo household while growing up as a child:

> Each morning began with a prayer. We, the children, would wake with sleep in our eyes. We would count the beads of the rosary several times and recite several 'hail Marys' and say the 'Pater nosters'; and these almost always caught us, the children, dropping off to sleep again on our knees. And on waking, we sometimes got punished for falling asleep during prayers. Christopher was always grumbling at the corner. I think we had a surfeit of religion as children, and that no doubt, affected our attitude to church in adult life.[17]

It is clear that the Okigbo children grew up in the shadows of strict Roman Catholic parents, who tried to enforce a firm religious upbringing on their children.

From 1930 to 1935, the Okigbo family moved through three mission stations, from Onitsha, Ugwuoba and to Amawbia. Life for the children of a teacher seemed constantly dynamic. It is easy now to overlook the impact of so much movement. One clear advantage was that the Okigbo children became exposed to different places, peoples, cultures and lifestyles. These contacts helped them evolve a broader, more cosmopolitan attitude in life. But they also became almost culturally alienated, uprooted early from their indigenous world. We sense this in Okigbo's double consciousness. Schoolmasters like Mr. Okigbo tended to live with their families in serene isolation in mission school compounds, away from the host communities. It was a form of spiritual exile.

In 1935, Anna Okigbo died of cholera at Amawbia. That year witnessed a particularly vicious cholera epidemic. Anna's death had been sudden and unexpected. She had not been ill previously and her death had come quickly. She had slumped down that morning while preparing her children for school and making breakfast. When she collapsed, the alarm was quickly raised. A desperate effort to revive her proved fruitless. The children did not go to school that day. They were quickly sent to the home of the Onubogus, close family friends of the Okigbos. While they were there they observed the unusual flurry of activity around the mission school compound.

A crowd began gathering in the schoolmaster's home. Somehow as Lawrence, Anna's eldest child, recalled several years later, the children knew that something had happened to their mother. They refused to eat the food brought to them by Mrs. Onubogu. The three older ones – Lawrence, Pius and Susan – were especially alert to the sense of tragedy. Even little Christopher must have felt the tension of the moment, for he was said to have remained unnaturally subdued at the Onubogus. The children remained restless and anxious to find out what was amiss with their mother. So when the chance presented itself, they sneaked out of the Onubogu house. Lawrence had Christopher straddled on his back, while Pius took little Victoria and, with Susan walking along, they went back to the mission school compound. Only then did they discover their mother's death.

The schoolmaster was inconsolable. He wept bitterly for his dear wife. His children joined him and soon mourners who had been touched by Anna's death surrounded them. Word was quickly dispatched to Ojoto, and preparations began for an elaborate funeral. The Okigbo family left with Anna's corpse and the funeral party at noon that same day from Amawbia. The cortege arrived in Ojoto at night. There was an even larger crowd and greater commotion than at Amawbia. Anna was laid in state on a splendid bier in Godwin Okigbo's father's house. Like most Africans, the Igbo people had always celebrated the passing of individuals, especially illustrious ones, with great fanfare, in colorful rites of passage, and often with elaborate and expensive ceremonies. Such was the one for Anna.

Dirges were sung. There was a lot of weeping, for Anna had been a truly popular woman in Ojoto. The next day, her corpse was taken to St. Odelia's church at Ojoto for an elaborate funeral mass, after which she was interred in the church cemetery. Young Christopher had witnessed all the misery – the tears, the dark solemnity of passage, the sense of finality invoked in death – and it became engraved in his memory. Quite early in life he absorbed the true nature of anguish, an experience that would prove significant in the evolution of important aspects of his character, especially in his tendency to relapse into sudden, aloof and gloomy silences.

It is a tribute to the power of his memory nevertheless, that he remembered the details of events around Anna's death and funeral, although he was only five. One of the most moving sequences in *Heavensgate* ('The Passage') is a poem in which Okigbo vividly describes the solemn procession of the Christian funeral ceremony held for his mother at St. Odelia, and grapples with the terrifying scene as it unfolds in a child's vision:

Silent faces at crossroads:
    festivity in black...

Faces of black like long black
    columns of ants,

behind the bell tower,
into the hot garden
where all roads meet:
festivity in black...

O Anna at the knob of the panel oblong,
hear us at the crossroads at the great hinges

where the players of loft pipe organs
rehearse old lovely fragments, alone – [18]

Old St. Odelia's church stands about a fifteen-minute walk away from the Okigbo compound and is approached from the rear, where the bell tower rises against the sky. The church, with its Gothic architecture, would have seemed quite splendid in its time.

Its extensive grounds still occupy a central place in the Ojoto community, with the old primary school and the church cemetery at different ends of the mission compound. From the Okigbo home, it might have taken a long funeral procession more than thirty minutes to reach the church.

The large Okigbo clan lives in a cluster of compounds belonging to several branches of the family, lying mostly southwards and downhill from St. Odelia. Moving uphill towards the church, the funeral procession must indeed have seemed like a 'long black columns of ants' in the eyes of a child. The solemn procession on that blazing afternoon, that minor difficulty of getting Anna's coffin through the church door, and even the music wafting from the church organ are fully captured in Okigbo's verse with startling poignancy. Several years later when the poet began to write, he recollects the gathering at the graveside – a powerful and defining moment for the young boy. Today, Anna's tombstone stands alone in the old church cemetery, the only surviving memorial of the dead buried at St. Odelia.

Anna's tragic death was when her children were still young and tender. Lawrence, the eldest child, was only thirteen years; Pius was eleven years, Susan nine, and Christopher and Vicky were five and three years respectively. Of all her children, Christopher may have been the most affected by the death of his mother. He was just old enough to retain a sense of his mother. She became a fleeting essence, a painful absence; yet, his acute mind understood the finality of death. He was alert enough to recoil from the loss. There were those moments in his life when he felt deeply alone and sad, longing for maternal consolation. Anna assumed the force of a myth which transformed her into an eternal metaphor in her son's imagination – the absent goddess: part mother, part lover – her image recurring consistently in his poetry. All his life Okigbo tried to grapple with that absence. Anna was like an intangible presence who left an emotional void in his life. His greatest struggle was to reconcile himself to his mother's death. Part of the way he dealt with her absence was to escape from attachments and responsibilities: to be amoral.

Another aspect of Christopher Okigbo's personality was his Oedipal desire to connect with an absent mother, which may explain his complex relationship with women. Christopher Okigbo's perennial quest for sexual experience as conquest – what became his habit of compulsive womanizing in his adult life – may indeed be connected to a fundamental sense of the emptiness he felt as a child and his inconsolable longing for his late mother. Freudians may discern in his melancholy, and in his sexual appetite, the longing for a secure childhood, disrupted by the death of his mother.

Idoto became a surrogate mother in Okigbo's poetic consciousness. Anna thus assumes a perpetual and powerful presence in her son's poetry, reified into the goddess, and thus an object of worship, the single most dominant archetypal figure of Okigbo's mythic imagination, the basis of an existential dilemma, the live-die option. Around her, the poet constructs his poetic or imaginative quest – a pursuit which approximates that 'fable of man's perennial quest for fulfillment'[19] or for healing power of memory, captured in *Heavensgate*:

> strains of pressed orange leaves on pages,
> bleach of the light of years held in leather…[20]

Anna's death occasioned profound changes in the Okigbo family. Faced with the unanticipated problem of raising a family of very young children without his wife, the headmaster nearly despaired. His professional commitment to the Catholic mission schools at a most active and demanding phase of his career presented a dilemma for a single parent. James Okigbo found some solution: he sent his two eldest sons, Lawrence and Pius, to boarding school at St. Andrews, Adazi, to complete their primary school education. From Adazi, the boys later went to Christ the King College (CKC), the recently established Catholic Grammar School for boys at Onitsha. Susan went to a Catholic convent from where she later went on to Teachers College. Christopher and the last child, Vicky, remained in the care of the busy schoolmaster.

Young Christopher became ever lonelier as a child. With his three eldest siblings away at boarding school, he had an acute sense of abandonment. The isolation of the mission compound in which the schoolmaster lived led him to feel even more alone in the world. He especially missed his favorite brother and closest friend, Pius, with whom he had a unique bond. Christopher looked up to Pius, who was to remain his most influential role model. The most painful separation at that time, however, was when his immediate elder sister Susie left for boarding school at the Catholic convent in Adazi. Susie was closer to him in age and was his playmate and friend. They quarreled frequently but made up just as quickly.

Christopher always longed for affection. He felt a deep need to be noticed, to be at the center of attention. By all accounts, his tendency for extravagant actions comes from this moment in his life when he would stage one event after another simply to attract attention: to amuse, certainly, but also to assuage his sense of loneliness. When Anna died, Victoria, the baby of the family, seemed to Christopher to command all the attention. Whenever she cried, there would be a flurry of adults to console her. Christopher, more used to Anna's attention, suddenly felt himself ignored. Soon his quick young mind discovered the easiest way of getting adults to notice him. Whenever he felt the need, he would purposely make Victoria cry. It was soon discovered that Christopher was the cause and Christopher learned to take reprimands quite calmly. But sometimes he would cry for such a long time that his father would come to console him. Christopher Okigbo came to live a life of such drama because he suffered from insecurity, from the absences in his life. Sometimes this need for attention took the form of the derring-do.

His younger sister Victoria told of the occasion when Christopher jumped from a tall oilbean tree with his eyes closed, just to prove a point. The Okigbo children were then attending school in Ojoto, sent by the schoolmaster to live at home with his extended family. The close of the school day was something of a carnival. The children trooped homewards and found opportunities from which to make innocent mischief on the way. They would fight and quarrel, settle private rifts and dare each other. Sometimes, the young schoolboys would climb trees, especially the oilbean trees that lined the path home. They would pluck the first, fresh sprouts of its flowering for its nectar.

The nectar of the oilbean in its early inflorescence is cool and refreshing when it is sucked. Its sweet flavor is not unlike honey. On this occasion, Christopher had climbed a really tall oilbean tree with some other boys. Having sucked his fill of the nectar, he threw down some bunches for the girls who would not climb the trees. When it came to climbing down, Okigbo rejected the idea of simply climbing down from the tree in the conventional way: he insisted that he would come down only by jumping.

An argument broke out on the ground. While some of the children tried to restrain him, the more adventurous boys goaded him, daring him to fulfill his claim. Victoria was in tears. Christopher was going to kill himself. He enjoyed the attention. Seeing that he had created enough interest, Christopher Okigbo suddenly declared that he would not only jump from the tree but that he could indeed do so with both eyes closed. The crowd of school children who had by then gathered got excited. Victoria was crying and appealing to Christopher to stop. The boys cleared a space in anticipation of the great fall. They started counting to five, at which Okigbo hauled himself from the tree and landed successfully. Except for a few bruises, he was otherwise unhurt. He loved such moments, and often staged a drama for its provocative effects.

On another occasion after school, Okigbo made a bet that he would get home in that acrobatic fashion popular among the boys when they walked along on their hands. And sure enough, with his hands firmly clutching the earth, his legs raised high up, as he made his way homeward through the dust of the stony road uphill from St. Odelia. He never once faltered. His playmates cheered and sang encouraging songs until he got home to his father's house. 'Christopher was like that. Anything that was difficult to accomplish attracted him. And he will go ahead to do them successfully. He had too many amazing abilities,' his sister Victoria recalled many years later.[21] This propensity to live at the edge gave his personality an undoubted vitality.

In spite of his mother's death, Christopher Okigbo lived a relatively cushioned and carefree childhood. He was considered spoilt and over-indulged both by a doting father and by the women in his life who loved him dearly – for the young Christopher had a bright and sunny side that made him very personable. He was a child whose amazing abilities, generosity of spirit, sense of humor and stubbornness made him attractive. Christopher's father had nonetheless noticed the impact in the life of his son of his many departures. One of the things he did to alleviate Christopher's loneliness was to invite companionship. First, at various times he brought Christopher's cousins to live with them in the mission stations. As a pioneer educator, James Okigbo not only symbolized the highest intellectual achievement in a period of great ferment, but he was also a role model in the community. His relations found it worthwhile to send their own children to live in the schoolmaster's household in order to get properly educated. Among the Okigbo cousins were Bede and Godwin, both of whom distinguished themselves many years later in different fields: Professor Bede Nwoye Okigbo became famous as an agronomist, while Godwin Okigbo became a banker, lawyer and administrator. Bede Okigbo's father, Nnaebue, was Christopher's eldest uncle. Though he was not educated in the 'white man's ways' he nevertheless saw that his own son would be better served by living with his brother, the schoolmaster. Thus was Bede adopted at the age of eight into the household of James Okigbo who took full charge of his life from 1935. Fate may have had a hand in this: Bede Okigbo's own mother had also died about the same time as Anna.

Bede Okigbo, four years older than Christopher and Susan's exact age, was so fully integrated into the schoolmaster's household that many people did not know that he was not one of the schoolmaster's natural children. 'We grew up thinking that Bede was from the same womb as the rest of us,' Susan, said many years later.[22] The schoolmaster took many of his extended family to live with him at different times. In the Igbo concept of a close-knit extended family of the same bloodline, Bede could rightly be counted as one of Christopher's brothers. But it was an aspect of the schoolmaster's character which would shape much of the outlook of his son – the open, liberal, generous, boundariless notion of the family.

Christopher Okigbo became especially fond of his cousin Bede, although they were temperamentally opposite in character. Bede Okigbo was studious, religious, and took life seriously. He was, as Pius Okigbo recollected, 'the kind of boy whom Lawrence especially liked.'[23] Christopher was restless and active, a thorough truant. He was to be found in the whirlwind of things – in a fight, in a game of football, in any serious argument, and in every wild and elaborate mischief. Ironically, it was the contrasting nature of Bede's temperament that Christopher admired – his emotional stability – as well as his precocity. Susan recalls that Christopher Okigbo loved to mimic Bede's deep baritone voice, which was a source of hilarity among the Okigbo cousins. Christopher was the soul mate of his other cousin Godwin, who came to live in the schoolmaster's household at Asaba. Godwin and Christopher had the same instincts for adventure. These two, from all Okigbo's numerous cousins with whom he lived, were possibly the closest to him. Of all these good Catholic boys it seems that Bede was the one who was most influenced by the schoolmaster's deep Catholicism. Christopher Okigbo later joined Bede to become an altar boy.

Shortly after his mourning period James Okigbo remarried. A woman was needed around the house, since it seemed the schoolmaster was unable to cope. The new woman – Elizabeth – the headmaster hoped would provide the needed maternal care to Anna's young children. But Christopher quickly resented this marriage. He developed a most difficult relationship with his stepmother. For Elizabeth found Christopher exasperating and thought him spoilt and over-indulged; a truly tempestuous, rebellious and headstrong child. Intrepid and outspoken, he often went to unorthodox lengths to prove his points. Nobody intimidated him. He had all the undisciplined habits of a child with scant maternal oversight. He learned early to muster his own reserve of strength as a protection against his vulnerabilities.

Elizabeth was much younger than her husband, and uncertain about her maternal role. Her relative inexperience left her unprepared for the challenge of nurturing five adolescent stepchildren. This inexperience complicated her relationship with her difficult stepson. She had not developed the emotional resources or the methods for raising an impetuous, emotionally vulnerable child like Christopher. Elizabeth was impatient with Christopher and until many years later, a close relationship between the two was practically impossible.

The Okigbo sisters remembered the numerous fights between Christopher and their stepmother. On many occasions, Elizabeth smacked Christopher for one domestic infraction or the other. Christopher would wait patiently, biding his time. He would find the right moment, especially when he felt the protective shadow of his father lurking close by to deal a retaliatory slap on his stepmother. Thereafter, he would run away. Elizabeth would complain bitterly to the schoolmaster who often rebuked Christopher sternly. Christopher nevertheless learnt to stand his own ground. His father would counsel and admonish him, but he equally championed his right to speak his mind.

This combination of justice and paternal indulgence sharpened Christopher Okigbo's personal sense of justice – for even as a child it was impossible to deny him any part of his humanity. He often resisted any such violation of his individuality firmly. He craved to speak, to act out this sense of justice. He equally expressed his individuality in habits like chewing his cud or twitching his ears in a very amusing way. These traits hardened into personal mannerisms in adulthood. His friend Ben Obumselu suggested that these distinctive habits were 'the quirky habits of an adolescent who had no mother to watch his manners.'[24]

The conflicts with his stepmother sharpened Okigbo's sense of justice but they became a source of worry for his father. It was for that reason that he invited his first cousin, Eunice, to live with them. She too had known pain intimately, as she was scorned and abused by her husband for her childlessness. Eunice had lived in Ahoada but had abandoned her marriage when the abuse became intolerable. From 1936 she returned to Ojoto to the Okigbo household, sometimes staying for long stretches. She became for Anna's children, perhaps more than anyone else, a mother figure, a nurse and a companion. She died in 1988 in ripe old age, under the care of Pius. Eunice was described as grand and colorful – one of those Igbo women bred to affect the life around them with ease and confidence. She had learned to take the vagaries of life with grace. She endowed her maternal affection on Anna's children as a way of assuaging her own deep longing for children of her own. With Eunice, Christopher found more than companionship. As his sister Susan recollects, Christopher clung to Eunice, who herself loved him dearly, and is said to have willed her estate at Ahoada to him in the event of her death.

Among many other virtues, Eunice was a gifted musician. Her song could drown sorrows and lift dullness from common occasions. She was the salt of communal gatherings, festivals and feasts, and her warmth found expression in social communion and play. Pius Okigbo especially recalled Eunice's 'happy knack of breaking into song with spontaneity.'[25] He painted the picture of a joyous and beneficent spirit, one whom adversity had made tender and affectionate. Pius Okigbo also recalled Eunice's 'elegance and sense of style.'[26] She was a great storyteller. Eunice's impact on Christopher Okigbo's childhood is significant. Always more tolerant of his individuality She overindulged him. Eunice allowed Christopher to express fully his active, restless and rebellious spirit. Eunice's most significant influence on Christopher Okigbo, however, was an original love for music: from her, Christopher Okigbo first learnt the rhythm of the earth, and much of the folklore which deepened the essence of his poetry. Out of Eunice's lyrical soul, Christopher plucked music from a diverse repertoire of profound experiences.

One of Christopher Okigbo's childhood traits was to insist that he be saddled on Eunice's back while she did chores around the headmaster's compound, singing some of her beautiful melodies. It was while thus strapped as a child, listening as the wind replayed fragments, that Christopher Okigbo felt the first stirring of music in his soul. This would later resolve into poetry. In a footnote to 'Fragments out of the Deluge', the ninth movement of his *Limits*, Okigbo wrote in acknowledgment a nostalgic recollection of his childhood nurse Eunice (also Yunice), whom he described as 'known for her lyricism':[27]

> Eunice at the passageway,
> Singing the moon to sleep over the hills,
> Eunice at the passageway...[28]

These lines are Okigbo's debt of memory to Eunice, and explain in part both the evolution of his personality and the lyricism of his poetry.

His maternal grandmother at Ire, Ojoto influenced him towards his first true encounter with the legend of the water spirit, Idoto, around which Okigbo later developed his idea of an alternative or surrogate mother. Pius described their grandmother as 'a source of great folklore.'[29] She had not converted to Christianity and was still steeped in the traditional rituals of Idoto's worship. The Okigbo children came home to Ojoto regularly to spend the holidays. Their grandmother would lavish attention on her late daughter's children who delighted in her cooking. On these visits she regaled Christopher with the enchanting lore of the goddess. It was his grandmother who convinced him that he was the true incarnation of Idoto's priests. She too believed like everyone else that Christopher was her husband, Ikejiofor, reincarnated. She often used terms of endearment such as '*Ikejiofor*', '*Obuluokpochie*' or

'*Omeghaluigboanya*,' which were the honorifics of her late husband.

Okigbo was also especially close to his maternal uncle, Nweze, who became the priest of the Ajani. Nweze was a source of profound knowledge of the ancient world – a passing world which was being lost rapidly to modernity. Nweze constantly used to prod Christopher about his duties to the shrine. He was also especially fond of his nephew, and loved to emphasize Christopher's unique place in the shrine, and never tired of regaling the children about the exploits of their redoubtable grandfather, Ikejiofor.

Susan recalled how their uncle Nweze used to spend endless hours with Christopher, telling stories about the origin of Idoto in Ojoto, and how she became the spirit-mother of all Ojoto. He told him about family lore and legend and about his place within it. He frequently reminded his nephew that he, Nweze, was a mere actor, a passing regent, for he Ifekandu was naturally in line for the priesthood of Idoto. He would share anecdotes, explain mysteries, and on each of their visits take him to assist in the performance of the seasonal rites to the water goddess. Nweze also loved to address Christopher by the titular names of his late father such as '*Obuluokpochie*'. He used say to Christopher Okigbo solemnly, 'One day, when you have gone round and round the world, and have become old, you will come back here and do your duties to our mother ... Mark my word.'[30] Okigbo and his uncle developed a warm friendship; with the uncle treating the young Christopher almost as a peer. 'Those two were inseparable. Each time we visited our maternal home they would be bantering, laughing and behaving like equals. Our uncle communicated easily with Christopher', recalled Susan Anakwenze.[31]

Okigbo loved those stories. He absorbed from those encounters with his uncle and grandmother at Ire, Ojoto the complexity of the Igbo world; a sense of the communal myth of the goddess on which he later depended in his search for identity,. 'I do not know what he liked more, the stories or our grandmother's cooking. He had great appetite for both,' reminisced Pius Okigbo.[32]

Apparently, Christopher Okigbo took the stories of his priesthood more seriously than was obvious at the time, for many years later when he felt his secular world in ruins, he turned to mother Idoto for spiritual anchor. He chose a different route to Idoto. He went through a western humanistic education with all its colonial ideology – a form of symbolic spiritual exile – but returned to the goddess, also symbolically, through an abstract sense of priesthood. In time he began to relate to Idoto unconsciously as a surrogate mother. Okigbo's attachment to Idoto of course was mostly intellectual; its myth later grew and afforded him the central idiom of his poetry. His choice of Idoto was a way to reconstruct, and articulate a personal narrative of the poet's alienation from the source of life and memory; a means by which to re-invent the self after a traumatic moment of self-questioning later on in his life.

Life at Ojoto, each time the schoolmaster's children visited, was lively. It was certainly different from the seclusion of the mission compounds. There were the numerous uncles and cousins. Some of Okigbo's uncles had been among the earliest Igbo men of their generation to attain sufficient schooling in the English education system of the early years of colonialism. Some had converted to Christianity and become active in the Roman Catholic Church, some had relapsed and become nominal Christians, while quite a number of these uncles chose not to be converted and retained their foothold in traditional society. Thus there were still numerous relations in the Okigbo clan who remained steeped in the traditional practices and life of the Igbo people. Some of Christopher Okigbo's uncles had gone to work for the white man: some went to work for the Railways in Aba, Port Harcourt, Lagos, and even up to the

North; some had gone to work as clerks in the colonial administration in Lagos; while some had gone to do business in Onitsha and other places. They had spread out in all directions, but there was the convergence of these relations at Ojoto, especially during the holidays and festive seasons.

Holidays in Ojoto were thus always an opportunity for the headmaster's children to interact freely within a large but close-knit clan. Like many other children of that generation who received English missionary and colonial education, the Okigbo children experienced the double consciousness of the dual exposure – in part European, and in part traditional. Frequent contact with the traditional life in Ojoto mitigated the destructive impact of the deculturised existence of mission school compounds. The conquest of traditional society by colonialism might have registered significant cultural shifts, yet the strong ties, the abiding currents of life in traditional society persisted with its intricate rituals, its experience of the deities of the Igbo world still intact. Its great folklore and the ethos of a collective engagement were still within the bounds of communal memory. The Okigbo children were thus exposed to two powerful influences: the western, Euro-Christian world and the deeply oral, ritualized, Igbo world. One was in the ascent and the other in slow decline. These worlds would clash in Christopher Okigbo's consciousness, and would find full expression in the idiom and spirit of his poetry later on. His work was a hybrid of classical western modes of thought with the experience of the Igbo ethical worldview, transmitted through a complex ritual landscape, deriving its energy from that society in which the poet had grown. The Igbo world of the 1930s and early 1940s had not completely disappeared, nor lost its spontaneity, its ancient mores, or the energy of its idioms. On the one hand, he was deeply influenced by the fervent Catholicism of his family. In spite of his father's deep Christian faith, Christopher Okigbo found important connections with the spiritual heritage of the Igbo. This gave foundation to his poetic practice.

Like many of the children of this conflict generation; Okigbo was born and raised 'at the crossroads of culture', as Chinua Achebe, came to put it years later. Achebe himself, born in November 1930, was growing up at the same time as Okigbo in Ogidi, only about twelve miles from Ojoto. Another novelist of the future, Vincent Chukwuemeka Ike, was born close by at Ndikelionwu. Benedict Obumselu, the literary critic of this generation, was born in Oba, near Onitsha.

These leading cultural figures of that generation, born at the same time, were growing up in the same milieu, were shaped by the same historical forces. Christopher Okigbo and Chinua Achebe had fathers who were both missionary educators, although they were on either side of the Christian divide. There was great rivalry between the Roman Catholic Mission (RCM) and the Anglican mission under the Church Missionary Society (CMS). These missionary groups kept each other at arms length in those years. V.C. Ike may have heard accounts of the Okigbo family while they lived nearby in Ekwulobia, about five miles from Ike's home in Ndikelionwu, but they may never have met socially in elementary school. There was another boy in the vicinity, Alex Ekwueme, also son of a mission schoolteacher who became an architect and later Vice-President of the Federal Republic of Nigeria. He came in contact with the Okigbo family when they moved to Ekwulobia in 1939-40. Alex Ekwueme recalled the serious rivalry between the missions, which marked the nature of relationships among the boys of Okigbo's generation and that 'The CMS and the Catholic boys were never allowed to play [football] against each other.'[33]

In 1936, the Okigbo family moved to Adazi and Christopher Okigbo was registered in school in the infant classes at St. Joseph's RCM School. Adazi was one of the earliest, important centers of the Catholic Church in Eastern Nigeria. The Catholic Church had established a strong missionary presence there by building schools, hospitals and a monastery. By the 1930s Adazi had become a semi-urban environment, vastly different from the mostly rural locations to which James Okigbo was often sent to work. Meanwhile, serious events in the world were reverberating everywhere with the rise of Adolf Hitler in Germany and the eruption of war between the nationalists and the republicans in Spain. On 26 April 1937, forty-three aircraft belonging to the Condor legion bombed Guernica, killing a thousand civilians, and virtually wiping the ancient Basque town, with its famous oak tree, from the face of the earth. Many world famous intellectuals – poets, journalists and other leading cultural figures, volunteered on the republican side in the Spanish civil war. The poet García Lorca was one of the casualties. This fact was to become significant to Christopher Okigbo many years later.

At St. Joseph's, young Christopher Okigbo had his first experience of formal schooling. But as his brother Pius recalls, 'he was a boy of many gifts and talents,'[34] and he had mastered the alphabet on his own before coming to school. The Irish reverend sisters who ran the infant classes taught nursery rhymes, like 'Little Bo Peep.' which Okigbo would later mimic as '*etru bo pi ashe*'. This was his reflection on the impact of colonial education, and the distortions in a child's consciousness of life of alien speech recollected in fragments. Okigbo completed two years in the infant section and one year of standard one at St. Joseph's, Adazi.

In the 1939–1940 school year, Okigbo's father was transferred to St. Joseph's Ekwulobia as headmaster. By this time, Lawrence and Pius, the two older sons, were at CKC Onitsha. The eldest, Lawrence, soon graduated from secondary school at Christ the King College, Onitsha and was on his way to the University of Aberdeen, Scotland, where he would study engineering and forestry. Lawrence was a strict, serious-minded and disciplined elder brother. He typified the firstborn in a traditional Igbo family system. He bore the brunt of the family's expectation and did not allow himself the luxury of frivolity. The relationship between Christopher and Lawrence was always cautious. There was the age difference, but most importantly, Lawrence always seemed to Christopher to be too much of a figure of authority who was relentless in his sense of responsibility and propriety. Lawrence was intolerant of the whimsical and quixotic aspects of Christopher's character. He was one of the few who would openly chastise him for his numerous follies, and never seemed able to comprehend his younger brother's unorthodox temperament. Unlike Pius, Lawrence always seemed to Christopher Okigbo to be unable to take a good joke. Christopher was intimidated by his seriousness and he had a respect for Lawrence bordering on fear.[35] Christopher's relationship with Lawrence was marked by absences – to the boarding schools, and soon after, to Scotland for university. To Christopher's young mind, he was mostly away, and he returned like the Ijele – the venerated masquerade of the Igbo upon whom rarity conferred a profound mystique. Beyond the apparent severity of his persona, there was evidence of genuine warmth and affection. The Okigbo children cared deeply for each other, perhaps because of a common grief shared, and a common expression of faith in each other. They were mostly protective of Christopher – intense and vulnerable.

Christopher's truest friend was Pius. He was the more liberal, more colorful elder brother who accommodated Christopher's sense of drama and style. Pius Okigbo was something of a child prodigy. His academic brilliance had become legendary by the time he left school in 1942 with his graduating class at Christ the King's College, which included Chukwudifu Oputa, Uche Omo, Anthony Idigbe, and Gabriel Onyiuke, a constellation of the brightest legal brains of that generation in Nigeria. Onyiuke became Attorney-General of Nigeria, and the others ended up on the Nigerian Supreme Court. Pius himself later gained international acclaim as an economist, and as one of Africa's most original thinkers in the twentieth century.

Pius Okigbo's accomplishments as a young scholar appealed to his younger brother's imagination. Christopher was in the early stages of primary school at St. Joseph's Ekwulobia when Pius was already in his last year of secondary school. Pius of course, spending his holidays in Ekwulobia, always cut a dashing figure in the '…cream and blue striped CKC blazer much admired by primary school pupils'.[36] Pius was admitted into the then prestigious Yaba Higher College, Lagos when Christopher was in standard four at St. Joseph's, Ekwulobia. Pius's successes inspired him as it did many other young boys of his generation. Alex Ekwueme puts in perspective a sense of Pius Okigbo's early accomplishments in the 1940s, and provides insight into how Pius Okigbo symbolized everything which Christopher found inspiring. Of Pius Okigbo, Alex Ekwueme wrote:

> He was at CKC for only four years and passed the senior Cambridge School certificate at 16 in December 1940 in Grade one with exemption from the University of London matriculation examination. Bearing in mind that the minimum age for matriculation in London University was 17 at that time, it was obviously no mean feat for a pupil in 'backward' colonial Africa to qualify for matriculation at 16. But that was Pius…. For his brilliance (and a few other escapades…) Pius was well known in Onitsha academic and social circles. His multi-talented capacity for multi-disciplinary work was astonishing and inspiring. Until his (and Chike Obi with an external M.Sc. in mathematics and a few others') emergence on the scene, those who took external degrees of the London University managed to scrape a pass or at best a Third class Honours. There was the very occasional 2nd Class Honours (Lower Division) degree. But Pius shattered all that myth. Not only did he, after obtaining the intermediate B.A., also obtain the intermediate B.Sc. (Economics) and the intermediate LL.B of the London University, when he did offer himself for the final B.A examination, he came out with a 2nd Class Honours (Upper Division) degree (in History). There was, of course, no doubt that if he had been an internal degree student, he would have come out in the First Class…Pius' brilliance, indeed genius, could not go unnoticed… while working as a development officer, he completed the London B.Sc. degree in Economics again coming out with a Second Class Upper Division. Thenceforth, Economics became the major field of his interest…[37]

When he returned to Nigeria from Achimota, Pius went to teach in a private school in Onitsha and worked as a reporter for the *Spokesman*, one of Nnamdi Azikiwe's newspaper chains. Already earmarked for higher things in the Catholic School system, Pius Okigbo's decision to teach in a private school rather than in the local Catholic Secondary School, ruffled some feathers in the Catholic Church hierarchy. He had contemplated the priesthood but discovered that he was most suited to a secular life and to a life of the imagination. The choice he made, and the challenge to the powerful Catholic Church in Onitsha put Pius under public scrutiny.

In the 1940s, Onitsha was the center of intellectual activity east of the Niger. A very politically active generation of young men was driven by scholarly and nationalist ambition. Many of them taught in school while studying privately for the external degrees of the University of London. Many of those young men later held distinguished public positions in post-colonial Nigeria. This was the Onitsha of Chike Obi, Chukwudifu Oputa, Chuba Ikpeazu, and Sylvanus Cookey. It was cosmopolitan and drew its population from as far away as the Sierra Leone, the Gold Coast, and the Caribbean. The Saro and Caribbean population had long established a professional middle-class elite of doctors, lawyers, teachers and engineers in the public works department. The city throbbed with commerce. It was a centre of anti-colonial and nationalist activism. This was the city of Mbonu Ojike, Osita Agwuna, the Nwafor Orizu, the Mbazulike Amechi, Mokugo Okoye, Nduka Eze and other vital figures of the radical Zikist movement.

The din of war was always in the background. For every school boy of Okigbo's day, the Second World War, although fought in the far and distant shores of Europe and Asia, seemed immediate and present. Everyone in the British colonies was made to contribute towards the war effort. As headmaster of the Catholic mission schools, for instance, Christopher Okigbo's father was required by the British colonial authority to coordinate the local community war efforts to 'buy the final nail for Hitler's coffin.' Young school children in the colonies were made to pick palm kernels in the bush as their own contributions to prevent Hitler from overrunning the entire world. It was a war, they were told, which Great Britain and her allies were fighting to guarantee global freedom. The war spawned Christopher Okigbo's generation, which began to glimpse the complexity of a 'brave new world'.

By the 1940s Onitsha had developed a virile printing and publishing industry, churning out what later came to be known as the Onitsha market literature. Pius Okigbo's home soon became a haunt for his circle of socially active intellectuals and colorful friends. Pius brought his cousin Godwin to live with him, who was to become influential in banking and business. Christopher began to visit Pius frequently on holidays. Pius Okigbo's life most likely accounts for Christopher's sense of social style; the epicurean; the courteous and polite charm, intellectual refinement, courtly manners, and worldliness of the intellectual aristocrat. Christopher replicated his brother's gait, the manner of his speech, and his display of erudition. Sunday Anozie later wrote that Pius '... typified for him (Christopher Okigbo) perhaps that sense of achievement-orientation which some people associate with the cultural psychology of the Ibo (sic) people'.[38]

Pius was deeply influenced by the liberal thinkers of the twentieth century. He has been described as 'one of the last Keynesians.' But his main appeal lay in the mould in which he was cast as a renaissance intellectual, well grounded in his various pursuits as a classicist, historian, economic theorist and as a gifted musician. It was Pius Okigbo who first taught Christopher how to play the trumpet, the clarinet and the piano – all instruments that Pius played with facility and style. Christopher copied his flourish on the trumpet, his manners on the piano, and played the same notes, in the exact way that Pius played them. Dr. Pius Okigbo later said, 'In many ways I understood Christopher... his volcanic ego, the basis of his artistic soul'.[39] It was a soul, which he said, was Promethean; it had to be unbound. Pius encouraged Christopher Okigbo towards self-discovery.

Behind the mask, Christopher was in many respects emotionally insecure, although he veiled it all with his bold and dramatic actions. He needed forms of affirmation at every point in his life. Victoria recalled: 'Pius always had a lot of time for Christopher. My brother could sometimes be withdrawn. Most people did not really see this aspect of his character. Christopher could be lonely at times. But every time Pius returned home, especially during holidays, he brightened. Those were Christopher's greatest moments as a boy. He looked up to Pius.'[40] Pius understood and empathized with Christopher Okigbo's compulsive nature and his need to experience life grandly. Both came to be believers in the same Whitmanesque sense of a large world. They shared a lot in common except that the poet had the restless instincts of the gypsy while his brother the economist had the discipline and rigour of a high-minded scholar.

Christopher was active as a young boy in the Catholic Church. At some point he was head of the altar boys in Onitsha. The Irish priests Reverend Fathers Flanagan and Leidan were two important missionary educators in Eastern Nigeria. Father Flanagan was later iconized by Okigbo in *Limits* as a figure of religious propaganda, who 'sowed the fireseed among grasses';[41] of Father Leidan, Okigbo wrote: 'arch-tyrant of the holy see'.[42] It is important to see why they appear in his poetry as symbols of the proselytizing mission of the church. Catholic missionary work in Igboland intersected many of the frontiers of Okigbo's personal life and private experiences. Father Flanagan was not only an influential priest in Onitsha in the 1940s, he was Principal of the Christ the King College when Christopher's two elder brothers were students there. Father Leidan was manager of Catholic mission schools while Okigbo's father was schoolmaster in Adazi and Ekwulobia. He was later instrumental in the founding of Stella Maris College in Port Harcourt, which opened in 1945, the year Christopher Okigbo was entering secondary school in Umuahia. Leidan rode about on his powerful Triumph motorcycle and was the subject of much mythology woven by schoolboys who associated him with the power of the Holy See and of colonialism. Leidan went on surprise inspections of the Roman Catholic Mission schools. The young Christopher no doubt heard from many adult conversations numerous tales of Leidan's tyrannical goings and comings on his roaring motorbike. European missionary educators, driven with zeal, were often impatient with their local agents who bore the brunt of any general tardiness associated with local schools. As poetic metaphors in *Heavensgate*, Leidan and Flanagan speak to Okigbo's later critique of the church and the entire missionary venture in his poetry.

But the teachings of the Catholic Church dominated his consciousness in his formative years. Christopher's participation in the Church was typical of his need for performance – to experiment with the form rather than the substance of the lived experience. According to Pius Okigbo, 'When he became an altar boy, Christopher was persuaded more by the ceremonies and glamour in its performance, rather than by any deep faith in the church.'[43] His ambivalence later about the church may indeed be because as children growing up in the schoolmaster's household, the Okigbo children had 'a surfeit'[44] of religion. This was bound to impact on the poet in some way. In fact, by the time Christopher began to write poetry, he had fashioned a form of private religion, which he explained later on in his 1965 interview with Marjory Whitelaw, verged on syncretism, a hybrid of the Christian and the traditional. Growing up however, he was fascinated by 'the grand rituals and ceremonies of Catholicism'[45]: the ceremony of mass, the mystery of the Eucharist, the procession of the Corpus Christi (when adherents marched with the host through the 'pagan' streets to the mystification and fascination of non-adherents), the stations of the cross, and the ceremony of novena, which lent themselves to the acute imagination of the poet, and later found expression in the early idiom of Okigbo's poetry.

Christopher was nine years when his father was transferred from Adazi to Ekwulobia to become headmaster of St. Joseph's RCM School. Christopher blossomed in Ekwulobia. The Okigbos spent three years there and the Ekwulobia landscape is heavily represented in Okigbo's *Heavensgate*. Ekwulobia, a little town not too far from the provincial headquarters at Awka, was the center of an important colonial district court. Like many other Igbo communities it maintained a network of clans and interlinked communities. It was an early center of missionary education in Igboland. St. Joseph's, the main Catholic mission in Ekwulobia, had acquired some importance in the Onitsha Roman Catholic ecclesiastical area in the 1940s. The school compound was situated at Agba village, at the boundary between Ekwulobia and Isuofia and was built in the grove of the spirits, or what was then known as 'Agu nwa Agba.'[46] The mission compound, about one mile from the school, compound, was close to the Eke Ekwulobia market at the central crossroads where meet the roads running from Awka to Orlu and from Nnewi to Igboukwu.

The Agueke native court, the Eke market with its forbidding shrine, and the Catholic mission compound formed one complex, according to Dr. Augustine Onyeneke, who also went to school in St. Joseph's Ekwulobia. All teachers resided at the mission compound at Eke and walked the mile uphill to St. Joseph's school, past the Eke shrine and its intimidating sacred grove. According to Okigbo's sister Susan, 'Christopher always thought he heard the endless pounding of the mortar by the priest of the Eke shrine at midnights.'[47] (This probably doubly resonates in his refrain 'And the mortar is not yet dry' in *Heavensgate*, although one immediately sees the transposition in meaning of an original poem by Eliot.)

Christopher grew up with other boys whose parents came to live and teach in Ekwulobia. Some of those boys would later become significant public figures: James Ezeilo became one of Nigeria's best known mathematicians and, later Chancellor of the University of Nigeria, Nsukka. He was also one of the scientists that headed the Research and Production (RaP) team that worked on the Biafran rocket development project during the civil war. There were the Anwunah brothers – Edward and Patrick – whose father became headmaster of St. Joseph's after James Okigbo was transferred to Asaba. The boys later met up with Christopher at the Government College, Umuahia. Edward Anwunah became a medical doctor and his younger brother Patrick later went to Sandhurst with Yakubu Gowon, Alex Madiebo and Mike Okwechime. Patrick would become General Ironsi's Principal staff officer as Military Head of State. He was later to be Ojukwu's principal Staff Officer in the Biafran resistance. There were also the Ekwueme brothers who had just returned to their village nearby in Oko: Alex went on to King's College, Lagos from the CMS School at Ekwulobia in 1945. Alex Ekwueme's younger brother Laz, the musicologist of later years, was to meet Christopher again at Umuahia in September 1948. This group of boys growing up in Ekwulobia came to be part of post-colonial Nigeria's elite.

Rivalries between clans and faiths kept some of these boys at a distance from each other. The Christians looked at the 'pagans' – those who had not converted – with a deep sense of superiority and even curiosity. They were considered to be an unclean and quite backward lot, because the Christians emblematized the sense of progress and modernity. Chinua Achebe has recounted how Christian converts lived openly segregated lives, and abandoned traditional modes – including the arts – because they stood for pagan, primitive behavior and value. Christian children were not allowed to participate in traditional rituals or eat in the homes of their 'pagan' neighbours lest they be fed with 'unclean food.' Among the Christians there was also the rivalry between the dominant Catholic mission and the rival Church Missionary Society. Alex Ekwueme recounts how these rivalries played out in Ekwulobia:

> His [Christopher's] father was a Roman Catholic school teacher (headmaster) and this meant that they moved from town to town generally within the area of the Onitsha Catholic ecclesiastical province; my father was an Anglican Church teacher and we moved from town to town within the Awka district of the Anglican Diocese of the Niger. In the course of

these movements, Mr. Okigbo was posted by the Catholic mission to head the Catholic school in Ekwulobia which then read only up to standard four. Our own movement brought us home to Oko and I enrolled as a pupil at the Anglican (CMS) central school, Ekwulobia. Not surprisingly, although we were 'age mates', we did not see much of Christopher in those days. I say not surprising, because at the time, it was considered a mortal sin for RCM (Roman Catholic Mission) pupils to associate too closely with CMS (Church Missionary Society) pupils. We never played football against each other; RCM Ekwulobia would play against RCM Adazi or RCM Nimo, while CMS Ekwulobia would play against CMS Nnobi, CMS Nnewi and CMS Practicing School Awka. But we did see more of Christopher's cousin Bede who regularly passed in front of our house on his way from Ekwulobia to Isiogwugwu stream in Oko to fetch water, Ekwulobia somewhat considered an arid 'Agbaenu' location. We remember Bede's occasional encounter on his way to the stream with not so sane but adorable Edward of Oko who lived nearby and once succeeded with amazing marksmanship to target Bede's head with a pebble thrown from a distance. After a few years, the Okigbos moved from Ekwulobia to another location.[48]

By the time he came to live in Ekwulobia, Christopher's ears were already tuned to the nuances of the spoken word. Kepkanly was one of the vivid characters who came to populate his poetry. His teacher in standard four was, according to Sunday Anozie, 'noted for his pompous howlers before his class'.[49] Kepkanly spoke Igbo with the rough and quaint accent of the upland – the '*agbaenu*' Igbo. Okigbo's description of Kepkanly as a 'half serious, half comical' character derived essentially from this rather humorous turn of speech which was an infinite source of amusement to the children at St. Joseph's. As the physical education instructor, Kepkanly also had the duty of preparing the pupils for the Empire Day parades at Awka. We now know from Sunday Anozie's work that the character 'Kepkanly' in *Heavensgate* comes from the Igbo compound of '*aka ekpe–aka nli*'[50] ('left-right') bawled out, military style, during school parade. Kepkanly died in 1945 possibly from a heart attack – 'from excess of joy',[51] when the Haragin commission paid workers arrears of salary. Okigbo sees this new alertness to the human landscape of words in terms of a ritualized experience: the baptism:

> mystery which I, initiate,
> received newly naked
> upon waters of the genesis
> from Kepkanly[52]

Poems like *Heavensgate* and *Limits* resonate with Okigbo's recollection of Ekwulobia – a mnemonic breadth that encompasses details offered in succinct poetic particulars, such iconic, almost transcendental experiences, out of which he constructs eternal idioms.

One of the most charming characters Okigbo brings alive in his poetry is Jadum – the 'half-demented village minstrel'.[53] He came from the nearby Eziagulu village and went about Ekwulobia without let, spinning witty shibboleths, gained from an uncommon insight into the nature of the world. Jadum was a complex contradictory character. He was not mad in a clinical sense, and had utter clarity of thought. Jadum nestled in a halfway zone between madness and sanity. He was the classic case of one who could be said to have been possessed by that capricious deity Agwu – patron of poets, musicians, artists, visioners, prophets and herbalists. Jadum was something of a giant, but with incredibly mild manners. He was a frequent visitor to the schoolmaster's home, where he would often be given food and sent merrily on his way to his usual haunt, the Eke shrine nearby Ekwulobia market square. He danced to his own rendition of 'jan-jan, dum-dum,'[54] an onomatopoeic reconstruction of the tone of the drum, from which he fittingly earned the sobriquet, 'Jadum'. Laz Ekwueme said of him: 'He was incapable of violence. He was known mostly for his penetrating wit.'[55]

The more adventurous young boys, like Christopher, often only needed to prod Jadum to get him to utter some of his famous witticisms. Whenever anyone asked Jadum about the state of the world, he would reply with one of his most hortatory responses: 'All the gourds in the tapsters home have broken into shards.' This witticism captures Jadum's idea of chaos, or the inevitable normlessness of the physical world. Yet he was never an anarchist. There was an inner beauty in the workings of his troubled mind. He entered into local mythology.

Laz Ekwueme told of the day Jadum was arraigned before the District Officer's Court, which sat at the Native Court at Ekwulobia, on a charge of public indecency. Jadum had apparently killed one of the vultures that hovered around the Ekwulobia market – and made a lively meal of it. It was against the law in colonial times to indulge in such 'unhygienic' activities, and Jadum forcibly was brought to the courts on a warrant. The English District Officer asked Jadum why he should not be punished for his transgression. Jadum stood ponderously and, after taking a deep breath, addressed the District Officer. He asked the court clerk to help him inform the District Officer about the foolishness of his question. 'Please, also help me ask the D.O., if he eats his chicken, does it taste the same as the vulture? Do I ask him why he eats his chicken? *Uwa bu onye na nke ya, onye na nke ya.*' ('The world is to each man his own....').[56] The logic was unassailable: the English District Officer should keep to his own laws and the privilege of his chicken, while Jadum be left to his preferences. He was acquitted for insanity. On another occasion, Jadum went through a house in Ekwulobia and removed the window curtains which he promptly tied around his waist. He was again brought before the court, charged this time with theft. Again asked to defend himself, Jadum implored the court to explain what sense there was that a people had such an excess of clothes that they hung some on their windows, while a full adult like himself had not a single piece to cover his manhood. 'Are they not ashamed to see this thing jangling between my thighs?' Jadum had a felicitous way of conveying morals by default.

One day, a newly crazed young man came to Ekwulobia. He had come to see Jadum, as he said, to see who was more insane. Quickly Jadum came upon an idea. They would have to resolve the question by competition. They would go round and round the Eke Ekwulobia to determine who was the most mad. Soon enough, they both set off. On the seventh round, the young fellow became tired and sat down to rest. Jadum went past him, came again and saw him sitting down and again went past him, not uttering a word. At the next round, the fellow was still sitting, at the same spot. This time Jadum went to him and gave him a knock on the head: 'You young folk do not have the patience to learn. Now, look at you. Whoever told you that the serious business of madness is for the fainthearted?'[57]

One particular day Jadum returned from a neighbouring, where he had gone to visit another famously mad colleague. As the story went, each time Jadum went to visit his friend at Umuchu, there was a dead dog lying around. They would roast it and have a hearty meal. Yet at Ekwulobia, Jadum rarely found meat to eat. So on this day he visited his friend again, and another dog lay dead to serve their delight. At the end of their feast, Jadum asked his friend how he had such luck in Umuchu while Jadum hardly managed to scrape by at Ekwulobia. His friend laughed and informed Jadum that his people in Umuchu truly appreciated his work, which was why they ensured that their cars knocked dead a dog for his regular supply of meat. Jadum bore that in mind, spent a wonderful day with his friend at Umuchu and returned to Ekwulobia. On his return, he took a gong round the town, proclaiming that the Ekwulobia people should go to Umuchu and see for themselves how people treated a mad man as though he were royalty.

Jadum was a source of profound wit whom Okigbo turned into a symbol. Okigbo reconstructs, even appropriates Jadum's philosophy as a valid aesthetic possibility:

Do not listen at keyholes,
After the lights,
To smell from other rooms,
After the lights –

Singeth Jadum from Rockland,
after the lights.[58]

Jadum's legends thus constitute meaning found deep in Okigbo's childhood. Iconic figures like Jadum point to Okigbo's love of drama and performance.

Another character appropriated by Okigbo was 'Up Andrew' – the traveling minstrel who appears as 'Upandru' alongside Jadum and Kepkanly in *Heavensgate*. Upandru was a gifted, handicapped performer from Achina who sang in the Ekwulobia market. Performers like Upandru were romantic figures for Okigbo, traveling men who enjoyed the freedom of the open air. They were citizens of the world witnessing history and social change. Upandru used humour, biting sarcasm and satire to make comments on social morality. In that sense, Upandru appears in Okigbo's poetry like Tiresias – blind and prophetic. It is towards that voice of prophecy which Okigbo's poetry aspires in his witness to violent change. Ekwulobia offered symbolism to the poet of *Labyrinths* at a crucial moment of his life – the moment of innocence from which the eyes could observe and the ears hear words from minstrels driven by the urge for utterance by the poetic deity Agwu.

In 1942 the poet's father was transferred once again to become headmaster of St. Joseph's RCM School, Asaba. Christopher moved with him, because St. Joseph's Ekwulobia had only classes to Standard IV, and Okigbo had to register for Standard V and VI. Meanwhile, Christopher's cousin Bede Okigbo had sought admission at Christ the King College Onitsha, but the principal Father Flanagan rejected him, on account of an earlier disagreement involving Pius Okigbo. Nevertheless, Bede was admitted into the prestigious Government College, Umuahia in 1943.

A new age was coming. The allied forces were the verge of a crucial victory in the Second World War. In Nigeria, the colonial government was being confronted by a vociferous nationalist alliance led by Herbert Macaulay and Nnamdi Azikiwe who had organized the NCNC. Students at King's College in Lagos had organized a march in protest against forced recruitment to military service. Many had been expelled. Some of them had been conscripted and sent overseas to fight for Great Britain. One had died in battle. Another of them, Anthony Enahoro, the radicalized son of a school master, had joined the nationalist movement, and then worked for one of Azikiwe's numerous publications. These events would not have escaped the attention of the curious minded Christopher. His own brother, Pius, had been among the group of students sent off to Achimota College in Ghana to complete their diploma when the Yaba Higher College had been closed down following nationalist agitations against the war.

Although Asaba was more cosmopolitan urban than Ekwulobia, life was just as idyllic. Resting on the west bank of 'the lordly Niger,' there was a lively interaction between the town and active commercial Onitsha. Asaba had been one of the earliest, administrative centers of colonial Nigeria, and gained importance as a major trading post and missionary center in the nineteenth century. It was while briefly living in Asaba that Okigbo first encountered the legend of Onishe – the river deity of the Asaba people which was worshiped by his adherents in an elaborate, colorful, annual ritual at the mysterious waterfront with its shrine at Cable Point. Many years later, Okigbo reconstructs this ritual in 'Siren Limits':

> Hurry on down –
>     Thro' the high-arched gate –
> Hurry on down
>     Little stream to the lake;
>
> Hurry on down –
>     Thro' the cinder market –
> Hurry on down
>     in the wake of the dream;
>
> Hurry on down -
>     To rockpoint of Cable…[59]

He wrote this section following his visit years later with the English critic Gerald Moore to Cable Point. He described that spot in *Labyrinths* as 'a sacred waterfront with rocky promontory, and terminal point of a traditional quinquennial pilgrimage'.[60] The 'qinquennial pilgrimage' was actually an annual ritual. Okigbo probably came to think of this ritual procession – the 'quinquennial journey' – in an exalted way. By then it had acquired a particular symbolic significance, which described his own pilgrimage, his ritual odyssey to the past. Onishe became closer to the Arthurian 'Lady of the Lake' in telling the experience of her poet acolyte. Onishe was, like Idoto, the water spirit that sustained all life. The legend of the water goddess appears among communities in Igboland with marine cultures, who often see manifestations of the essence of the same goddess, Idemili.

Okigbo's early fascination with the Onishe cult was equal to his imaginative attachment to Idoto; Onishe had the same primal essence of the river goddess. The headmaster's home stood close to the bank of the River Niger at Asaba. The waterfront endlessly fascinated Okigbo. Driven by his impulse for drama and adventure, the fourteen-year-old Christopher would wander alone by the river with the great trading town beyond at Onitsha. He would watch the canoes sailing off into the twilight, until they disappeared into the timeless horizon, merging with the silhouette of the great river, 'Christopher loved the magic of the river,'[61] his brother Pius Okigbo said. The legend of the watermaid is the most constant poetic image in Okigbo's creative invocation. The Great River at Asaba indeed provoked mystery and its own legends. But the river was also the source of great sport and entertainment. His sister Susan remembered how Christopher sometimes went off with other local boys to swim from Cable Point and to the UAC piers at Onitsha; a dangerous venture, which tested the skill of the finest swimmer.

The move from Ekwulobia did not dampen Christopher's impishness. Susan noted that Christopher was a source of constant anxiety for his father because of his irreverent and mischievous sense of fun, which sometimes clashed with local Asaba norms or taboos. In the 1940s, non-indigenes living among the Asaba people were still regulated by the many sacred laws of the Asaba. The Asaba people were highly suspicious of strangers living among them. Asaba people have always been very proud of their magnificent culture and heritage. Their women were elegant and graceful. Perhaps this was why they established that form of benign segregation, which excluded and isolated non-indigene families like the Okigbos, who came to live and work at Asaba. The segregation was even sanctified by ritual. There was a point at the river in Asaba called the 'Ngene Ugbomanta', from which outsiders were restricted. Only Asaba women could bathe on that spot. Not even Asaba men from the age of puberty were allowed to enter that part of the river. Asaba women were settled in the knowledge that no one had broken this taboo for hundreds of years. Yet Christopher would go to Ngene Ugbomanta while the women were taking their bath and throw himself merrily in their midst, splashing water in every direction. The Asaba women would quickly cover their nudity and raise a cry in the village. The women would refuse to cook for their husbands until they had been sufficiently cleansed. A crowd of hungry men would march to the schoolmaster's house to demand justice. The headmaster would usually plead and make amends on his son's behalf. He would give them the money required for the elaborate cleansing ritual. The schoolmaster would seriously reprimand Christopher and warn him against further breaching of the taboos of Ngene Ugbomanta. But it was to no avail. He always went back, to that same spot where only Asaba women took baths. Susan recalled 'In Asaba, any man who throws water on an Asaba woman was required either to marry the woman or perform a very expensive ritual to cleanse her. Christopher's idea was to splash water on as many women as possible. He wanted to marry all of them.'[62] Hardly fourteen years of age at this time, the prospect of marriage was certainly a distant proposition for Christopher. His father was thus left with the burden of settling his many violations of an ancient taboo so dear to adherents of this traditional system.

Perhaps as a way of redirecting his son's hunger for adventure, the schoolmaster took Christopher on occasional hunting expeditions. James Okigbo was a first-rate marksman, and he relished hunting game. He was indeed reputed to be a great hunter of bush fowls. The Okigbo men loved firearms, both for sporting value and prestige. All of Christopher's uncles owned guns and some were fine marksmen. The elemental tension echoing in the ears of a hunter, and the mysteries of the world resolving themselves in the utter solitude of the forest are unique experiences from which Okigbo's young mind would have gained as he accompanied his father to hunt. With a sensitive apprehension of his environment, his good ears, and his deep power of observation, the young Christopher was moved early by the power of the natural world. He communicated the result so beautifully in his poems: his mimicry of the song of birds, his fascination with the organic world, his understanding of fauna – all would become central to his poetic experience and invocation.

It must have been a source of great relief to the schoolmaster when his restless son left home for a prestigious boarding school in January 1945. Christopher Okigbo took the Standard Six examination and the entrance to the Government College, Umuahia in December 1944. He received the letter of admission to Umuahia in December, and was among the boys interviewed by the new principal, William Simpson. He entered Government College, Umuahia on 12 January 1945.

## NOTES

1   Christopher Okigbo, *Labyrinths with Path of Thunder* (London: Heinemann, 1971), p. xi.
2   C. L. Innes and Bernth Lindfors, eds, *Critical Perspectives on Chinua Achebe* (London: Heinemann Educational Books, 1979).
3   Interview with Pius Okigbo, 1994.
4   Interview with Suzanne Anakwenze, 1994.
5   Ibid.
6   Chinua Achebe, *The Trouble with Nigeria* (Enugu: Fourth Dimension Publishers, 1983).
7   Interview with Uzo Maxim Uzoatu, 1994.
8   Ibid.
9   Interview with Susan Anakwenze.
10  Interview with Susan Anakwenze and Victoria Okuzu, Nsukka and Lagos, 1994.
11  Pius Okigbo, 'A Toast of Christopher Okigbo', *Glendora Review* 1 (2) 1995 (34–39) Lagos.
12  Christopher Okigbo, interview with Marjory Whitelaw, Ibadan, 1965, published in *The Journal of Commonwealth Literature*, Vol. 9, July, 1970, pp. 28–37.
13  Christopher Okigbo, Introduction to *Labyrinths*.
14  Evelyn Waugh, *Remote People* (London: Duckworth, 1931).
15  George Orwell, *Shooting an Elephant and Other Essays* (London: Secker and Warburg, 1950).
16  James Coleman, *Nigeria: Background to Nationalism* (Berkeley: University of California Press, 1958).
17  Interview with Pius Okigbo, 1994.
18  Christopher Okigbo, *Labyrinths*, p. 5.
19  Christopher Okigbo, Introduction to *Labyrinths*, p. xiv.
20  Christopher Okigbo, 'The Passage', *Heavensgate*, *Labyrinths*.
21  Interview with Victoria Okuzu, FESTAC Town, Lagos.
22  Interview with Susan Anakwenze in Dr. Uzodinma Nwala's residence on the campus of the University of Nigeria, Nsukka, 6 March 1994.
23  Interview with Pius Okigbo, 1994.
24  Interview with Ben Obumselu, Lagos, 2 August 1992.
25  Interview with Pius Okigbo.
26  Ibid.
27  Christopher Okigbo, *Labyrinths*, p. 32.
28  Christopher Okigbo, *Limits* IX.
29  Interview with Pius Okigbo, 1994.
30  Interview with Susan Anakwenze.
31  Ibid.
32  Interview with Pius Okigbo.
33  Alex Ekwueme, 'Remembering the Weaverbird', opening remarks at 'Song for Idoto': A Celebration of Christopher Okigbo, National Museum, Enugu, 2 November 1996.
34  Pius Okigbo, 'A Toast of Christopher Okigbo'.
35  Interview with Victoria Okuzu.
36  Alex Ekwueme, 'Remembering the Weaverbird.'
37  Ibid.
38  Sunday O. Anozie, *Christopher Okigbo: Creative Rhetoric* (New York: Africana Publishers, 1971).
39  Interview with Pius Okigbo.

40  Interview with Victoria Okuzu.
41  Christopher Okigbo, *Limits* VII, *Labyrinths*.
42  Ibid.
43  Interview with Pius Okigbo, Enugu, 1995.
44  Ibid.
45  Ibid.
46  Interview with Revd Father (Dr.) Augustine Onyeneke, Institute of African Studies, University of Nigeria, Nsukka, February 2000.
47  Interview with Susan Anakwenze.
48  Alex Ekwueme, 'Remembering the Weaverbird.'
49  Sunday Anozie, *Christopher Okigbo: Creative Rhetoric.*
50  Ibid.
51  Christopher Okigbo, *Labyrinths*, footnote, p. 7.
52  Christopher Okigbo, 'Initiations II', *Heavensgate*, *Labyrinths*.
53  Christopher Okigbo, *Labyrinths*, footnote, p. 8.
54  Interview with Laz Ekwueme, University of Lagos, Akoka, Sept. 1994.
55  Ibid.
56  Ibid.
57  Ibid.
58  Christopher Okigbo, 'Initiations II', *Heavensgate*, *Labyrinths*.
59  Christopher Okigbo, 'Siren Limits', *Limits*, *Labyrinths*.
60  Christopher Okigbo, *Labyrinths*, footnote p. 26.
61  Interview with Pius Okigbo, Enugu, 1995.
62  Interview with Susan Anakwenze.

# 2

## *Sportsman, actor & 'effortless genius'*

### UMUAHIA 1945–50

For he was a shrub among the poplars,
Needing more roots
More sap to grow to sunlight,
Thirsting for sunlight...
(*Limits* II)

...the quadrangle, the rest, me and you...
('Initiations')

The Government College, Umuahia, an all-boys boarding school, was established in Eastern Nigeria in 1929 as a colonial model of the English public school. It was extremely elitist. Umuahia admitted talented boys mostly from Southern Nigeria after a competitive entrance examination. Candidates also came from other parts of British West Africa. Barry Cozens, one of the English men who taught in Umuahia at the end of the Second World War, described this process of selection to the American critic, Robert M. Wren. Cozens (who later became Principal) recalled that about three thousand boys sat exams annually for the thirty available places in Umuahia's one-stream classes. Wren reports in his book, *Those Magical Years*:

> They all sat for the entrance examination at centres throughout Nigeria and Western Cameroons (then a British protectorate). The entire staff worked to create 'a short list of about two hundred'. Of these, 'the first twenty or thirty picked themselves; thereafter, quite frankly, any of the next two or three hundred –'. He stopped, with a helpless look, resignedly embarrassed about the process by which hundreds of worthy candidates failed to get a place. 'We invited the first hundred and thirty for a two night visit at our expense, for interview, and to check that they were indeed the boys who sat for the examination.'[1]

The Nigerian musicologist Laz Ekwueme was one of the lads who were admitted to Government College, Umuahia in September 1948. Writing in 1992 he said:

> ...Several factors in my judgement, account for the immense contribution in the arts by Umuahians. First is the intellectual material of which the Umuahian is made. It was a known fact that only the best brains from the length and breadth of Nigeria and the (then British) Cameroon went to Umuahia. In those days when money was very hard to come by, and even the five shillings entrance examination fees proved a burden for most parents, only those pupils who were sure of their mental endowments dared attempt the very competitive examinations and only the very best, and it must be added lucky ones made it to Umuahia![2]

Before the expansion of colonial education in the West African colonies, the British left the establishment and administration of educational institutions in the hands of

Christian Missions and voluntary agencies. These agencies established and ran their schools – mostly grammar schools and vocational institutions – according to their own convictions or religious beliefs. There were a number of well-known mission schools in the south-east of Nigeria, like the Hope Waddell Institute in Calabar, the Methodist Colleges in Oron and in Uzoakoli, and the Dennis Memorial Grammar School, established by the Anglican mission in Onitsha in 1925. There were schools for girls, such as St. Monica's College at Ogbunike near Onitsha, long established by the CMS. The Catholics established St. Patrick's College at Calabar in 1929, followed by the Christ the King College, Onitsha in 1935. Christopher Okigbo's two elder brothers, Lawrence and Pius, attended Christ the King College, Onitsha from 1936 to 1940. Christopher also took the entrance exam to CKC Onitsha and to the newly established College of Immaculate Conception (CIC) at Enugu, and could most likely have headed in either direction had he not been admitted to the prestigious Government College, Umuahia.

The Government College was special. It was conceived by the British colonial administration to educate a select category of 'natives' who were to be recruited into the colonial administration, following the loss of some of England's most talented young men in the First World War. Administrators of the empire created local equivalents of Eton, Harrow and Winchester, to train the elite who would assist in running the colony. This policy became even more urgent with the Great Depression of the late 1920s.

The first of the government colleges – King's College – was established in Lagos in 1909. Twenty years later, in January 1929 three more Government Colleges were established at Umuahia in the East, Ibadan in the West, and Zaria (Barewa College) in the North. These Government Colleges were located at least ten miles away from town and near agricultural research stations (Umudike in Umuahia, Moore Plantation, Ibadan and the Samaru station, Zaria). They had teachers drawn mostly from English men who themselves had been educated at Cambridge and Oxford. These teachers were employed through the colonial civil service as education officers rather than through the missions. Their mandate was to provide the best English education to a select elite, trained and prepared in the English mould. Government College, Umuahia became generally known in Nigeria as the 'Eton of the East.'[3]

The Reverend Robert Fisher, founding Principal of the school, already well known in the intellectual circles of colonial society in British West Africa, was commissioned by the colonial education board to open Government College, Umuahia in December 1927. By the time he arrived at Umuahia, Fisher had not only acquired extensive experience in colonial education administration in the Gold Coast, but his reputation gave him the advantages necessary to secure unstinting cooperation from the colonial authorities to establish a model school. Born on 24 May 1887 at Groombridge, Sussex, where his father was vicar of the church, Fisher studied at Marlborough and later at Pembroke College, Cambridge. He then served briefly as curate of St Mary's Church, Tottenham, London, before being drawn to the colonies by missionary activity. He went initially to Gold Coast, now Ghana, where he was appointed as priest in charge of Christ Church and Principal of the Anglican Grammar School in Cape Coast. He moved on later to Accra to become priest of Holy Trinity Church. In 1920, Robert Fisher transferred from missionary work to the education department of the Gold Coast, where he took part in the founding of the famous Achimota College, Accra, which was often to be regarded as Umuahia's sister school.

Government College, Umuahia opened its gates to its first students in January 1929. Fisher nurtured the dream of Umuahia for nine years, strengthening the foundation of the college and its highly elitist ideal. So dedicated was he to building Umuahia into a fine boarding school for boys, that he rejected an offer to become a Bishop of the Anglican Church. Nestled in a valley on the road to Ikot-Ekpene, ten miles away from the Umuahia railway town, the school's reputation would later justify Robert Fisher's hard work. Following the outbreak of the Second World War, Fisher returned to England, becoming vicar of West Den. Government College, Umuahia was closed in January 1939 so as to be used for three years as an interment camp for German and Italian prisoners of war from the Cameroons.

In 1942, however, a set of new boys was admitted to the school. They were attached to King's College, Lagos, and quartered at a building on the old Customs Street, in downtown Lagos, from where they attended classes at King's. This 1942 class was known as 'Umuahia class one,' preparatory to the re-opening of the Government College, Umuahia in January 1943, on its old compound in Umudike, Umuahia. Okigbo's first cousin Bede was among that set of boys admitted to Umuahia in 1943. In the early period of its re-opening, the school managed without a substantive Principal, administered intermittently by education officers sent from Yaba Higher College or from the colonial education department in acting capacities. Then one of the masters, Mr Hicks, took on the duties of acting principal until William Simpson took over in January 1945.

When William Simpson arrived in Umuahia in December 1944 as the new principal of the school at this crucial period, he began a remarkable resuscitation of Umuahia and ushered in a golden age. William Simpson's eight years at Umuahia brought on a remarkable generation. He rebuilt the Government College to its pre-war eminence, strengthened its academic standards, and generated a literary spirit through Umuahia's 'magazine culture.' Young students at Umuahia, at the time the only Government College in Eastern Nigeria, had the privilege, and luxury of a well-stocked school. Saburi Biobaku recollects one of the distinct aspects of his work in Umuahia, as the challenge of creating a national elite, a talented tenth, upon whom the future of independent Nigeria would be consolidated. However, The Second World War was heading towards its ferocious climax. Simpson arrived at the time of Christopher Okigbo's admission to the new class of January 1945.

Okigbo was the only boy from his school, St. Joseph's Primary School, Asaba, to gain admission into Umuahia in 1945. He had walked eight miles from Asaba to Ibuzo, the provincial headquarters, to collect his admission letter to Umuahia. According to the novelist, Vincent Chukwuemeka Ike, who was also admitted in 1945, the portly and kindly William Simpson was soon to be nicknamed 'the Dewar', after a whisky bottle of that shape. Umuahians nurtured under his remarkable authority became known as the 'Simpson generation.'

The question has been frequently asked: how did so many of the most exciting writers in the second half of the twentieth century in Nigeria come from Government College, Umuahia? How did such distinct voices as Gabriel Okara, Chinua Achebe, Christopher Okigbo, V.C Ike, Elechi Amadi, I.N.C. Aniebo and Ken Saro-Wiwa emerge? These boys were shaped by an ethos in Umuahia that demanded high achievement and allowed for individuality. William Simpson was assisted by a crop of extraordinary teachers who came to teach in the 1940s and 50s such as Mr. Wareham, The poet and cricketer Charles W. Low was to have a particular input on Christopher Okigbo. Mr. Stone and Mr. Cozens were authors of the successful book on tropical biology. Among the African staff were Saburi Biobaku, G. T. Ifon, Mr. Ohiwerei, Mr. Longe, Mr. W. Alagoa, Mr. I. D. Erokosima, J. C. Menakaya, Mr. Opukiri and the legendary Reginald Jumbo; Mr. Jerry Enyeazu was later to be one of Nigeria's most distinguished sports administrators. These were among the pioneers of modern Nigerian education in the twentieth century.

The Government College, Umuahia had a stimulating environment for learning. Chinua Achebe wrote in 2000 of his own experience at Umuahia: 'My school had a wonderful library and a regulation that forced us to use it. I was not one of those who grumbled about that particular imposition! I was entranced by the far away and long-ago worlds of the stories, so different from the stories of my home and childhood.'[4] This mythical, far-removed world excited the imagination of many young Umuahia boys.

It is apt therefore briefly to examine the impact of this English educator on this generation of school boys. William Simpson's benign authority, belied his deep intellect and innovative spirit. He was a mathematician with an eclectic taste in poetry, sports and the classics. The historian Saburi Biobaku described him as 'a man of quick, well-rounded intellect who was open to debate, who had a keen knowledge of the old world, and was comfortable in the new world.'[5] Okigbo's cosmopolitanism stems in large part from his experience of Umuahia under Simpson.

Born early in the twentieth century on 7 August 1901 in England, Simpson attended Gresham's School, Holt. He was admitted to King's College, Cambridge where he studied mathematics and established a reputation as an all-round athlete, representing his college in the sprints and at the pole vault. He also played excellent cricket and narrowly missed a 'blue' in rugby.[5] Simpson was elected a member of Hawke's, a club which admitted only outstanding sportsmen and scholars.

Simpson spent two years as a tea planter in Ceylon (Sri Lanka). He began his career in the colonial service in the southern provinces of Nigeria in 1927 as Superintendent of Education. He was later posted to King's College, Lagos and taught temporarily in 1933 at the Government College, Ibadan. From there, Simpson moved on in 1934 to be acting Principal of the Yaba Higher College in Lagos. He worked throughout Eastern Nigeria until 1940, when he moved back to Lagos on special duty at the Department of Land and Survey. He returned to the East as senior education officer in Calabar, from where he was transferred to British Cameroon. On 4 December 1944 he went to Umuahia. V.C. Ike wrote thus about Simpson some years later in 1979 in a reflective tribute:

> It is appropriate that although he spent a quarter of a century in Nigeria he is remembered pre-eminently as principal of Government College, Umuahia. As a leading article in the Eastern Outlook rightly stated, 'no story of post-war Umuahia can be complete without a special reference to the devoted and selfless service which Mr. William Simpson gave to the college from 1944 to 1951. Many schools take decades to come to limelight. Umuahia under Simpson took no time to establish an enviable reputation for all-round excellence'. One man (and this is a true story!) was said to have held the school in such high esteem that when his son failed to realize his greatest ambition - to gain admission to Umuahia - he wrote to Mr. Simpson offering not only to pay the boys entire fees for the six-year course in one installment but to add a very generous 'jara' for the principal, if only the boy could be given a place!
>
> An all-round sportsman himself, Mr. Simpson did all in his power to turn his boys into thorough sportsmen, not just men who always played to win. Schools which lacked the spirit of sportsmanship (and there were such schools in which the players were brutally caned if they lost a match!) were not allowed to play Umuahia. He could not stand undue showmanship, or playing to the gallery, in sports; I still remember how unsuccessfully I tried to suppress a giggle one morning watching him demonstrate to the whole school how NOT

to bat! In the days when our boxing opponents from friendly schools announced themselves as 'Bandit Kosoko' and 'kid from Chicago,' the Umuahia boy climbed into the ring as plain 'Okafor' or 'Kurubo,' using his surname and relying on the power in his fist rather than on whimsical names to cow his opponent...[6]

The success of Simpson's work in Umuahia can be measured by the sheer fact that within a generation, the boys who passed through the school became leaders not only in science, engineering, medicine and military science, but also in the arts. The products of the Simpson era included those boys whose works would be pioneers of modern African literature written in the English language.

A decade after leaving the Government College, Umuahia, one of those 'Simpson boys' would write the definitive novel of his generation. The boy, Albert Chinualumogu Achebe, was admitted into the Government College, Umuahia in January 1944. Chinua Achebe, as he chose to be known on his books, preceded Christopher Okigbo by one academic year. However, by the time Okigbo's set arrived the school in 1945, Achebe was one of the seven gifted boys in the 1944 class who had 'double promotion' for their brilliant performances and were made to join the class of 1943. So Achebe went to the intermediate class to make up for a shortfall, and joined Okigbo's cousin Bede, who was later to become an agronomist and plant pathologist.

Among Christopher Okigbo's classmates in 1945 were numerous boys who were to became prominent in public life in Nigeria. Vincent Chukwuemeka Ike, a tall, reserved boy from Ndikelionwu, became a university administrator and novelist. The economist Johnson C. Obi rose to become Nigeria's Federal Director of Budgets. Mmaju Onwuka (later Mmaju Kazie) became a structural engineer. Festus Emeghara emerged as one of the most powerful mandarins of the Nigerian public service. Celestine N. Egbuchulam became the Government Surveyor-General. Eno Namsey, who trained both as a lawyer and as a pharmacist, was also Nigeria's international cricket captain. John Owhochukwu and E. M. Jack were Permanent Secretaries in the government of the Rivers State after the civil war. Austin Ugwumba was Head of the Civil Service in Biafra during the civil war. Patrick Ozieh studied at Trinity College, Dublin and at Oxford and then worked for British Petroleum. Wilfred Chukwudebelu's work in the area of reproductive health and maternal care became internationally renowned. Ebong Etuk distinguished himself as a physician working among the poor in rural Etinan. Francis 'Jazz' Egbonu became a doctor in Onitsha, and later served as the chair of the governing council of the University of Nigeria Teaching Hospital in Enugu. Sinclair Amabebi became a Permanent Secretary, first in the Eastern region before the war in Biafra, and later in Rivers State after the war. Egbonu and Amabebi had been admitted into the 1944 class with Chinua Achebe, but came down to repeat with Christopher Okigbo's class in 1945.

Dark clouds had already gathered over the British Empire as it began its descent towards disintegration. The mood in colonial Africa did not convey the sense of drift that was pervasive in post-war Europe. There was an awakening among Nigerians in that era and they rallied to the movements for political freedom. Young, radicalised Africans who had fought in the war broke the myth of European invincibility. They had seen the human side of the colonialist, his weaknesses and fears in the battlefield. Fighting side by side with European men in the trenches inspired a new confidence among returning soldiers, some of who came to play crucial roles in organizing the African liberation movement. Those colonial subjects who fought in the war on the side of the allies understood that the colonial powers could no longer justify the political subjugation of their so-called colonial subjects. Young educated men like the political essayist Mokugo Okoye and the journalist Smart Ebi, along with Fred Anyiam, M.C.K. Ajuluchukwu, Kola Balogun, Raji Abdallah, and Saad Zungur, were important in organising the revolutionary Zikist movement, the radical wing of the anti-colonial struggle which was formed in that period.

Thus in post-war Africa there was a new mood. In India, Gandhi provided a vital example. Nnamdi Azikiwe's *West African Pilot* thundered the same message of political, economic and cultural freedom through peaceful but consistent agitation. These were the forces of history that would ultimately shape Okigbo's consciousness. The way in which the Second World War inaugurated a new fear about the destructive capacity of modern civilization, with the Hiroshima and Nagasaki bombs, had brought in Aldous Huxley's 'brave new world'. Soviet communism and the United States of America were divided by an iron curtain. Following the conference at Yalta came the withering of imperial Great Britain as a dominant colonial power, which was coterminous with the rise of America. The decline of the European powers gave the sense of a broken world in Europe.

Okigbo's generation would struggle between its high modernist aspirations and the sober realities of modern life; but it would also plant dreams among a newly decolonised people. When they began to write, national renewal framed their vision.

The year 1945 was significant in Nigeria's political history. Nigeria was consti-tutionally redesigned as a federation of three regions. Southern Nigeria, with its capital in Enugu, was broken into two: the Eastern region retained Enugu as capital, and Western Nigeria, with an administrative capital in Ibadan. Lagos remained the seat of colonial government. Kaduna remained the administrative capital of the mammoth Northern Nigeria, left intact as a region. This restructuring came as Sir Arthur Richards assumed office as Governor-General in Nigeria. His mandate from the Colonial Office was to initiate the slow transition towards self-rule. One of the elements of that plan apparently was carefully to select young boys for secondary school who could be fashioned to take over the British colonial bureaucracy and to maintain English values and interests in a postcolonial Nigeria. Most of the boys admitted to the elite government secondary schools in that period became from 1957 the first set of Nigerians to be appointed into the restricted administrative cadre of the colonial civil service.

A maximum of thirty students were admitted each year to Umuahia in the 1940s, many from very distant places. Many of those boys saw for the first time at school modern utilities like electricity and pipe-borne water. Many of the boys were on government scholarship which was the only way they could afford Umuahia's elite education. Umuahia's diversity was its strength. There was the story in Umuahia about a boy admitted from a remote school in the Cameroons, who trekked for one week to the Government College to take his place. That boy, Dr. Endeley of the 1929 class, later became premier of the Southern Cameroons. Many of the boys came from such humble backgrounds. However, the bond of brilliance, the acuteness of their minds, and an ambition to reach their highest personal goals linked these boys to each other. Going to a place like Umuahia was an entry into privilege. It was also an important opportunity to be of service to one's community – and no wonder that many communities raised contributions and pooled funds to see some of these boys through an Umuahian education. A few of the boys like Okigbo, however, were considered already socially privileged: he was born to relative comfort in one of those bustling new townships of the East – Onitsha – the town the novelist Achebe would later describe as 'the gift of the lordly Niger'. Okigbo was aware of the dynamics of township life and the nature of modern conveniences. Christopher's relative social privilege derived from his father, who was by then a highly respected headmaster of Catholic mission schools and a figure of the colonial establishment. Christopher's eldest brother, Lawrence, was already studying abroad at the University of Aberdeen in Scotland, and his other brother Pius had just returned from Achimota College in Gold Coast. Pius would soon join the elite administrative service of the Nigerian colonial civil service after qualifying for his full honors degree as an external candidate of the University of London in 1947.

At Umuahia, Okigbo was admitted into School House and placed under the care of Donatus Opara of the 1942 class, who later became a distinguished harbour engineer and head of the Nigerian Ports Authority. Don Opara was one of the students who had returned from King's College in 1943. Regarded in his days at Umuahia as an all-rounder in sports and academics, Don Opara was made school captain as well as the captain of School House. His younger brother later to become actor and broadcaster, Ralph Opara, came to Government College in 1947, two years behind Okigbo, and was also admitted to School House. Ralph Opara was one of the junior boys like Edward Bayagbona, Lawrence Amu, Chu S. P. Okongwu, and David Okali who radiated around Chris Okigbo. Ralph Opara remained close to Okigbo through university and through their lives as young professional men in Ibadan and Lagos in the 1950s and 60s. Opara recalled that Okigbo was one of the earliest people to spot the true thespian in him: 'I remember Chris used to make me stand up on one of those lockers in School House common room, and he would say 'okay, *ooin* [*ooin* is a Government College term for 'juniors' introduced into the school lexicon in the 1940s] start singing!' and I would sing and dance! He used to have so much fun watching me improvise and he would laugh so much. But that was probably my first introduction to the stage.'[7]

Okigbo indeed loved the stage. He felt a keen sense of the world and life as performance. His brother Pius called him a 'recondite raconteur'[8]. Pius, a man of high style, exposed Christopher from secondary school onwards to the pleasures and manners of high society. He was influenced by Pius's deep love for books, an attribute undoubtedly sharpened by the traditions at the Government College, Umuahia. This tendency to explore and read widely on diverse subjects became one of the most enduring features of Christopher Okigbo's life. Pius first exposed him, through his impressive collection of the classics, to the Greek poets and Latin historians. Latin was not taught at Umuahia until his third year, but Okigbo had begun reading Catullus on his own, instructed by Pius. It was Pius who first introduced Christopher to the great beauty of language and classical culture by interpreting the finer nuances of the classical texts to him, a fact which became important later on in Christopher Okigbo's eventual decision to read for a Classics degree in the university. Incidentally, Pius had been the best student of Classics in his year at the Yaba Higher College to which he was admitted in 1942. He had actually considered taking his degree in Classics, but abandoned that for the combination of economics and history. Pius nevertheless retained his love for the classics and impressed on Christopher Okigbo the notion that they were the domain of truly enlightened men. Pius also influenced Christopher's early taste in fashion and notions of the sartorially elegant. The Okigbo brothers saw themselves as men of taste and leisure. Christopher thought of himself an impeccable dresser, although by the time of his death he had abandoned the formalism of English suits for the more casual style of the shirt and pair of shorts – reflecting his adherence to the lifestyle of the Beat movement – or the long casual caftans of the Nigerian bohemian. But in the 1940s in Umuahia, Okigbo appeared on more than one occasion at school in a sharply cut, expensive, 'senior service' dinner suit which was quite the fashion in elite colonial society; the clothes were apparently borrowed from Pius Okigbo's wardrobe. The cricketer Namsey Eno vividly recollected the day that Okigbo had appeared at school in a stylish Saville row tuxedo dinner suit, collars and all, and 'caused quite a stir among the boys.'[9] It was all part of Okigbo's sense of high drama, that propensity for showmanship and his love for the centre stage. Okigbo always had an impulse to display, a need to amuse and entertain which drew him to excel in any performative act. Okigbo was small framed, and loved to prove himself through physically demanding activities like sports. But Okigbo's flamboyance and competitive-ness was a mask for deep fear of inadequacy that many Freudians may find to be a compelling symptom of his neurosis. This tendency to prove himself perhaps ultimately drew him to the incredible heroism of the battlefield in which he tragically died.

In those years, Christopher spent his holidays with Pius at his home at Ogbor Hill in Aba. The Okigbo brothers often played music together. It was not unusual, as Okali U. Okali later remembered, to visit Pius's home in Aba and to find the brothers engrossed in frenzied, expressive jazz, with Christopher on the piano and Pius on trumpet. Peter Chigbo, who also spent his holidays in Aba said of those years: 'It was remarkable to see them at play together. They had a very powerful chemistry. Pius shared everything with Christopher – his clothes, his books, even the same girlfriends! At seventeen, Christopher was already worldly beyond many of his peers because Pius introduced him very early to the life of the socialite. They were that close.'[10]

Pius Okigbo's early professional life was already notable when in 1947 he moved to Aba as Development Officer (DO), a member of the senior colonial administrative service. Prior to 1946 no Nigerian had been appointed to administrative positions in the colonial civil service. The key leaders of the nationalist movement had long argued for greater indigenous participation in the country's administration. As a way of pressing home their demands, the labour alliance called for a nationwide strike in 1946, with the nationalist figure Nnamdi Azikiwe and the labour organiser Michael Imoudu playing key parts. As part of the resolution to the nationwide strike, the new governor general Sir Arthur Richards set up a panel to look at local grievances. With the example of India in mind, Richards recognized the inevitability of self-rule. The work of that panel set the tone for colonial disengagement in Nigeria and put in motion a transition process that involved leaders of the anti-colonial movement such as Azikiwe. Among its recommendations was the political restructuring of Nigeria into three regions in 1945. Another recommendation was the establishment of the Asquith panel which led to the formation of the University College at Ibadan in 1948 to train a new generation of Nigerians to administer the post-colony. But more important was the guarantee of the British colonial policy of disengagement, the principle to begin a gradual recruitment of qualified Nigerians into senior administrative service positions of the colonial service. As the historian Michael Crowder wrote:

> Eight Nigerians, including Dr Nnamdi Azikiwe, sat on the commission, which recommended that no expatriate should be recruited where a suitable Nigerian was available. McPherson also appointed four Africans to his executive council, and with the appointment of Dr S.L. Manuwa as the first Nigerian Director of Medical services; this made five, since his post gave him a seat ex-officio.[11]

So began the policy of Nigerianization both in the public and the private sectors of the colonial government, with Pius Okigbo, Simeon Adebo and Abdulaziz Attah (on returning from Oxford) becoming the first three Nigerians appointed to the senior administrative service in the colonial government. Pius's position as Development Officer conferred immense social status on him.

Among the benefits of Pius's position was accommodation in the Government Reservation Area (GRA) at Ogbor Hill, built originally for the exclusive use of the European officers so they would not have to mingle with the natives. The colonial service had maintained an apartheid system which sequestered European civil servants and officers in the European commercial establishment. Hardly an African was admitted to the local country club, or allowed to be treated at the exclusive nursing homes that hitherto served only European officers and their families. These alien privileges marked entry into a new social status during political transition. Pius owned a motorcar, moved in important circles, and dressed elegantly. At quite a young age, Pius Okigbo had become one of the most distinguished Nigerians of his day.

In the 1940s, Aba was beginning to grow from a little garrison town into one of the bustling commercial cities of the East. With its growing urban character, lying on the corridor to Port Harcourt, it pulsated with the new energy of the returnees from the Second World War. As Development Officer, Pius Okigbo's duty was to plan and oversee the methodical growth of this new urban society.

A number of Umuahia boys came from Aba, many of whom had passed through St. Michael's School. The school was run by the legendary Mr. Okongwu , whose son Chu S. P. Okongwu – later to be Nigeria's economic minister – came to Government College, Umuahia in 1947. Chu Okongwu was reputedly the smallest boy admitted into his class in 1947 and was also sent to School House. He soon fell under the spell of Chris Okigbo who is reputed to have introduced him to a lot of schoolboy pranks. Okigbo's classmate Johnson Obi recalled how Christopher would sometimes take the young Okongwu to the lower fields in midnight forays to raid the school orchard. Armed with their pillowcases, they would plunder as much fruit as they could. Okigbo didn't particularly like oranges, but he loved the adventure. There were many other such 'Aba boys' who came to Umuahia, and with whom Okigbo spent memorable holidays: Godfrey and Christian Momah; Okali U. Okali and his brother David, who became a forest pathologist; Edward Chukwukere later trained as a metallurgist.

Government College, Umuahia had extensive grounds which gave an adventurous youngster ample opportunities for natural exploration. It had a nine-hole golf course, cricket pavilions, athletic fields and two football pitches at the upper and lower fields. Wilberforce Alagoa, a teacher in Okigbo's time, described the school as 'a jewel shining in the armpit of a valley.'[12] There was a heady, aesthetic grace to the Umuahia compound. Okigbo's classmate Namsey Eno described the experience of coming to Umuahia:

> We came into Umuahia in January 1945 from several places. I was admitted from Jos where I was living at the time. There was a sense of beauty in the whole environment as one came in. But soon, you found that there were those among your seniors – especially those who were one year your seniors – who would sooner put you down to your place... you know the sense of things in Umuahia – every first former was an *ooin* – a little, inconsequential decimal, to be seen but not to be heard. But not Nixton! Nixton came to Umuahia, an *ooin* alright, but he was prepared to be seen and heard by all means! He was smallish, but he could stand up to any one – that sort of fellow. From his second year, and I remember clearly, Nixton had already started walking it to WTC [Women's Training College] ... he was like that![13]

Chukwuemeka Ike also recalls that Christopher Okigbo 'was a fearless and an unorthodox sort of fellow. He broke rules with finesse. He broke the bounds of convention and he could get away with most things which would mean trouble for most people. But the really remarkable things about Chris were in the sort of very strange things that he did – like chewing his cud. He could recall meat, which he had eaten two days earlier, and everybody who knew him liked him enormously for his entertaining nature. He had amazing abilities at sports and was very popular with especially the younger boys at Umuahia.'[14] Ike also recalled Okigbo's amusing habit of twitching his ears. His open charm, his ease and willingness to make friends quickly, endeared him to many people. Small, wiry, broad faced, with a wide smile, Okigbo had an infectious charm. Sam Onyewuenyi remembered, as many did, that 'Chris was a rascal ... a pleasant kind of rascal. He was a charming rogue; very bright and loveable.'[15]

Onyewuenyi, a stylish cricket batsman, encouraged Okigbo to play the game in which he would excel. Onyewuenyi was regarded as one of the finest schoolboy cricketers in his time in Nigeria. He became both Captain of Niger House as well as Captain of cricket at the time Okigbo went to Umuahia. Onyewuenyi took a special interest in the slightly built boy from Onitsha province who later became a star athlete in Umuahia. Onyewuenyi became a power engineer in Nigeria, in those years when engineers were icons of modernity, symbols of the transformation of the built space, embodying the potential of new, post-colonial nations to rise to industrial power. He also rose years later to be head of Nigeria's national electricity monopoly, the National Electric Power Authority (NEPA).

Most of Okigbo's Umuahia contemporaries remembered him as an outstanding sportsman, an effortless but distracted genius who was excellent in the subjects he liked. They remark on his great appetite, especially for beans, the type locally called, *okpodudu*. 'Chris could eat beans literally with weevils!'[16] recalled one of his seniors in School House, John Onwuka, who later worked as Sales Manager of the Nigerian Tobacco Company in Ibadan while Okigbo was living in Cambridge House. Onwuka was among his closest contemporaries who witnessed Okigbo's evolution as a poet in Cambridge House, Ibadan – one of those whom Okigbo trusted with the various revisions of his poems as they evolved in Ibadan. Onwuka, for instance, preserved a signed original version of Okigbo's *Limits*. Although he did not proceed to the university like the rest of his peers in the 1940s and 50s, John Onwuka was nonetheless considered the best student of English in Chinua Achebe's 1944 class in Umuahia, and always retained his fascination for poetry and for the elegance of language. Onwuka thought of Okigbo in Umuahia as having an 'appetite as large as his spirit!'[17] But Christian Chike Momah, later United Nations Librarian in Geneva and still later at the Dag Hammarskjöld Library at UN headquarters in New York, provided the best insight into Okigbo's appetite. C.C. Momah was Okigbo's senior by one year, but always his team mate in cricket, both at the Government College, Umuahia, and later at the University College, Ibadan. Momah wrote thus about their time in Umuahia:

> ... I thoroughly approved of an original idea of the principal's to group boys in the dining hall by their eating ability. The aim was to reduce food wastages. By this arrangement, those of us who were great eaters had more food than the others. Christopher Okigbo, of blessed memory, slim and small as he was had a reputable appetite, especially for beans and rice, and was numbered among us. Where all the food he ate went, I'll never know to this day but he remained as trim at the end of the experiment as at the beginning. He must have been endowed with extraordinary metabolism. The experiment itself was unfortunately short-lived, perhaps some of us were gaining weight too rapidly for Mr. Simpson's comfort...[18]

Christopher Okigbo would sometimes trade all his meat for beans. He came to be, in spite of his slight build, a physically tough, confident opponent in a fight. William Simpson had instituted a rule about fighting in Umuahia. Its aim was ultimately to check physical battles among the rural boys brought to school in Umuahia. The rule was quite simple: fights in the school should not be reduced to the crass, street side brawl of uncivilized men. Being himself once a redoubtable pugilist, the principal decreed that disagreements that led to fighting in Umuahia be made to follow the fair, 'civilized' process of umpired sportsmanship.

Boxing was thus made into the art of the gentler classes at Umuahia. Boys caught in a private fight were summoned before the housemaster, under whose strict umpiring they would then engage in a 'proper' fight. The boys would form an arena around the pugilists, cheering each man to victory. The idea, according to Laz Ekwueme, was to encourage the young boys to fight their own battles and take care of themselves. On the other hand, boys who were not sure of their own strength would be better off if they did not find people to provoke. It also inculcated a sense of fairness in dealing with opponents. In one incident, Christopher Okigbo fought his classmate and friend Ebong Etuk, an Etinan boy and son of a prominent education officer, who was quite tall for his age. The difference in height between Etuk and Okigbo did not stop Christopher from showing his paces, by giving 'a surprisingly good account of himself'.[19] From this encounter arose an old school legend that Dr. Ebong Etuk's good six feet in height of later years came from the several uppercuts he received from the smaller Okigbo. An exaggeration, no doubt, but a good indicator of the person of Christopher Okigbo: physically tough, resilient, highly determined and extremely competitive. It was not surprising that he made the Umuahia boxing team, which won the Parnaby Cup among schools in Eastern Nigeria from 1948 to 1950.

One of the most important influences on the boys at Umuahia in the 1940s was the stylish tutor Saburi Biobaku. With his distinctive English manners he cut the image of a truly cosmopolitan figure, a man of the world, an intellectual aristocrat. Just back from Cambridge, Saburi Bisiriyu – as he was then known – taught English and history at Umuahia from 1946 to 1949. Professor Saburi Biobaku became an historian, the first Nigerian registrar of the University College, Ibadan, and Chancellor of the University of Lagos. He became a cult-hero for the Umuahia boys. A thoroughgoing anglophile, he would model his manners in imitation of the ways a proper Englishman might bat at cricket. He would, for instance, after a late cut, brush back an imaginary lock of hair. In teaching English, he always tried to impart the perfect Oxbridge elocution. He also brought elegance to the study of history in a school that was distinctly science-oriented. He was the quintessential picture of the truly modern man of letters. But in trying to affect the panache of the well-bred English gentleman, Biobaku became a true advertisement of what a Cambridge education did to an African. Part of his appeal was that he embodied the possibility of high intellectual attainment in an era when only a handful of people attained a university degree in Nigeria.

Biobaku had earned Oxbridge honours, the high mark of English education, the preserve, in the mind of the boys, of only aristocratic Englishmen. He was also open and approachable, a man of voluble spirit; an engaging teacher who took a special interest in his students, especially the talented ones whom he took under his wings. Vincent Ike, who was known to be Biobaku's favourite student at Umuahia, said. 'He was one of the early, truly influential examples that Christopher tried to emulate. He even copied Biobaku's, close cropped hairstyle with the path in the middle!' Ike suggested that Okigbo admired Biobaku for the same qualities he admired in his elder brother Pius: erudition, intellectual energy, enlightened grandeur, a great cosmopolitan spirit and a sense of style. Both Biobaku and Pius Okigbo were cast in the same mould of the bright new intellectual aristocrats – renaissance figures – Pius with his chain of degrees, and Biobaku with his Cambridge degree in tripos. 'He was by far the most colourful of the Nigerian masters at Umuahia,' recalled Don Egbue, one of the boys admitted to Umuahia in 1946, the year Biobaku came there to teach. 'And we all wanted to be like him!'[20] Biobaku declared to his boys at Umuahia: 'scientists are Bushmen!'[21] As Chukwuemeka Ike recalled, Okigbo took that declaration quite literally.

Christopher Okigbo loved English and history, and was soon to be counted among the 'Biobaku boys' – those who showed the highest aptitude and proficiency in the English language. Biobaku had evolved a grading system in which students were placed on a descending scale of performance and measured against stiff criteria. Once placed in a certain performance bracket, a student would require a landmark improvement to score above the given average. Okigbo was one of those boys whom Saburi Biobaku conceded the higher marks for their performance in English. Professor Biobaku recalled Okigbo's complex character:

> I knew his needs were for a private, sometimes totally unfathomable isolation. He could just withdraw into himself! It was a new kind of experience for me. Christopher was all below the surface. He was vigorous as a sportsman, but beyond the effervescence of his character, the public face, there was the deeper private one; perhaps it was the manifestation of an artistic impulse – the need for silence. He was occasionally subdued by bouts of melancholy. The Christopher I knew was a highly sensitive child. I knew his imagination was unorthodox. That Christopher was unconventional really was only an indication of his great genius. He was a highly intelligent boy, who sometimes needed a lot of attention. The inwardness of his being, I think, was provoked, and expressed itself through poetry later.[22]

It was this tendency to withdraw that first drew Biobaku's attention to Okigbo early in 1947:

> Christopher was a complicated child. Outwardly he was so full of life and activity, but there was a deep sense of gloom and loneliness, an agony, which was very real in his life at the time I knew him in Umuahia. He could just withdraw totally from his world and stubbornly cocoon himself in his private existence, and he would resist attempts to draw him out...[23]

As housemaster of School House in 1947, Biobaku took a special interest in Okigbo. This highly sensitive boy fascinated him. He immediately sensed that the young Christopher Okigbo needed to be gently but firmly nurtured, and quite literally coaxed to aspire to the highest performance – willingly to unlock his reserve of abilities. 'Christopher was an effortless genius; he could do very well in any of those things he chose to do, but he had to be made – literally forced – to do it!' Professor Biobaku reminisced.[24] He challenged Okigbo by getting him deeply involved in the less routine aspects of life at Umuahia; he encouraged that competitive impulse that felt released in outdoor activity. When a new radio set was installed in the school at the Assembly Hall on 22 September 1949, Biobaku convinced the Principal to put Okigbo in charge.

Biobaku was also engrossed with his own academic research for his doctoral thesis, which he later published in his landmark book on African history. Much of that work was done at Umuahia with the students. As part of his ethnographic study he designed fieldwork that allowed him to interview local informants in the surrounding communities in Umudike. As a Yoruba with an English education, his interaction with the local Umudike community would have been hampered by his inability to communicate in the local Igbo language. Biobaku solved the problem by taking some of the Umuahia boys along, principally to aid his communication with his local sources, but most importantly, as a way of exposing them to the process of historical research. He involved Chinua Achebe, Christian Momah and Benjamin Uzochukwu. From Okigbo's class, he frequently took V.C. Ike, Celestine N. Egbuchulam, Vincent Aniago, Festus Emeghara, Johnson Obi, and Chris Okigbo. These were the students closest to Biobaku who usually performed above average in Biobaku's subject – the English language.

There is evidence that these excursions helped to stimulate some of these boys to an alternative worldview, a different perspective of their traditional societies, different from the colonial history taught them at Umuahia. As Biobaku himself noted: 'the boys who went with me to these villages in Umudike, and Christopher (Okigbo) was one of them, began to see and hear a new version of the truth and were very inspired by what they heard.'[25] The imperial view of history in an English-type public school, at this time in the 1940s, presented a distorted picture of Africa. Africa had no history worth recovering or telling. Saburi Biobaku was one of the great pioneers of African historical research in the twentieth century, who tried to prove the contrary by showing that African history was rich and complex. Biobaku influenced Okigbo's intellectual development in an important and profound way; ultimately he diverted his interest towards a liberal, humanist education rather than the career in the sciences to which he was naturally headed. Biobaku was instrumental in convincing Okigbo that the pursuit of the arts was not only enlightened, but indeed that only individuals of style – 'civilized men' – studied the liberal arts. Biobaku himself embodied that credo.

Okigbo's sporting life came to be one of the most important aspects of his life in school. He was a first-rate sportsman, one of Umuahia's best-known schoolboy athletes, whose colourful performances made school sporting meets exciting. Okigbo became a famous national sporting figure through his involvements in sporting life at Umuahia, particularly in cricket and football. Biobaku was also the master in charge of football, assisted by the science teacher, a young Englishman Mr.Boll. Biobaku took great interest in Okigbo's development as a formidable inside right attacker for the Umuahia Football team. Saburi Biobaku's insistence that Okigbo turn from a left foot player to a deadly right was a 'modest epic.'[26] It took persistence on his part to realise Okigbo's potential. 'At first,' Biobaku said, 'he resented my attempts to turn him to a right center player. He saw it as interference with his physical coordination. He was quite stubborn.'[27] But Biobaku insisted, and coaxed him in the long run into 'one of the most exciting schoolboy footballers in the Eastern region of the 1940s'.[28]

Okigbo generally showed far less interest in academic work. His contemporaries acknowledged his brilliance but his school records reveal he academically was an average student. He did not muster the discipline necessary for the scholastic grind. He simply coasted along. 'He was the kind of boy who took his incredible talents for granted. He knew he did not need to do much to do well.'[29] This contradiction perplexed Mr. I.D. Erekosima, who taught chemistry and mathematics, in which subjects Okigbo excelled. He was also the master in charge of the Umuahia hockey team of which Okigbo was a member. Erekosima said: 'his sporting life just served his greater need for the outdoors and for showmanship. He was bored with academic discipline and rigour, but you know, Christopher had an effortless genius…he was actually very aware of his most innate possibilities…he could accomplish anything if he put his mind to it. He was just brilliant. He did not have to make an effort!'[30]

The jolly Wilberforce Alagoa was master of School House and had spent almost his entire and professional years in the school. He said, 'I went to King's, but Umuahia was without compare.'[31] He saw some of his best boys become the leading men of their generation. His nephew, Ebigwere J. Alagoa, was admitted to Umuahia in September 1948 and later became an eminent Nigerian historian. As master of School House, Mr.

Alagoa developed a very close relationship with the young boy from Ojoto. 'I should say this,' Alagoa said, 'of all the Government Colleges, Umuahia chose the finest.'[32] Christopher was known by his contemporaries to be Mr. Alagoa's favourite student in Umuahia in the 1940s. Alagoa's recollection of the young boy from Ojoto bears testimony to that relationship:

> Christopher ... that boy was one of my forward terrors in football alongside that other rascal Francis Egbonu! You know, Christopher's brother, Pius, who was in the civil service in Aba became my friend and Christopher was one of the unforgettable boys whom I had the privilege of teaching. He had the temperament of a genius even then. He could do just anything from running a mile race to solving problems in algebra, only if he chose! Come to think about it, he was very good in his sciences and could have studied for a science degree, if he chose.[33]

Okigbo's extracurricular interests in Umuahia were diverse. He was an active member of the Art Society and the Chess Club. Okigbo was also active in the Drama Club and showed an early talent as an actor. He participated keenly in the entertainment programme at Umuahia, which required that each house take turns in evening performances before the entire school. These house concerts featured singing, drama and poetry reading; they starred boys like Donald Ekong on the piano and Ralph Opara performing some skit. With the help of Mr. Farmer, a fine pianist, but also a carpenter, the students designed and constructed their own stages. Mr. Alagoa recalled 'the naughty Christopher breaking into that scintillating jazz he so often rendered on the piano. I always wondered where he learnt to play like that, you know, with so much spirit as if his soul resided in the tunes ... and any way, we never taught the boys jazz at Umuahia, Farmer taught them the classical stuff.'[34] On one of those evenings, it was the turn of Okigbo's School House to entertain the school; they had improvised a drama sketch in which the characters appeared only in silhouettes on a cloth background. The housemaster himself had played the part of a surgeon who was about to operate upon a patient played by Christopher Okigbo. Alagoa recalls that they both put on such splendid performances that at the end of the play, the house master's then seven-year-old son kept muttering to his father, 'Daddy, you killed that boy, Daddy you killed that boy...'[35] On another occasion Okigbo played the part of defending counsel in the production of a play, 'The Trial of Hitler.'

Okigbo apparently enjoyed a rounded experience in Umuahia, and in turn affected the life of the school with his unusual and dramatic ways. His classmate, Johnson Obi's most vivid recollection of him was of a rambunctious and active student: 'Christopher was most likely to be found in the thick of things; he was restless and lively, and full of innocent mischief.'[36] Okigbo fell quickly under the spell a senior student, Anthony K. Sam Epelle of the 1942 class. Sam Epelle, who later became Federal Director of Information after Cyprian Ekwensi, had in 1943 returned from King's College, Lagos, where he had taken part in an anti-war revolt. Already firmly established in School House when Okigbo was admitted in 1945, Epelle found kinship with this mischievous junior from Ojoto, and took him under his wing. Soon enough, Okigbo became his closest collaborator in the muck-raking school press. The authorities at the Government College, Umuahia, considered Sam Epelle a rebel and something of a nationalist agitator; but he had been put in charge of the school's ancient radio set in the Assembly Hall. A.K. Sam Epelle was drawn ideologically to the heady nationalist activity of the new Zikist movement. Epelle was known for his voracious interest in world news and was always to be found fiddling with the radio, and would post a bulletin of events following any breaking news. 'More than anybody else, Sam (Epelle) was responsible for feeding the school with the news of the world, and with the activities of the allied forces in the closing periods of the Second World War.'[37] His closest friend in Umuahia, the cricketer Sam Onyewuenyi remembered that Sam Epelle was the first boy in Umuahia to get hold of Nnamdi Azikiwe's influential book, *Renascent Africa*, which had ruffled the feathers of the colonialists. Zik's book and other nationalist literatures were forbidden in the school because they were regarded as 'provocative and not fitting works of the intellect.'[38] Zikists were regarded as provocateurs and their writings as exerting a 'bad influence' upon young colonial schoolboys. The Government College authorities did not wish for any form of nationalist literature to provoke emotions and affect the tranquillity of the Umuahian temperament, as had happened in Lagos in 1942 with the riots at King's College. Sam Epelle not only read Zik, but somehow managed to smuggle those forbidden newspapers, *The West African Pilot* and the *Nigerian Spokesman* into the school compound, where they were read avidly by students underground. A.K. Sam Epelle was editor of the school magazine, *The Umuahian*. Okigbo's first contact with any form of politics, especially of the 'revolutionary' kind, his engagement with the rhetoric of nationalist struggle, could indeed have been through this early association with Sam Epelle at Umuahia. Epelle not only provided the grounds for the early radicalisation of Okigbo's adolescent unconscious – 'that left wing part of him,'[39] as his friend, the journalist, Ignatius Atigbi, later described it – but also introduced him to an early interest in literary journalism. His involvement in the school's magazine accounts for his intellectual disposition towards radical politics. Young Okigbo's political consciousness also evolved with the nationalism of the radical Zikist movement, which Epelle so admired and followed. It was complemented by the liberal education offered at Umuahia. While the authorities in Umuahia subtly censored certain forms of nationalist literature, they nevertheless encouraged a tradition of literary debate and even dissent through the school's magazines published by the students. Peter Chigbo recalled that there was a regular subscription to *The London Illustrated News*, the *US News & World Report*, *Life* magazine and many others. The well-stocked library widened the imaginative horizon of the boys. Chinua Achebe, as already mentioned, acknowledges this library as important in the evolution of his own creative consciousness:

> …I still remember walking into this long room with incredibly neat bookshelves. I'd never seen so many books in my life. When I finished from the University, I came back…and I taught for a little while at a school at Oba – just a few miles below Onitsha – the Merchants of Light School. They had no idea of a library. This was a revelation to me, to see that at Umuahia we were so privileged.[40]

The Government College, Umuahia school magazine, *The Umuahian*, became the first nurturing space for the school's aspiring writers. Literary culture thrived around it. In addition to the school magazine, there were various house magazines to which every boy was required to contribute an article. Each of those house magazines chose the best-written materials with an eye for balance between the seniors and juniors. The house magazines were often handwritten. The boy with the most dexterous pen was always appointed secretary to the editorial board. Such a boy was required to possess correct spelling habits and high draftmanship. The covers were done by the house artist, who also did the illustrations to most of the stories in watercolour. At the end of production, each house presented their magazine with great fanfare at the school assembly. This was always a grand occasion, which attracted great interest and criticism, or even praise, from students from other houses. At the end of term, the house magazines were taken from various house common rooms and archived in the

Umuahia library. Umuahia students took the magazines seriously. The result of course would be demonstrated much later. This tradition accounts in large part for the emergence of the literary talent from Umuahia. Many boys, who never knew that they had such abilities on coming to Umuahia, suddenly discovered themselves to be potential writers.

In 1947/48 for instance, Chinua Achebe was editor of the Niger House magazine. In the 1949/50 session, Okigbo co-edited with Chukwuemeka Ike the School House magazine, *The Athena*. Ralph Opara was the secretary of that editorial board. *The Athena* had the motto:

> Our government is not like the government of our neighbours.
> We are an example to them rather than they to us...[41]

As Chukwuemeka Ike remembered, Christopher Okigbo especially loved the sentiment in the School House magazine's motto. It was Horatian, and it appealed to his sense of individual heroism and competitiveness.

Christopher Okigbo was also on Sam Epelle's editorial team for *The Umuahian*. There is nothing, however, to suggest that Okigbo had more than a passing interest in writing in these early involvements, or that he would emerge as a poet from any writings he did in the school. In fact only a few of his earliest efforts were published and they were unremarkable. Christopher Okigbo's literary output in Umuahia was simply too lean to constitute any significant insight to his later development. But he got an important stimulus through Umuahia's literary culture and magazine tradition.

The literary impulses of students at Umuahia were also sharpened by William Simpson's 'Textbook Act,' which decreed that no student was allowed to read any prescribed school text in the evenings on Mondays, Wednesdays and Fridays, or after hours on Saturdays and Sundays. It was a rule enacted by the Principal to dissuade the 'swots,' from 'murdering the night,' endlessly trapped in their books rather than engaging in other activities. I. D. Erekosima summed up the rule and the circumstance that led to its enactment: 'Simpson did not want the boys simply to leave the Government College merely as bookworms. He wanted them to have a healthy appetite for books as well as for life, as truly well-rounded individuals.'[42] Laz Ekwueme later wrote about this:

> The reason for the *Down – Text – Book Act* was very clear. No boy playing soccer, cricket, hockey, tennis, rugby, rounders or any of the numerous games played at Umuahia one time or the other felt cheated by those who were not playing during games periods. Everybody could therefore take part in sports to the best of his ability without losing out in academics. Furthermore, these text-book-Act's free evenings were recognized as meeting days for culture oriented clubs and societies such as the Art club, the debating society, the Dramatic society, the music group, the Dancing club and the like. One therefore got a rounded education at Umuahia, with lots of opportunity to learn those things not directly concerned with classroom work – to be truly educated. These above all provided opportunities for students to read novels, magazines, newspapers, religious books, and journals of various kinds freely provided in the school library.[43]

The Umuahians were thus made to encounter and explore works of great literature on their own terms. They were exposed to the great English classics. The most popular book among the Umuahians seemed to be R. L. Stevenson's *Mutiny on the Bounty*. Johnson Obi recalls that Okigbo was also always to be found in those years clutching a library copy of Anthony Hope's *Prisoner of Zenda*, 'a novel which he never quite seemed to finish'.[44] The average boy at Umuahia was therefore expected to be an all-rounder: not only well read, but a scholar, a man of culture and an athlete – a truly well adjusted, renaissance intellectual. It seems apparent, that Okigbo's life at least, bears testimony to the effect of Simpson's philosophy of education: he was not only an avid and varied reader in his life, but his later pursuit of diverse vocations testifies to his truly renaissance impulses.

One of the most influential teachers in Umuahia in the 1940s and early 1950s was the Australian poet, cricketer and classicist, Charles W. Low. He was a bohemian intellectual who arrived in Umuahia in December 1946 to teach English and Latin. He had taken his degree in the classics from the University of Melbourne. Later, he studied at Cambridge, where he was a cricket blue. Charles Low was a casual and eccentric figure, mostly seen smoking his pipe and carrying on in the most carefree way, often wielding a cricket bat. Low invested much of his energy revolutionizing the game in Umuahia. He soon created a cult following! Umuahia's finest cricketers were his truest friends and companions. He demonstrated his passion for the game in a public way when in 1948 he grew a shaggy beard, in commemoration of the centenary of W.G. Grace, the grand old man of cricket. The boys fondly nicknamed their Australian teacher, 'Mad Low'. He had little respect for routine. He was a mediocre administrator, but he was deeply intellectual and distracted. Low was a typical housemaster who was interested in everything that was going on in the school. He frequently ignored his beautiful wife for a life of sport, the imagination, and occasional tipples. The Umuahia boys of Okigbo's generation remembered Charles W. Low's wife, Moira, as a striking beauty and a talented pianist who often played at school assemblies. But above all, she was known as the indulgent wife. While Low went about living wildly, Moira was the long-suffering and martyred woman to a carefree scholar. 'Low was a truly unusual fellow who had such an impact on the boys. He had an infectious personality,'[45] said Professor Saburi Biobaku. There was much of Charles W. Low in Okigbo, particularly replicated in his passionate and distracted relationship with his wife, his love of cricket and poetry, his decision to study the classics, his interest in the stage, and his life as a teacher.

Low's direct relationship with Okigbo began almost as soon as he arrived at Umuahia to take over from the English teacher, Adrian Slater. Mr. A. P. L. 'Apple' Slater was reputed to have established a high standard for English at the Government College, Umuahia. When Charles Low arrived, he conducted an English proficiency test for the entire school. The seniors and juniors took the same English written test. But when the results came out, it was not one of the senior boys who wrote the best paper, as would be expected. Festus Emeghara in Okigbo's second form class scored highest in the entire school! On the average, Okigbo's class performed better than the rest of the school in Low's test and attracted him to the boys of the 1945 class. He involved them in more collaborative activity. When he arrived in Umuahia, he was writing a play called *West Flows the Latex, ho!* based on his experiences as a colonial officer in the British Cameroons. He would occasionally bring drafts to class, getting the students to discuss its plot and develop the next scene. That experiment helped to provoke the dormant literary interests of some of the boys in Umuahia.

The Drama Club, of which Low was patron, staged *The Mikado*, the musical opera by Gilbert and Sullivan. Chukwuemeka Ike recalled that Christopher Okigbo was very involved in the production, and was one of the boys with whom Low worked closely. They engaged in endless hours of discussion about the play in which Ralph Opara played the lead, perhaps his first major role in an acting career that became illustrious. Low began something of a literary soirée in Umuahia. Sometimes, he would invite his favourite students like Okigbo to tea at his bungalow in the teachers' quarters. They would spend the afternoon tackling Latin and discussing the Greek classics, especially the tragedies that Charles Low loved. Low's intellectual and philosophical predilections were much like Eliot; he believed in the majesty of western civilisation and its traditions, and he communicated this grandeur of the European world. The sense of a usable past would form the plank of Okigbo's own revivalist spirit, a sense of the majesty of the African past on which he later based his recovery of the legend of Idoto.

But the event that most inspired the literary aspirations of these young Umuahia boys occurred in March of 1948. The event was occasioned by a letter from Moses Udebiuwa of the 1942 class who went on to Yaba Higher College in 1947. One day at Yaba he found himself confronted by an embarrassing situation. Udebiuwa had invited a girl from town to his room at the College but it was the first time he had been so close to a young woman. He became tongue-tied and felt so embarrassed by his lack of social skill that he suddenly lost his nerve and quickly escaped from his room. He had been, like many Umuahia boys, sequestered from female company and a novice in the ways of the world. As an all-boys boarding school without a girls school around, Umuahia had little opportunity for boys to interact with the opposite sex. The closest female schools were the Women's Training College in Old Umuahia and the School of Nursing at the Queen Elizabeth Hospital. Moses Udebiuwa thought it was his duty to prevent the future embarrassment of other Umuahia boys unaccustomed to female company. So he wrote a letter to Mr. Simpson, his former principal, describing his experience and recommending that the Government College Umuahia authorities find a way to expose the boys coming behind him to good female company.

On receiving the letter, Mr. Simpson considered the suggestion worthwhile. He quickly set in motion preparations for a rousing social evening. The stylish Mr. Bisiriyu (Saburi Biobaku) was put in charge. An elaborate rehearsal was put on. The boys went to the dining hall in the evenings to learn proper social manners. They watched with fascination as Biobaku demonstrated how to ask a lady properly for a dance. Biobaku demonstrated how to make a well intoned 'May I?' while approaching a lady in the relaxed, unhurried and confident manner of a dashing paramour. The boys were taught to end the dance courteously with a 'thank you' intoned with the same proper manners of well-groomed gentlemen. It was all grand. Biobaku felt duty bound to impart these skills which he did with his usual, affecting dash and enthusiasm. Chukwuemeka Ike recalled, 'By the end of that week the whole school was agog with preparations to host the girls from the Women's Training College in Old Umuahia. At every corner, you would find the boys practising Biobaku's flawless manners. Christopher (Okigbo) as usual was in the thick of it'.[46] Okigbo's social interests, especially a sexual interest in women, was already far more advanced than most of his peers. 'By the time he was in class two, sixteen years old Christopher was already walking the seventeen miles to WTC Umuahia in search of sexual conquest,'[47] Johnson Obi recalled. His other classmate, Eno Namsey always thought that Okigbo's high social confidence, and sexual awareness was as a result of an early exposure to women and the high society through his equally, socially restless brother, Pius Okigbo. Nevertheless, the visit of the WTC girls to Umudike became a *cause célèbre*. The social evening was a roaring success. It included a game of netball played between the Government College, Umuahia boys and the WTC girls. The Umuahians lost, although apparently without regret. The redoubtable master of Niger House, Reginald Jumbo declared in the school Assembly on the following Monday that the Umuahia boys had lost the game because they 'left the ball to catch flying breasts!'[48]

On Monday morning after the memorable weekend, the school awoke to find a poem penned by Charles W. Low reconstructing the weekend of games between the Umuahians and the young women from the Women's Training College. The poem captured the not so innocent concerns of some of the more adventurous boys, like the memorable lines on Bassey Inyang, who later became an Army Surgeon:

> Oh where is the capon-lined belly of Bassey
> A rogue with an eye for a nice female chassis
> he is under the stars with a slim little lassie
> The WTC are here![49]

There were also, of course, the casualties like Okigbo's own classmate Celestine Egbuchulam whose innocence in such matters, Low canonized in these lines:

> Alone at the corner Egbuchulam glowers
> Regretting how Oliphants wasted his hours
> You do not learn from Durell how to say it with flowers
> The WTC are here![50]

This poem would unchain the poetic soul of so many. Chukwuemeka Ike's vivid recollection of the event, places the occasion in its proper historical context:

> One morning, we went to the board and found this poem written by our Australian English teacher, Charles Low. Low was an amazing man with several amusing tendencies, but we never reckoned before then, that he was also a poet! As far as many of us were concerned and in our thinking in those years, poets were dead men! And so you could only imagine the impact when we discovered that we had one living among us. It is not like these days – the later generation is lucky – because you see writers and poets around you. In our days they never quite walked on the streets or so we thought! They lived mainly in fiction! But when Charles Low came out with this poem, 'The WTC are here,' many of us began to see the possibilities of becoming poets. Chris actually went about trying to construct one line or two of poetry, although I hardly think he came through to it at that time. I think he abandoned the whole idea entirely after the initial euphoria and went back to his old ways. He never did write much in Umuahia. But he was struck like many of us. Charles Low had offered us that day something new in ourselves.[51]

Low had made the figure of the writer come alive. He helped to convey the truth that writers were not just dead, mythical people read only in books. It was a signal moment. Okigbo himself, affected by the event, wrote one of his earliest schoolboy poems, he titled, 'Flute calls at the Quadrangle,'[52] inspired by Low's poetic invocation of the WTC girls. Charles W. Low's influence on the poet of *Labyrinths* was more significant in Okigbo's later choice to be 'nothing other than a poet.' In his last year at school, Charles Low gave Okigbo a copy of Eliot's *Ara vos Prec* and the book of essays on poetry and criticism, *The Sacred Wood* as gifts. Doubtless, it was an impulse from which Okigbo drew several years later when he began his own writing. The story of Christopher Okigbo, and indeed those Umuahia boys who later emerged as important figures of modern African literature in the twentieth century, can truly be connected to the impulse awakened by Charles Low's incidental poetry, in an environment made suitable for it by the philosophy of the principal William Simpson who believed in giving the Umuahia boys 'a rounded education.'[54]

This philosophy of education could easily explain the genius of Chinua Achebe, who on switching from medical school at Ibadan, proceeded to take a degree in English, History and Religion; or why the novelist Elechi Amadi, after taking degrees in Physics and Mathematics, engaged the literary world with the inspired genius of his novels; or the versatility of the poet Okigbo, who, without substantial preparation in Latin, still went on to register for and take a degree in the classics. 'Any of those boys,' said their mathematics and chemistry teacher, Dagogo Erekosima, 'could have taken any degree. Christopher could easily have taken a science degree ... he had excellent grades in mathematics, physics and chemistry. But he chose to study for the Arts and was not the worse for it. It was the type of education we gave them...'[55]

Until Low's arrival at Umuahia, the Government College was essentially a science school. Classical studies were marginal, although Simpson tried to emphasize a general liberal education. This emphasis on the sciences accounts for the overwhelming number of the boys in Okigbo's generation in Umuahia who were guided to careers in science, medicine or engineering. It was an accident that Achebe and Okigbo were headed towards careers in medicine before a twist of fate turned them towards a humanistic education. Charles Low introduced Latin first to Okigbo's class in 1948, when Christopher Okigbo was in form three. Of course, as a Roman Catholic and a former altar boy who had gone through Catholic primary schools, Christopher Okigbo had already been exposed to some Latin. His brother Pius also gave him an important introduction and private tutoring. Okigbo's class, to which Latin had been first introduced, did not show too much interest. Only a few like Christopher Okigbo apparently paid attention. Latin always fascinated Okigbo. To Okigbo, Latin was the language of ritual, of history, of poetry and the great classical romances and tragedies of the powerful western civilisation: it was in short, the language of the intellectual aristocracy. Chukwuemeka Ike remembered 'During class, it was often Christopher who would end up bantering in the language with Charles Low.' The principal, Mr. Simpson, had also shown considerable enthusiasm for the subject. Although a mathematician, William Simpson was quite proficient in Latin and Greek and sometimes came in to help Low teach Latin to Okigbo's class. Some of Okigbo's classmates could recall how Christopher would find a way to make the Principal pronounce the Latin words 'ama bunt.'[57] The class would be unable to contain its laughter, as Simpson's potbelly would bounce to the stress of 'bunt.' It was, of course, part of Okigbo's nature to find entertainment in that kind of human drama.

Simpson took a special interest in Christopher, perhaps because he noticed Okigbo's 'effortless genius' – which was exactly how he described Okigbo in his meticulously kept reports of the boys under his charge. Simpson made a point of allowing the boys to speak up, to seek healthy adventures, and to reach for the great possibilities of life. William Simpson understood that Okigbo needed a measure of freedom to express his full humanity. He also perceived that Okigbo had remarkable abilities. He possibly also noticed that the young Okigbo's exuberance obscured deeper anxieties that forced him to express himself in dramatic ways – as if to prove himself. By Christopher Okigbo's third year in Umuahia, he was already proving himself to be a venturesome teenager, Mr. Simpson drafted a burly prefect, Moses Udebiuwa, from Niger House to School House and specifically told him to 'keep an eye on Okigbo.'[58]

On one occasion, Okigbo's attempts to prove himself ended in extravagant failure, much to the joy of his junior classmates. For many years at Umuahia, junior boys had the responsibility of washing and stacking the college china set after dinner. The task was divided between the first year boys, the *ooins*, who would wash the plates, and the *monsieurs*, the second year students, who stacked the plates in the pantry. This chore continued until Okigbo's time. But it all came to an end one Saturday night in the second term of the 1946 school year. Rain fell that evening in the deafening torrents of a tropical downpour. The rain began just before dinner and continued while the junior boys were engrossed in the chores of washing and stacking the college china in the pantry. Suddenly, a voice broke through the dining hall: 'Make way for Nixton! Make way for Nixton!' It grew into a refrain as other junior boys joined in the chant. They were clearing the way for a smallish lad, who had stacked too many of these expensive pieces of china on top of each other until the pile towered high above his small frame. He was hurrying along to ensure that he got safely to the pantry. It was Christopher – young, impatient, determined to complete the task quickly and to accomplish an unusual balancing act. But he slipped in the process, and the pieces of college china, with the college crest embossed on them, fell and smashed into smithereens. The next Monday, the principal banned the juniors from washing and stacking the plates, thus relieving them – to their utmost joy – of that chore. When Okigbo was asked by his friends why he had packed so many plates at once, he replied that he wanted to get the whole chore over quickly so that he could curl under his blankets and get a good night's sleep under the rain. It was the kind of night when boys longed for dreamless sleep without the interruption of Big Ben, the college bell that roused everyone to activity.

Christopher had many memorable encounters with Mr. Simpson. For instance, in 1946, in his second year at Government College Umuahia, the football team was preparing to play a match against Dennis Memorial Grammar School in Onitsha. Younger students who could not be trusted to take care of themselves were not allowed to travel with the school's teams outside Umuahia. Christopher Okigbo loved football as much as he loved to travel, and was determined to go to Onitsha. So he convinced his friend, Peter Chigbo who was in class one to accompany him to see Mr. Simpson. The 'Dewar' bulk alone intimidated many a student. Even the most daring of the seniors were in awe of him. Nevertheless, with Chigbo in tow, Okigbo walked up to the Principal's office and made a convincing case for 'special permission' to travel with the football team to Onitsha. Peter Chigbo remembered the occasion well: 'Chris was calm. He had no fear.'[59] Chigbo, himself also a rather gutsy junior, had a fleeting sense of disgrace; the least of the punishment for that occasion, Chigbo thought, would be Simpson's 'six-of-the best!'

> 'And what else would you be doing in Onitsha?'
> 'We only want to watch the football match sir' Okigbo replied.
> 'Do you have anybody to stay with at Onitsha?' Okigbo and Chigbo replied in the affirmative.
> They had families in Onitsha. Simpson heaved his great bulk from the chair and said:
> 'That settles it then. You may go and watch the match, but make sure you return with the school lorry tomorrow. Have a great time boys...'

Both of them uttered their 'Thanks' and went out of the Principal's office and did a great joyous dance together. They went to Onitsha, watched the match and came back. Peter Chigbo's most distinct impression of that incident was his sense of Okigbo's remarkable intrepidness. 'That was Christopher. Once he put his mind to anything, he did it.'[60]

Another memorable incident involving the Principal happened much later in his senior year. Christopher Okigbo had convinced his friend and classmate, Chukwuemeka Ike, to accompany him to the principal's office one Sunday afternoon. Ike recalled the event many years later:

> 'Good afternoon, sir' Okigbo said.
> 'Hello boys' Simpson replied.
> 'May we speak to you sir about something?' Okigbo asked.

'Yes, my boy, what about?'
'I'd love to drive your car, sir'[61]

Ike recalled Okigbo's calm, fearless self-assurance, as if it was the most normal thing to ask the Principal's permission to drive him home in his car. He equally remembered that Mr. Simpson was momentarily caught by surprise. No other student could have made such a daring request. The bemused Principal was intrigued by Okigbo's calm audacity. William Simpson was a liberal, fair-minded man. After a calm appraisal of the matter, he asked:

'Do you know how to drive, Christopher?'
'Yes, I do sir'
'Well then, I suppose it's alright if you try.'[62]

The truth, as Ike recalled, was that Christopher Okigbo had discovered a manual on driving in the school's library and had been studying it since morning. So Simpson assented on one condition, that Chukwuemeka Ike, a more sober student, would join them in the car, just in case Okigbo had something else in mind! Thus it was that Okigbo drove the Principal home from the Administrative block, with V.C. Ike sitting beside him. It was no ordinary feat for a seventeen-year old secondary school student to be able to drive about in a car. In contemporary context, it would be like allowing an unlicensed teenager to fly a Boeing airplane, for in Nigeria in the 1940s, cars were a luxury reserved for a handful of individuals. Aside from some of the English staff members at Umuahia, the only African teacher who owned a car was Wilberforce Alagoa, the master of School House. Indeed he was one of the few Nigerians who owned an automobile in the whole of the Eastern region during those colonial years. The man who came closest to this privilege at Umuahia was Mr. Opukiri, in charge of the adult education centre, who owned a motorcycle. The legend of Okigbo's superlative performance that afternoon came to endure as part of the school's lore, surviving in various versions among generations of Umuahia boys.

For the young Okigbo manipulating a car was certainly a new and exhilarating experience. His display of bravado satisfied his sense of the difficult. Cars fascinated him both as mechanical and aesthetic mysteries. Okigbo's love of fast cars would last all his life. After driving Simpson home that day, Okigbo earned the right to drive around in Mr. Alagoa's car. Alagoa was also a man of indulgent and liberal disposition, much beloved by his students. Wilberforce Alagoa did not hide the fact that Christopher was his special student. The jolly master of School House also loved his whiskey now and then and, usually after a tipple, he would drive down during games to the lower field, often joining the boys at the cricket pavilion for a round of cricket. Sometimes when he got too engrossed with the game, the boys would seize the opportunity to fiddle with Alagoa's car. Christopher Okigbo often took advantage of Mr. Alagoa's distraction and would get into the car and drive around the school. The master of School House did not mind.

Many years later, Mr. Alagoa remembered very clearly the first time Okigbo came to him to ask permission to drive his car: 'He said "Excuse me sir, I want to drive your car ... I can drive..." and I said to him: "Look here my boy, any day you show me a driving license you can have my car to drive anytime..." One week later, he came again clutching a driving license and said: "Sir, I've got a driving licence!" And I said he had my permission to drive my car in the college compound, but it was a different question whether he could drive outside...'[63] But Okigbo was restless. His adventures with driving led him to trouble. One day he drove the school's five tonne lorry into town without permission. He wanted to prove to Mr. Alagoa that he could drive beyond the school. For his efforts, Mr Simpson gated him for the last six weeks of the term. All these incidents demonstrate important aspects of Okigbo's character: his love for drama and adventure, and a life-long fascination for what was difficult and dangerous.

Okigbo deservedly earned a reputation as a rebel in school. But he was an equally outstanding sportsman. Okigbo was a true jock – an all round sportsman who won his highest honours in football (soccer), and cricket, and gave outstanding performances in hockey, boxing, and athletics. He was without doubt one of the finest amateur athletes in Nigeria in the 1940s. Okigbo's sporting life as a student is an important part of his personal narrative. The sporting season was the occasion for sportsmen to enjoy certain social privileges unavailable to regular students. Christopher Okigbo excelled, and enjoyed the life of a sportsman because it offered him the best opportunity both for the outdoors, and for a sense of drama, excitement, and showmanship. In 1948 he made the Government College, Umuahia Hockey second XI, and the rugby team when the Australian master Charles Low, introduced it to Umuahia in the same year. In the 1949/50 school year, his last year at Umuahia, he was made the captain of School House boxing team, 'scoring impressive victories in the intramural matches in the 9-stone and 9-stone-7 division.'[64] But his finest exploits however were in football and cricket. Here again, Charles Low was a great model for him. Within months of coming to Umuahia in 1946, Charles Low gave cricket a boost. He brought what the boys thought was unparalleled elegance to this very elitist English game, and it became even more appealing. Low's own passion was very infectious: the cricket master was often seen after lights out, practising the most delectable late-cuts, late into the night with boys like Chike Momah, Christopher Okigbo, Patrick Ozieh, Kelsey Harrison, Eno Namsey, Wilfred Chukudebelu, Etim R. Akpan and many more of his favourite Umuahia cricketers. Okigbo became an ardent cricketer mostly because it was a stylish and complex game; and he quickly made the Umuahia cricket first XI team from 1947. According to Namsey Eno, Charles Low encouraged Okigbo in his unconventional batting style and turned him into one of the most remarkable cricket batsmen of his time in Nigeria. Low however could not make him play the classical straight bat. Okigbo insisted rather on playing his unorthodox cross bat, with devastating results for his opponents at the wicket. Christopher Okigbo played alongside some of the finest cricketers in British West Africa: people like Eno Namsey, an all-rounder who captained the Government College, Umuahia teams, in cricket, football and athletics. After Umuahia, Namsey also captained the Nigerian national teams in cricket and hockey simultaneously for twenty-five years. There were others like Chike Momah, Wilfred Chukudebelu, and Kelsey Harrison – later recipient of the prestigious Nigerian National Order of Merit for his achievements in Medical Science – all of whom played internationally for the Nigerian National Cricket team of the 1950s. Sportsmen in Umuahia had opportunities to travel regularly and Okigbo loved the opportunities which this offered. But more importantly, the sporting life often brought fame to the schoolboy athlete in the 1940s. In 1948, Christopher Okigbo won national acclaim for a splendid performance at Warri against the rival Government College, Ibadan cricket team during a tour of the west. The Umuahia cricket team won the series of cricket matches among the Government Colleges in the 1940s. The school's teams used to travel annually across the Niger, to compete against sister Government Colleges in Ibadan, Warri (later Ughelli) and Lagos (King's College). The 'Western Tours,' as the events used to be known, were usually one weekend of games, which any of the schools would host. The Government Colleges in the west also travelled across the Niger for the 'Eastern Tours' which were often hosted in Umuahia. At the Warri cricket quadrangular in the 1948/49 Cricket season, Christopher Okigbo, batting for the Umuahia team, became one of the earliest Nigerian batsmen of his generation to score a century in a test game, in the match against the rival Government College, Ibadan.

The Government College, Ibadan had its own array of fine cricketers, like Leslie Harriman, later to be one of Nigeria's finest diplomats; Olumuyiwa Awe, a physicist, was to be one of Nigeria's most acclaimed scientists; Femi Odunjo who was to become a pathologist; Victor Awosika, the medical doctor who later founded the famous Holy Trinity Hospital in Lagos; the zoologist Caleb Olaniyan; Femi Esan, the power engineer who was to head Nigeria's Energy Commission; and Femi Olutoye, who became one of the first generation of Nigerian university graduates to join the officers' cadre of the post-colonial Nigerian army and rise to the level of General. Okigbo would meet all of them again later on as students at the University College in Ibadan. But in that competition at Warri, in which the Umuahia team walloped the Ibadan team, Okigbo won a cricket bat for his outstanding performance. He would repeat this feat the following years at the King's College cricket oval, again against the Ibadan team, thus consolidating his reputation as one of the finest cricket batsmen of his generation. Indeed, *The Umuahian* magazine of 1949/50 reported the following:

> Okigbo had a successful batting season, scoring two centuries. He was presented by the school with a bat for his score against Ibadan. He always attacked the bowling and punished lose ball severely with his favourite shots, the hook and cover-drive. His late cuts have improved, though he occasionally gave chances to point or second slip. His fielding at cover continued to be good.[65]

These games sowed the seeds of life-long friendships between schoolboy sportsmen from rival schools who met frequently on the sporting field. Most of them would indeed play important parts in the evolution of post-colonial Nigerian society.

It was through these games that Okigbo met two of his best friends in life: Leslie Oritsewenyimi Harriman and Eugene Olufemi Odunjo were both playing for the rival Ibadan team. They had initially met in 1947 when the Government College, Ibadan team travelled eastwards to Umuahia to play cricket. They would meet again during the 1948 Warri cricket quadrangular. It was during these cricket matches that Christopher Okigbo also met and began his lifelong friendship with Wole Soyinka, who was scorer for the Ibadan cricket team in 1948 at Warri. These occasions for competitive sports helped to break down ethnic and religious barriers. As Caleb Olaniyan reflected many years later: 'We grew up as Nigerians; it was not important where anyone came from – that fact was in fact de-emphasised for us.'[66] The Government Colleges specifically emphasized a pan-Nigerian view by bringing together, for the first time, teenage boys from different places to live together, interact and forge close friendships across ethnic and religious lines in a truly difficult society. Many of these boys later came to the pioneer University College, Ibadan, and later on, met in their professional careers working in Nigerian public life. They were all products of a hybrid culture: a generation uprooted early from their traditional, indigenous cultures, and put through the elitist mill of English education. The result sometimes was that ambiguous creature of the empire – the native Englishmen – wearing the Fanonian white masks under black skins. In time, many of these boys felt the deep insufficiency of both worlds, and the fragmentation of their consciousness, which became the source of their deepest conflicts. Okigbo's life reflected that conflict, that sense of an inner disturbance, inherent in the dual consciousness of an Anglo-African identity. Cricket – that most English and aristocratic of sports – symbolized this reality, for it emphasized values so alien and colonial in its performance.

Okigbo was equally accomplished in other sports. By 1948, he was regularly in the Umuahia football first eleven playing teams from Dennis Memorial Grammar School, Onitsha, Hope Waddell Institute, Calabar, Aggrey Memorial, Arochukwu, the two Methodist colleges at Uzuakoli and Oron, St. Patrick's College, Calabar, Stella Maris College, Port Harcourt, College of Immaculate Conception, Enugu, and various schools around the Eastern region. Umuahia suffered numerous humiliating defeats from the Catholic schools. There were, of course, memorable exceptions, as when C.I.C. Enugu, parading a formidable team, fell to the Umuahia team by a lone goal scored by Sam Izuora with a combination from Okigbo and Egbonu playing in the center forward and on the right flank. There were also slim victories over Dennis Memorial Grammar School and Methodist College, Uzuakoli in 1948; games in which Okigbo was 'radiant' to use the description of his teammate B. N. C. Uzochukwu, himself one of Umuahia's finest athletes in the 1940s. Okigbo's reputation, as one of Umuahia's most skilful soccer players whose exploits entered the sporting lore in colonial Eastern Nigeria, was based on solid performance. Mr. Alagoa remembered how sometimes during crucial matches, Okigbo and Francis Egbonu – both of them in the same class and in the same School House – would suddenly feign illness, knowing how indispensable they were to the school's football team. They would use such an occasion to draw attention and to dramatize their importance to the school team. It would take a combination of Alagoa, the football master, Biobaku and virtually the entire school to coax them to play. 'Sometimes the whole school would troop down to School House to plead, cajole and pet the two back to the fields, where they would nonetheless give good accounts of themselves'[68] recalled Lawrence Amu. Lawrence Amu who became the Group Managing Director of Nigeria's National oil corporation, the NNPC many years later, was also a renowned sportsman who entered Umuahia in September 1948. As the Government College, Umuahia magazine of 1949/50 also reports: 'Okigbo proved to be a useful goals scorer, often because the defence was drawn out of position by the other two inside forwards and he was left unmarked to receive the expected pass, and shoot.'[69] He played in the center-forward position.

Okigbo's football skills indeed, not only won him acclaim in sporting circles, but also the admiration and love of a young woman, Felicia. It was a forbidden love. Felicia was the wife of the formidable Chuba Ikpeazu, a prominent Onitsha magistrate, who later became a distinguished high court judge and chairman of the Nigerian Football Association. He had been a great admirer of the young Okigbo, whom he knew through his brother Pius, a contemporary at CKC Onitsha. During the 1949/50 season, the Government College Umuahia team played a football match against Dennis Memorial Grammar School at Onitsha. Ikpeazu, an avid patron of sports, often hosted visiting school teams who came to play in Onitsha and entertained them lavishly in his home. At such a gathering, Christopher and Felicia met, became intensely attracted to each other and fell in love. Okigbo was only nineteen, and was just entering his senior term at school. Felicia was twenty. She was the first woman with whom Okigbo fell madly in love. Born to a prominent Onitsha family – the Ayalogus – she had recently left Queen's College, Lagos and married Chuba, who had just returned from studying law at Cambridge. A striking beauty in those years, she apparently felt unfulfilled in an arranged marriage to an older man, with whom she possibly had little emotional connection. Her love for Christopher was instant, deep, physical and redeeming. Okigbo's ardent love offered her passion, and his sense of adventure awakened her to the truest, physical and emotional expression of her most intimate desires. They carried on an illicit relationship which lasted into Okigbo's freshman year at the University College, Ibadan, before it was discovered and blown up into scandalous drama. The adulterous relationship between the young spouse of a famous man and a restless schoolboy, needless to say, became the subject of much gossip in Onitsha society. For days, Okigbo harboured Felicia at the Eleyele campus of the University College, and agonised over the scandal. He began to make elaborate plans to elope, but it proved to be an impractical proposition. 'Christopher was mostly moved by chivalry in his decision to contract this marriage', Ben Obumselu reminisced later, 'but it did not happen.'[70] Apparently, wiser counsel, and pressure from his father, prevailed. There are indications that Chuba Ikpeazu's agents threatened the young Christopher with both physical and legal harm. The threat of violence against Okigbo was so real that he disappeared from Onitsha for a while. But here again, the crisis was resolved with deft diplomatic moves by Okigbo's friends and relatives, especially through Pius, who waded into the matter, using his many connections in Onitsha society, his enormous goodwill, and his close friendship with Chuba Ikpeazu to bring the matter to a close. In the end, Felicia's marriage ended and she was sent off to England by her family to study law. She was to become the first Igbo woman to qualify as a lawyer and to be called to the English bar in 1959.

Okigbo was affected by this incident enough for him to reflect upon it many years later when he began to write. Poetry provided healing, and allowed him to resolve the significant moments in his past from which he wished to be exorcised. Although Felicia was only a year older than Christopher, she offered him maternal consolations: 'she offered me love thinking me a child'[71] – he wrote in the 'Four Canzones'. Felicia was indeed like the rest of the women in his life, moulded into the same complex figure of the goddess, mother and lover, rolled into one. Okigbo wrote the commemorative poem in *Heavensgate* on her return from England in 1961. Felicia resurrects in Okigbo's poetry as the sophisticated 'maiden of the salt – emptiness' in the poem 'Watermaid', whose:

> Secret I have told into no ear,
> save into a dughole, to hold, not to drown with -
> Secret I have planted into beachsand…[72]

We recognise here, as much Ovid's tale of King Midas, his secret ears and his barber, as the Igbo folktale about the inexorable choice of silence by the tapster in the fable, who, from the top of his palm tree, witnessed the act of adultery between a man and woman. His recourse is to dig a hole and confess the act he had witnessed into the hole, absolve himself of the burden of guilt, and avoid the consequence of vicarious involvement associated with not telling what he had seen. But it was also the act of ritual silence for the sake of sustaining the balance and harmony in nature and in the community. Okigbo appropriates this tale to hint at his own love story. The story of this futile love affair, and its devastating finale was part of Okigbo's initiation into a world of conflict. As Chike Momah would say later, people were struck by 'a natural amazement that a boy so immature as Christopher could get embroiled in an affair so potentially explosive.'[73]

By his last year in secondary school, while preparing for the university matriculation examination to Ibadan, it became apparent that Christopher Okigbo had decided to forgo an earlier ambition for a science degree, and pursue an Arts degree in the University, probably influenced as much by Biobaku's view of scientists as by his absolute distaste for geography. Chukwuemeka Ike recalls that Okigbo hated geography 'more than he hated oranges and was prepared to demonstrate that point even if it meant a zero in his final examinations.'[74] Christopher Okigbo's class had taken the Cambridge School certificate examinations in May 1950. On the day of the geography examination, Okigbo signalled his intention to leave the hall. Mr. Wareham, the geography master, who was invigilating looked at Okigbo and said,

> 'Well, Okigbo, you've made a capital mess of your geography paper, I reckon!'
> 'I'm sorry about it sir,' Okigbo replied keeping a straight face, 'But I do not want to continue with the exam sir.'
> 'What did you say my boy?'
> 'I said you can fail me sir!' Okigbo replied calmly.[75]

Mr. Wareham was dumbstruck. He took him to the Principal, who interviewed Okigbo. Mr. Simpson tried by all means to cajole him, and even allowed Okigbo to take as many books as would help him into the examinations, but Okigbo was resolved not to take geography. Without geography, however, Okigbo would be deficient in one paper, and would not be eligible for a place at the University College, Ibadan and would be unable to take the matriculation examination. It was then that Christopher decided to replace geography with Latin. 'And it didn't bother him that he had done only three terms of Latin previously in the class three. Umuahia did not offer Latin for the Cambridge School Certificate examinations,'[76] Chukwuemeka Ike said. Without a solid preparation in Latin it seemed unlikely that he would pass the tough university college matriculation examination. But that was the kind of challenge that inspired Okigbo: in a typical demonstration of his natural abilities, Okigbo went ahead and prepared for Latin, and not only passed with remarkable results in the university matriculation examination, but went ahead to enroll for the full honours degree in Classics at the University College, Ibadan.

In his penultimate year at Umuahia, tragedy struck. It was an Umuahia tradition to organize a picnic the week before the Cambridge School Certificate examination for the senior boys. The picnic was organized by Professor Biobaku at the Imo River to help relieve the inevitable tension leading to the tough exams. On this particular occasion in December 1949, two schoolboys, Green and Derima, drowned, 'sucked in mercilessly by the eddies of the river.'[77] No one expected the tragedy because both boys were great swimmers from the riverine Ijaw area. The incident itself had a profound effect on the college. Biobaku was personally shattered. He felt a personal sense of guilt, and chose to leave the College at the end of the term. He went back to Cambridge to complete his doctoral research in African history and by 1950, when Okigbo entered the University College, Ibadan, his English and history master Biobaku, had returned to assume a new role as the Registrar of the University College.

Okigbo was sent off from Government College, Umuahia with a rousing farewell, organised by junior classmates Kelsey Harrison and Ralph Opara. It was a real measure of Okigbo's personality and his popularity in school that he was the only boy in his class of 1945 for whom the juniors organized such a send off. Okigbo had frequently championed the causes of younger students, standing up for them against the inbuilt tyrannies of a regimented, British-style public school. Indeed, Okigbo was too restless and unconventional to be made a prefect. It was an amusing sight, to see him, already a senior boy, doing 'the runs' – that punishment which involved running one and a half miles of the school mostly uphill in six minutes – and quite cheerfully, with the juniors.

Okigbo left Umuahia in June 1950, with a Division Two in the Cambridge School Certificate Examination taken in March 1950. He had distinctions in Mathematics,

Physics and Chemistry, and credits in Biology, British Empire History, English Language, and English Literature, and a pass in Geography, and he won the Latin prize. This result, overall, placed him fifteenth in a class of twenty-six boys who sat for the exam. He was however, among the fourteen candidates from Umuahia invited to sit for the University College, Ibadan entrance examination in March 1950, and was one of the ten who passed and was admitted to the University in 1950, to study Classics.

In some respect schooling in Umuahia represented the beginning of Okigbo's conscious uprooting from his primal world: his spiritual exile, his straying from roots towards the new gods of modernity. English education disconnected him from the ancient priesthood and his functions to Idoto. The English ambience and traditions of the Government College upon which he was nurtured, introduced him to a deeply western European sense of the world, and symbolically forced him away from Idoto. Okigbo was assimilated into a western unconscious, as was every 'privileged' member of his generation who had the same opportunities of an elitist English education. The allure of their intellectual pursuits led them all towards deeper encounters with western cultural values. Through their distinctly English education they grew apart from the rest of the community. This fact would explain Okigbo's sense of the contradiction of his existence as an African moulded consciously in the image of Europe, seeking ultimately to deal with a double heritage and a dual consciousness – the conflict which Chinua Achebe would describe as the 'confluence of cultures.'[78] Okigbo would later attempt to resolve his conflict through his poetry. But as a schoolboy in Umuahia, he was still like the 'poplar' in his poem, 'needing more roots, more sap to grow to sunlight.' Thirsting indeed for the 'sunlight' of this new world increasingly dominated by the European values foisted upon him and the rest of his generation of Africans as colonial subjects through the school system.

## NOTES

1  Robert Wren, interview with Barry Cozen, *Those Magical Years* (Washington DC: Three Continents Press, 1984).
2  Laz Ekwueme, 'Umuahia and the Arts' (unpublished essay), 1992, Lagos.
3  Interview with G.K.J. Amachree, Marine Road, Apapa Lagos, 1992.
4  Chinua Achebe, *Home and Exile* (New York: Oxford University Press, 2000).
5  Interview with Saburi Biobaku, Ilupeju Lagos, 1992.
6  V.C. Ike, *The Umuahian Magazine* (Enugu: Nwamife Publishers, 1979).
7  Interview with Ralph Opara, Savage Crescent, GRA Enugu, 1995.
8  Pius Okigbo, 'A Toast of Christopher Okigbo' *Glendora Review* 1 (2) 1995 (34–39) Lagos.
9  Interview with Namsey Eno, Lagos, 1994.
10  Interview with Peter Chigbo, Umuoji, Anambra State, 1995.
11  Michael Crowder, *The Story of Nigeria* (London: Faber, 1978).
12  Interview with Wilberforce Alagoa, Harold Wilson Drive, Port Harcourt, 1994.
13  Interview with Namsey Eno, Ikeja, Lagos 1994. 'Nixton' was Okigbo's nickname in school, taken from the name 'Christopher'.
14  Interview with V.C. Ike, Lagos, 1994.
15  Interview with Sam Onyewuenyi, Lagos, 1994.
16  Interview with John Onwuka, Lagos, 1994.
17  Ibid.

18 Christian C. Momah, *The Umuahian Magazine* (Enugu: Nwamife Publishers, 1979).

19 Interview with Johnson C. Obi, Ikoyi Lagos, 1993.

20 Interview with Don Egbue, Lagos, 1993.

21 Interview with Chukwuemeka Ike, Lagos, 1993.

22 Interview with Saburi Biobaku, Ilupeju, Lagos, 1993.

23 Ibid.

24 Ibid.

25 Ibid.

26 Ibid.

27 Ibid.

28 Ibid.

29 Interview with I.D. Erekosima, Port Harcourt, 1993.

30 Ibid.

31 Interview with Wilberforce Alagoa, Port Harcourt, 1993.

32 Ibid.

33 Ibid.

34 Ibid.

35 Ibid.

36 Interview with Johnson C. Obi, Ikoyi, Lagos 1993.

37 Interview with Sam Onyewuenyi, Lagos, 1993.

38 Ibid.

39 Interview with Ignatius Atigbi, Lagos, 1994.

40 Chinua Achebe cited in Robert Wren, *Those Magical Years* (Washington DC: Three Continents Press, 1981) p. 57.

41 Interview with V.C. Ike.

42 Interview with I.D. Erekosima.

43 Laz Ekwueme, 'Umuahia and the Arts'.

44 Interview with J.C. Obi.

45 Interview with Saburi Biobaku.

46 Inteview with V.C. Ike.

47 Interview with J.C. Obi.

48 Interview with V.C. Ike.

49 Charles Low, 'The WTC Are Here', *The Umuahian Magazine* (Enugu: Nwamife Publishers, 1979).

50 Ibid.

51 Interview with V.C. Ike.

52 Interview with J.C. Obi.

53 Interview with J.C. Obi.

54 Interview with I.D. Erekosima.

55 Ibid.

56 Interview with V.C. Ike.

57 Ibid.

58 Interview with Moses Udebiuwa, Lagos, 1992.

59 Interview with Peter C. Chigbo.

60 Ibid.

61 Interview with V.C. Ike.

62 Ibid.

63 Interview with Wilberforce Alagoa, 1993.

64 Report in *The Umuahian*: Umuahia Government College Magazine (1949-50) quoted in

Bernth Lindfors 'Okigbo as Jock' in *When the Drumbeat Changes,* (eds) Carolyn Parker and Stephen Arnold (Washington DC: Three Continents Press, 1981) pp. 199-214.

65  Quoted in Bernth Lindfors, 'Okigbo as Jock', in *When the Drumbeat Changes.*
66  Interview with Caleb Olaniyan, GRA Ikeja, Lagos, 1993.
67  Interview with B.N.C. Uzochukwu, Lagos, 1993.
68  Interview with Lawrence Amu, Ikoyi, Lagos 1993.
69  Quoted in Bernth Lindfors, 'Okigbo as Jock'.
70  Interview with Ben Obumselu, 1992.
71  Christopher Okigbo, *Four Canzones* (1956–61), *Black Orpheus* 2, 1962.
72  Christopher Okigbo 'Watermaid,' 1961, *Heavensgate, Labyrinths.*
73  C.C. Momah's e-mail to author, 2005.
74  Interview with V.C. Ike.
75  Ibid.
76  Ibid.
77  Chike C. Momah, *The Umuahian* (Enugu: Nwamife Publishers, 1979).
78  Chinua Achebe, *Morning Yet on Creation Day* (London: Heinemann, 1972).

# 3
## Cricket, classics, politics & urbane dissipation

### IBADAN 1950–56

Me, away from home, runaway. Must leave
the borders of our Land, fruitful fields
must leave our homeland.

('Song of the Forest', *Four Canzones*)

The University College, Ibadan was established in 1948. For many years the colonial administration struggled to come to terms with the realities of demand for higher education in the English colonies. There was an immediate practical consideration for the formulators of colonial policy: the two great wars in Europe in the twentieth century had reduced the number of hands trained to run the far-flung empire. With the increasing cost in administration of the colonies, it was urgent to recruit a local elite who would assist in maintaining the objectives of the empire in the colonies; a local gentry, in other words, fashioned in the image of the English. In the post-war years, as the reality of independence dawned, it became even more necessary to train the indigenous elite for the administrative services of the post-colonial state. This policy was behind the founding of the Government Colleges, Yaba Higher College and eventually University College. By the end of the Second World War, agitation for wider opportunities in higher education had grown in the colonies. Yaba Higher College had been established in 1931 to offer limited diplomas. Many Nigerians desiring higher education either went abroad or took by correspondence the tedious external degrees offered by the University of London. Agitation continued until the Asquith and Eliot commissions recommended the establishment of the University Colleges in Ibadan and Legon to join Fourah Bay College in Freetown, Sierra Leone in catering for British West Africa, and Makerere in Uganda, for the East African colonies. The opening of the University College, Ibadan in 1948 marked the end of Yaba Higher College, as students from Yaba moved over to University College, Ibadan to complete their programs. UCI had a 'special relationship' with University of London, from which students actually earned their degrees. This affiliation to London defined the character of the university for many years, until Ibadan's charter as an independent degree awarding institution was ratified in 1962. For many of its critics however, the University College, Ibadan bore the uncomfortable seal of empire.

Christopher Okigbo arrived at the old Eleyele campus of the University College, Ibadan on 17 October 1950. By all accounts, Okigbo introduced himself to the UCI society in his usual flamboyant style. His fame had preceded him to Ibadan as Alex Ekwueme recollects:

Christopher moved to Ibadan to read classics. Coming from Umuahia, essentially steeped in science, we considered this either the biggest joke or the biggest wonder of the 20th century. It was alright for students from mission schools or King's College, who were well grounded in Latin to read Classics at University – Dickson Igwe, J.T.F. Iyalla, Bola Ige or even my own classmate Kalada Hart – but somebody from Umuahia to attempt to read Classics, or even Law, was an entirely new development. Christopher Okigbo did it in grand style. I understand that in the three months between leaving secondary school and entering the University, he had gone through Books I, II and III of *Latin for Today* and that by the time the University resumed he was almost as ready as any of his colleagues in the Classics department to tackle university course work.[1]

Okigbo was admitted to the University College only two years after it opened, and thus belonged to its first generation of undergraduates – pioneers of modern university education in Nigeria. Ibadan was highly elitist; its community was isolate, its conception bourgeois, and the students were highly conscious of their extraordinary privilege. Okigbo took his assured place in the new society for granted, as did most of his peers. Martin Banham, who came later to teach drama in Ibadan towards the end of the 1950s, summed up the mood and character of the period:

On the campus were the young intellectuals and the young potential politicians. The students saw themselves very much I think as the natural rulers of the future. There was a certain arrogance about them…I went out there as a young socialist, fire in the belly and all the rest of it, thinking that I was going into a situation with all the clichés of colonialism, but finding myself in the middle of a body of very elite young men and women whose main concern in life was how soon they could get their car allowance, and their car, and take over this or that position…there was innocence in this attitude…[2]

Admission to Ibadan was extremely competitive. A lot of resources were dedicated to the nurturing of this select class of young Nigerians – 'the most talented scholars in that generation'[3] – drawn from across wide shores. There was a broad mix of students who came to the university from all over English-speaking West Africa, which in those years included the part of the Cameroons under British trust. Nevertheless, from the university's admission records of 1948, boys from Okigbo's alma mater, Government College, Umuahia, accounted for the highest number of students admitted to the new university at Ibadan in the first five years of its founding.

Going to this English-style university meant further separation from primal roots. Students were nurtured on a diet of European manners, but many would struggle to retain some connection to their ancestral worlds. In time, this experience of alienation created a sense of permanent disjunction and ambiguity: a crisis of identity among the educated members of Okigbo's generation. It is this sense of disconnection, of uprooting, which Okigbo equates to his own spiritual exile from Idoto, and to which he makes a grand gesture of reconciliation and expiation as he began to write poetry:

Emigrant with air borne nose,
I have had my cleansing…[4]

In Okigbo's case, going to boarding school in Umuahia symbolically marked this early uprooting from Ojoto and, therefore, from his symbolic duties at the Ajani shrine. European education meant that Okigbo must abandon his roots for the modern urban society in an era of rapid transition. It was the fate of people born in his generation to straddle that new world, and in doing that, achieve a near erasure of ethnic memory and identity. '*And the cancelling-out is complete,*'[5] Okigbo wrote also in *Limits*, describing the imaginative or psychic disruption of the mind conditioned by colonialism, an event which the poet likens to the violence and chaos of Picasso's 'Guernica.' Okigbo's sense of alienation was completed by going to Ibadan, a place that powerfully symbolized a physical, as well as spiritual separation from the traditional Igbo world.

The steady disintegration of traditional society had commenced with his father's generation who had converted to Christianity, abandoning the rites of the ancestors. Okigbo's generation was only to mark the completion of that historical process. Okigbo's upbringing was dominantly Christian. He remained nominally a Roman Catholic, still attending mass in the early years at the university, though he had become increasingly ambivalent and skeptical. His connection to the ancient Igbo world was tenuous, expressed merely as a lost arcadia. However, as he told Marjory Whitelaw, the Canadian journalist, in Ibadan in March 1965, he kept up his responsibility to Idoto even as an undergraduate by the symbolic gesture of money sent home to his uncle at Ojoto for the upkeep of the Ajani shrine – a token of the prodigal who had strayed off to the glittering lights of modernity.

The campus of the University College was originally located in the rehabilitated military barracks at Eleyele, reconditioned by the Public Works Department. With a little over three hundred students enrolled in the arts, the sciences, engineering and the medical school, it was a close-knit place. The Eleyele Campus was serene. By Ben Obumselu's account, the Ibadan campus had the egalitarian atmosphere of an English provincial town, with its simple architecture of wood framed bungalows. Obumselu himself was admitted to the University College, Ibadan in 1951, coming one year after Okigbo. He retained a vivid memory of the place: 'I came to the University when it was still at Eleyele,' he said to the American critic Robert Wren. 'I remember it with a great deal of pleasure and nostalgia. It is really for me, and to most people who lived in it, a lost paradise. And the reason for that: one, there were very few students, and we knew one another…'[6] It was possible in that environment to gain instant fame or notoriety. Okigbo quickly threw himself into the social life on campus. He enjoyed the ambience of the close-knit community and soon was reckoned among the most prominent of the socialites and politically active students.

Intellectual life in Ibadan was rigorous in its early years even under conditions that were makeshift. Ibadan was a colonial experiment: its umbilical cord was attached to London, its curriculum designed from the syllabus of the University of London, emphasizing a Eurocentric pedagogy. The university drew its faculty from first-class scholars across the world. They were mostly romantics: individuals who were driven by curiosity to discover an alternative world and settle its old myths. Kenneth Mellanby, the first Principal of the University, was a romantic figure – a brilliant and colorful intellectual who appealed to the imagination. Mellanby and his wife, then Jean Copeland, were both impressive liberals. Jean Copeland had been a member of the British House of Commons before coming to teach history in Ibadan. Ulli Beier, the German Jewish scholar who came to teach in Ibadan's English department in October 1950, said: 'Dr. Mellanby had the appearance of a mischievous but likeable schoolboy.'[7] There were lots of such other remarkable men and women who came to shape the intellectual climate and character of the new university.

There was Dr. Geoffrey Parrinder – who had spent many years in Ivory Coast working as a Methodist minister, studying African religions on which he had published a book. There were the Sansomes – one of the few expatriate couples who were both professors at Ibadan. They were among the few who genuinely tried to break the social barrier with the UCI students in that early period. There was James Welch, one-time chaplain to King George VI and journalist for the BBC whom Mellanby brought in as Professor of Religion, and there was Keith Buchanan in Geography. In English, there were equally interesting people: Alex Rodger, Eric Robinson and Paul Christopherson. Christopherson was already developing his new concept of phonetics, for which he would become world famous. In history, there was John Potter, whom the novelist Achebe described as 'a very eccentric man. A former Anglican priest who lost his faith and became agnostic.'[8] E.A. Cadle, who taught Latin to Pius Okigbo at Yaba Higher College, had moved over in 1948 to establish Ibadan's Classics department in 1948. He and Okigbo became especially close. Cadle's interest was classical drama, and he was patron of the Drama Society at Ibadan. He tried to guide Okigbo's interest to the stage. For a time, Okigbo was active in the Drama club, although he became increasingly less active from 1954. Eugene Cadle was also Okigbo's university tutor. John Ferguson was also teaching Classics. He too was a man of the theatre – an accomplished actor and stage director who once staged *Toussaint l'Ouverture* at Ibadan. He earned considerable reputation in Ibadan for directing plays. Okigbo also got to know and enjoy the friendship of Professor Molly Mahood who came as Professor of English, taking over as head of the department when Paul Christopherson left in 1954.

There were also some key Nigerian pioneer educators on the staff of the new University College: Okigbo's former English and History teacher at Government College, Umuahia, Dr. Saburi Biobaku, was the University Registrar, and Nathaniel Adamolekun was Assistant Registrar. On the academic staff, there was the historian, Professor Kenneth Onwuka Dike who revolutionized the research and teaching of modern African history at Ibadan, and a few years later became the first Nigerian Principal of University College. There was also Hezekiah Oluwasanmi in Zoology, the parasitologist Dr. Sanya Onabamiro, Olumbe Bashir in Chemistry, Dr. Andrew Okechukwu Ikejiani in the medical school, and Chike Obi in Mathematics. Professor Kodilinye, the highly Europeanized Nigerian professor of medicine at Ibadan, used to introduce himself as 'Kodline from Obosai', and, it is said, wear gloves to shake the hands of his rural kinsmen at Obosi on his infrequent visits home. Wole Soyinka was to satirize him later on in his novel, *The Interpreters*. All of these men were leading intellectual lights of their time who became role models for Okigbo's generation.

When Okigbo arrived at UCI, a decidedly European aesthetic held sway. Recounting her experience of Ibadan in its earliest years, history Professor Jean Mellanby said: 'When I went out in 1949 I found the students were in ferment with ideas, intellectual ideas. They admired Europe very much. They were at the stage of not coming to terms with anything African, partly rejecting that, but not completely. They were torn in several directions culturally...'[9] Mellanby no doubt refers to the condition of dual consciousness, which Fanon and Dubois had examined as symptoms of subjugation and alienation in the colonial unconscious. The condition expresses itself through patterns of cultural consumption and assimilation, through the instability of identity from which the product of a colonial experience suffers. Okigbo's experience undoubtedly exemplified that condition of profound doubleness.

Before long, the notion of an African aesthetic began to express itself at UCI. In the intellectual circles in Europe, especially in Paris, a new generation inspired by developments in the interwar and post war years, had developed a profound romance with black African culture. Ulli Beier, then at the University College's department of Extramural Studies, was present at the 1952 Paris conference on new Black and African literature which introduced Léopold Sédar Senghor to a wider audience. The Senegalese scholar-statesman and poet was already a leading cultural figure in Paris and counted the philosopher Jean-Paul Sartre and the Martiniquan poet Aimé Césaire among his close associates. The journal *Présence Africaine* edited by Birago Diop was active in propagating the ideas of a new black aesthetic. Beier introduced the writings of the negritude poets to the Ibadan undergraduates. Senghor's ideas became quickly influential in the 1950s within the nationalist intellectual circles at Legon, Makerere and Ibadan. Rallying to a black aesthetic for political and cultural philosophy gave increasing form to their notions of identity. There was much talk then, of the 'African personality' which must negotiate the nature of hybrid consciousness and trans-culturality, and at the same time remain authentic. Although he was to reject it later as too sentimental, Christopher Okigbo was fascinated with the essential ideas of negritude as a young undergraduate, as Sunday Anozie has noted. His early works exhibit the influence of negritude and of Senghor particularly. Okigbo also later came to admire the works of Tchicaya U Tam'si, whose sublime and tortured consciousness spoke of Africa, but whose surrealism flowed more from Rimbaud than Senghor. The romantic image of the new Africa on the doorstep of a new history, sharpened the intellectual response of Christopher Okigbo, like many members of his generation, to the notions of his new identity – the point from which his poetry would later flow.

At Ibadan, Christopher Okigbo felt free, unencumbered by the demands of social responsibility. His life as an undergraduate pointed in many directions – he pursued his musical talents, he dabbled in entrepreneurship and entered Chike Obi's left-wing politics. Obumselu who was one of Okigbo's closest friends at the University College Ibadan in the 1950s and throughout Okigbo's life, has written that Okigbo soon discovered he was no scholar, but was taken by the pleasurable, sybaritic existence of 'a man of leisure' and 'urbane dissipation.'[10]

There were three main student residence halls at the Eleyele campus: Halls One and Two were for the male students, and Block Zero was for the female under-graduates, of which there were only twelve at the university in 1950. Every year, UCI appointed government and university scholars from the best students in competitive entrance exams. The preferment included more private quarters. Although, he was not one of the 'University Scholars,' Christopher Okigbo nevertheless had his room in the scholar's block. 'No one knew exactly how Chris got a room in the scholar's block,' Caleb Olaniyan noted years later, 'but he came with a solid reputation as an all-round sportsman. He had great charm and was very likeable and could get around.'[11] In the early years at Eleyele, the rooms were divided into fairly large spaces partitioned with raffia mats, nets and wood. Okigbo's block stood at the western end of the Eleyele Campus, behind the temporary building of the College of Medicine. In his first year in 1950, he shared a room with Agiobu-Kemmer, a Classics scholar, who later became a distinguished permanent secretary of the Federal Government of Nigeria. In 1951, Okigbo's roommate was Demas Akpore who was also studying the Classics. Many years later, after a successful career in education, the height of which was as the famous principal of the Government College, Ughelli, he was elected deputy governor of Bendel State, in Nigeria's second republic from 1979 to 1983. Although Demas Akpore was more socially conservative, he got along easily with Okigbo. Next door was Gamaliel Onosode. Even in those years, Onosode was a born-again Christian of the Baptist faith, whose social life and worldview contrasted sharply with Okigbo's. Onosode's recollection of the times with Okigbo reveals the camaraderie of life on campus in Ibadan in the 1950s, as it especially emphasizes the character of the poet as a libertine and rebel. Onosode wrote:

> Apart from politics I was also very active in the religious sphere of activities in Ibadan. Initially I was of a fundamental kind of persuasion particularly in my first two years, when most of my activities were church centered. This baffled and irked Christopher Okigbo, my

next-door neighbor, who simply got fed up with the routine and the regularity of my church attendance especially on Sundays when I used to go to worship in one of the Baptist Churches. There was a particular one on Salvation Army road and on Saturday I would hire a bicycle, so I could ride to town on Sunday. One particular Sunday when he couldn't take it anymore, I woke up to find my hired bicycle had been locked and the key had disappeared. I was baffled and was looking all over the place for the key, when Okigbo came round and confessed that he had confiscated the keys because he couldn't understand why I should be going to church every Sunday. I said I couldn't see how else I could spend a Sunday without going to interact with Christian people and joining the Christian worship. My persistence did not really leave any impression on him. He only changed his tactics of discouragement, by simply carving a hole in the mat which partitioned our rooms so I could have a full view of activities which were going on his side of the mat. Maybe he hoped that I might catch a glimpse of what I was missing by living a church centered life. That did not in any way interfere with our friendship. We only agreed to differ and respect each other's views.[12]

Many of those who encountered Christopher Okigbo in the University College, Ibadan in the 1950s, remembered him as restless, highly intelligent, very friendly, unconventional and very socially involved. The poet and scholar, Michael J. C. Echeruo came to study English at the University College, Ibadan in 1956, when Okigbo was repeating his degree examination in Classics. He remembered Okigbo vividly on campus: 'You couldn't help but notice Christopher Okigbo. It was impossible to miss him on campus. He was active, restless, everywhere. He cut the picture of a young rake...'[13] Okigbo was a socialite, a sportsman, a musician, and even a politician of the radical bent; he was far less a scholar in the orthodox sense of it. 'He recoiled instinctively from the drudgery of undergraduate discipline.'[14] Although he was too distracted to be a scholar, Okigbo read widely and voraciously. As Michael Echeruo again puts it, Okigbo 'could make more of a hint than the most omnivorous reader could.'[15] But Okigbo saw himself in Ibadan neither as scholar nor even a poet. His life was devoted to the pursuit of pure pleasures, and of other youthful passions. Obumselu in his reminiscences provides a vivid description of Okigbo as an Ibadan undergraduate:

> He wrote nothing as a university student. He had come to Ibadan trailing the clouds of an awesome reputation as a cricketer, footballer, hockey player and pianist. Even in those early days, he had begun to cast his eyes on the possibilities of the wider world with its great careers, great loves and great fortunes. He socialized, talked and played the piano. That he chose to study Latin and Greek literatures meant that he had ambitions in humane learning. But he could not become a scholar because he was an athlete. Nor could he become an athlete because he dabbled in the bogus politics of Chike Obi's Dynamic Party. Nor could he be a political activist because he was tempted by the urbane dissipations of a man of leisure. He was incapable of that merciless lopping off of the heads of sundry distractions upon which solid achievement must depend.[16]

He proposed originally to read Chemistry or Medicine at Ibadan, and was given distinctions in the sciences in the Cambridge School certificate examination. But he suddenly changed his mind, and chose instead to pursue full honors in Classics. Okigbo's sudden decision to change course demonstrates that spontaneous, almost capricious quality of his persona. During the cricket season of 1949/50, Okigbo's last term at school, the Government College, Umuahia cricket team, captained by Patrick Ozieh, had gone to play the King's College, in Lagos. Both schools always had a keen rivalry in academics and in games. Alex Ekwueme refers briefly to this in his account of the visit of Umuahians to King's College in 1950:

> We both played first eleven cricket for our schools although we rather looked down generally on the quality of cricket at Umuahia, notwithstanding such flashes in the pan as Namse Eno,

Christian Momah, Kelsey Harrison, Christopher Okigbo, Wilfred Chukwudebelu, and a few others. I heard a lot about Christopher from my younger brother, Laz who was at Umuahia but did not get to see him much until a group of six Umuahia boys came to Lagos after the Cambridge School Certificate Examination to attend the Federal Government Scholarship interview. They were quartered in my dormitory at King's and as the prefect in charge I had the duty of looking after them for the duration of the stay. Christopher was easily the most fascinating of my guests. He was warm and very pleasant. He moved around King's as if he had been there for five years, made friends with many students and generally exuded a level of charm and self-confidence we had not thought possible from a student brought up in a rural setting such as Umudike-Umuahia![17]

Students at King's College generally thought of themselves as epitomizing civilization and cosmopolitanism, because it was the only one of the Government Colleges established in an urban centre, and it stood close to the heart of government in Lagos, the capital of Nigeria. It was during this visit that Rex Akpofure, captain of the King's College cricket team, declared that the boys from Umuahia were 'Bushmen' because they not only lived miles away from civilization, but they could never study the humanities as they only went for the science degrees. Okigbo took up the gauntlet and with typical passion argued that Umuahia students were all-rounders – renaissance men who would not only beat King's at cricket, but could read anything they chose, including Classics. Okigbo offered to make good the claim by going to Ibadan and reading Classics. Rex Akpofure expressed incredulity – it was the biggest joke of the year – as Umuahia did not even offer Latin. Okigbo had planned to take the matriculation for a science degree with assurances of a government scholarship, but chose to forfeit his scholarship to pursue a degree in Classics to prove the point eloquently that he was 'a renaissance man' and up to the challenge. This incident was confirmed later by Akpofure, who said, 'it was quintessential Christopher'[18] – that sense of his drama and impulse; and his love for the difficult. Contemporaries of Christopher Okigbo in the classics department went on to distinguished careers in the new Nigeria.

A few had been teachers of Latin in various secondary schools, before coming to the University College to earn a degree and advance their careers. The department included relatively older students like S.A. Osinulu – 'the flying president' of the Students Union who had transferred from Yaba Higher College. He was the first president of the Ibadan Students Union. He had presided over the appropriate sharing of chicken in the dining hall. Osinulu later became a minister in the Methodist Church and Principal of the Methodist Boys High School in Lagos. The novelist John Munonye, two years ahead of Okigbo, later graduated in 1953 with a first class degree – the first in the University College. The politician and lawyer Bola Ige, called the 'Cicero of Esan Oke' for his oratory, became Governor of the old Oyo state in 1979, and many years later in 1999, Nigeria's Attorney General before he was assassinated.

Okigbo's classmates in Classics at Ibadan in 1950 include Augustus Adebayo and Kalada Hart, both of whom entered the post-colonial civil service. Kalada Hart became secretary to the government and head of civil service of the old Rivers State. In the same 1950 class were Muhammad Bello, later Chief Justice of Nigeria, Buba Ardo and Mamman Nasir, all of whom later served on the Nigerian Supreme Court. Three of them were admitted from Northern Nigeria, on a special program for two years studying for the inter B.A. in Latin at the University College, Ibadan, before proceeding to England for their legal studies at the Inns of Court.

It was remarkable how many among the first generation of Classics scholars at UCI ended up in the Foreign Service. Okigbo would have liked to have joined them

67

but his career was to take a different path. J.T.F. Iyalla from King's College, was to become Nigeria's Ambassador to the United States. Dickson C. Igwe was Nigeria's Ambassador to the Organization of African Unity secretariat in Addis Ababa when it was established in 1963. Godwin Onyegbula became Permanent Secretary in Nigeria's Foreign Ministry and later headed the Biafran Foreign Service. Ignatius Olisemeka served for many years as Ambassador and later as Nigeria's Foreign Minister in the 1990s. There was also Blessing Akporede Clark, elder brother to the poet John Pepper Clark who became Nigeria's Ambassador also to the UN. Emeka Anyaoku was to be the first African to become Secretary-General of the Commonwealth.

The Classics Department was next door to English where Chinua Achebe, was pursuing his degree. Achebe had come at the top in the University College matriculations examination in 1947/48 and was admitted as a government scholar into the foundation class of University College, Ibadan Medical School. But he left medical school, forfeiting his scholarship to study English, Religion and History in 1949. Achebe's English class included people like Mabel Imokhuede (later Mabel Segun) and Christian Chike Momah, Achebe's best friend from their days in Umuahia, who later became the Librarian of the Dag Hammarskjöld Library of the United Nations. Rex Akpofure arrived with Okigbo in 1950. He was to become the first African Principal of King's College, Lagos and, later Federal Director of Education; he and Okigbo remained great friends, and played together in the Ibadan cricket team. The 1951 English class included V.C. Ike and Ben Obumselu, who became a leading literary critic of that generation and was to play important roles in the crises of Okigbo's life; Ignatius Atigbi, a prominent socialite on campus who became the West African manager of Reuters news agency. He reported the constitutional conference in Lancaster House in 1957/8, leading to Nigeria's independence, and had been Reuters Paris correspondent. Peter Chigbo, who had been one of Okigbo's closest collaborators since their days at Umuahia, was also in that class. He had a career in the civil service before becoming in 1963 executive director of the newly established African Development Bank. After the Nigerian civil war, he took an MBA at Stanford and later became the President of the Nigerian Stock Exchange. Wole Soyinka remembers that one of the most amusing sights on campus was to see Okigbo struggling to keep the cap on his head from the wind and holding fast to Peter Chigbo, as they sped off on a motorbike on the unruly Ibadan roads, seemingly impervious to danger – until one evening, while speeding along the precipitous road to Mapo hall, Okigbo crashed in a close shave with death. Wole Soyinka himself, 1986 Nobel laureate for literature, was admitted into the Ibadan English department in 1952. This group was remarkable because of the intensity of the talent gathered in one place; even though Wole Soyinka came later to describe it as 'the wasted generation'.[19]

Okigbo's wide social contacts enriched his undergraduate life in Ibadan. Besides his personal contacts in the city, Okigbo also had close family members in Ibadan. His eldest brother Lawrence had returned from Dublin and was employed as a forestry officer at Moore Plantation. He later moved on to the Umunede Agricultural Extension station, where Okigbo and his friends visited him frequently. His cousin, Bede, was also living at Moore Plantation before he traveled abroad to the United States for study in 1952. Interaction outside the small, closed, isolated community of the University was also important to reduce the tedium of scholarship.

However, it was Leslie Oritsenweyinmi Harriman from Warri and Eugene Olufemi Odunjo from Abeokuta, who formed, with Okigbo, a memorable triumvirate at the University College. 'Inseparable' was how Ben Obumselu described their friendship.

'They were something of the three musketeers.'[20] They had first met in 1947, while playing cricket during the 'western tours' at Warri and their friendship blossomed at Ibadan. They constituted a fascinating trinity on campus – Okigbo in Classics, Harriman in Zoology and Odunjo in medical school. Obumselu noted that, while Okigbo and Harriman were extrovert in their involvement with life on campus, Femi Odunjo's introversion allowed him to share in their social performances in a more amused way. He provided a balance in colour to his more high-spirited friends. Obumselu later reminisced. 'He simply sat back and watched, and loved to enjoy the sometimes outrageous things which his friends cooked up; he was the observer but he was deeply involved with them at an intellectual level. It gave him pleasure to just watch them.'[21]

Arriving at the university with a formidable reputation as a sportsman – a brilliant cricket batsman, soccer star and all-round athlete – Okigbo quickly made the University's soccer and hockey first eleven, as well as the cricket team from 1950. Leslie Harriman who also made the University's cricket XI, remembered with great amusement their first cricket match on coming to Ibadan, for which they traveled to Lagos in December 1950. It was a selection game for the Nigerian national cricket team billed to play Ghana in 1950/51. Arrangements were made for the team to be quartered in Simeon Adebo's home along Ikorodu Road where they were to stay till the Monday, when the boys would go for the trials. Simeon Adebo, another nascent ambassador, was to become executive director of the United Nations Commission on Trade and Development (UNCTAD.) Adebo, although a man of great warmth, was a stickler for form, the result of his strict Christian faith. Apparently to prevent any youthful mischief, Simeon Adebo had locked the Ibadan team inside his compound for the night. But Okigbo and Harriman particularly wanted to visit the nightclubs. Soon they plotted an escape. They waited till it got adequately dark, and sneaked out, while everybody was asleep, through an unbarred window in Adebo's house. They went into the city to the Rex Club nearby at Alagomeji, Yaba where they danced the night away.

They had enjoyed themselves tremendously at the Rex Club, recipients of Alfred Rewane's renowned hospitality. They did not reckon, however, that Adebo would notice their absence. They returned to the house in the early hours, just as the clouds of dawn were lifting, only to find to their chagrin that their host had discovered their escape route and had locked his windows. They were stranded, and had no alternative but to wait outside at the gates, until the morning. Adebo took them in, bleary-eyed, and led them, with the rest of the team, to church that Sunday. Church service, under the stern and watchful eyes of Simeon Adebo, was an ordeal. They longed for sleep. After Sunday lunch, they went for cricket practice at the oval of the Railways club in Ebutte-Meta. Leslie Harriman made some runs but Christopher Okigbo was out for 'ducks'. In spite of this performance however, Okigbo's batting was adjudged remarkable enough to earn him a place in the Nigerian National Cricket team. The famous national cricket coach, Morocco Clarke praised Okigbo's batting style, which although unorthodox, was elegant. He preferred to play the cross bat because it suited his sense of the unconventional. Okigbo won his colors at UCI, playing alongside such Nigerian cricket greats as Caleb Olaniyan, Rex Akpofure, Christian Momah, Wilfred Chukwudebelu, and Kelsey Harrison who had been in his Umuahia team. There were others like Leslie Harriman, George Alele, Ebens Ikomi, Henry Enahoro, Afolabi George (later, Ogunlesi), Sam Okudu, Olunloyo, and Ignatius Atigbi, who were the stars of the University College, Ibadan, as well as the Nigerian national cricket teams. Okigbo featured prominently in the West African Universities games, held annually among the English-speaking universities in West Africa, at Ibadan, Legon and Fourah Bay. He toured with the University College, Ibadan team to Ghana in the 1950/51 season, during the first West African Universities games in Legon in March 1951, for which they stayed in Achimota.

This trip to Ghana in 1951 was probably Okigbo's first travel outside Nigeria. In that game, he played brilliantly against Fourah Bay College, for which he earned his caps. He was possibly Nigeria's best cricket batsman from 1950 to 1953. The American literary critic Bernth Lindfors has admirably documented Okigbo's life as a sportsman, in his essay, 'Okigbo as Jock.' Lindfors highlights Okigbo's significant athletic prowess, reflecting on his activities as a highly decorated national athlete and scholar sportsman. This record calls into question Ali Mazrui's representation of the man in his novel *The Trial of Christopher Okigbo* as an effete or 'frail aesthete'[22] who was disdainful of robust activity; a withdrawn and lonely character marked by a 'distaste for some of the sports which were organized at school, the mixture of insecurity and arrogance as he cultivated a style of social distance.' Ali Mazrui's description of Okigbo's character could not be further from the true character of Christopher Okigbo; for Okigbo, as the Lindfors account shows, was anything but 'a weak, introverted, cold, ineffectual and wholly unimpressive individual whose poetry is charged with surprising power.'[24] If anything Okigbo was the direct opposite: he was active, extrovert, warm and charismatic, and was deeply engaged in the social life on campus.

Indeed according to the *University Herald* edition of 1950, Okigbo was actively involved, playing in the attacking center forward position with the football first eleven and was working 'to build a strong football club from the decrepit form into which it fell [the year before his arrival] owing to bad administration.'[25] One of the finest tributes paid to Okigbo as a university athlete, a reflection of his influence and contribution to the sporting and social life of the university, is in the testimony published in *The Bug*, lamenting the state of the UCI football team in 1954: 'Had old-timers, who had made names for themselves at the school such as Okigbo…been playing [this season] the team would almost have attained perfection.'[26] By 1954, Okigbo had given up active sporting life, seduced by other adventures, but not as Lindfors suggests, 'in order to concentrate on his studies.'[27] Ben Obumselu puts Okigbo's interest by this time in 1954 in clearer perspective: 'He could not be an athlete because he dabbled into the bogus politics of Professor Chike Obi's Dynamic Party.'[28] But above all, also in that period, Okigbo had begun to 'cast his eyes on the possibilities of the wider world with its great careers, great loves, and great fortunes.'[29]

Alfred Rewane modeled such an endeavor. He owned the Rex Club in those years. A young businessman and socialite on the make, Rewane was a flamboyant figure in Lagos society, driving around in his famous Jaguar. He later became one of Nigeria's most powerful businessmen, prominent in Nigerian political life as a financier of the Action Group Party, and one of the closest confidantes of the politician Obafemi Awolowo. He exercised great political influence up to the time he was tragically assassinated in 1995, apparently for his vigorous opposition to the Sani Abacha dictatorship. But in the 1950s, his club, the Rex Club, was the regular haunt of the colorful, jet-setting, upwardly mobile men of colonial Lagos. He courted the young undergraduates of the University College. Rewane was also Leslie Harriman's cousin, and so they were often treated with lavish hospitality when they went to the Rex Club. Alfred Rewane grew close to them, and his home in Yaba soon became their occasional rendezvous during holidays in Lagos. Rewane's reputation in the small circle of elite Lagos society where he held regular court was already legendary. He drove about in flashy cars. His style as a socialite impressed Okigbo very much.

In 1953 Okigbo and Ignatius Atigbi went to dance at the KitKat, a popular nightclub on Igbosere Road in downtown Lagos. There was a dancing competition that night, in which several dancers, including Okigbo, participated. Atigbi was adjudged the best dancer, and won a silver mug for his effort. 'As I recall,' he said years later, 'it was Christopher (Okigbo) who began to sing my praises, and called me *Rex Mamborum*, that is, King of the mambo dancers; and the next week, Ignatius Olisemeka, writing in *The Bug*, recounted the great dancing feat of Ignatius Atigbi, *Rex Mamborum*... that was how I became known at Ibadan as *Rex Mamborum*! It all began with Christopher...'[30]

UCI's social life in its first two years revolved mostly around evenings of formal entertainment organized by student clubs. The dancing club was the most popular. The scientists Dr. and Mrs. Sansome were among the few expatriate academics who tried to break racial and social barriers by socializing with the students at Ibadan in the dancing club and the cricket club. As patrons of the dancing club they infused it with a sense of glamour. Ben Obumselu wrote in *Our U.I.*:

> Dancing was all the rage at Eleyele when I entered the university in October... I distinctly remember my friend Christopher Okigbo insisting with his characteristic love of what is arcane or difficult, on doing only the tango reserved usually for the advanced class. It was like him too that he often let his hair down at the end of the day's session by breaking loose into frenzied jitterbug, or if we were in the games room, he would engage the grand piano waiting in a corner for the Sunday service in a delightful conversation on the theme of *Star Dust*.
>
> *All men are dancers and their feet*
> *Move to the barbarous clangour of the gong...*
>
> We had to dance, I suppose, because we were young...[31]

The annual foundation dance was the greatest dancing event of them all: it was a ballroom affair, which normally took place on 17 November, to mark the founding of the University.

There were other small groups on campus: the Takonists, champions of liberty and defenders of female rights, that had formed around the leadership of Takon, an undergraduate from the Southern Cameroons and who preached weekly in the pages of *The Bug* on the virtues of chivalry. There was the irreverent Low Gisting Club, which formed around Anthony Oseni – known as 'Osonorous' – who was an undergraduate in Botany. At Ibadan he invented the seductive art of ribald understatement. The Low Gisters was an informal and amusing circle, which met under the trees, with many students gathered to seek and exchange new humorous *bric à brac*. Okigbo loved Low Gisting, and its subversive use of language. Okigbo and some of his friends – Leslie Harriman, Femi Odunjo, Kofi Duncan, James Ezeilo – formed the Tombo Club in 1951. The Tombo Club had noisy parties and put the rooftop of Kuti Hall to bacchanal use. On one such occasion, the Tombo Club had taken Francesca Pereira's younger sister to drink with them up on the Kuti Hall roof. Pereira's sister, a student at the Catholic girls' school Holy Child College, got very drunk in the company of the Ibadan sybarites. It was an occasion for great scandal. *The Eagle*, the Pyrates newspaper edited by Wole Soyinka, known for its crusading editorials, took up the gauntlet and criticized those 'shameless undergraduates who had no qualms at all in defiling a poor holy child!' Wole Soyinka was, coincidentally, also Francesca Pereira's boyfriend.

Social intercourse was sometimes hindered by the absence of female company. Ibadan male undergraduates of the 1950s had few female colleagues. There were only twelve in 1950 and most were already married before coming to Ibadan. There were thus a limited number of dancing partners in Ibadan in those days when entertainment involved mostly the dances on campus. However young women were invited from the neighboring school of nursing at Eleyele, and from the various girls colleges in Ibadan, such as St. Anne's, St. Theresa's, U.M.C. and Queen's School, Ede. Ibadan under-graduates thus had their flings and found outlets for amorous escapades. Christopher Okigbo, for instance, was a notorious visitor to the school of nursing where he had female admirers and more than one affair going on at the same time. There was not much else to do in Eleyele in those early days.

Okigbo first met Judith Safinat Atta in 1951 during one these events on campus when girls were invited from outside. They fell madly in love. Safi was an Igbira princess, daughter of the eminent Attah of Igbira, one of the most powerful monarchs in Northern Nigeria. She was in her senior year at St. Theresa's, a Catholic Girls College in Ibadan, when she met Okigbo who started wooing her from the first day. According to Atigbi, 'It was in my house, at Oke-bola in 1955, when I was teaching at the Ibadan Grammar School that Christopher first made love to Safi. I remember it all.'[32] The beautiful Safinat was Okigbo's archetype of femininity; at once the illusory goddess of *Limits* and at the same time the redemptive muse, in part mother, and in part lover, who always figured as an incandescent presence in Okigbo's poetry. Okigbo likened the frustrations of wooing Safi to masochism, that demonic obsession which lured him to Yola 'in pursuit of the white Elephant.' Okigbo's pursuit of Safi had all the drama of his passionate life; it was one of stubborn insistence, frustration and difficulties. It was, as Pius Okigbo would describe it, 'very epic.'[33] In a letter to Ignatius in the early years of his courtship of Safi Attah, Christopher wrote: 'There is an innocence and purity about Safi. Sometimes I think no man has a right to her. Sometimes she reminds me of an inscrutable wraith. I'm madly in love with her, more than it is possible with any woman.'[34] That phrase 'an inscrutable wraith' resonates in the line 'Queen of the damp half light' in 'Siren Limits.' The seed that had been sown that day in February 1951 in Ibadan, would blossom into turbulent love and marriage. Their relationship was to be marked by absences, for Safinat soon left Ibadan, first to teach in the Native Authority schools in Ilorin, and then in 1954 to the University of Dublin where she read History and Geography. She later went on to the University of Reading in 1958 where she studied for the post-graduate diploma in education. Perhaps Safi's absence inspired Okigbo's longing and need. He was sexually adventurous, and extremely unfaithful but he was committed to her in his own unorthodox way.

Socially active undergraduates like Okigbo scoured the city for pleasure and crawled the nightclubs, looking for all kinds of drama in the sprawling metropolis. Ibadan was like the shards of two broken moments, modern and ancient, fused to add color to the sprawling and bustling city, then the largest metropolis near the African west coast. Its landscape was divided by the gentle vigor of the Ogunpa River, which broke the inner city of Inalende away from the bustling Mokola – an area which the poet J. P. Clark described in his poem 'Ibadan' as 'broken china in the sun.'[35] Sometimes they took a walk from Eleyele through the famous Dugbe market, uphill to Oja Oba – where there was always a colourful spectacle of people around the Bower Tower, a monument to Ibadan's chronotypical modernity. Mokola was the soul of Ibadan's city life with its highlife clubs, its brothels, its nightclubs and bars, its excitement and its noisy celebrations. A favorite place was the African Club, where African members of the colonial civil service in Ibadan entertained themselves, and also the Paradise Hotel which was a prominent city hangout.

Ekotedo was the red light district in the city, a haunt of the sexually adventurous undergraduates at University College, who would 'turn left' quite often, seeking illicit consolations. It was of such significance to undergraduate life in Ibadan in those early years that Wole Soyinka modeled his character Simi, in the novel *The Interpreters*, after an Ekotedo courtesan of the same name. Simi in real life was a prostitute, with whom some of the students consorted, 'in her lair'[36] in Ekotedo. Christopher Okigbo knew Simi well, and according to Harriman, Okigbo loved to dance with her and enjoyed her favours. She was a dark, beautiful woman, who had taken to the free life, but had a sense of her own place. She had exclusive tastes. Most of her clientele were young undergraduates in Ibadan, along with some well-heeled city cats seeking occasional company. Ekotedo was the hub of nightlife, the underbelly of the city. Okigbo and his friends were often to be found at the African club, or at JMJs, a club owned by Johnson Modupe Johnson, prominent socialite and leading NCNC politician who later became Nigeria's first federal minister for sports. JMJs was the popular rendezvous for those seeking lively fun outside the ordered pace of the university.

The Paradise Hotel was another regular haunt for Okigbo and his close circle of friends in Ibadan. Okigbo was occasionally invited to Paradise to play with bands on the stand. Aside from the clarinet and the piano, Okigbo also played the trombone well. Most of these musical instruments were self-taught, but he played each with professional dexterity and verve. Music was indeed his first real passion and he went on the occasional jam sessions with the bands at Paradise Hotel. Sometimes when people like the famous musical superstar of those years, Bobby Benson, came to Trenchard Hall to perform, Okigbo, and his friends Harriman and Atigbi would jump onto the stage, singing songs like Lord Kitchener's 'London is the Place for Me.' The influence of music, the collage form and the spontaneity of jazz, and the formal compositional elegance of classical music, are evident in Okigbo's poetry. Choral elements came fully to play in his unpublished 'Dance of the Painted Maidens' written at the birth of his daughter in 1964 and which was to be performed at the Commonwealth Festival in London in 1965. But this was all in the future.

In 1952 University College, Ibadan moved its campus from Eleyele to its modern, spacious, permanent site on the road to Oyo. The first batch of medical students moved ahead to the new site. Among the great benefits were the improved facilities for entertainment and cultural life on campus. There was a brand new performance hall, Trenchard Hall, which was opened in 1952, built by an endowment from Lord Trenchard, then Chairman of UAC. This hall hosted Okigbo on a number of occasions. One memorable evening for instance, he had accompanied his friends, Wole Soyinka and the actress, Francesca Emmanuel, on the piano, as they sang a duet. On another night, Okigbo led Wole Soyinka on the piano, in his performance of the song 'Amabola'. Perhaps Okigbo's most memorable performance was a solo rendition on the piano of one of the hit songs of the day, Bing Crosby's 'Moonlight Becomes You' for which he received a standing ovation during the May Havana of 1954.

Okigbo was a founding member of Mellanby Hall, a hall of residence known as 'the hall of gentlemen.'[37] Most of the campus socialites somehow found themselves there. The new environment inspired a new social outlook. Okigbo originally subscribed to the dancing club, until it experienced an internal crisis, and ultimately broke up in 1952. Two new clubs emerged from the factions – the Social Circle and the Sigma Club – and they became intense rivals. Each claimed the allegiance of the so-called socially prominent students on campus. Chinua Achebe, already editor of the University paper, *The Herald*, and his assistant Mabel Segun, for instance, became active in the Social Circle. Okigbo and others established the Sigma Club as a pre-eminent university society on the campus. Both the Social Circle and the Sigma Club were very formal and bourgeois in character. However, in the course of time, the Sigma Club came to dominate the social scene in Ibadan and became the most exclusive of the student clubs on campus.

But preceding the Sigma Club was a secret fraternity, called *pi phi psi*, which Okigbo formed with his closest friends. They clothed it in mystery and tried to cultivate a sense of a secret brotherhood. The *pi phi psi* did cause a stir among the students at Ibadan, because of its intriguing ceremonies. Leslie Harriman, who was an active participant in its rites, told how they would go silhouetted in darkness from the student halls, walking in a single file with their lit lanterns and in dignified silence cross to the university pavilion. There, they would sit in a circle and have their beer. Sometimes they took the ritual walk to Ekotedo. According to Ignatius Atigbi, who was also one of the original founders of the *pi phi psi*, the idea itself came from the magistrate Odumbaku who always bought them drinks at JMJs. Odumbaku came to the club often to relax at the end of the day. Although already quite elderly, he loved the company of the young UCI undergraduates. He used to talk to them about the Freemasons, of which he was an active member. The idea of freemasonry fascinated Okigbo and his friends – it must have been its sense of mystery and its secret rites. They decided to replicate on the campus 'a society of the intellectually and socially elect'[38] in Atigbi's words. They registered the club taking their seal from the Greek mathematical symbols. Atigbi and Harriman both agreed that it was Okigbo who suggested the name and symbols for the club. The Greek symbols were meant to lend gravitas to what was at best a regular drinking session of some imaginative undergraduates. Okigbo loved that kind of drama.

Their 'bottle parties' were always preceded by rituals: once a month *pi phi psi* met in the Mellanby junior common room during dinner clothed in Roman togas, improvised from bedsheets. 'It was nothing, if not theater,'[39] recalled Atigbi who described the ceremonies. Bearing a lighted candle or 'taper,' they would file into the room solemnly. Suddenly, someone would switch off the lights, and the room would be washed in the glow of candlelight. The Archpriest of the *pi phi psi* fraternity was Banjo Solarun, who led the ceremonies. Banjo, (son of a Methodist minister) was one-year Okigbo's junior in Classics. He would mutter prayers in an arcane mix of Latin and Greek, and, at the end, would say the grace in Latin: 'Sit nomen benedictum, per Jesum Christum salvatorem nostrum', and everybody would say 'Amen!' Then the Archpriest would say, 'Now the communion!' and the lights would suddenly come on and the 'brothers' would drink and have their dinner merrily. These strange rituals provoked bewilderment on campus, which was what Okigbo and his friends intended. It also incited outrage and suspicion that a secret cabal was growing in the new university. Father A.J. Foley who was master of Mellanby Hall and Professor of Chemistry, was one of those who felt horrified by the *pi phi psi* fraternity. Father Foley was also the Roman Catholic chaplain who regularly held the Catholic mass on campus. He quickly fired off a letter to the registrar, Dr. Biobaku, seeking a permanent ban on the activities of *pi phi psi*. He would have been even more horrified if he had known his own contribution to the fraternal meetings.

Father Foley was the unknowing supplier of the beer which members of the *pi phi psi* fraternity drank in their meetings. Harriman recalled how Okigbo, who had been close to the Catholic priest, devised an ingenious way to supply beer for some of those meetings by raiding Foley's stock. Father Foley was in the habit of leaving his windows open against the tropical heat of Ibadan, so entry was always easy. He would enter Father Foley's bedroom by the window and take some of the reverend gentleman's beer, which was usually kept in crates under his bed. Harriman also confirmed that he always had to be the lookout for Okigbo, just in case Father Foley came along suddenly during one of Okigbo's heists. Outraged by what he thought was motivated by a dark influence, Father Foley caused the *pi phi psi* fraternity to be banned by the University. Foley then invited both Christopher Okigbo and Femi Odunjo to say their confessions as good Catholic boys from illustrious Roman Catholic homes. Harriman was left out. He was not a Catholic. At confession, Father Foley asked the two young 'Cultists' to say the Rosary, and as an act of penance, suggested that they stop their association with Leslie Harriman whom he described as an 'evil influence.' He threatened to write to their fathers, whom he knew as schoolmasters of Catholic mission schools, if they continued to fraternize with Harriman. The two 'penitents' left Foley and quickly went to Leslie, to tell him Father Foley's opinion of him as 'an evil influence'! Leslie Harriman put on a mock rage, and he promptly walked straight up to priest and attacked him.

The ban on *pi phi psi* motivated Okigbo and his friends to found the Sigma Club in 1952. Although the revised official records of the club at the university in Ibadan for some reason omit the facts, the Sigma Club was originally conceived with Okigbo playing a central role. Among the original founders were Okigbo's closest associates at Ibadan – Eugene Femi Odunjo, Leslie Harriman, Ignatius Atigbi (*Rex Mamborum*), Felix Nkendu, Carolus Gomez (its first treasurer), and S. O. Olojede-Nelson, its first president. There were also Banjo Solarun, E. E. Nsefik (the mayor of hospitality), Richard Akpata, 'the great' Etudo, Agu Ogan, Kofi Duncan, Ndeghede and a few others. Christopher Okigbo was not only one of its moving spirits, but had suggested the name – 'The Sigma Club'.

According to Harriman and Atigbi, both of whom remained honorary members of the club to their deaths, even though the name of the Club derived from Okigbo's interests in the classics, it is also possible, that he had first heard the name 'Sigma' from his elder brother Pius Okigbo, who was already at university in America, where the sigma clubs were famous. It is possible that Okigbo tried to inspire a club in the tradition of merit and excellence, which the Sigma fraternities claimed in the universities in the United States.

The Sigma Club soon blossomed and earned its reputation as the club for stylish young men at Ibadan: the club rules emphasized a strict dress code of sartorial elegance at all times. Sigmites were to be properly dressed in suits and bow ties as befitted men of stature and importance. Okigbo adopted the image of a grandee with his tobacco pipes. Atigbi adopted a long elegant cigarette holder, while Leslie Harriman was already known for his fat Cuban cigars. In 1953, Okigbo, Harriman, Odunjo and Atigbi had their suits made by Fagbowo, the most expensive city clothier of that period in Ibadan.

The Sigma Club initiated in 1952 what became the most famous annual event – the May Havana – which introduced a colorful dimension to student life at Ibadan, so much so that for a generation, the pulse of society was gauged by attendance at the annual event. Atigbi remembered the preparations for the first Havana:

> We had just moved in to the new, very modern permanent site in 1952. Actually, the medical students had preceded the rest of us to the new place, and many of them were already resident. We thought about organizing the Havana in a very big way, in a way that would let out the young, ebullient spirit of the socialites among us. Christopher, (Okigbo) of course was very active in the plans, it was his kind of thing. He was among the ones who had to arrange for the elaborate entertainment. Leslie (Harriman) was sent off to Ghana to arrange

for musicians. In actual fact, we came to Lagos, to Kofi Duncan's mother, a very sociable woman, and she helped us in the preparations for the Havana. She used to run a very large and successful sewing institute, and she allowed us to take some of her girls. And once the first Havana happened, it became the most important feature of the social life on campus. And Christopher (Okigbo), as always, was the soul of it![40]

The name 'Havana' was Atigbi's suggestion, the result of his love of the Latin dances of the time. For many years the May Havana attracted visitors of every shade from as far away as Lagos and Accra. Many important dignitaries from Ibadan and Lagos, came to its elaborate annual evenings of entertainment.

The May Havana brought the musical superstars of that generation in West Africa to the Ibadan campus – highlife legends like Bobby Benson, Victor Olaiya, and Rex Lawson. For the first Havana, Okigbo accompanied Harriman to Ghana to invite the famed Ghanaian highlife musician, E. T. Mensah to play at the event. The Havana also organized a costume parade in which, for many years, the actor and broadcaster Ralph Opara, was a popular participant. He was the most colorful dresser, often turning out in costume of the captain of an Arab pirate ship. Ralph Opara became the Cap'n of the Pyrates confraternity, after Wole Soyinka left for Leeds in 1955. The Pyrates were the real non-conformists – the counter face to the Sigmites. For a long time social activities in Ibadan were characterized by formal dinners and huge ballroom dances in an English collegiate ambience with hall masters and wardens presiding. This formalism was borrowed from the Oxbridge tradition and established in Ibadan from its inception; the students came to dinners in suits and academic gowns. It was against this rigid formalism that Wole Soyinka and his friends rebelled. One evening during dinner, Soyinka and the nucleus of people with whom he started the Pyrates confraternity – the 'pyratical seven' – dramatized their disdain for form by appearing in open necked shirts at the dinner table in Mellanby Hall. The Pyrates confraternity was thus formed in response to the colonial mentality in the U.C.I. Community. The Pyrates became symbols against the elitism of the Sigma Club with its exclusive pretensions, its bourgeois formality, and its idea of the gentry, which aped the worst of the English colonial lifestyle. The Pyrates' credo 'against convention,' must certainly have appealed to Okigbo, for his real temperament was to be against convention. But he was equally drawn to the high idealism of the Sigma Club which rested on its own credo: 'for all that is pure.'

In hindsight, however, both the Sigma Club and the Pyrates confraternity – each different in its orientation – represented the level of social awareness that typified the generation of students who founded these clubs in the 1950s. The Sigma Club – bourgeois and exclusive – attracted individuals driven by the aristocratic ideal of *noblesse oblige*, while the Pyrates – more populist and unconventional – stood against the privileges and exclusivity of the university, isolated from the rest of the community. The original founders of the Pyrates confraternity – Wole Soyinka, its first 'sailing Cap'n,' who was known as 'Cap'n blood of Tortuga;' Ralph Opara; Ikpehare Aig-Imoukhede; Pius Oleghe; Nathaniel Oyelola; Olumuyiwa Awe and Chris Egbuchulam – were all Christopher Okigbo's friends, with whom he shared social and intellectual kinship. The idealism of the 'four compass points and the seven Rudder blades' contained in the Pyratical scroll, its rejection of social convention, were values which Okigbo also understood and shared. The 'humanistic ideals' of the Pyrates may even have appealed enormously to him, but he still at that time preferred the flamboyance, the cult of the aristocracy, and the high endeavour, which the Sigma Club proclaimed at Ibadan. Christopher Okigbo would come closer to the 'piratical' quest later in his life;

as he made his transition from the 'aristocrat destined for the higher bureaucracy'[41] to the poet-chronicler of his generation.

In *Distances*, when Nigeria's history took a violent turn in the first republic, he paid a moving tribute to the deep friendship and ideal of the 'original seven' Pyrates 'sealed and mated in a proud oblation'.[42] Okigbo would adopt the revolutionary stance of the Pyrates as poetic symbolism. He utilized the context of their intimation, their rejection of injustice and their revolutionary principle to analyze the disruptions of post-colonial history. The events of 1964 permitted a parallelism by which he weighed the events of that history against the idealism contained in the original vision of the Pyratical seven, conspirators for revolutionary change, and sworn to silence. When he was writing the first sequences of 'Lament of the Drums', the poet's political views were still slightly moderate, possibly even resigned and ambivalent. But moderation soon gave way to increasing frustration and anger with political developments, and by the time Wole Soyinka was arrested late in 1965 in Ibadan over the Radio station incident, Okigbo himself had progressed ideologically towards the credo of the Pyrates: 'We are tuned for a feast-of-seven-souls...'[43] Okigbo equated the revolutionary involvement of members of the Pyrates confraternity in Ibadan as a precursor to the larger revolution – the Ifeajuna coup which aspects of the 'Laments' prefigured. But it all began when as young men at UCI they were animated by the social and political realities of the times.

Christopher spent many a vacation together with his friends, traveling and visiting places such as Warri, Lagos, Sapele, Onitsha, Enugu, or Port Harcourt. They were elegant and self-aware. Their presence in these cities during their vacations was often notable. They were attractive as young suitors and made the most of being such an attraction. The journalist and writer Adaora Lily Ulasi had young socialites like Okigbo in mind when in 1955 she wrote her exhortation in the *Daily Times*, 'Beware the Gay Adders', warning young women about these elegant heartbreakers on holidays. Christian Chike Momah distinctly remembered one of those vacations, and 'The day he (Okigbo) popped up in Chief Z. C. Obi's house in Port Harcourt, while I was vacationing there from University College, and told me he had an eye on one of the great man's daughters, and could I help him get to her? As things turned out, I married Ethel, the young girl in question.'[44] Early in the 1950s, there were some other ambitious young men on the make who cultivated friendships with Okigbo and his group of young Ibadan socialites and feted them whenever they were on vacation in Lagos. Cyril Akpom lived on what became Herbert Macaulay Street in Yaba and worked as a clerk in the customs services: he was to become a professor of biochemistry at the McGill University in Canada. Michael Kubenje was another: he had been Ignatius Atigbi's 'fag' at Government College, Ughelli. On leaving Ughelli, Kubenje went directly to work for the CBS, first as a produce examiner in Lagos, but in the 1950s, Kubenje lived at a place which they fondly called 'Ogogon lodge' on Catholic Mission street in downtown Lagos. It was in this one-story house that Okigbo and his friends spent many a memorable holiday. Years later, after studying in the United States, Kubenje became the CBS correspondent in Lagos from the 1960s to the '70s and so he reported the civil war in which Okigbo would die. Dominic Okwuraiwe, also in the customs, shared a flat on Hawley Street with Sonny Odogwu and Talabi A. Braithwaite, who both worked for a British insurance company in Lagos and who would become giants in the corporate world in Nigeria. Another close friend was Billy Dudley, who lived in the coastal city of Warri. Like Mike Kubenje, Dudley was employed as a produce examiner before he proceeded to the university and became one of the most outstanding political theorists of his time in Nigeria; he also became national secretary of the NCNC, and later distinguished professor of political science at the University of Ibadan.

Okigbo was not a disciplined scholar at Ibadan. He was far too enthralled by adventure. One of the most striking things about Okigbo, however, was his capacious memory. His power of recall was extraordinary. An old Umuahia schoolmate and contemporary at the university, the sprinter E.J. Ekong, remembered 'one of those evenings of debate in the Kuti Hall senior common room in 1955,'[45] when Christopher Okigbo had been handed the voluminous Gray's *Anatomy* and challenged to read it, and to answer questions, after summarizing the content. 'Okigbo astounded everybody with his immense power of recall,'[46] E.J. Ekong said. 'It was so impromptu, yet he was effortless and spontaneous. But that was Christopher!'[47]

Okigbo was reputed to be more than capable of holding his own in any of the serious debates that characterised the social intercourse on campus. The residential halls organised debates as intramural events, for amusement and for edification. Okigbo often proved his versatility on such occasions. Ignatius Atigbi remembered one evening in 1953 when Christopher Okigbo, speaking for Mellanby Hall, had participated in a long and intense debate with his friend Richard Akpata, from the sciences. Akpata was Okigbo's team-mate in the university's hockey team, but on this occasion they had sparred on the theme 'Sex and Human Repression'. Richard Akpata had taken the theological view of sex as a hallowed act, in which indulgence must be regulated. Okigbo however kept faith with his own more liberal world view, arguing for indulgence as a redemptive act often conveyed in the natural pleasure of sex for its 'common salutary sake.'[48] Okigbo had intended to outrage his listeners. His conclusion in the debate with Akpata was that 'sex unlocks the human emotional door. The hidden man is found by indulgence, freed from the anxieties of moral inhibition...'[49] Banjo Solarun, his contemporary in Classics at Ibadan said, 'Christopher's ideas outraged the moralists. But it seemed so new and unorthodox. And Christopher was quite an unusual person, anyway.'[50] Okigbo had apparently just discovered the works of the psychoanalysts Freud and Jung. He must have been impressed by Freud's theories, which were not yet taught at Ibadan. Okigbo's postulations in that debate were echoed years later in a rejection of Christian orthodoxy and morality in his poem, 'Initiations':

> so comes John the Baptist
> with bowl of salt water
> preaching the gambit:
> life without sin, without
>
> life; which accepted,
> way leads downward
> down orthocenter
> avoiding decisions.[51]

Here Okigbo, seems to equate a 'sinless' life – a life without the deeply sensual experience – with the death of consciousness; a counter view to the Christian idea of original sin and its ethic of salvation which derives from a disavowal rather than an awareness of the body as the site of pleasure. Okigbo's hedonism, his sense of the libertine rebelled against that notion of 'Christian salvation' or asceticism. Okigbo's rebelled against self-denial.

In many ways, Okigbo was the prodigal: freed from responsibility, and preceded by two already successful elder brothers and a prominent father, Okigbo had no great need to exert himself. His choice was to live free of domestic or material burden. Although he was driven sometimes to extreme competitiveness, Okigbo wanted to make his fortune in big business, but he lacked the discipline or the shrewd resolve of the entrepreneur. These contradictions form the 'irreconcilable elements of his life,'[52] to which he refers in the introduction to his final volume of poetry. His poetry became a means, in later life, for coming to terms with the contradictory conditions of his humanity. Much of his lifestyle at the university indeed reflects this ambition for a life of the high society, not so much for a life of scholarship. But he neither had the discipline nor the inclination, as Obumselu has hinted, to pursue anything to its conclusion. Each pursuit nevertheless showed Okigbo's versatility and polymathic abilities. He did not consider himself in those days a scholar, rather a man of the senses, a renaissance intellectual whose broad reading was quite obvious even in class. Kalada Hart had been the top student in Okigbo's 1950 class, and he placed Okigbo's undergraduate quest in fine perspective:

> He was the sort of fellow who would normally not bother about university education. Chris knew just about everything he wanted to know, and was probably cleverer than many of us his classmates and if he wanted, would pass his examinations effortlessly...and that is if he decided to put his mind to it! But he just didn't care or bother about such things. It is still a surprise to me that he went through all that rigor of university. He wasn't cut for that kind of life. Not Chris! His great love was pleasure – sports, music, politics, and travel.[53]

The University of Ibadan was nevertheless important in shaping the intellectual life of the poet as it did the most important writers of his generation in Nigeria.

By 1951, Chinua Achebe was already editing the student newspaper, *The University Herald*, which was publishing serious articles and short stories, and had people like Mabel Segun, Chukwuemeka Ike, Agu Ogan, and Tam Oforiokuma on the editorial board. However the most popular student publication at Ibadan was *The Bug*, an irreverent rag which was a great purveyor of college scandal and gossip. It published cartoons and lampoons, directed mostly against the few women – the 'acada girls' – on campus. By its history *The Bug* became the first paper to host the early literary sallying of most of the first generation of Nigerian writers who were undergraduates at Ibadan. Christopher Okigbo also published a newspaper on campus, which Ben Obumselu edited. The story of the *Varsity Weekly* typifies part of the Okigboan spirit: he was the financier, the business manager, the circulation manager and the vendor, and he did translations of Greek poetry for the paper, while Obumselu wrote most of the stories and produced the paper. Although it was called a weekly, Okigbo's paper came out at Okigbo's whim, or when he had spare cash. Chukwuemeka Ike recalled that Okigbo devised a unique marketing strategy for the *Varsity Weekly*. Whenever an issue of the paper appeared, Ike recalled, Okigbo would go from room to room launching the 'Christopher Okigbo relief fund.'[54] 'It didn't matter whether you wanted to buy or not, Chris would just hand you the paper and take your money. If he came to your room, and you were not there, he simply would leave a copy of *Varsity Weekly* and take money from your pocket, and would leave a note to tell you, if he wanted.'[55] It does seem early on that Okigbo and his friends saw themselves embarking upon a literary path. It is telling however, that Okigbo saw himself not as a writer, but a facilitator – at the entrepreneurial end of the cultural endeavor.

He was different, in that sense, from Achebe who had graduated. When, in 1954, Chinua Achebe left the University College, Ibadan, 'with a good second class' he first went to teach at Merchant of Lights College in Oba, a few kilometers from Onitsha in Eastern Nigeria. A few months later he went to work at the Nigerian Broadcasting Corporation as a talks producer, and began writing his novel, *Things Fall Apart*. Wole Soyinka was also already clearly determined to be a writer, and had written a student play in secondary school. He had been admitted to the University College, Ibadan in 1952 after working as a clerk in the government medical stores in Lagos. He came onto the Ibadan scene with 'a wild play,' which he had written titled *The Cock's Tale* which was obviously influenced by the new absurdist drama coming out of Europe. This play, later acted over the radio by Ralph Opara, Ben Obumselu, Pius Oleghe and Wole Soyinka himself, had an electrifying effect on the campus. It was Soyinka's debut as a playwright.

Soyinka came to Ibadan to study for a general degree in English, and left in 1955 for Leeds after his intermediate degree at University College, Ibadan. Ibadan did not yet offer a full honors program in English. Because he did not want to take a general degree, or wait for the honors program to commence with the arrival of Molly Mahood as professor of English in 1955, Soyinka left for Leeds under a western regional scholarship where he studied with Wilson Knight, theatre director and Shakespearean scholar and worked for a short time at the Royal Court which was the most avant-garde theatre in London. Drama was at the center of cultural life in Ibadan in the 1950s. The university stage witnessed the advent of actors like Ralph Opara, Wole Soyinka, Pius Oleghe, and Christine Clinton (who would later marry Ben Obumselu). For a generation, they were the greatest figures of Ibadan's drama society.

The Drama Club produced Synge's *Playboy of the Western World* and Bernard Shaw's *Androcles and the Lion*, in which Rex Akpofure played the lead role. First year students on their first social evenings in Ibadan many years later would come to see the poster of a man bearing a lamp announcing the drama season on campus: and they would soon discover Rex Akpofure as that mythical personage of the posters. Wole Soyinka, the leading dramatist of his generation first introduced himself to the stage at Ibadan one social evening on campus, by singing the ballad of a dying man.

The poet John Pepper Clark was admitted into the University in 1955, in Okigbo's final year, to read English, although he had to defer his admission for another year. He resumed for classes with the 1956 set, the year Okigbo also returned to repeat his degree examinations in the classics department. There is no evidence that Okigbo and Clark moved in the same circles in this period, although they shared close mutual friendship with Emmanuel Ifeajuna. But they became close personal friends later. The novelist Elechi Amadi came to Ibadan to study Mathematics and Physics in 1955 after studying briefly at the survey school in Oyo. He had been Okigbo's junior by three years at Government College, Umuahia, and they did not seem to have interacted closely. Chukwuemeka Ike graduated from the English department in 1956, and he stayed at the university where he had been given the job of Assistant Registrar first under Biobaku, and then under Nathaniel Adamolekun. It was in this job, and in that period, that he gathered much of the material for his novel, *Toads for Supper*. Their lives at the University College, Ibadan of the 1950s give only a slight insight into the literary community that was emerging. Many of them had been active student journalists, writing in the fiery polemical spirit of that age.

Okigbo read voraciously. His greatest literary ambition as a student at University College was to translate the *Aeneid* into English from its Greek original. Okigbo loved Virgil. One of his habits was to inscribe long passages from the *Aeneid* on the wall of his dormitory room. Olu Akaraogun, who became a newspaper columnist in Lagos, came to the University College, Ibadan to study Physics in 1956. He was one of those freshmen who gravitated towards Okigbo, and used to spend long evenings debating in his room in Kuti Hall. He noticed that the walls of Okigbo's room were filled with graffiti. On closer study he recognized that they were translations of Greek poems. Akaraogun was curious about this practice. So he tried to find out from Okigbo why he did such a quaint thing as translating lines of classical poetry on the wall. Okigbo told a story of the cave art. Okigbo's theory was that this early form of documentation was more effective, both as signifier and as a mnemonic prompt. He was experimenting to see how much of the deliberate order of Greek poetry he could retain by scripting it on the wall. 'I like my Virgil on the wall. It's my concrete parchment really and it's easy to read, you know'[56] he said to Akaraogun.

Okigbo's 'Virgil on the Wall' may have been one of his strategies to equip him with the fine architectural order of his own poetry when he began to write. He always believed that poetry was, above all, a matter of craft – a technae. By 1952, Okigbo had begun to translate classical poetry from the original. He did a lot of poetry translation for the *Varsity Weekly*, and he acquired more than an ordinary grasp of the structure of classical poetry. The heavy influence of the classics evident in his own early writing is reflective of his absorption with the form and nuance of classical poetry. 'He was very good at it,'[57] said Pius Okigbo 'He tried frequently to translate from Greek to Latin then to English, to get as close a resonance as possible'[58] He loved to quote long lines of Virgil from memory, and mystify his audience with a sense of his versatile reading. Ben Obumselu remembered Okigbo's particular fascination for the 'cult of the difficult'[59] and suggests that his translation of Virgilian verse was a particular expression of this.

Of his closest friends at Ibadan, Benedict Ebele Obumselu eventually played the most prominent part in Christopher Okigbo's evolution as a poet. Few critics have attempted to evaluate the extent of Obumselu's contributions to Okigbo's work. Lalage Bown, who was active in the Ibadan circles in the later years of the Mbari movement, told Robert Wren that Okigbo's 'main mentor was Ben. But he did consult with other people…on a literary level they respected each other. That's one reason for their closeness…'[60] The brilliant Obumselu shared not only deep friendship but also a true intellectual kinship with the poet. Obumselu's contemporaries had been extravagant in their praise of his abilities at Ibadan. Leslie Harriman once said of him 'Ben was the best of my generation.'[61] Obumselu worked well with Okigbo because 'he was his own best poetry.'[62] He indeed confessed that he was always quite aware that Okigbo was rather fond of him 'and that always flattered me greatly.'[63]

Ben Obumselu had come to the university from Dennis Memorial Grammar School, Onitsha with a reputation for academic brilliance. He was the university scholar in the arts for the 1951 session. While at DMGS, Obumselu wanted to study Mathematics, but he changed his mind later, and was admitted into the arts in Ibadan. He took a general degree in English. Obumselu wanted to take the honors degree and thought seriously about taking it in Classics since it wasn't offered in English. 'I was one of those who used to advise Ben (Obumselu) to take his degree in Classics. He was so brilliant, and so very widely read in the classics,' recalled the lawyer and politician, Bola Ige, with whom he was also deeply acquainted in the 1950s at Ibadan.[64]

Obumselu had earned acclaim as the best student of his years in the humanities at University College in the 1950s, having traversed the terrain between the classics and modern letters. He later took one of the early honors degrees in English at Ibadan, graduating at the top of his class in 1957. A tragic event resulting in a landmark court case illustrates the esteem to which Obumselu was held in his day. In his last year at the university, his girlfriend, Bisi Fagbenle, the vice-president of the Ibadan Students Union, died allegedly while Obumselu was trying to perform an abortion on her in his students lodging in Mellanby. The case dominated the front pages of newspapers around the country. Bisi, one of the few female undergraduates at Ibadan, was from a prominent family in Western Nigeria. Obumselu was arraigned and prosecuted for manslaughter. In the landmark decision, the judge acquitted Ben Obumselu, only on the ground of his great 'promise as a scholar.' He became one of the key figures of modernist criticism of the emergent literatures from Africa. Okigbo admired his versatility, and the discipline of his scholarship. Although they were born roughly fifteen miles apart from each other in the same part of Eastern Nigeria, they met for the first time at the University College, Ibadan in 1951. Their great friendship began one evening in October 1951 when Okigbo came unexpectedly to Obumselu's room and proceeded to read an excerpt from *Euripedes* to Obumselu in its Greek original, at the end of which he said, 'They say you're very bright, and that you know many things. But you do not know this one!' They discovered a mutual admiration for each other and for the classics. Soon they began to collaborate on their papers.

In later years, Ben Obumselu helped to shape Okigbo's poetic impulses towards aesthetic clarity. By his own accounts, Obumselu had somehow always acted as editor, and so Okigbo learnt early to trust Obumselu's judgment as a more rigorous craftsman. They collaborated on an undergraduate essay on the Greek tragedies written for E.A.Cadle's class on Greek drama. From then, when he had a class paper to write in the Classics department, and was faced with other distractions, Okigbo would say to Obumselu: 'Ben, I don't have time, do it!'[65] and Obumselu would write the paper. Okigbo eloquently acknowledged Obumselu in *Labyrinths*, his final collection of poetry 'for criticisms that continue to guide me along the paths of greater clarity.'[66]

The generation of young people across the world in the 1950s – products of the experience of the global war – began to seek alternative meanings to the universal questions. The absurdity of modern life and its impact on human consciousness in the middle of the twentieth century began to define the late modern era. The age of the atomic bomb, the beginning of the cold war, the rise of the iron curtain, and the western challenge to communism fueled a sense of modern dystopia. The sense of futility rose, as the world grew in the Orwellian sense of catastrophe. Christopher Okigbo, as his brother Pius Okigbo would affirm years later, was touched by the mood of an edgy world. He became aware of the existentialism of Martin Heidegger and Jean-Paul Sartre although, as Pius alludes, he was to reject its nihilism as inaction. The Dadaist movement fascinated him although he would reject its manifesto by Crosby.

The late modern Euro-American imagination in the post-war years discovered a new form of cultural expression exemplified in the angry outbursts of the absurdist writers like Harold Pinter, and the counter-culture of writers of the Beat movement. The poetry of Allen Ginsberg, Ferlinghetti, Duncan, Brother Anthonius and the rest of the Beat generation valorized decadence, rebelled against the certainties of mainstream western culture, and powered a moment which captured the desolate mood of the post-war years. The angst had not percolated among the young intellectuals at Ibadan. It was difficult to find an equivalent mood of an 'angry young generation' in the African unconscious. The closest expression was the young Wole Soyinka's early undergraduate play at Ibadan about a hanging. But while the general response of the student population at Ibadan to the social questions of the anti-colonial years was far from disinterest, it was nevertheless more restrained in its effusion and less revolutionary in character. The British political scientist, Ken W. Post who came from Cambridge to teach in Ibadan as a Leverhulme Scholar later in the 1950s, has given an account of those years:

What I noticed more than anything was already some disillusion with politics. There had been some concern and student activity in connection with the constitutional conference in '57...they were literally negotiating the day of independence. They seemed to have been disillusioned by it all being handled in such a gentlemanly way, a very British way, and a very Westminster way. I think they had really wanted independence to come more dramatically and not in this kind of negotiated fashion, with the politicians obviously being very concerned to keep control of things and make sure the power devolved to them when independence came.[67]

Among the more politically active students, like Christopher Okigbo however, there was at least a desire 'to stir things up a bit' – to emphasize an ideological rejection of the 'negotiated' process of decolonization.

The 1950s were indeed a busy period politically. Okigbo's arrival at Ibadan coincided with the 1950 constitutional conference held in that city which set the tone for British disengagement and the firm transition towards self-government. Okigbo's early years at UCI also coincided with the western regional elections, (1951–52), whose controversial outcome marked an important shift in the character of the nationalist anti-colonial movement. Home rule had been inaugurated in the regions following the constitutional conference

Okigbo's close friendship with the Odunjos placed him in close contact with some of the colorful political actors of the day and exposed him early to the politics of decolonization in Ibadan in those crucial years that set the tone of Nigeria's postcolonial politics. In 1952, Femi Odunjo's father, Mr. J.F. Odunjo, was appointed minister for Land and Labor in the Western Regional government under the premiership of Obafemi Awolowo following home rule. Before then, he had made a name as a writer of the *Alawiye* books. Like Okigbo's father, he had been a famous educator in the Catholic Mission school system. The Odunjos lived in the Oke-bola area of Ibadan, and Okigbo and his friends were frequent weekend guests, with Mrs. Odunjo playing a surrogate mother to Okigbo. She took them joyously into her maternal care and treated them with great hospitality. Ignatius Atigbi described Mrs. Odunjo as a lively and spontaneous woman, who made sure that the young men enjoyed themselves. Atigbi said, 'She was especially fond of Christopher, who had no mother of his own, you see. She lavished affection on him.'[68] Mrs. Odunjo sharpened their taste for highlife music, especially for the music of the irrepressible Israel Woba Njemanze, which she would unfailingly play, and to which they would all dance whenever they visited. At the end Mrs. Odunjo would always say, 'All musicians will go to heaven!'[69]

Woba Njemanze had been brutally murdered. His body dumped, by his unknown assailants, on the rail tracks in Yaba, Lagos, and his minstrel's tongue brutally plucked from his mouth. The reports of his death and the mutilation of his body had played very prominently in the news. It signaled early on for Okigbo the paradox of the artistic conscience and the dangers that a committed, politically conscious artist faced in this society. The violent suppression of artistic truth, symbolized in the Njemanze tragedy was a possibility which Okigbo himself glimpsed in *Path of Thunder* when he wrote:

If I don't learn to shut my mouth, I will soon go to hell,
I Okigbo, town-crier, together with my iron bell.[70]

Israel Woba Njemanze was the archetypal figure of the artist from which Okigbo made that invocation. Njemanze had invented the form of highlife music, which combined a charged, soul-stirring, mellifluous tune with a social, satirical content, played in palmwine bars. The musicologist Sam Akpabot once compared Woba Njemanze to

Fela Anikulapo-Kuti, and noted that they both combined in their music a harsh critique of powerful figures of society. Akpabot suggested that Fela indeed drew the idiomatic sources of his music from Israel Woba. Woba was the first to utilize Pidgin English, the language of the new urban underclass, to great effect. He modernized the satirical elements of Igbo minstrelsy. The minstrel in the Igbo world was like that character, Upandru, in Okigbo's *Heavensgate* – a social critic. Woba Njemanze was to Okigbo's generation what Fela Anikulapo-Kuti became for a later generation – a powerful, stirring, satirical voice, a musical conscience that challenged political and social morality. He was killed on account of this. It was believed that Woba Njemanze had been murdered by the paid thugs of one of the most powerful political figures of the time in western Nigeria whom he had satirized frequently in his music. Woba Njemanze's example doubtlessly reverberated in Okigbo's life and poetry.

In 1951, Okigbo's sophomore year, the Western region assumed home rule with political headquarters in Ibadan, and was followed by the Eastern region in Enugu in 1954. Limited sovereignty gave the Southern regions a chance to do a test run in preparation for full national independence. The political drama which had taken place on the floor of the Western regional parliament in Ibadan dramatized the emerging character of Nigerian postcolonial politics: intricate moves by Obafemi Awolowo's Action Group party led to the 'carpet-crossing' incident. A sudden shift in alliance had been engineered to make it impossible for Dr. Nnamdi Azikiwe, an Igbo and leader of the anti-colonial nationalist movement, to form a government, and become the head of the Western region. His party, the NCNC, which had led the agitation for decolonization, and its political affiliates, had apparently won a majority of seats in that election, enough to form the government. But Obafemi Awolowo, who had organized the Action Group party in 1948 'to safeguard Yoruba interest' managed to play a shrewd hand – some say the ethnic card – by convincing the NCNC affiliates to move over to the aisle of the Action Group, giving Awolowo the crucial votes to assume the head of government and leaving Azikiwe, the leading figure of the nationalist movement, as leader of opposition.

Political historians have judged that move to be the single most compelling incident in modern Nigerian political history, one which introduced the ethnic color to the character of Nigerian politics with important implications in the first half of the twentieth century. Among its most long-lasting effect, the 'carpet-crossing' incident ushered in distrust, and the sense of sharp disillusionment with the political process among University College undergraduates in the period. The novelist Chinua Achebe described in his book, *The Trouble with Nigeria*, how as an undergraduate he sat as a witness that day in the gallery in the Western regional parliament in Ibadan. Years later, Achebe told the American critic Robert Wren 'What I do remember in the '50s as a source of great disillusionment was the introduction of ethnic politics, with the arrival of the Action Group on the scene.'[71] Christopher Okigbo was equally a perceptive observer of those events; and like the rest of the Ibadan undergraduates who were nurtured under the pan-Nigerian idealism of the nationalist, anti-colonial movement, he may have been disillusioned by the turn of events in 1951. It could well have affected the texture of Okigbo political thoughts, beliefs and actions.

Political activity on the campus of the university was intense. Okigbo was elected into the Students' Representative Council – the student parliament at the University College – from 1951 to 1953. As a student political activist, Okigbo was in the thick of these nationalist debates. Ibadan undergraduates formed various platforms to canvas their positions and to enact debates on controversial questions of the day. These debates served as a barometer of the national politics, taking up such issues as the Enugu coalmine incident of 1949; the constitutional conference of 1950; the 'carpet-crossing' incident of 1951–52; the 1954 move by Anthony Enahoro on the floor of the Federal House of Representative in Lagos calling for full and immediate independence, which was rejected by the Northern delegation; the stoning of the train conveying the Northern delegation back to the North; and the imprisonment of members of the radical Zikist movement. So UCI ticked not only with social and cultural activity, but also with political activity in the high-minded debates in the Students Representative council.

Many of the debates had also broken along ethnic, party, and ideological lines with the fierce rivalries. By 1951, for instance, the NCNC, the Action Group, and to some extent the NPC, had their student members in the students' council. Students like Bola Ige and Akin Mabogunje became leaders of the student wing of the Action Group. It was also at this time in Ibadan in 1953 that Okigbo and Leslie Harriman came under the influence of Dr. Chike Obi and his Dynamic Party. Okigbo may indeed have embraced political activism as a means of being intellectually engaged, maintaining his social presence or involvement in an alienating culture and in an era of rapid political transitions. But this involvement with Chike Obi's Dynamic Party was also mostly play.

Okigbo was attracted to Chike Obi's 'bogus politics'[72] because it had elements of the theatre of subterfuge. Chike Obi was a cultural and intellectual icon among a generation of Nigerian students in the 1950s. He was widely regarded as a mathematical genius. He had earned his degrees with high honors in Mathematics as an external candidate of the University of London, and in 1950 became the first Nigerian to take a doctorate in Mathematics while at Pembroke College, Cambridge on the strength of his 'studies in mathematics, biology and military history.' He had established his reputation as the most radical Nigerian intellectual. Left-leaning and mercurial, Chike Obi's brand of politics was flamboyant, and aimed at upturning the staidness of emerging political thought and action. He aimed to teach as well as radicalize the political thinking of Ibadan undergraduates. Chike Obi was a very unusual and remarkably eccentric character. His informality marked him out: his common touch and openness in a conservative place such as the University College, Ibadan campus, made him enormously attractive and popular among students. He joined the undergradutes in pubs. He made powerful arguments against 'the idiocy of the emerging political class.'[73] He broke new boundaries as a scholar-politician, a renaissance figure around whom the students loved to gather and listen, because they could easily relate to him. He became famous on campus as the mentor of Ibadan's radical students.

As a doctoral student in Cambridge in the years following the Second World War, Chike Obi had moved in radical socialist circles and had been present at the 1948 Pan-African conference in London. He came under the influence, at Cambridge, of the English philosopher Bertrand Russell and his work in analytic philosophy, mathematical and symbolic logic and the philosophy of mathematics. Obi was also attracted to Russell's radical politics, his hardiness in the face of countermanding authority, and his ease with common men and their ease with him. He was in London when Lord Russell delivered the first Reith lecture for the BBC on 'Authority and the Individual' in 1948, and it made a great impression on him. Chike Obi's own Olympian disdain for convention was Russellian. He returned to teach mathematical theory at the new University College, Ibadan, in 1950. Chike Obi attempted to rekindle his radical Cambridge politics in Ibadan.

In many ways Okigbo's admiration for Chike Obi stemmed from awe for his profound intellect and his accomplishments as a scholar. But far more importantly, he was attracted to the unorthodox in Chike Obi. 'He was a restless genius... with a charming liberal disposition, a certain lovable "madness"', said Leslie Harriman 'and Christopher loved this quality of "madness".'[74] Christopher had first met Chike Obi through his brother Pius, who was Chike Obi's friend and contemporary in school at Christ the King College, Onitsha, and later on at Yaba Higher College. Chike Obi was ahead of Pius Okigbo in school by one year and had already earned a reputation for himself at CKC as a brilliant rebel. After Yaba Higher College, he had, like Pius, embarked on a teaching career in Onitsha. They were all active in the social and political life of Onitsha, a city replete with small presses and popular literature, and the anti-colonial journalism. Chike Obi and Pius were already famous young men in this provincial town, the commercial and intellectual nexus of the East and epicenter of Igbo urban life in the 1940s. Christopher Okigbo grew up absorbed and inspired by their legends as young over-achievers. Chike Obi naturally adopted Chris Okigbo as his 'younger brother' when he retuned to teach mathematics at Ibadan in 1950.

With such social affinity, it was easy for Christopher to become Chike Obi's closest confidante and political collaborator at Ibadan, at a most exciting moment of Nigeria's political development and transition. It gave Okigbo the opportunity of a unique and intimate involvement at the radical end of the highly charged anti-colonial politics of the early 1950s. Chike Obi's radical politics were anchored in the notion of direct political action, or what he termed 'dynamic collectivism.' He was an advocate of the elevated role of the intellectual as the repository of national political conscience. Any attempt to discern the evolution of Okigbo's political thought and action, even those irreconcilable aspects of his politics and life, must ultimately take into account this early political association with Chike Obi and its impact on his political consciousness. Pius Okigbo later described Chike Obi's politics as 'bogus' - tending towards 'the lunatic fringe; very near the anarchic side of the political divide.'[75] Fringe or not, the Dynamic Party provided the kind of alternative that attracted Christopher, because it appealed to his natural rebellious instincts and provided him ample grounds for adventure. Chike Obi introduced him to the political philosophy of Bertrand Russell, the modernist vision of Kemal Ataturk and the nationalist politics of Abdul Nasser. Dr. Obi began to organize the socialists on campus through the Dynamic Party around his praxis of Kemalism. The fundamental basis of Chike Obi's 'bogus' politics was his belief that 'a sort of benevolent dictatorship by a dedicated corps of enlightened and patriotic Nigerians for an interim period is essential to the successful welding of the diverse tribal linguistic groups of the country into a strong and industrialized nation in as short a time as possible.'[76] Chike Obi summed up the political program of the Dynamic Party, outlined in the pamphlet, *Our Struggle*, the manifesto published in 1953 by Etukokwu Press. It described 'Kemalism' and its praxis as:

> 'Totalitarianism of the left' as opposed to the 'totalitarianism of the right', which differs from the former in that the latter believes in force as a permanent way of maintaining order, whereas the former when resorting to force is used only in order to quicken the pace of progress... Kemalism is a philosophy which in recognising the vital urgency for a backward country, to introduce western technology into her borders also recognises the necessity for the backward to introduce into her borders western administration, language, way of life as much of these as is inseparable from western technology, and the suppression of any local pretensions which might be an obstacle to the declared westernisation.[77]

The Party wanted to divide Nigeria into fifteen states, seek an alliance with Europe and America for economic and cultural progress, and stem 'the mad rush towards self-government.'[78] The Dynamic Party's opposition to rushed self-government led it into an alliance with the Nigerian Self-Government Fiasco Party, on the basis of Obi's belief that 'self government was impossible in a country where…apathy and ignorance were widespread.'[79] Because it had been 'born' under the constellation Aries, the Dynamic Party chose the ram as its symbol. Years later, Chike Obi recollected: 'Those politicians negotiating independence were only interested in creating huge financial empires for themselves, and replacing the British as the lords of Africa, at independence. And so my main purpose was to organize a resistance, and I brought radical, enthusiastic boys like Christopher to work with me.'[80]

But he was also allied with the dominant national political organization of the moment: the NCNC, Azikiwe's party. The NCNC had lost its momentum in the political events that occurred between 1947 and 1948, when the party leadership lost control of its rank and file, and allowed the opportunity of becoming a truly national movement slip by. Nnamdi Azikiwe's handling of the Zikist movement, the radical wing of the NCNC, disappointed radical intellectuals like Chike Obi. Awolowo's party, the Action Group, did not appeal to him either, on account of what Obi himself saw as the 'narrow, perfidious politics that was going on.'[81] There was talk in those years, Dr. Obi recalled, of how the British had helped to organize the Northern Peoples Congress, and how it had funneled slush funds to form the Action Group as a way of undermining the nationalist momentum of the NCNC.

The Dynamic Party at best, however, was a paper tiger. Its appeal was very narrow. If the party made any impact at all, it was in providing an intellectual, discursive climate, an alternative to the political thought process at that time: but it was also a movement ironically limited by its own agenda, its appeal and location in the ivory tower, University College, Ibadan, although it tried to fashion itself on a radical populist ideology. Leslie Harriman suggested that one of Okigbo's apparent motivations in working with the Dynamic Party was the opportunity for frequent travel and robust adventure off campus. Okigbo felt intellectually dissatisfied and unmotivated by the routine of work in the university. He needed something more to stimulate his curious and hungry mind. His truancy at Ibadan was the result of boredom with academic life, and so Okigbo welcomed the 'distractions' of life on the road with the Dynamic Party.

Okigbo was especially active in the party from 1953 to 1956, traveling frequently with Chike Obi on Dynamic Party business. Okigbo's real political convictions were of course contradictory: intellectually he was left of the center, but his lifestyle was epicurean. As Ben Obumselu said, 'He could not be anything other than a man of leisure.'[82] On the whole, Okigbo's political involvement did give him valuable insight into the larger political questions of his time, something which later sharpened his poetic insight. Okigbo, was drawn towards the sense of subversion – the seduction of the profound but inexplicable beauty of the unusual, which the Dynamic Party offered him.

The Dynamic Party had a small operation run by Chike Obi, assisted by Okigbo and Harriman who became indispensable to him from 1953. He recruited them into the Department of Propaganda and Spiritual Education. They worked hard, campaigned vigorously, and although the party could never garner the popular appeal of the bigger, mainstream parties in the crucial politics of the era, they nevertheless recorded some spectacular successes. The Dynamic Party won five seats in the Eastern region. Dr. Chike Obi was elected in 1953/54 to the Eastern House from Onitsha, the home constituency of Dr. Nnamdi Azikiwe. This was no mean achievement. Chike Obi's party became a magnet for radical undergraduates on campus like Emma Ifeajuna, who would later play a significant role in Nigeria's political history. The Dynamic Party served to foreground Okigbo's political consciousness and his later involvement at the epicenter of national events.

They had many unforgettable adventures. Leslie Harriman recalled some of their experiences campaigning. On one occasion in 1954, they had traveled from Ibadan to Aba in Eastern Nigeria for a political meeting. They were waylaid on Ngwa Road and attacked by thugs at Aba, a formidable NCNC stronghold. Harriman remembers fleeing into the bush while Christopher Okigbo managed a spectacular manoeuvre in the car he was driving and found his way to the nearby Ngwa Road police post to get help. Dr. Chike Obi was severely manhandled by the thugs, and might have been even more badly mauled had the police not come just in time to rescue the eminent mathematician. They had cause to return quickly to Ibadan. Okigbo drove all day from Aba through the midwest of Nigeria and by the time they reached Akure they were suffering from exhaustion and headed for Akure General Hospital where Leslie Harriman had a girlfriend, a nurse, and a cousin, Dr. Ebenezer Ikomi, who was a House Officer. They made plans to spend the night in Ebens Ikomi's apartment in the hospital quarters. Leslie Harriman, however, decided that he would rather stay with his girlfriend for the evening. Apparently feeling more keenly entitled to feminine consolation, Dr. Chike Obi made advances to Leslie's girlfriend and a minor argument ensued over territorial rights until Dr. Ikomi intervened.

If they had not been so overwrought that night, they would have noticed that while Leslie and Chike Obi were arguing, Okigbo had quietly slipped into the night and disappeared. No one knew where he had gone, and they searched around the hospital but could not find him. The next morning they discovered to their dismay, that Okigbo had found convenient lodgings in the maternity ward of Akure General Hospital. He just found an empty bed and slept off. The next morning a nurse on her rounds had discovered him in innocent sleep, and the pregnant and nursing mothers raised quite an alarm upon the discovery of male company in their midst. From Dr. Ikomi's flat, they heard the ruckus in the maternity ward, and knew immediately that Christopher Okigbo was its likely cause. They hurried quickly to the scene, and came just in time to see Okigbo walking calmly away from the noise, a big grin on his face. Leslie Harriman later summed it up: 'He was always one step ahead in his own world... always clipping at the edge of what is considered normal or acceptable.'[83]

The Aba incident remained a source of deep reflection of the emerging character of Nigerian politics for Okigbo, as he grew away from active involvement in partisan politics of the first republic. Much of politics brooked little regard for life and this shaped the character and history of later events. Suddenly aware of their vulnerability, the Dynamic Party decided to hire an Ibadan thug, a strong-arm, who went by the name 'Broken Bottle.' Christopher Okigbo had to literally scour Ibadan's inner city to find a man suitable enough to calm Chike Obi's tussled nerves. Broken Bottle was just the right man: Leslie Harriman described him as a giant of a man who had 'greater brawn than sense,'[84] whose lair was the Molete Motor Park. Bottle was a product of the violent politics of that period. The market for hired hands was booming in the atmosphere of incipient postcolonial politics. Broken Bottle had once traveled with the political entourage of that 'stormy petrel of Ibadan politics', the colorful 'Penkelemesi' – Adegoke Adelabu, one of the most remarkable actors in Nigeria's political theatre of the 1950s. Harriman's account is that Okigbo had found Broken

Bottle through his numerous underground contacts in Mokola. The negotiations were delicate. Party loyalties were fierce. Broken Bottle agreed to join the Dynamic Party because Okigbo conceded to pay him ten shillings more than what he got normally from the Adelabu camp. Broken Bottle also knew exactly what was expected of him. He quickly became their personal security.

Soon after the Aba incident, Chike Obi committed an inadvertent *faux pas*. The Dynamic Party was touring the East on campaign. A meeting had been arranged at Ihiala, and the local branch of the Dynamic Party had arranged for a representative of the party to wait near the main market square to bring Chike Obi to the meeting, where he was billed to address a rally of party supporters. There was an unfortunate mix up, however. Chike Obi and his group arrived in Ihiala earlier than anticipated and had to wait at the Ihiala junction. While they were ruminating on their predicament, a man suddenly appeared and approached them, and inquired if they were waiting for anybody. Still smarting from the memory of the past ambush at Aba, Chike Obi mistook the whole scenario, and thought he had discovered another ambush. He flared into an Olympian rage against his sudden interlocutor who was rendered speechless. The gentleman tried to mollify the angry don assuring him earnestly that there was some mistake and that he meant no harm. But Dr. Chike Obi, fortified both by righteous indignation and by the towering presence of Broken Bottle, was determined to give his presumed assailant a bit of his mind. It turned out that the man whom Dr. Obi so thoroughly abused was, in fact, his host at Ihiala who had been waiting patiently for the Dynamic Party entourage to arrive, and had spent most of the day scouting for them! When he realized his error, Dr. Obi offered profuse apologies. But for a long time, this incident remained a source of great amusement for Christopher Okigbo, who used every opportunity to remind Chike Obi that even great mathematicians and military historians could be irrational on occasions and short on tactics.

Working closely with Dr. Obi gave Okigbo the right to drive about the university campus in Obi's famous Oldsmobile – a black, rambling American car. It enhanced his standing in a community in which ownership of a car was a status symbol. On one occasion in 1954, the Dynamic Party needed vehicles to organize its political campaigns in Ibadan. They did not have the money for the down payment required. They went into a wet lease negotiation with the United Africa Company, the major car dealership in Ibadan. Chike Obi had promised Okigbo and Harriman that he would relinquish his Zephyr 20 model to them if they succeeded in procuring the cars on hire purchase from UAC. Leslie Harriman recounted how he and Okigbo went one morning to the UAC show room in Ibadan and put forward their request for hire purchase on behalf of the Dynamic Party. To dress appropriately for the occasion, Okigbo had gone into town to borrow a lawyer's wig and gown from a friend of his who practiced law in the city, and acted the part of the Dynamic Party's legal representative. They remarked to the English manager that they wanted the cars and motorcycles for the campaigns in the crucial 1954 elections because the Dynamic Party was opposed to the 'mad rush towards independence,' a message which they intended to canvass widely, and which would require great logistical support. The UAC, a British conglomerate, was active in funding pro-British political interests and seeking to protect its investments in Nigeria, and was apparently not in support of independence for the colonies where they made much of their wealth. The manager quickly processed their hire purchase agreement, 'without fulfilling all the terms of hire purchase.'[85] Okigbo carefully choreographed this elaborate sham. They had a great laugh afterwards, when they came out of the UAC offices with the cars. Harriman justified it as 'sheer and necessary theatre.'[86]

For the Dynamic Party, hampered in its campaigns by limited resources, Okigbo's acting skills had come in handy. They justified their actions by invoking Machiavelli's axiom that good men should seek power by whatever means, for the good of the commonwealth. Months later, the party was faced with the problem of raising money quickly to pay off the hire purchase; and they again thought up a scheme, this time of getting Broken Bottle to push one of the cars which they got from UAC over the hills in Ibadan to raise 'insurance' money, and to forestall payment by the Dynamic Party of the full hire purchase agreements. Again, Machiavelli was invoked: the end justified the means. The end, for the Dynamic Party, was decolonization, even if it required duping colonial institutions and its agents like the UAC to achieve that. The campaign to elect Chike Obi into the Eastern Nigerian House in 1953/54 paid off. But they lost their deposits in the Western elections in the Ishan, Kukuruku, Egbado and Ekiti Divisions where it had fielded candidates, winning only 4,841 votes or 0.4% of the total votes cast in Western Nigeria.

The experience with the Dynamic Party was crucial to the growth of Okigbo's political consciousness, and subsequently, his evolution as a national poet, an artist whose significant political involvement within the post-colonial society was both aesthetic and active. The political experience provided him with an acute perception of the workings of his society in rapid transition. There are hints in his poetry about the sensitivity with which he apprehends and relates to the social and political events in post-colonial Nigeria. The extent to which these events affected him could also be gleaned from his involvement later with the Ifeajuna group. Okigbo's acute, poetic interpretation of events much later in his life, from the 'glimpse of the dream' of an independent nation, through the nationalist struggle, the metaphor of spiritual renewal in *Heavensgate*, to the catatonic events of the national crisis, which inspired the dark vision of *Path of Thunder*, owed much to his political awakening and his early involvement with Chike Obi.

As an acute and sensitive observer of his society, Okigbo's poetry places him within the threshold of early nationhood and situates him as Nigeria's national poet, the most important poetic chronicler of his time and milieu: from its disruptions by the alien forces of colonialism, to its self-immolation in the post-colonial era. Dubem Okafor has detailed Okigbo's imaginative response to Nigeria's national politics in his book, *A Dance of Death*, suggesting that Okigbo's intimacy with the fabric of social and political issues of his day, and his close contacts with leading characters in the nationalist struggle, doubtlessly ignited Okigbo's later creative consciousness. His search for a more humane social order, which he eventually discovered through poetry, flows from his early political activism as a student in the crucial years of decolonization.

Okigbo belonged to a generation of students at Ibadan who had been roused politically by the journalism of Dr. Nnamdi Azikiwe and his *West African Pilot*. In Africa, the process of decolonization stimulated an imaginative response against the empire; and within the seemingly staid complacency of the University College campus, this response took the form of cultural politics – as when Achebe's undergraduate English class questioned the authenticity of the African character in Joyce Cary's *Mister Johnson*. The appearance of Amos Tutuola's *The Palmwine Drinkard* in 1952 triggered much debate on the nature and value of African writing. The arrival of Ulli Beier in 1950 to teach in the English department, and his attempts to revolutionize and Africanize the discourse of literature also added stimulation to the cultural and aesthetic consciousness incipient among that generation of students. Okigbo's cultural and political consciousness was nurtured in the ambience of such discourse. All these would in time, shape Okigbo's aesthetic response, and impact in a fundamental way on his intellectual life and his artistic vision.

Okigbo's years at Ibadan saw the emergence of such leading student political activists as Ben Obumselu who became president of the Students' Union from 1955 to 1957 and was the first national president of the National Union of Nigerian Students (NUNS) when it convened in 1957. Bola Ige also cut his teeth politically in that period; he later became executive governor of the old Oyo state (1979–83) and rose to become Attorney-General and Minister of Justice until he was assassinated in December 2002. Tunji Otegbeye was a Marxist student who took the unprecedented step of going for medical training in the Soviet Union, despite intense scrutiny from the colonial security police of anyone seen as a 'communist sympathizer'; when he returned, he founded the Socialist Workers Party and the Ireti Hospitals. The geographer Akin Mabogunje, later awarded the Nigerian National Order of Merit, was a leader of the Action Group Party on campus. There was Edward Kobani, one of the 'Ogoni 4,' tragically murdered years later in the Ogoni crisis for which the writer Ken Saro-Wiwa was arraigned, tried and subsequently hanged. There was Emmanuel Ifeajuna, who led the first military coup of January 1966. There was also Sam Agbam, Ifeajuna's intellectual and ideological comrade at Ibadan, who was later executed by firing squad by Odumegwu-Ojukwu during the Nigerian civil war. Gamaliel Onosode rose from the humble politics of the student years to be a leading captain of industry and figure in the board room politics of some of the key corporations in Nigeria. Sam Okudu later made his name as the registrar of the University of Ibadan. Godwin Adopkaye became head of Mobil in Nigeria. They were all key figures of undergraduate politics at Ibadan, with whom Christopher Okigbo closely associated.

Okigbo belonged to the wing of student politicians which sought independence and political freedom as a revolutionary imperative. They were wary about freedom handed down 'on a platter of gold.' There was something dissatisfying and incomplete about the ordered nature of Nigeria's anti-colonial struggle. Okigbo's group saw themselves principally as nationalist revolutionaries. They first began to meet in Kuti Hall to seek a radical completion of 'the unfinished business called Nigeria,'[87] as Ignatius Atigbi put it. In 1954, Okigbo was among the group of 'troublesome' students removed from Mellanby Hall to start the new Kuti Hall when it opened, joining freshmen like Emmanuel Ifeajuna, Sam Agbam, and Anthony Ukpabi Asika, who gravitated towards Okigbo. Soon, his room became the nightly rendezvous of the radical students on campus, and Kuti Hall earned the reputation in Ibadan as the hall of 'hotheads.' The fervent nationalism of the period, shaped by the looming presence of Nnamdi Azikiwe in Nigeria, and the radical examples of Abdel Nasser in Egypt, and Kwame Nkrumah in Ghana provided the Kuti Hall 'hotheads' with grounds to interrogate the course of Nigeria's modern political and social history. Abdel Nasser particularly was an important model for Okigbo's generation. They admired his radical challenge to imperialism, and his efforts to secure the solidarity of the politically marginal societies still under colonial rule in Africa and the Middle East. Many years later, the 'federalist' Anthony Asika who was appointed the Administrator of the East during the Biafran war in which Okigbo, Ifeajuna and Agbam died, mused: 'Chris was in the center of it all. He was leader of the radical caucus in Kuti.'[88] So it was that in Kuti Hall, apparently, the earliest ideas for a political revolution in Nigeria's post-colonial society germinated.

Ifeajuna was clearly the star of that generation. He was already a much celebrated athlete before arriving at Ibadan. He had won the gold medal in the 1954 Commonwealth games in Vancouver and set a new record in the high jump. Okigbo's close friendship with Emmanuel Ifeajuna began in Ibadan. Brilliant, charismatic and attractive, Ifeajuna came to the University College, Ibadan in 1954, four years after Okigbo. They became close friends and collaborators from shared interests in sports and politics, long before he joined the army and led the coup of 15 January 1966. Alex Olu Ajayi was not a student in Ibadan, but he associated closely with both Ifeajuna and Okigbo in later years. He observed that: 'Emma always had deep respect and great affection for Chris Okigbo. In some ways he looked up to him from their days in Ibadan. It must have been for the kind of social presence which Christopher already had on the Ibadan campus, as much as for the breadth of his intellect.'[89] It was mutual admiration. Okigbo loved Ifeajuna too. They came to share the same revolutionary vision for their emerging nation. They became active political collaborators on campus, and were both of a revolutionary persuasion – at 'the anarchic end' of the spectrum, as Pius Okigbo later put it.

As Director of Information of the University College, Ibadan Students' Union in the 1950s, Ifeajuna was a great mobiliser of students for great political causes; he was a great propagandist and public speaker. He was central in organizing the protest over the Queen's visit to University College in 1956 and in the picketing of the federal parliament in Lagos over a proposed defense pact between Nigeria and Great Britain. The revolutionary spirit was marginal in Ibadan's highly conservative ethos, but the sense of the intellectual man of action was deeply ingrained in the souls of the more radical students who absorbed the revolutionary ideas of Chike Obi. Their sense of civic involvement came to be reflected in the later actions of these Ibadan intellectuals: whether it was Ifeajuna leading out troops in the night to topple a government, or the masked figure of Wole Soyinka entering the newsroom of a radio station to force at gun point a change in the unjust announcements of a government, or Okigbo running guns for a secessionist government, these acts took root in the left-wing political action of the UCI campus of the 1950s.

Okigbo's generation of Ibadan undergraduates, guided by a sense of itself as the intellectual elect, sensed its 'manifest destiny' as agents of change: they learnt to express dissent against the norms of convention and orthodox morality in ways that were quite remarkable given Ibadan's conservative moorings. Okigbo's early poetry expressed this consciousness defined by the urge to be freed of the burden of a colonial past - that led the orphic persona in Okigbo's poetry towards a 'homecoming'. The central figures of Kuti Hall's left-wing politics were all drawn inexorably into the drama of tumultuous national events, and became the tragic victims of the post-colonial state when their failed revolution led to war, and the war led to their deaths or failure.

There were many other aspects of Okigbo's life in Ibadan other than left-wing politics. Many of his contemporaries remembered his sense of fun and playfulness and his capacity for innocent mischief. Okigbo loved to party with his friends on the roof of Kuti Hall, which overlooked the female hostel. Sultan Bello Hall originally served in the interim as a women's hostel at the university in the 1950s when the female population of the university began to grow. From the roof of Kuti Hall it was easy to see what was going on inside the female hall. Okigbo would routinely go up there in the cool Ibadan evenings to drink beer 'and observe the ladies in their habits!'[90] It was an act of protest, for the university had constructed a barricade to prevent access from Kuti to Sultan Bello. Students like Okigbo argued that it was a backward decision, which did not take into consideration the freedom of choice that defined social intercourse on a university campus, and were prepared to frustrate it.

Ifeajuna for instance, led a dramatic student rebellion in 1957, for which many students were rusticated. This incident became one of the most enduring legends in the annals of the university: the gate leading to Sultan Bello Hall – the female residence – from Kuti Hall suddenly disappeared in the middle of the night, yanked off its hinges! The idea of that gate rankled students who felt it incongruent with the normal freedoms of a university.

Christopher Okigbo failed his degree examination in 1955, and left the university to work briefly for the Nigerian Tobacco Company as trainee Sales Manager from March to September 1955. Okigbo made it known to his friends and relations that he was not prepared to return to the university and repeat his degree exam. However, he eventually succumbed to boredom and family pressure, and left the NTC to return to University College in October 1955 to resit the examination. Leslie Harriman believed that Okigbo's decision to return to the university was in part because: 'he actually liked the university environment. It suited him. Moreover, he still had so many of his friends around on campus, so it was easy to convince him to return.'[91] The second factor was even more important: his father, the old school master, had put considerable pressure on him. Okigbo rejected all entreaties. It was a struggle of will between the schoolmaster and his tempestuous son. Okigbo's father had to call a family meeting. The discussions went nowhere until his eldest brother Lawrence intervened. He sat Okigbo down and had a long talk with him. Lawrence quickly realized that he had to employ a little guile to lure Christopher back to his studies. 'I cajoled, I pleaded, I threatened Chris,'[92] he recollected, years later. In the end, he offered his Ford as a bribe. It was the only condition upon which Christopher agreed to return to the university and complete his degree.

Thus bribed with a car, Okigbo returned to Ibadan, and resumed residence in Mellanby Hall, his original hall, from which he was sent to Kuti. He began using the Ford as a taxicab to make extra income. But he was virtually living with Chike Obi at the professor's quarters, and was found always driving about in Dr. Obi's Oldsmobile with Harriman, helping the Dynamic Party with the 1956 elections. Chike Obi's home was their evening rendezvous, where they learnt among many other things, to mix potent cocktails; remarkable incendiary experiments of those years, which they called, 'Sabo Chemistry.'[93] According to Harriman 'Sabo Chemistry' was a great cocktail of Jamaican rum, mixed with krola soft drink, and laced with a good quantity of marijuana. They drank with relish, toasting to life and to coming political independence. 'It had the effect,' Harriman said, 'of inducing sobriety.'[94]

Okigbo also came under the influence of the Beatnik craze at this time. He had become aware, through Pius who was at Northwestern University in Evanston, of the new Beat movement in America. He was intellectually drawn to their challenge against orthodoxy. His sense of fashion was radically transformed by this new influence. A group of Lagos boys entered university in 1956 and came with this new fashion and its sassy attitudes. They went about casually in shorts and simple beach shirt tops, with a cap. One of those Lagos boys, Dapo Falase, later became a formidable leader of the Students' Union, and many years later, also a distinguished professor of medicine at the University College Hospital, Ibadan. But as an undergraduate, he was of a bohemian spirit. Okigbo expressed his interest in Dapo's clothing style. The next day, Dapo Falase had two outfits for Okigbo. According to the journalist Olu Akaraogun, 'Chris was so thrilled that he called Dapo and gave him all his expensive suits and shirts retaining in his wardrobe only those two new clothes that Dapo had given him!'[95] To illustrate the striking nature of the new fashion, the journalist, Olu Akaraogun recalled how a freshman had stopped at the gates of University College. He saw Dapo Falase decked out in this bohemian fashion. Mistaking him for a university porter, the freshman called out to Falase, and commissioned him to carry his luggage to the hostel. Falase obliged, took the luggage on his head to Mellanby Hall, earned a tip and left most graciously. But come evening at dinner, the Ibadan freshman was shocked to find Falase among a retinue of friends chatting boisterously, all turned out in the same casual fashion. He soon discovered to his chagrin that Falase was not only an older student, but was one of the leaders of the Students' Union too. He went over and apologized and they all had a hearty laugh.

It was in that bohemian style of clothes that Alex Olu Ajayi first encountered Christopher Okigbo at Ibadan. Alex Ajayi would be important, two years later, in Okigbo's life, and in his eventual emergence as a poet. In 1956, Ajayi had just returned from Fourah Bay College, and was engaged in research for Durham University at the Africana Library of the University College. At first, he lived in the university quarters with his cousin, the Deputy Registrar of the University College, Nath Adamolekun. But he felt he needed to move into the student residence to socialize with other students. Mr. Adamolekun helped him secure lodgings at Mellanby Hall, and Ajayi soon found himself in a close friendship with Bola Ige. Like Okigbo, Ige had also returned to UCI to repeat his final exams. Bola Ige made a great event of preparing for the final exams in Classics and he went about campus with his head tied in a towel soaked in cool water – 'to hold the Cranium,' he loved to say. Bola Ige's room in Mellanby, was next to Okigbo's. Each time Alex Ajayi came to visit Bola Ige, he recollected that he always saw this 'smallish fellow, who was extremely carefree, and always carelessly shod, with his buttons all down ... and he always came with an unrestrained loudness. You could not miss him. He was particularly infectious'.[97] This 'loud' fellow was of course Christopher Okigbo.

Ajayi was immediately drawn to Okigbo. He thought him very sociable and lively. He recalled that Okigbo's room in Mellanby was a constant hive of activity. Sometimes, because of his intense preparations for his examinations, Okigbo would refuse to take a bath for upwards of two days, and would resist all attempts by his friends to lure him to the bathroom. On one occasion, unable to take it anymore, some of his friends conspired to carry Okigbo physically into the bathroom and give him a thorough bath. They hoisted Okigbo up in the air and into the bath, in spite of his protestations, and turned the shower on him. Soon Ajayi and Okigbo discovered that they shared similar intellectual interests, especially a love for Virgil. But it was largely Okigbo's sense of fun that intrigued Alex Ajayi: 'He was always in the center of the most outrageous of events.'[98] Ajayi found certain aspects of Okigbo's rather eccentric lifestyle fascinating, like his careless disregard for danger. 'There was something intriguing, subversive and edgy about the way he lived, it was almost suicidal.'[99]

One particular memory of Ajayi's illustrates Okigbo's capacity for the unorthodox. Okigbo owned an old shortwave radio. In truth, it was nothing more than the skeletal remains of what was once an electric radio set. It was almost inoperable. But Okigbo used to plug it in by holding two dry sticks to both ends of the wire, and manipulating them with this naked current! 'It was very dangerous. But it was the funniest thing ever, to watch Christopher operate that thing. The way he went about it...the casualness of it. Any mistake would have meant instant death, but that never seemed to bother him.'[100] Alex Ajayi also recalled asking him why he took that risk when he could afford a newer radio. Christopher replied that he was putting to use his skills in physics. Besides, he was very fond of that ancient radio. 'That was more important, his long attachments. The radio had great sentimental value. That sums Christopher. He had a great sentimental soul. He was loyal to old things – friends, loves, anything that embodied his past.'[101]

In June 1956, two months away from his twenty-sixth birthday, Christopher Okigbo finally graduated with a third class degree in Classics, majoring in Latin, Greek and Ancient History. Okigbo's genius lay trapped within the conflicts of his soul, and the dilemma of his irreconcilable nature. His eyes were nevertheless, trained towards the great careers for which he was prepared. The cleaners who came to clear his room when he left the University found piles and piles of university library books, which Okigbo had read but never returned. There were so many of them that it took many goings and comings to clear them all up. People wondered how he was able to collect and keep so many books without fines from the strict university librarian, Mr. Harris. But apparently, Okigbo had become great friends with Harris, who indulged him.

Although he was not much of a scholar, Okigbo's contemporaries at Ibadan however were unanimous in acknowledging his natural genius – the fact that he was well read and acute. Alex Ajayi said 'Christopher of course could not make much of a scholarly life but it was not for lack of ability. He was never ever settled enough to anything, never took seriously to the academic chores. He had very little time or patience for examinations. Ibadan did not challenge him; it was too much rote, and he was bored by its routine. He was an instinctual rather than a committed scholar. He read widely, without any specific goals to be attained.'[102] Eugene Cadle, who was Okigbo's academic advisor, came also to appreciate Okigbo's 'restless genius.' According to Obumselu, although Okigbo failed his degree examination in 1955, Cadle wrote a moving testimonial for Okigbo, acknowledging that he wrote the best essay on Greek tragedy ever submitted by any student in the Classics department of his time at Ibadan.

## NOTES

1 Alex Ekwueme, 'Remembering the Weaverbird' opening remarks at the exhibition 'Song for Idoto': A Celebration of Christopher Okigbo, National Museum Enugu, 6 November 1996.
2 Quoted in Robert Wren, *Those Magical Years* (Washington DC: Three Continents Press, 1981) .
3 Interview with Sam Okudu, Lagos, 1992.
4 Christopher Okigbo, *Limits* I–IV, 1961, *Labyrinths with Path of Thunder* (London: Heinemann, 1971).
5 Christopher Okigbo, *Limits*, XII, 1961/2, *Labyrinths*.
6 Quoted in Robert Wren, *Those Magical Years*.
7 Ulli Beier, quoted in Robert Wren, *Those Magical Years*.
8 Chinua Achebe, Robert Wren, *Those Magical Years*.
9 Quoted in Robert Wren, *Those Magical Years*.
10 Ben Obumselu, 'Christopher Okigbo: a Poetic Portrait'. Essay delivered at 'Song for Idoto': A Celebration of Christopher Okigbo, National Museum, Enugu, 2 November 1996.
11 Interview with Caleb Olaniyan, Ikeja GRA, Lagos 1993.
12 Gamaliel Onosode, in *Our U.I.* (ed.) Bunmi Salako (Ibadan: Lyntana Books, 1990).
13 Quoted in Robert Wren, *Those Magical Years*.
14 Ben Obumselu, 'Christopher Okigbo: a Poetic Portrait'.
15 Quoted in Robert Wren, *Those Magical Years*.
16 Ben Obumselu, 'Christopher Okigbo: a Poetic Portrait'.

17  Alex Ekwueme, 'Remembering the Weaverbird'.

18  Interview with Rex Akpofure, Victoria Island, Lagos, 1994.

19  Wole Soyinka's Agip Lecture, 1984.

20  Interview with Ben Obumselu, Lagos, 1994.

21  Ibid.

22  Bernth Lindfors, 'Okigbo as Jock', *When the Drumbeat Changes* (eds) Carolyn Parker and Stephen Arnold (Washington DC: Three Continents Press, 1981) pp. 119–214.

23  Ali Mazrui, *The Trial of Christopher Okigbo* (London: Heinemann, 1971) pp. 52–3.

24  Bernth Lindfors, 'Okigbo as Jock'.

25  *The University Herald* 3:3 (1950) quoted in Bernth Lindfors 'Okigbo as Jock' *When the Drumbeat Changes* (eds) Carolyn Parker and Stephen Arnold (Washington DC: Three Continent Press, 1981) pp. 119–214.

26  *The Bug* magazine 5:3 (1954) p. 11.

27  Bernth Lindfors, 'Okigbo as Jock'.

28  Ben Obumselu, 'Christopher Okigbo: a Poetic Portrait'.

29  Ibid.

30  Interview with Ignatius Atigbi, Surulere, Lagos, 1994.

31  Ben Obumselu, in *Our U.I.* (ed.) Bunmi Salako (Ibadan: Lyntana Books, 1990).

32  Ibid.

33  Interview with Pius Okigbo, 1994/5.

34  Christopher Okigbo's letter to Ignatius Atigbi, 16 May 1956.

35  J. P. Clark, 'Ibadan' in Gerald Moore and Ulli Beier (eds) *Modern Poetry from Africa* (Harmondsworth: Penguin Books, 1963) p. 115.

36  Interview with Leslie Harriman, Apapa Boat Club, Lagos, 1992.

37  Interview with Ignatius Atigbi.

38  Ibid.

39  Ibid.

40  Ibid.

41  Ben Obumselu, 'Christopher Okigbo: a Poetic Portrait'.

42  Christopher Okigbo, *Silences*, 1964, *Labyrinths*.

43  Ibid.

44  Chike C. Momah's e-mail to the author, 2005.

45  Interview with E.J. Ekong, Festac Town, Lagos, 1993.

46  Ibid.

47  Ibid.

48  Interview with Ignatius Atigbi.

49  Ibid.

50  Interview with Banjo Solarun, Ikeja Golf Club, Lagos, 1994.

51  Christopher Okigbo, 'Initiations', *Heavensgate* 1961, *Labyrinths*.

52  Christopher Okigbo, Introduction to *Labyrinths*.

53  Interview with Kalada Hart, Chez Therese, Aba Road, Port Harcourt, 1992.

54  Interview with Ben Obumselu.

55  Interview with V.C. Ike, Lagos, 1994.

56  Interview with Olu Akaraogun.

57  Interview with Pius Okigbo.

58  Ibid.

59  Ibid.

60  Quoted in Robert Wren, *Those Magical Years*.

61  Interview with Leslie Harriman.

62  Interview with Ben Obumselu.
63  Ibid.
64  Interview with Bola Ige.
65  Interview with Ben Obumselu.
66  Christopher Okigbo, *Labyrinths*.
67  Quoted in Robert Wren, *Those Magical Years*, pp. 62–3.
68  Interview with Ignatius Atigbi.
69  Ibid.
70  Christopher Okigbo, *Path of Thunder* 1966, *Labyrinths*.
71  Quoted in Robert Wren, *These Magical Years*.
72  Pius Okigbo, 'A Toast of Christopher Okigbo'.
73  Interview with Chike Obi, UNTH Enugu, 1996.
74  Interview with Leslie Harriman.
75  Interview with Pius Okigbo.
76  Kalu Ezera, *Constitutional Development in Nigeria* (Cambridge: Cambridge University Press, 1960) p. 103.
77  Chike Obi, *Our Struggle* (Onitsha: Etukokwu P, 1953) pp. 55–6.
78  W.J.H. Mackenzie and Kenneth Robinson, *Five Elections* (Oxford: Clarendon Press, 1960).
79  Ibid.
80  Interview with Chike Obi.
81  Ibid.
82  Interview with Ben Obumselu.
83  Interview with Leslie Harriman.
84  Ibid.
85  Ibid.
86  Ibid.
87  Interview with Ignatius Atigbi.
88  Interview with Ukpabi Asika, National Museum, Lagos 1992.
89  Interview with Alex Olu Ajayi, Surulere, Lagos, 1992.
90  Interview with Leslie Harriman, Apapa Boat Club, Lagos, 1992.
91  Ibid.
92  Interview with Lawrence Okigbo, Skoup, Enugu, 1994.
93  Interview with Leslie Harriman.
94  Ibid.
95  Interview with Olu Akaraogun, at *Daily Times*, Ikeja Lagos, 1992.
96  Interview with Alex Olu Ajayi.
97  Ibid.
98  Ibid.
99  Ibid.
100  Ibid.
101  Ibid.
102  Interview with Kalada Hart.

# 4

## Colonial civil servant, covert businessman & bankrupt

### LAGOS 1956–58

They cast him in mould of iron,
And asked him to do a rock-drill –
Man out of innocence –
He drilled with dumb-bells about him.

('Fragments out of the Deluge')

In 1956, there were less than three thousand Nigerians with a university education. Those naturally formed part of the elite of the colonial society. The colonial civil service offered attractive incentives to these new graduates to enter its Administrative Service. Christopher Okigbo's generation of Nigerian university graduates, newly recruited into the senior service, were given comfortable subsidized accommodation in the exclusive Government Reservation Areas. These exclusive areas known then as 'European quarters,' and once reserved for European staff of the colonial administration, came with a full complement of cooks and stewards. These Nigerian recruits suddenly had access to privileges formerly reserved for European members of the senior civil service.

The few multinational corporations, in the spirit of Nigerianization, were also expanding their African personnel. Some of the new graduates headed to well-established multinational corporations like the United African Company (UAC), the Unilever Group, the British-owned Nigerian Tobacco Company (NTC) which guaranteed them comfort and career advancement. Looking to the emergence of post-colonial opportunities in business, they wooed these new graduates with salaries that made civil service prospects pale in comparison. However many young university graduates owed bonds to their communities or to the government, and needed to pay off debts as quickly as possible, while maintaining a lifestyle commensurate with their new social status. Obi Okonkwo in Chinua Achebe's *No Longer at Ease*, shows the demands on new graduates. It was into this social and material environment that Christopher Okigbo entered.

On graduating in June 1956, Okigbo returned to the Nigerian Tobacco Company, in Ibadan, as Regional Sales Manager with control of western operations. NTC was the biggest corporate organization in Ibadan, from where it oversaw its vast national operations in Nigeria. Okigbo's job was to organize sales campaigns, inspect his brands for quality control, and replace stock where necessary. He had to liaise with NTC distributors in the western district. It was an outdoor job which suited his temperament, his disdain for routine and his love for travel.

Okigbo rented a flat near Eleyele station in Ibadan and was assigned an NTC Land Rover. He frequently toured north to depots at Jos and Kaduna, west to Ijebu-Ode and Benin City and controlled distribution in places as far as Asaba. The NTC job paid well but it did not challenge his intellect. Travel gave Okigbo the opportunity to gain an appreciation of the complexity of Nigeria's people and landscapes. He had a comfortable, bachelor existence and lived prodigally. The NTC paid more than double what he later received in the civil service. This stint with NTC, however, was short-lived. First, there was the lack of challenge. He soon became bored with the routine of the sales job. Before long he perceived the racism of his English colleagues. Okigbo, Alex Ajayi recalled, '… he choked under its pressures. He could no longer stand the stupidity of it all.'[1] Okigbo '… felt like he was only part of the window dressing for the policy of Nigerianization.'[2] Okigbo felt increasingly under-utilized, sidelined, and isolated. He had no real authority. Even as area sales manager he was not allowed freely to run his own operations. Authority at NTC was within the hierarchy of the expatriate British staff. Okigbo fell under the meddlesome supervision of much younger, and even sometimes less educated, expatriate NTC staff who were supposed to be under his supervision. Many of the English managers had grown cynical of independence and Nigerianization. They found subtle ways to humiliate their Nigerian employees. It was therefore not too surprising that he lost interest quickly, and moved on.

Okigbo's experience in this regard was by no means unique. As part of the new labour regulations enacted in the transition towards decolonization, international companies operating in Nigeria were obligated to employ new Nigerian university graduates in executive trainee positions. Cynicism often defeated the lofty idea behind the employment programme aimed at providing Nigerians the opportunity to acquire skills that would equip them to run complex systems in the post-colonial economy. Alex Ajayi recounted the incident which led his friend to leave the NTC. Chris had gone to Ijebu-Ode, a three-hour drive from Ibadan on the old trunk B road, to inspect his depots and meet his distributors. He traveled to Ijebu-Ode quite frequently in those years where he had many old friends from UCI. Safi Attah, whom he was wooing seriously by this time, was on holiday from England, and had also brought along her best friend, Felicia, later Professor Onitiri. They rode in the NTC Land Rover. Okigbo had planned to spend the weekend in Alex Ajayi's bungalow on the compound of the Ijebu-Ode Grammar school where he was teaching Latin and English. It was a rollicking weekend for Okigbo, except for an unforgettable incident which ruined their last evening. They were returning from a late party. Ajayi was driving the NTC Land Rover with Christopher Okigbo next to him while the ladies who were sitting behind were having a lively conversation. Okigbo suddenly asked a surprised Alex Ajayi to pull off the road. Quickly, Okigbo switched places with him. He had spotted some of his English colleagues from the NTC driving quickly towards them. They pulled up to ask Okigbo why the NTC Land Rover was out late in the night, reminding him about the company policy which required that NTC vehicles should be parked after the day's business. It was lucky they had not seen Ajayi driving the car. Okigbo felt the humiliation of that open reprimand, especially in the presence of his girlfriend whom he was trying to impress while she was on holiday from England. This incident was followed by an official inquiry when he returned to NTC offices in Ibadan. Alex Ajayi explained how Okigbo felt it; that it was all unjustified. 'Christopher was very sensitive to that sort of thing, more especially because, he felt a justifiable sense of superiority with his better education, and even better experience, over the "small boys," (as he called them) who had issued the query; and even more so because they too were driving in the night. It was a truly displeasing experience for him; it affronted his sense of dignity.'[3] Okigbo felt that remaining at the NTC, which denied him equality, fairness and the courtesy due to his station was untenable. So he left.

Early in 1957, he took a new job with UAC in Lagos, along with two of his closest friends, Leslie Harriman and Peter Chigbo. They were all designated Trainee Managers in their letters of employment signed by the chairman Lord Trenchard. Okigbo and Harriman shared a flat at Alagomeji, Yaba, then a serene suburb in this bustling area of Lagos. Peter Chigbo and George Nwanze also shared a flat in Yaba where most of the new African business and professional middle class lived. They lived on Abule Ijesha road, behind where the Federal Technical College now stands. Michael Ibru, who later became one of Nigeria's wealthiest businessmen, was also a Trainee Manager, who lived in a bungalow on Pierce Street. It was a lively community of stylish and ambitious young men, with their eyes set on the opportunities that new nationhood offered. Yaba was an enchanting place with its dizzying parties and social activity with its late 1950s fragrance. From all accounts, Okigbo lived fully in the socially active, middle class ambience of late-1950s. Okigbo and Leslie Harriman spent many an evening at the nearby Railway Club at Ebutte-Metta where they played cricket and hockey, and drank beer and socialized in the English country club atmosphere. The life of a young bachelor with a university degree and great prospects was enriching in the glamour of the intense city. The UAC paid well, and the young men lived wildly.

Sometime, early in 1957, Christopher Okigbo traveled to Ojoto and brought back with him two rustic country damsels, intact in their bucolic sexuality, their rough beauty and innocent ways. They were certainly different from the sophisticated city girls with whom Okigbo and Harriman were better acquainted. These young women were between the ages of seventeen and eighteen. They had apparently been entrusted by their relations in Ojoto for Okigbo to act as their guardian in Lagos, a city notorious for its loose morals and strange appetites. It was Okigbo's idea that the two country beauties would live with them 'acting both as housekeepers and as mistresses.' But there was a snag: one of the two girls had arrived with a fresh sore on her leg, which was just healing when she came to Lagos. Who would keep her as mistress? Christopher Okigbo and Leslie Harriman argued over this for a while, and eventually resolved the matter, at Okigbo's suggestion, by flipping a coin 'in the fashion of deck gamblers on a pirate ship.'[4] Okigbo won. Thus these two restless and adventurous young bachelors in their early twenties began to cohabit with the girls, 'whose innocence denied inhibitions'.[5] They lived freely, crawled the bars of Lagos, made love to the two young women, and had a wonderful time. Then there was a dramatic fall-out between Leslie and his fiancée and the young women had hurriedly to be sent back home.

Leslie Harriman had become engaged to the passionate Clara Edewor who was madly in love with him. She lived on Military Street in the heart of Lagos with her parents. Her brother James Edewor, had become great friends with Christopher Okigbo. Even while, courtesy of Okigbo, he was having his affair with the country belles, Harriman continued his relationship with Clara. He felt an occasional sense of guilt. 'But Christopher led me into all sorts of troubles in those days,'[6] Harriman recalled with a laugh many years afterwards when he described 'a very compromising and embarrassing situation.'[7] His relationship with Clara could have ended permanently one day in 1957, when she came unexpectedly to the Alagomeji flat and saw to her chagrin that Leslie was in the grip of intercourse with one of the young women. Okigbo himself was engrossed in intense intercourse with the other. Clara became uncontrollable in her rage and even slapped her brother James, who had come with her. In vain, Leslie tried to appease Clara who fled in tears, resolving to end the relationship with him. Sobered by the turn of events, Okigbo initiated elaborate schemes to help Leslie win back Clara's affection. 'Christopher was full of ideas. He was very fond of Clara actually. Besides, he shared my sense of guilt!'[8] Clara's brother, James, became a useful intermediary. Okigbo took the blame for leading Leslie into temptation. In the end the efforts worked. It is an indication of Okigbo's character that he retained Clara's confidence and affection in spite of that incident.

Clara Harriman explained this later in an interview. She came to understand the unique bond between Leslie and Christopher. Clara became an important part of their friendship, and a witness to the turbulence of Okigbo's life in colonial Lagos which was intimately intertwined with the life of the man she married. 'It was pointless to fight it. They were very wild young men.'[9] Clara not only understood the dramatic impulses of Okigbo's character, but she was also attracted to the 'pure innocence of Christopher's soul'.[10] She discovered in Christopher Okigbo a quality of openness, warmth and compassion: 'Even in the wild, turbulent life he always led, Chris was an amusing person who was difficult to dislike. There was no dull moment with him. He was so full of life and laughter and so open. Nothing was sacred, only friendship. He was without envy. He bore no ill will to anyone ... and he was especially very loyal to his friends. That was an aspect of Christopher's life that stood out in his relationship with people: he was the chivalrous and dedicated friend. He was very protective of me.'[11] These were Clara Harriman's reminiscences of Christopher Okigbo, one somnolent evening, several years later, while sitting over some club sandwiches and beer with the sea breeze coming from the Lagos lagoon at the Apapa Boat Club. The tide lashed sadly against the stone surfaces of the barrier protecting the Boat Club in front of which stood the modest house, where Clara had then retired with her husband Leslie, after he had spent a distinguished career in the diplomatic service, rising to be Nigeria's Ambassador to the United Nations. Decades after Okigbo died, Clara still recalled wistfully Chris's role as a mediating force in their marriage. Okigbo used to bring to her a box of 'Black Magic,' chocolate which Leslie always sent to appease her after every clash of will accompanied with the words in the song: 'When money goes love flies away through the window'.

Okigbo also served as Leslie's best man when they married in August 1957. The Harrimans had planned a private wedding restricted to a handful of their friends and close family in Lagos. The wedding service was to take place at Holy Cross Cathedral on a Saturday morning. That morning Okigbo had driven into the compound of the Catholic Mission near the Race Course, only to see Clara in tears, and Leslie looking very worried and subdued. Okigbo soon discovered the reason for the bride's distress. It turned out that Father Foley, the priest who taught Chemistry at University College, Ibadan, had dispatched a letter to the Catholic Bishop in Lagos warning against the danger of wedding the 'amoral and irreverent young heretic.' Father Foley had apparently not forgiven Leslie over the *pi phi psi* incident in Ibadan when Harriman, Okigbo and their friend Femi Odunjo had gone out late, bearing lanterns and dressed like Roman senators, to drink their beer and 'frolic wildly' at the university pavilion. The *pi phi psi* fraternity did not survive the session, but Leslie Harriman's quarrel with the Catholic priest which began then, came to a head as he stood at the altar before his bride. And there indeed he was, stranded that morning with his fiancée in tears. There were other complications: Leslie was not a Catholic, and Clara was pregnant. In the scandal-mongering society of colonial Lagos, with its Victorian sensibility, it would have been a blight on the Harrimans in 'decent circles' for a young man who had just been appointed to the important post of Assistant Divisional officer for the city.

Following Foley's letter, the Catholic Bishop had given orders to Father McCarthy, the Irish parish priest who was to wed the couple, to stop the wedding until the matter was clarified. Left to Harriman, they would just have settled for the civil ceremony in the court where their marriage had been registered anyway. He did not care for the elaborate rites of the church and appreciated even less the humiliating conditions to which they had been exposed that Saturday morning. But for Clara, a devout Roman Catholic, it was unthinkable not to be wed in church. Christopher Okigbo quickly reassured Clara and walked purposefully into the pastoral offices from where he was heard arguing vigorously in his high-pitched voice with Father McCarthy. The pastor emphasized the rules of the church and the orders of the Bishop. Okigbo on the other hand put up a compelling argument that, as the best man in the wedding, and a decent Catholic himself, he too deserved some respect. Soon Christopher Okigbo's argument prevailed, and Leslie and Clara Harriman had their marriage vows administered in the chapel of the Holy Cross Cathedral.

The entire event infuriated Christopher Okigbo so much that he soon hatched a plan with Leslie Harriman to dramatise the deep-etched hypocrisy of the church. As Harriman recalled of the incident that later took place, Okigbo felt that the Catholic Church and Father had acted outside the dictates of Christian charity. In those years, a sense of awe remained around the Catholic clergy who ran the church, conducted the rituals and enacted the myth of priestly infallibility. But the church was silent about the cases of, mostly Irish, priests whose sexual dalliances with female parishioners left behind mulatto children. The priests were shielded from the consequences of their human foibles. Duped parishioners held them in deep awe. Okigbo had grown skeptical of the church – although he remained a sentimental Catholic all of his life. Okigbo's attitude to the dominant presence of the Catholic church in his life and its mission in Africa is seen in his figuration of the famous missionary priest at Onitsha, Flannagan – 'who sowed the fireseed', or Father Leidan, the 'archtyrant of the holy see' in the original version of the *Heavensgate*. Okigbo's argument, that many of the Irish priests whom he knew early in his life acted too powerfully and arbitrarily over the lives of their African adherents, was borne from close experience. He saw in McCarthy's refusal to wed Harriman that same form of tyranny and racism with which he struggled emotionally. He felt that the humiliation which Clara suffered because she was pregnant was undeserved and should not be allowed to pass without remedy. His solution was to find a powerful, symbolic way to expose the hollow morality of the church and its clergy.

Okigbo and Harriman wanted to cure Clara of her fanatical devotion to the church. They plotted a scheme borne of a great sense of mischief to show how human foibles, even from the sacral, vivify the dreariness of moral absolutes. One weekend not long after the wedding, Okigbo stopped over at the Catholic mission and invited Father McCarthy over to Leslie's house for lunch. Okigbo had become quite friendly with the priest at that point. The Harrimans had just moved to Fowler Crescent in Ikoyi in 1957. On their way to Ikoyi, Okigbo stopped over at the Kingsway stores and bought a dozen bottle pack of Heineken beer. At the Harrimans, Okigbo set the beer before the priest, and they engaged him in a long, engrossing conversation, and urged him on until he had exhausted the beer. Having made him very drunk, Okigbo dropped him off at the church in a state of inebriation. Near the race course, the padre vomited all over his cassock, Okigbo helped him remove the cassock and made the reverend gentleman take the short walk down to the Catholic mission. Okigbo hoped that the Reverend Father would walk, in his drunken state with the vomit all over him, straight into the Bishop. For Okigbo it was all a big joke – it was what Leslie Harriman described as his 'sense of innocuous mischief, not intended to harm, just for the laugh.'[12] His real target was the church.

Clara was scandalized. After much pleading, she retrieved the Reverend Father's cassock from Okigbo, washed off its vomit stain, ironed it neatly and returned it to the hapless priest, who had been sobered and remained grateful to the lady. The priest thenceforth became wary of Christopher Okigbo. Although Harriman did suggest that Okigbo's treatment of Father McCarthy was all an 'innocuous joke,' there was something very cruel about it; indeed, sometimes Okigbo's sense of mischief was of such cruelty that it might be difficult to balance with his equal gestures of extreme kindness. Okigbo's irreverence demonstrated his belief that the truly experienced life consisted of a lived drama, the pure was not an act of the highest morality. His was a rejection of moral absolutes. The perfect life for the poet was not the 'life without sin,' but consisted in the truth of individual frailty. This view is echoed in his poetry, in a line in 'Initiations' in which he admits the 'pure line' drawn between the conflicts of the moral or psychic life, 'At confluence of planes,' are where 'man loses man, loses vision.' An inessential life, for Okigbo, could lead to spiritual death. The highest form of the moral life for the poet was of a life 'whose innocence denies inhibition.' Okigbo conceived of his own life in those terms – dependent on that primal state of innocence. This state of innocence was equally symbolic of the African past, which conventional Christianity disrupted with its hollow rituals and morality.

Okigbo had become sceptical about his Roman Catholic faith by the time he graduated from university. He arrived at a state of hybrid humanism framed around a platonic ideal. His poetry evolved from a unique mix between the symbols of European Christianity, the pagan cults of classical Sumeria, and the offerings to a matriarchal African deity, Idoto, by which he inscribed his quest for identity. His repudiation of Christian orthodoxy was a demonstration against its usurpation of the traditional religious mores. In his actions against Father McCarthy, Okigbo was apparently responding, although in his typically extravagant and dramatic manner, to the emergent mood of self-awareness among a new generation of educated Africans who began to affirm their identity by symbolically rejecting their ties to the symbols of European colonization. Okigbo's prank was tantamount to unmasking the Christian *egwugwu*. This rejection of Christianity coincided with the rapid decolonization in the middle of the 1950s.

The revivalism that began to occur around this period of the 1950s inspired the search for the new 'African personality.' African intellectuals began to question the image of the African long sustained in the canons of western scholarship and journalism, as 'primitive and cultureless,' views held in the powerful novels and writings of the nineteenth century, which were promoted to justify Europe's 'civilizing mission' in Africa. A new sense of freedom and autonomy was sweeping through the African continent in the closing years of colonialism.

By 1956, talks about independence for Nigeria from Great Britain were at the final stages. A transitional government was soon to be elected. Okigbo's generation of university educated Nigerians began to enter the civil service, preparing to take over administrative functions from the British colonial officers. The year 1957 was the culmination of a transition period which had begun in 1948, when Sir John McPherson appointed a commission to make recommendations about the recruitment and training of Nigerians for senior positions in government service. Prior to then, only a handful made it to the administrative service: Simeon Adebo was the first Nigerian to be so appointed in 1946; Pius Okigbo had been appointed Development officer in 1947; and the Oxford-trained Abdulaziz Attah, was posted to Southern Cameroon in 1948.

Christopher Okigbo left the Unilever group (UAC) in March 1957 and entered the colonial bureaucracy. According to Harriman, 'The letter from Lord Trenchard designated us as Trainee Managers. But we were not treated as such. We were just marking time.'[13] The policy of Nigerianization was proceeding more rapidly in the public sector, and there was a greater need for university graduates in the civil service. The government therefore sent out a warrant for all graduates who had held government bonds and scholarships at Ibadan. Leslie Harriman said, 'We were at home one day when Peter Chigbo came to announce that the government was looking for us all to serve out our bonds.' Positions in the administrative service also conferred a greater sense of dignity – a view that was confirmed by another Ibadan contemporary Ikpehare Aig-Imhokhuede: 'In those years, the stints with NTC or UAC were regarded as play, quite like extending your youth. One was regarded to have settled down when one took a civil service position. You became more stable and put an eye towards a career.'[15]

Aig-Imokhuede himself had entered journalism by chance. He was hired as a features editor in 1956 by the *Daily Times*, then a Nigerian subsidiary of the London *Mail* group. After taking a general Bachelor of Arts degree from University College, Ibadan. Aig-Imokhuede wanted to take a full honors degree in English. Leeds University had offered him a place with a scholarship guaranteed by the new government in the Western region. But he found that he was enjoying journalism, and so he chose to forgo his scholarship to Wole Soyinka, his best friend at University College, Ibadan, to do his English honors at Leeds. By the time Ibadan signed on Professor Molly Mahood to begin the English honors program, Aig-Imokhuede had committed to a full time job with the *Daily Times* in 1956. He was also writing book reviews for the Nigerian Broadcasting Service, where Chinua Achebe was already talks producer. One of the books he reviewed was the new rage in literary circles at the time – Richard Wright's *Black Power*. 'It was the subject of a lot of talk in the intellectual circles in Lagos, particularly because of its criticism of the cults of power in Ghana and decolonizing Africa.'[16] Aig-Imokhuede recalled the literary and cultural mood of Lagos in that period of the 1950s: 'It was made up of a little circle of educated friends and colleagues; close peers really. Most of us were recently from the University College, Ibadan, and doing things in Lagos. I was writing leaders for the *Times*. Chinua (Achebe) was talks producer at NBC. Chris (Okigbo) was just busy having fun. He had moved to the Federal Ministry of Information. Ralph Opara arrived in Lagos and started in radio. Soon we were producing the famous radio play 'Save Journey' – Ralph and myself were doing the scripts. It was a hit. Peter Chigbo sometimes acted in the radio play. It was an intense place…'[17]

Christopher Okigbo and his friends were the very first set of graduates from the University College, Ibadan to join the colonial civil service in 1957 as Administrative Officers. He was soon deployed as an Assistant Secretary at the Federal Ministry of Information and Research. The rapid disengagement of colonial authority meant that more power was given to Nigerians. The departmental system of the colonial government had been effectively abolished in 1954 to be replaced with ministries, with ministers as their political heads. Nigerians had started taking such positions as ministers in the transition government. A Nigerian head of government, Tafawa

Balewa, had been appointed to lead a coalition government in Lagos. Full political independence was only three years away. There was so much going on. The 1957 London constitutional conference gathered the various leaders of Nigeria's political parties to write the independence constitution. In that year, Ghana had become the first African country to achieve independence. The celebration was deafening. The reality came upon Nigerians that liberty from colonial Great Britain was imminent.

The colonial administrative service was, however, still very elitist, admitting only a handful of young Nigerian graduates. Thus many of the first products of the University College, Ibadan came to embody this cast of the national elite in the post-Second World War nationalism that shaped them. Okigbo and his generation became the direct beneficiaries of the colonial program of transition. Leslie Harriman for instance, became the Assistant District Officer for Lagos in 1957. Before his time, the ADO, Lagos, was a position that was a designated a 'European post.' The significance of these changes for young Nigerians, trained in the traditions of British-type public schools and universities at Cambridge, Oxford and University College, Ibadan, was that they had been prepared to rule. Others of Okigbo's contemporaries were recruited in 1957 to administrative positions: Peter Chigbo, George Nwanze, Tim and Godfrey Eneli. Philip Asiodu and Allison Ayida, both classmates at King's College, Lagos, returned home after their studies in Oxford to be appointed. Many were products of the exodus to America, begun by the 'Argonauts', a group of Nigerians motivated by Nnamdi Azikiwe to seek education in America after the Second World War. The political scientist, Dr. Eme Awa, was Okigbo's colleague at the Federal Ministry of Information. He had returned after teaching as Assistant Professor of Politics at the State University of New York. Years later Eme Awa became Professor of Political Science at the University of Nigeria, Nsukka and then chairman of the Federal Electoral Commission in the Ibrahim Babangida years. But in 1957 he was appointed Senior Assistant Secretary – a cadre above Okigbo and the other new entrants. As senior service men they were entitled to subsidized homes at the low density European quarters of Ikoyi. They also had expense accounts at Kingsway and Leventis stores, the huge departmental chains. It was a comfortable life.

At that time, the colonial city of Lagos had not yet spread to the mainland. The Carter Bridge separated those two parts of the city. Years later, Lagos broke into a sprawling metropolis. Okigbo's Lagos of the 1950s was an organic urban space in which the small network of elite society was easy to identify. Gossip was rife. Celebrity was instant. There was still a distinct 'Lagosness' with its complicated ruses, its many broken images, and its unique contradictions. It was festive with highlife music; it felt celebratory with independence on the horizon.

Okigbo rented a house on Igbosere Road, in the city center. Not very far away from Igbosere was the Isale-Eko neighborhood, the nerve of city life in inner-city Lagos that harbored an acute social energy. It was the Harlem of colonial Lagos. Not far away was Ikoyi, subdued and exclusive, a vast European reservation with its elegant ambience and former norm of segregation. Okigbo felt able to capture the smells and the color of life among the 'mad generation.' It gave him a window into the soul of the city. He experienced life in 'the high society' of Lagos – the experiential source of the theme of 'Debtor's Lane.' There were colorful all night parties, with festive and exuberant drumming, often lasting a whole week: this festive aspect of the inner city stole the sanctity of the open air, from dusk to dawn of colonial Lagos. Igbosere Road gave Okigbo a panoramic view of colonial city life and the contradictions within its active social space. Okigbo actually refused an allocation of a house on McDonald

Avenue, in the low density Ikoyi area, preferring the busier part of the city. He wanted to be closer to the warmth of people, the laughter of the streets, the common pleasures of Lagos society in the 1950s. The life of colonial Lagos was not conducive to the contemplative life. Okigbo was busy constructing an identity as a city socialite, civil servant and businessman. In such a turbulent, socially charged ambience, Okigbo's ambition was not to be poet.

His home, was a rambling, one storey building at the junction between Igbosere Road and Hawley Street, behind the Supreme Court building. He shared the apartment briefly with his friend, Philip Asiodu, who had returned from Oxford University and was also an Assistant Secretary in the Ministry of Economic Development. The journalist Ignatius Atigbi suggested the location, since it was a convenient distance from his office at the Government Secretariat and close to his friends, Sonny Odogwu and T.A Braithwaite in Hawley Street. They were both starting out in the insurance business and already had their eyes on big finance. What they all shared in 1957 was ambition to create huge financial empires. Odogwu and Braithwaite apparently influenced Okigbo's abiding interest in big business. Okigbo was intrigued by great fortunes. As Philip Asiodu put it 'Christopher was contemplating all sorts of business schemes ... he just loved the wheeling and dealing that went on in Igbosere in those days.'[18] This pursuit of pleasure and wealth marked the high hopes of Africans in the era of independence.

It was indeed the age of highlife, with its percussion, its fast paced, soulful beats, its swing and its 'sherikoko'[19] insouciance. It celebrated the erotic. Much of that spirit is captured in the city novels of Cyprian Ekwensi, who had trained as a pharmacist. Ekwensi's first full-length novel *People of the City* had been published to great acclaim in 1954, and he had begun a career in the government information service. 'Lagos was one big festival. The background music was highlife. It was the sound that said "everything is possible, enjoy life",'[20] Cyprian Ekwensi noted.

It was in this social ambience that Okigbo began work at the Federal Ministry of Information and Research in what was arguably the busiest department of government in the period. Okigbo encountered the spirit of the new nation being born, and came to be a particularly close witness of the drama of social and political change in Nigeria's transition to independence. He loved his work as private secretary to the minister, the amiable Kola Balogun who was one of the youngest and most dynamic of Nigeria's emerging political leaders who animated the anti-colonial movement. He had been conditioned intellectually by the pan-Africanism of Nnamdi Azikiwe and by his stint as a newspaper editor before crossing over to England to read law. Kola Balogun had returned to become Secretary General of Nigeria's leading anti-colonial party, the NCNC. He had made his name as one of the main leaders of the banned radical Zikist movement. He had earned plaudits as one of the lawyers who defended nationalist agitators in their numerous brushes with British colonial authorities; these credentials came to play in his nomination by the NCNC as one of their six ministers in the broad-based transition government established in 1957.

According to Dr. Balogun, when he was invited to join the transition government in 1957, he placed an immediate request for a private secretary. One from the pool of English colonial officers was sent to him. But, he 'whispered', as he put it later, to the Chief Secretary of the colonial government, Sir Ralph Gray, to send to him one of the young Nigerian university graduates whom he hoped would then learn and grow through the system in preparation for a fully Nigerian Civil Service. That was how Christopher Okigbo came to work with him. Okigbo and the minister soon developed a working relationship based on mutual respect and admiration. Kola Balogun's lively spirit agreed with Okigbo's sense of adventure and the sensual. Many years later, after Christopher Okigbo's death, the former minister's recollection was vivid:

> When Christopher came to the ministry as my private secretary, we became very good friends. It went beyond the official relationship of a minister and one of his staff. He shared my dreams and I shared in his own life. We sometimes went off together and visited the same places; when my official duties allowed which I fear was not very often, because I suppose I was heading the busiest ministry at that time. We got along famously, however. I recall he visited me when I became high commissioner at Ghana. Chris was a highly intelligent and amusing fellow, highly intelligent! He was very open and very full of life and it was impossible to dislike or ignore him! There was a certain part of him, which I think blossomed into his poetry: it was the acute, passionate intelligence, which observed a world intimately, and with the remarkable finesse with which he did things.[21]

Okigbo was the minister's liaison man. As a political appointee, the minister often needed to maintain contact with the normal bureaucratic structure of the ministry. Okigbo was his channel. He planned the minister's itinerary, kept his diary and represented him in official situations in which he was unable to appear. Kola Balogun hosted numerous official parties and was guest at others. Okigbo was part of a bureaucracy at the Federal Ministry of Information and Research that was charged with setting up Nigeria's local and foreign intelligence services, its cultural infrastructure, and its agencies for dissemination at a most crucial moment of its transition to independent nationhood. He gained deep and valuable insight into the workings of government, the endless negotiations and indeed the contradictions of the emerging neo-colonial state. The political realities were often quite gruesome: there was widespread optimism about the impending end of colonialism, but the process of decolonization, the unresolved questions presented difficulties and contradictions which Okigbo perceived as dangerous to the emergent nation, and which he could not resolve. He was critical of the transition process. Leslie Harriman recalled many years later, 'One clear fact was that Christopher became quickly disillusioned by the civil service. He was always complaining, always worried by the manipulations which the British colonial officers, still heading the Nigerian civil service, deployed; he felt the dubiousness of some official policies. Certain critical questions were not clarified for him and he spoke his mind. You do not speak your mind in the civil service, and he quickly grew cynical after a while.'[22] His apprehension came from observing the contested results of the 1957 election and the hurried invitation of Tafawa Balewa, a key British ally to form the 'government of national unity,' the manipulations by key British interests of the process of political transition, and the emergent character of the indigenous political leadership. His disillusion led to alienation. Alienation led to the pursuit of distracting leisure. He was soon drawn towards a confrontation with the civil service.

Christopher Okigbo's years in Lagos are the bridge years in the evolution of his personality and poetry. They were the years of his ideological conversion from a member of the unconscious elite, to an engaged critic of the neo-colonial state. It was no longer enough to be simply symbolic. He gave up his quest for 'a great career' and sought the creative or imaginative life. It was the phase in which the tensions of his existence as a colonial subject resolved into poetry. Okigbo would not only fashion a creative role for himself in the emergent society, but he would realize his ancient calling as a prodigal who must return to his roots through poetry – to assume the creative role as Idoto's priest. He went through an emotional crisis, and came ultimately to a valuation of the worth of his life, of the factors that had shaped the deep conflicts of his personal life. He discovered poetry through a sense of rebirth. It was the phase that completed his cycle of spiritual alienation from this past – a past symbolized by Idoto, to whom he would later declaim at the beginning of his creative journey: '*de profundis clemari.*'

Okigbo's encounter with life in colonial Lagos, its high society and the 'mad generation', was to become in many ways a reflection of a larger dilemma. He was an individual struggling through an emotional crisis towards a full understanding of himself. The period prior to 1958 was marked by restlessness, as Okigbo expressed it to Leslie Harriman, 'in pursuit of alien gods.' A combination of events inspired his creative life in this period in Lagos. Although he found his voice later in Fiditi, this turbulent period led to his discovery of his creative consciousness. Okigbo's life in Lagos in the late 1950s constitutes a valid place to examine how it is possible to arrive suddenly at a conscious artistic clarity, how deep psychological shifts can become powerful forces in the life of the natural poet, and how tragedy, as in Okigbo's case, instigates a personal search to which poetry becomes a natural response. Is there an immutable law of poetry, one which accepts that a recumbent unconscious can suddenly awaken, possessed by a poetic power, or was Okigbo simply a sleeping genius needing the nudge of tragedy to awaken his dormant energy?

It is possible that Okigbo had contemplated the possibility of a poetic life as early as 1957. He told the Ugandan journalist Robert Serumaga who interviewed him in 1965, that he wrote his first poems in 1957. But the only creative work which seems to have survived from that period, according to Ben Obumselu, was his music and the constant translations he did from Greek or Latin poetry into English. 'He had a compulsion to do these translations.'[23] Okigbo spent most of 1957 working relentlessly on a musical score, which he wrote in his usual, unorthodox Dutch notation. He was trying to explore the possibilities of art and life, examining the progression of a traditional Igbo folk story line based on the trickster tale of the tortoise's heroic seduction of the great elephant, which he tried to fit into the expressions of the classical western musical form. He also played a lot of jazz and tried his hand at a few jazz compositions for clarinet modeled after Stan Getz. This background in music gave Okigbo's poetry its distinct, lyrical impetus and character.

Okigbo's fine craftsmanship, his technical dexterity as a poet, derives largely from his understanding of the harmonious structures of music and of classical poetry, which he brings into his conceptual strategy. His translation of the classics equipped him with the confidence to experiment on the poetic form when he began to compose his own poetry. For him there was an essential relationship between art and craft. By the time Christopher Okigbo abandoned music as a formal basis for his creative expression, poetry became the logical replacement with which he would incorporate the details of the life he lived. What he often felt in his poetry was that striving for sound, for music, for the harmony of the spheres. Obumselu reveals that Okigbo composed his poetry from some scansion in his head, which only he could hear or understand. Okigbo would write later in 'Lament of the Silent Sisters':

I hear sounds, as, they say,
A worshipper hears the flutes –

The music sounds so in the soul
It can hear nothing else[24]

He found it impossible to continue work on his musical scores apparently because he felt the limitations of music to convey his total experience of life. But he remained, all his life, sensitive to the subtleties of music, for music opened the floodgates of deeper feelings and emotions, animating his deep artistic instincts. He composed many of his poems with music in the background. He refers to this life-long fascination with music, in his interview with Dennis Duerden at the Transcription Centre in London, years later, when he had become a poet. That he became, as Chinua Achebe has said, 'the greatest lyrical poet of his generation in Africa'[25] owes something to his experiments with the forms of music. By 1958, late European modernism, expressed in post-war absurdism, was in decline after the flurry of the generation of angry young men of the 1940s and '50s. The African world and its unique experiences seemed suddenly to present a rescue from the sterility of modern literature written in the English language after Amos Tutuola's *The Palmwine Drinkard*, with its structural and linguistic 'quaintness,' was published by Faber in 1952. The vista of modern poetry was transformed in the works of the Senegalese poet, Léopold Senghor whose works came out in *Présence Africaine* with the Martiniquean Aimé Cesaire. The Negritude movement contained the ideological framework of a new African poetics. Africa was at the threshold of change. In Nigeria, the new generation born at the 'confluence of cultures' had matured through their hybrid experiences. In 1957 Ulli Beier started *Black Orpheus* magazine in Ibadan, which he co-edited with the German journalist and art historian Janheinz Jahn. He was soon to move from Ibadan to Oshogbo where he established himself with his wife, the artist Suzanne Wenger. But his impact as an advocate of the new literature and arts from Africa was already gaining attention. His mission was to try and build an interface between modern European aesthetics and the idiom of African art forms. His efforts gave rise to the Oshogbo art movement and the Mbari Club, two phenomenal contributions that deeply defined the emergence of modern Nigerian literary and plastic culture in the twentieth century.

Chinua Achebe had been living in Lagos since 1954 and working on the manuscript of *Things Fall Apart*. Achebe and Okigbo often met in Lagos in the evenings to share beer and talk. They often had the pleasure of the company of old school friends like the novelists Chukwuemeka Ike and Christian Momah, both of whom sometimes drove down from Ibadan, where they had taken positions at University College in the 1950s: Ike as Assistant Registrar under Mr. Nath Adamolekun and Momah as Assistant University Librarian. They too were aspiring writers. Christian Momah later became the founding Deputy Librarian of the University of Lagos and, many years afterwards, the Librarian of the United Nations in Geneva and in New York. One of his earliest writings, a short story, appeared in an anthology edited by Olumbe Bashir. Later he disappeared completely from the literary scene in spite of promise. These friends not only met regularly and informally, but they formed a community. Their informal meetings, their literary discussions, and responses to Aig-Imokhuede's reviews for NBS and the *Daily Times*, would later turn out to be auspicious. For these men, the literary and intellectual climate of the Ibadan–Lagos axis stoked their ambitions to become writers.

They had arguments. These seemed always centered on certain critical assumptions about the new writings from Africa. They were striving to arrive at their own interpretation of the African past and the African personality and what it all meant in the context of the post-colonial nation. Okigbo was one of the few people to see and read the manuscript when Chinua Achebe completed his first novel *Things Fall Apart*. 'He was very excited by it,'[26] Alex Ajayi recalls. Okigbo also shared with the intellectual circle of colonial Lagos the notion of the emerging African writer who had to be an interpreter of the distorted past. It was a theory which had by that time gained much ground. Okigbo drove frequently to Ibadan to visit Chukwuemeka Ike, who was working on *Toads for Supper*. Okigbo's intellectual response to the the emerging literature from Africa was sustained through these associations.

It is often said that Christopher Okigbo's poetic genius was trapped under the urban disorder of colonial Lagos, but he was constantly seeking kindred spirits. Christopher Okigbo would walk into Chinua Achebe's office at the NBC buildings at Obalende or into his house at Ikoyi in the evenings. Or they often shared a beer at the Empire Hotel bar. He needed the closeness of friendship with his peers to establish his own artistic validity. With the turbulence in his own life, it is important to sketch how Okigbo was stirred into a literary career by a combination of factors: first by his sense of personal crisis when his civil service career abruptly ended, followed immediately by the ruin of his private business schemes. The sudden emergence of Chinua Achebe, one of his closest friends, on the international literary map created a sense of possibility, a sense of rebirth.

Before then much of the writing in Nigeria took the form of penny books, mostly moral tales and love stories, which sold among boys and girls in the secondary schools or among clerks in the colonial service. These booklets were mostly produced by half-literate veterans of the Second World War who came at the heel of the surge in public education in the 1940s. Nwoga and Obiechina would study this rise of the penny press, which later became known as the 'Onitsha market literature', as part of the history and sociology of modern African writing. Cyprian Ekwensi's first novella, *When Love Whispers* (1947), was a more sophisticated example. Changes were happening to modern writing in Nigeria. Amos Tutuola's *The Palmwine Drinkard* and Dennis Osadebey's book of poetry *Africa Sings* had appeared in 1952. Both books generated appreciative attention, although they were still essentially defined by western paternalistic criticism. *The Palmwine Drinkard* had attracted what a lot of Nigerians saw as backhanded compliments in the English newspapers at the time – led by Dylan Thomas' review of the book for *The Observer*.

'*Négritude*' began to assume a much wider importance in this decade, with notable intellectual champions like Léopold Senghor, Léon Damas, Jean-Paul Sartre, Aimé Césaire, Germaine Crispin and René Maran. They established a passionate credo, to explain and recreate the idea of Black Africa and its unique aesthetic. Okigbo, like many other younger intellectuals of his generation, was attracted to Negritude (as it became known in English). The Guinean writer Camara Laye's book *L'enfant noir* had just been published and in 1954 was translated into English as *The African Child*. Ikpehare Aig-Imokhuede had given Okigbo a copy of Camara Laye's book as a present for his birthday in August 1957. He read it with great relish and in his excitement after reading the book he had driven to Imokhuede's *Daily Times* office, to praise it in 'his typically extravagant ways.' He declared: 'I love this book.... I just love it!' Okigbo read long passages from the book to Imokhuede and the broadcaster Femi Lijadu. *The African Child* fascinated Okigbo in part because of the shared nuances of biographical truth which raised aspects of Okigbo's own childhood and life. 'The power of the innocent voice, the simple gestures captured, the sense of the pastoral past of Africa's pre-colonial life and all its norms; all fascinated and touched Christopher,'[27] affirms his friend Ben Obumselu. What he found in Camara Laye was that sense of a powerful, recoverable and 'usable past' and a nostalgia for vanished moments; its sense of a lost arcadia would invade Okigbo's early poetry.

Okigbo apparently saw himself on a productive career path in the civil service, in spite of his own misgivings about its operations. Okigbo was among a handful of Africans in Lagos who owned a car – which gave him mobility and social presence. As Ikpehare Aig-Imokhuede, who was a regular visitor to Okigbo's lodging on Igbosere Road, recalled, 'There was no indication that Chris did not enjoy that life of the civil servant. He was basically a normal civil servant. He wore a suit around. He carried on with the normal dignity expected of the colonial civil servant. There was no difference.'[28] But it does seem that Okigbo remained irresponsible and defiant of the conventional rules and requirements of the civil service. Aig-Imokhuede himself lived then in Yaba, on the mainland, but worked at the *Daily Times* on Kakawa Street, in the heart of the city on this island. He recalled his daily routine of driving every morning first to drop off a friend of his at the Secretariat, not too far from where Okigbo lived, then using the opportunity to stop by every morning at Okigbo's home before proceeding to his office. 'There was always a different woman every day I came, and Chris would be dressing up to get to work at 9 a.m.; and each time he would say, "Oh Aig, you can drop her off." Just like that. And I would.'[29] Okigbo was embroiled in numerous romantic dramas in which he often recruited his friends. On one occasion, Okigbo had requested that Aig-Imokhuede escort him to a girl who worked at an office behind Catholic Mission Street in Lagos. Aig-Imhokhuede drove with Okigbo to a restaurant on Marina Street. Okigbo sat behind on the 'owner's side' of Aig-Imokhuede's little Volkswagen with his girl beside him, and when they got to Marina, said to Ikpehare, '"Okay driver, drop me off and you can go for the day". Me! Features editor of the most important paper in Lagos!'[30] It was a source of amusement many years later for Aig-Imokhuede to recall how Okigbo, just to impress a new girlfriend, turned him into a chauffeur. 'That was no problem. We would indulge Christopher, everyone of us!'[31] Okigbo's many love affairs, sometimes conducted with such elaborate schemes 'just to lure the girls to bed',[32] were a regular feature of his life in Lagos. It probably illustrates a deeper psychological complexity, an inner conflict within Okigbo, in which women were to be loved and conquered at the same time.

In the midst of all his romantic schemes, he managed a busy official life in the work of the Ministry of Information. About May 1958, for instance, Okigbo accompanied the minister Kola Balogun and Mr. Stocker, a senior Assistant Secretary, on a foreign mission to establish serious bilateral and diplomatic relations with the United States and Canada when Nigeria became independent. The 1958 trip was a public relations tour, aimed at exposing the potential of an independent Nigeria to political allies and economic investors. Nigeria was on the verge of establishing its own foreign service, embassies and high commissions, and Kola Balogun's trip was the first step taken to present Nigeria officially to these countries as an independent country. As Balogun recollected, the Nigerian delegation held a series of meetings with trade and state department officials in the hopes of establishing an information office to act as the Nigerian liaison office to the United Nations, the United States of America and Canada. On his first visit to America, Okigbo was involved in conducting high-powered bilateral negotiations which led to the establishment of the Nigerian Mission in the United Nations in New York and the Nigerian Embassy in the United States. According to Kola Balogun, Okigbo drafted the protocols for the establishment of the information arm of the Foreign Service.

For that trip, Okigbo was also acting as the accounting officer. Ikpehare Aig-Imokhuede recalls meeting him shortly before they embarked upon the trip when Okigbo had come to buy travelers' cheques from Barclays Bank in the Marina Street office. Aig-Imokhuede remembers that while they were talking, Okigbo was absent-mindedly signing the bundles of travelers' cheques. 'I reminded him that he should be careful to sign the cheques in the same, regular signature or he would have problems cashing them. He was just signing away! And he said, "Oh, it doesn't matter." But when he returned from the trip, he met me, and he said, "Aig, you were right you know?"'[33]

On their way home, they visited Britain. It was on that trip that Okigbo first proposed marriage to Safi Atta, who later became his wife 'after overcoming serious, initial impediments.'[34] Safi Atta was madly in love but driven distraught by Okigbo's numerous infidelities. It was to grow more complex, more passionate and more heartbreaking. In 1958 Safi was on the last lap of undergraduate studies in England, and she often went to visit Christopher Okigbo's elder brother Dr. Pius Okigbo, then living with his family in Oxfordshire while was a Leverhulme post-doctoral fellow and tutor at Nuffield College, Oxford. At the time that Christopher Okigbo visited, Safi was contemplating visiting home on holiday before graduation. Her prominent family in Okene also had plans for her.

As it turned out, Okigbo was not part of the plan. He was also not a fulfilled man in the colonial civil service. The Nigerian Foreign Ministry was created in 1957, and Okigbo sought unsuccessfully to transfer his service to the new Foreign Service. The Foreign Service department in the Prime Minister's office had begun to recruit young educated Nigerians to be groomed under the British Foreign Service program. Advertisements were placed in the government Gazette seeking new recruits. Christopher Okigbo applied, just like a number of his close friends and contemporaries: Dickson C. Igwe, Joe Iyalla, G. Onyegbula, Olujimi Jolaosho, Leslie Harriman, Godfrey Eneli, B.A Clark, Philip Asiodu, George Dove-Edwin, Ignatius Olisemeka and so on. All these men were recruited into the highly desirable service. Okigbo was not successful. He had gone through the interview, and was not lacking in qualification, especially with his classical education. He seemed ready-made for the Foreign Service and had his hopes turned in that direction. Besides, he had been closely involved in drawing up the program establishing Nigeria's diplomatic service, through his work in the Ministry of Information and Research. Okigbo's failure to secure a position in the Foreign Service had a lot to do with the politics of that era. As it happened, Mr. King, the English Permanent Secretary at the Ministry of Information and Research, had written a not very flattering report on him for the board of selection. It seemed that Okigbo was far too independent of will, far too disdainful of defined administrative structures, and even perhaps far too undisciplined, to fit into the model of the British Foreign Service training.

The Permanent Secretary was the archetypal colonial administrator who had an abiding suspicion of politicized 'natives' like Okigbo, who frequently openly disagreed with him. Okigbo was far too direct in his handling of official communications. As Eme Awa, his colleague in the ministry with whom he was very close, recalled, 'Christopher spoke his mind too often about those things. He was almost tactless, because frankly he could not fit into the civil service with all its slow, secret bureaucratic burden and codes of silence.'[35] Leslie Harriman would remember years later the impact of this on Okigbo emotionally: 'He was deeply disappointed.'[36] His failure to join that first set of Foreign Service Officers quickly disenchanted him and inspired his sense of disappointment, which was later heightened by the resignation of his friend, the minister, Kola Balogun.

Early in 1958, a brewing political disagreement climaxed in the crisis which swept the minister out of office. Balogun's party, the NCNC, had been split over questions of political alliances in the transition government under the Northern People's

Congress Prime Minister Tafawa Balewa. There was also the question of the succession to the premiership of the Eastern region from which the NCNC leader, Nnamdi Azikiwe, was soon to resign to take up the non-partisan role of Governor General of the federation – father of the new nation. Powerful party figures had taken hard line positions on the key question of whether the NCNC would remain under the leadership of the nationalist leader Nnamdi Azikiwe or not.

The disagreements led to a massive party feud. When it was over, Kola Balogun resigned his position from the federal cabinet in which Balewa had already been installed as Prime Minister by the British Governor-General. A new minister, the Southern Cameroonian Victor Mukete, like Okigbo, an old Umuahian, replaced Kola Balogun. Christopher Okigbo was disappointed by the events, and it sharpened his personal insight into emerging post-colonial politics. Throughout the constitutional conference of 1957 at Lancaster House, he was Kola Balogun's confidante. Okigbo became privy to some of the classified issues that led to the establishing of the modern Nigerian state. The result was that he soon developed antipathy for the emerging politics, and ambivalence to the new political elite. His cynicism took root from being a witness at very close quarters to the intrigues of the unfolding nation.

With Kola Balogun gone, Okigbo's connections in the civil service weakened. His sense of ennui led to his desire to find a different kind of fulfillment through a pursuit of love and private business. Okigbo experienced devastating disappointments on all fronts. These factors came to define his sense of tragedy, and his search for a different kind of healing through poetry. His alienation from the 'mad society' of colonial Lagos thus began sometime in early 1958, and had roots in his failed ambition and in bankruptcy. Okigbo's ego was bruised, and he felt left behind by many of his peers, which hardened his disenchantment with the colonial service. His best friend, Leslie Harriman, was among those that went for the Foreign Service training to London, late in 1957. Philip Asiodu, with whom he shared the apartment on Igbosere Road, moved on to the Nigerian office in the United Nations in New York. By this time, Okigbo's work in the Federal Ministry of Information and Research began to suffer. As Professor Eme Awa recalled, Okigbo was getting restless; he would often come late into his office, take a sweeping look at his desk and would begin an endless complaint about long memos. He could be heard saying loudly: 'What's all this about long memos?' or 'Can't they make them short and readable? I don't like long memos... I don't have the time!'[37]

Okigbo had a habit of barging irreverently into the Permanent Secretary's office at the end of the corridor. Mr. King, tested British colonial civil servant, Oxonian and groomed through the routine of rigid British bureaucracy was astonished by Christopher Okigbo's candour and audacity. He was bewildered by the younger man's disdain for form. He would sometimes try to sit Okigbo down and give him a lengthy lecture on good conduct. Christopher Okigbo would then get up again to attend to his long stream of female visitors, and in no time would roar off in his car, away from the oppressive official stuffiness of his Ministry into the streets of colonial Lagos in his endless pursuit of pleasure and adventure. At this time Eme Awa and Okigbo were the only two Nigerians in the administrative grade of the senior service in the federal Ministry of Information and Research. Mr. Ogwuazor, an elderly midwestern Igbo, was an executive officer who was coming to the end of his career. He was one of the few who had climbed strenuously through the ranks from the lower clerical rungs of the civil service to the senior service position. He felt threatened by the first batch of young, highly educated men who had come into the civil service in those twilight years of colonialism. His years in the service had equipped him with a respect for the methodical, conservative order and routine of the civil service establishment. 'He was a careerist…straight as a ruler!'[38] was how Dr. Eme Awa, described him. 'He could not fathom Christopher's disdain for the time-worn civil service routine and regulation.'[39] A few years later, Eme Awa himself moved on to academia, where he had a distinguished career. At the time he worked with Okigbo, however, Eme Awa was one of the rare people in the civil service of those years whose background prepared him both with an insight into policy formation, and with the discipline of a researcher.

Eme Awa one evening in 1993 gave a vivid account in this period of Okigbo who respected him, '…especially what he called my energy for work.'[40] Awa recalled him as 'frisky'.[41] He said:

> Chris always struck one to be in the wrong place in those years. He had an amazing energy, a brilliant and acute mind and a real capacity to generate laughter. I was more or less concerned with my work. The minister, Kola Balogun, often took one aside to handle some of the difficult jobs, which although not on my schedule, he felt I would be better suited to handle, than some of the British officers. One significant occasion was the case involving certain cattle rearers, which I remember I had to handle at short notice to prevent a major crisis. But Chris was closer to the minister; they often traveled around together and went to the same parties and shared the same appetite for beautiful women and the adventure which their pursuit pertains. But it seemed to me, and I think I was borne out, that he was apparently out of place; he was not satisfied with the civil service and apparently had his eyes in other things. He struck me in those years as very frisky.[42]

Eme Awa was already thirty-six when he went to work in Information and Research. Christopher Okigbo, despite the difference in age, was able to relate easily to him. Awa, the conscientious intellectual and bureaucrat, was the direct opposite of the irresponsible Okigbo but became Okigbo's closest confidant in the ministry, in an environment that was getting more oppressive for Okigbo. He was fascinated by Eme Awa's methodical routine and sense of order and the fact that he could be resilient in the face of significant odds in working with the British officers. Okigbo was far less willing to be domesticated into the high bureaucracy. Dr. Awa said that by early 1958 Okigbo, feeling increasingly bored, had withdrawn completely from most of his official engagements. He would often sit alone in his office with his legs thrown onto his desk with files strewn carelessly about him. Sometimes, he would step into Eme Awa's office next door just to prod him into a debate, usually about the sterility of the civil service. Okigbo believed that the colonial civil service allowed little personal initiative. He thought a modern, post-colonial civil service should provide room for more creativity. He favoured a more democratic civil service, 'shorn of the colonial mentality', meaningless routine and blind rules that favoured careerism rather than integrity and imagination. He would give Eme Awa reasons why he would certainly not last in the system; always concluding with: 'I don't want to become Ogwuazor.'

He turned to business. As a businessman, he was a complete failure. He had registered Kitson and Partners ('Kitson' deriving from his first name) while still an undergraduate at University College, Ibadan, late in 1954, long before he joined the civil service. Many of those who knew Okigbo closely, even as an undergraduate at Ibadan, recalled his numerous business schemes which usually failed. He loved the drama of high finance, and the shadowy world of business. But he lacked the discipline and shrewdness of the hard-eyed investor.

A streak for business ran in the Okigbo family. The poet's mother had made a reputation as a wealthy businesswoman with interests in textiles. Even his brother, the economist Dr. Pius Okigbo, with an international reputation as a scholar, bureaucrat, diplomat and international economist, developed a successful private life as a businessman in later years. Okigbo's Kitson and Partners was driven by a sober interest: he wanted to supplement his civil service earnings so as to sustain his expensive lifestyle and taste for fast cars and exquisite women. He earned far less working for the civil service, than when he had been at the Nigerian Tobacco Company and at UAC.

By the middle of 1958, Okigbo employed an assistant to run the office at Kitson and Partners and he devoted his spare time to this private endeavor to make himself a man of private means. Kitson and Partners depended mostly on the goodwill of his friends. His role was thus limited to making important contacts, taking orders for supplies, and ensuring that orders were quickly delivered. The assistant carried out much of the daily routine business. It was not a big operation. For a short while, Kitson and Partners handled only a few supply contracts. Okigbo's next step was dabbling in the high stake export and import business. He had received what seemed like a huge order to supply copra. He began to put all his energy into Kitson and Partners, and this would soon become the basis of his troubles with the civil service.

To understand Okigbo's dilemma, it is important to describe the kind of murky business environment in the late 1950s. Capital was moving from the major financial capitals of the world into Nigeria in anticipation of independence. Many of the businesses registered in that period turned out to be bogus; great hoaxes, and brilliant scams used to seduce money from other shady interests in the occult world of international finance. Kitson and Partners was also such a perfect hoax. There were spurious gains posted and spurious returns. There were those who wrote elaborate business correspondences and cut fast deals from international business interests, many at that time seeking new markets and partnership in Nigeria and other decolonizing nations. Once one particular scheme was exhausted, they turned to other things.

Okigbo loved the great scams in this age of adventure, when young men began to see themselves, with the approach of independence, as the new business class. The stories of success were few. Many simply savored only the excitement of risk associated with international financial transactions, happy to be playing the field. Others had great ambitions, visions of wealth, and large appetites. Okigbo fancied himself no less an ambitious speculator on the make. Ben Obumselu recalled: 'Christopher was intrigued by that kind of business…the complex nature of international finance charmed him much more than huge gains,'[43] In other words, Okigbo was fascinated more by the brilliance of these scams and their sense of intrigue.

Many of these new business offices sprang up in Christopher Okigbo's Igbosere neighborhood. Okigbo's choice of home on Igbosere Road, the epicenter of commerce in Lagos in those years, was thus deliberate and strategic and in tune with his entrepreneurial ambitions. Igbosere was where ambitious young men launched new businesses in posh new offices shrouded in dark secrets. The energy of new business endowed the street with the aura of the raw energy of the ascendant generation. It was the most fashionable and upscale street in the heart of the city of Lagos in the 1950s. Igbosere road was what Allen Avenue became in Lagos in the later surge of business in the 1980s and 1990s – the nexus of the new, sometimes dark, uncertain business and the numerous shady schemes of urban Lagos. The neighbourhood changed rapidly as new wealth was created and the elaborate moneymaking schemes were hatched. There were some private residences, built in the beautiful Brazilian architectural style. Okigbo had leased such a building. He used the top floor for his domestic residential needs, and turned the ground floor into offices for Kitson and

Partners, which was incorporated as a trading and supplies company. Although Kitson and Partners was registered as an import and export company, it dabbled in every kind of business.

Ben Obumselu had come to work briefly in Lagos after graduating from Ibadan in 1957. He followed Okigbo's business interests closely. Okigbo did not have sufficient capital to run the business of Kitson and Partners. It was mostly a shoestring operation. He had fulfilled a handful of contracts with the UAC and to the Greek owned Leventis group. He had established some of these contacts while he was working for NTC and for UAC, before he joined the civil service. He started his business on the leverage of those early contacts to get some small supply operation going, just to keep afloat. He kept looking for his big break. The environment for business was precarious. The Leventis Stores, the major distributor for Coca-Cola, was one of Okigbo's key clients. Leventis had given him the first contract to supply the wooden crates for crating soft drinks, but it kept him barely solvent. Later Okigbo and the manager at Leventis disagreed over matters involving kickbacks, which Okigbo refused to pay. Obumselu recalled: 'Christopher's feeling was that the man had asked for too much and so he refused to give.'[44] So, although Okigbo had done the first jobs successfully, he could not go back for more. Kitson and Partners was thus barely surviving with occasional little contract jobs. Obumselu suggested that part of his failings as a businessman were because '...Christopher couldn't understand the whole point of business, as a rat race.'[45]

In August 1958, Okigbo had collected an order from Buzotti to supply copra to Italy. The profit would be handsome, and so he put all his energy and resources into the business with Buzotti. He borrowed money from the bank and from some of his close friends and family. When he came upon an unexpected financial twist, Okigbo did not have enough capital to conclude the business or a strategy to recoup or minimise his loss. He had purchased the copra, bagged it and was preparing to make the first shipment when produce inspectors tested the produce at the wharf, and found it to be very low-grade. Okigbo's inexperience with the highly controlled produce market and the complexities of the international commodities exchange proved to be a handicap. He had simply bought sacks of the dried cocoa seeds and put them ready to sail to Europe. By the time Okigbo discovered the implication of what he had done it was already too late. He tried to recall the shipment but it was only waste. Okigbo was ruined. He had tied his entire capital on the business in anticipation of great returns which came to naught: this ambitious adventure became a nightmare. Ben Obumselu, followed the progress and failures of his business ventures. Sadly for Okigbo he was relocating from Lagos to Accra to join the newly established West African Examination Council as its first Assistant Registrar. As he recalled, 'Christopher was enthusiastic, full of ideas about the business. But he was also completely amateurish in matters of high finance and investment...he proved to be too adventurous in his calculations on the Buzotti business.'[46] There was another complicated aspect to this venture which Okigbo's friends always hinted at. Ben Obumselu had described Okigbo's business relationship with Buzotti as 'shadowy.' Buzotti apparently engaged in other businesses like the arms trade. In the flush of decolonisation, such European companies with vast stores of surplus from the Second World War were seeking ways to break into new markets. The Nigerian market had been a closed field controlled by the British. International companies like Buzotti, seeking to break the British monopoly, courted ambitious young men like Okigbo who were set to run things in these new nations. That was how Okigbo met the Italian arms dealers and agreed to be their representative in Lagos. For Okigbo, this was his big break – a chance to get truly involved in the complex world of international arms trade at this important time, just at the dawn of Nigerian independence. Christopher Okigbo's first contract to supply copra to Buzzotti was a test case. He had calculated that he would make enough to put Kitson and Partners on a firm footing.

Okigbo was soon embroiled in a controversy with the colonial civil service establishment. One morning the executive officer, the elderly Mr. Ogwuazor, discovered the documents of Kitson and Partners, with Okigbo's private stamp as managing director of the import and export company. This was against the general orders of the service. Ogwuazor promptly wrote a memo to the English Permanent Secretary, Mr. King, who instituted an administrative process to deal with the matter. The Chief Secretary, Sir Raph Gray, signed the termination of Okigbo's tenure in the service late in October 1958.

Eme Awa contended that Okigbo had made himself a target of the administrative machination of the English officers because of his independence of mind. 'Don't forget' Professor Awa noted, 'that the British were carefully recruiting and placing people who would maintain their structures in Nigeria during the transition period. Christopher was far too independent minded and frisky. He was not their kind of material, so he had to go.'[47] It is not impossible that the British mandarins of the colonial bureaucratic establishment deliberately '…hurt an innocent man,'[48] as Alex Ajayi also said many years later. It may equally be not be far off the truth, as the poet M. J. C. Echeruo put it, that Okigbo simply 'made a capital mess' of his civil service career because he was the 'prodigal.'[49] Philip Asiodu later observed that Okigbo's business failed because he lacked the rudimentary discipline of effective book-keeping and late in 1958 he had no one to depend on: 'I had moved to New York, and there was nobody to advise him on his finances. I used to do that. If I was around, Kitson and Partners would not have run into trouble.'[50] Okigbo, in Asiodu's words, was too careless and impulsive to be a good businessman. Unfortunately, Christopher Okigbo's dismissal from the Civil Service coincided with the collapse of his business. It was a most turbulent time in his life. He was suddenly faced with an uncertain future.

The picture of Okigbo's life late in 1958 was thus not attractive: from a promising career in the elite civil service, he suddenly became a social failure and an outcast from merciless high society. The ruin of Kitson and Partners left Christopher Okigbo with even fewer prospects. Without his civil service job, Okigbo quickly lost his privileges. His credit account with Kingsway was cancelled. His bank advances were canceled. Overnight, the colourful socialite was faced with the loss of self-esteem. There was also a sudden twist in his love life: his relationship with Safi had been uncertain, mostly because of the enormous pressure exerted on her by her powerful family over their relationship. At the same time, Okigbo was carrying on an intense love affair with a beautiful Lagos girl, Ibilola Smith, who was working as a nurse at the Massey Street Children's Hospital. Okigbo's whirlwind love affairs had run into trouble for a combination of reasons, but now Safi's doubts began to affect him. Okigbo's immoderate infidelities did not seem to deter women from falling madly in love with him; perhaps his lovers were highly attracted to the vulnerable, mercurial and passionate aspect of his character. Okigbo was often too deeply drawn to the drama of sexual pursuit to care truly for commitment. His relationship with Ibilola Smith was the most serious of his love affairs in Lagos. However, it ended with his single-minded pursuit of Safinat Attah, an affair rekindled as soon as she returned to Nigeria in 1958. Okigbo pursued her fervently until she agreed to get married. Lola Smith later married a wealthy Greek Lagos socialite.

But his plan for marriage was upended when Safi's family decided that they could not trust Okigbo, whose future clearly was uncertain at this time, following the scandal of his discharge from the civil service. Safi was not without prospects especially as she was the first Northern Nigerian woman to earn a university degree. Okigbo was too much trouble. 'They felt that Christopher was too unsettled for Safi,'[51] Christopher Okigbo's eldest brother, Lawrence, recalled this situation. This combination of events put a lot of emotional strain on Okigbo and deepened his sense of alienation and failure. Broke, in debt, and jobless, Christopher Okigbo's suffered the greatest trauma of his life, compounded by perennial melancholy for his lost mother. In the aftermath of his failures, Okigbo slid into a brief period of depression. For days, he locked himself in his rooms upstairs on Igbosere Road. He became deeply disillusioned with life and, by many accounts, even contemplated suicide.

This trajectory of events in his life late in 1958 would nevertheless offer catharsis. Sobered by adversity, Okigbo abandoned the world of the great career, of the elegant scams of international finance, and the rat race of the postcolonial elite. He decided to lead a life of contemplation, the charged impulse of which would soon explode into poetry. The events of his life in Lagos provided the background to the poem 'Debtor's Lane' in which Okigbo contemplates the terrible options then left for him in his terrifying circumstance. These were real questions that confronted Okigbo between November and early December of 1958. Alex Ajayi remembers that it took days of sitting around him and gently urging him to look at other options to get Okigbo off the track of possible suicide in 1958, a possibility hinted at in the 'Debtors Lane':

*And if the phone rang*
alas, if the phone rang...
Was he to hang up his life on a rack
and answer the final call?[52]

Vicious gossip about Christopher Okigbo's dismissal from the senior service had circulated in the Lagos rumor mill. This event can be appreciated in the context of the fictional material out of which the novelist Chinua Achebe created the character of Obi Okonkwo in *No Longer At Ease*. Lagos society had scant sympathy for a young, highly educated African, like Okigbo (or Obi Okonkwo), who succumbs to the terrible conflicts of the colonial society that had created him. The furor over Obi Okonkwo's arrest and arraignment in the court in *No Longer At Ease*, was much the same as was created over Okigbo's dismissal from the 'Senior Service' in Lagos.

On getting news of Okigbo's travails, and quickly perceiving the impact of the scandal in the elite society of colonial Lagos, Alex Ajayi quickly came to offer comfort to his friend. He spent a few days with him at his now lonely house on Igbosere Road. Christopher's mood was one of quiet despondency. Ajayi quickly sensed that Christopher had come to a dead end in his career and offered him a new direction. He convinced him to join him in Fiditi, and make a clean break with his past life. A fresh start would give him time to sort out his affairs. It was a fortuitous moment. Alex Ajayi had just been offered the position of Principal of Fiditi Grammar School. The founding principal of the school, Chief Adeyi, had become a minister in the Western regional government under Obafemi Awolowo. Fiditi Grammar School was in its infancy when Ajayi took over its administration. He lobbied for Okigbo to join him as the vice-principal to build a great school – and to free the voice trapped within. Okigbo accepted, chiefly because he had no better alternative at that moment, but equally important was that going to Fiditi Grammar School was the kind of challenge which appealed to Okigbo's sense of drama. He moved on – and Fiditi saved him.

## NOTES

1 Interview with Alex Ajayi, Surulere, Lagos, 1992.
2 Ibid.
3 Ibid.
4 Interview with Leslie Harriman, Lagos, 1992.
5 Christopher Okigbo, *Heavensgate* II 1961.
6 Interview with Leslie Harriman.
7 Ibid.
8 Ibid.
9 Interview with Clara Harriman, Apapa Boat Club, Lagos, 1992.
10 Ibid.
11 Ibid.
12 Interview with Leslie Harriman.
13 Interview with Leslie Harriman.
14 Ibid.
15 Interview with Ikpehare Aig-Imokhuede, Lagos, 1996.
16 Ibid.
17 Ibid.
18 Interview with Philip Asiodu, Lagos, 19933.
19 Interview with Sam Akpabot, Lagos, 1992. 'Sherikoko' was 1950s slang for city ladies, made popular in the song of the same title by Sam Akpabot.
20 Interview with Cyprian Ekwensi, Lagos, 1992.
21 Interview with Kola Balogun, Lagos, 1992.
22 Interview with Leslie Harriman.
23 Interview with Ben Obumselu, Lagos, 1994..
24 Christopher Okigbo, 'Lament of the Silent Sisters', 1962, *Labyrinths with Path of Thunder* (London: Heinemann 1971).
25 Interview with Chinua Achebe, Ogidi, 1998.
26 Interview with Alex Ajayi, Lagos, 1992.
27 Interview with Ben Obumselu.
28 Interview with Ikpehare Aig-Imokhuede.
29 Ibid.
30 Ibid.
31 Ibid.
32 Ibid.
33 Ibid.
34 Interview with Pius Okigbo, Lagos, 1994.
35 Interview with Eme Awa, Lagos, 1992.
36 Interview with Leslie Harriman.
37 Interview with Eme Awa.
38 Ibid.
39 Ibid.
40 Ibid.
41 Ibid.
42 Ibid.
43 Interview with Ben Obumselu.

44  Ibid.
45  Ibid.
46  Ibid.
47  Interview with Eme Awa.
48  Interview with Alex Ajayi.
49  Bernth Lindfors interview with Michael Echeruo, *Greenfield Review*, 1974, Vol. 3, No. 4, pp. 48–59. Reported in Bernth Lindfors (ed.), *Dem Say: Interviews with Eight Nigerian Writers* (Austin: African and AfroAmerican Research Centre, 1974).
50  Interview with Philip Asiodu, Lagos, 1993.
51  Interview with Lawrence Okigbo.
52  Christopher Okigbo, 'Debtor's Lane' (1958). *The Horn* 3: 2 (1959–60), pp. 6–7. Reprinted in *Black Orpheus* II (1962), p. 6.

# 5

# *Poetry gives purpose to his voice*

## FIDITI 1958–60

Here rather let us lie in a new haven,
drinking in the air that we breathe in
until it chokes us and we die

('Debtor's Lane')

The year 1958 was most certainly Christopher Okigbo's *annus horribilis*. He had turned twenty-eight in August that year; at the prime of youth he was ambitious, driven – but suddenly a failure. He lost his place in the world. He could no longer maintain a gentleman's establishment, or keep a gentleman's easy manners; nor could he, as Malcolm Cowley expressed it, sustain 'the magnanimity of a gentleman sure of tomorrow's dinner.'[1] He had become like the garret dwellers of Grub Street, subjects of Alexander Pope's venomous muse in the *Dunciad,* 'whose lives were spent dodging the bailiff.'[2] To Fiditi he turned, and to the bohemian life of the poet.

The tone of 'Debtor's Lane,' the first poem he wrote soon afterwards, suggests that Okigbo contemplated suicide. But fate intervened in the form of Alex Olu Ajayi. Ajayi had nursed him back to emotional health, and convinced Okigbo to move with him to Fiditi to teach Latin and Greek in a grammar school for boys. Fiditi proved to be a balm on his wounded soul. This rural forest community lay twenty miles from Ibadan, the cosmopolitan capital city of the Western Region, on the way to the ancient town of Oyo, one of the important centers of Yoruba civilization. Fiditi was thus a gateway to both these cultural centers. Also Fiditi Grammar School lay on the main road to Ilorin so it was easy to commute to see Safi at Queen's School, Ilorin.

When Alex Ajayi came to Lagos he inadvertently opened the creative chambers of an intense and repressed genius. It is in the realms of possibility that if Okigbo had not suffered the shock of misfortune, he would not have discovered poetry.

Alex Ajayi persuaded the board of governors to appoint Christopher Okigbo as vice-principal. Okigbo's appointment caused disaffection. Fiditi Grammar School was built by the efforts of the Fiditi community. It was their pride in an era when communities competed to build schools, using community taxes and levies. A young graduate from the Fiditi community was already earmarked for the position of vice-principal and had been lured from a government post to Fiditi; the idea was to groom him to take over as principal of the Grammar School after Alex Ajayi's tenure. He was already acting as Ajayi's assistant before the issue of Christopher Okigbo's appointment came up. In spite of a lot of local opposition, however, Alex Ajayi stuck to his choice of Okigbo, with the result that the young Fiditi man resigned in protest. Alex Ajayi preferred to let him go. Ajay still does not regret refusing to succumb to the enormous pressure exerted on him by the board of governors and the entire Fiditi community. Ajayi said some thirty years later that in his judgment, Christopher Okigbo was a greater asset to the young school. 'He would convincingly prove this and justify my insistence to hire him.'[3]

Ajayi not only stood his ground on the decision to appoint Christopher Okigbo but he also negotiated a salary far above what Okigbo earned previously in the civil service. This was not an unusual practice for those years. Many communities which had raised taxes and built grammar schools in the Western region sought to attract university-trained teachers by offering them higher emoluments than the government offered. Rural posts were considered hardship posts because many rural communities like Fiditi did not have the luxuries and amenities that modern city life offered to the upwardly mobile university graduate. Because there was a real shortage of such highly trained graduate manpower, such incentives were considered crucial if the new schools were to retain them. Moreover, community secondary schools were often in competition with the better-funded government and mission schools that were constantly looking for graduate teachers. Ajayi also confessed a private motive in negotiating good terms for Okigbo: 'I wanted to make certain that Chris regained the fullness of his spirit. His self-esteem was very low. He needed real support in that delicate transition, to explore the fullest possibilities of his creative nature.'[4] Fiditi, with its sylvan splendour, proved crucial.

Freed from material and emotional doldrums, and removed from the social distractions of colonial Lagos, Okigbo blossomed. He arrived in a moment of self-awareness: 'I decided to be nothing else but a poet…'[5] he was to recall some years later in his interview with Marjory Whitelaw. Okigbo quickly discovered an aesthetic alternative to the concerns of the ordinary life; he soon appropriated the power of a deeply felt experience to navigate the tension of his individual conflict as a way of projecting its collective, universal significance. Poetry was a way towards a clearer spiritual and emotional resolution of his sense of conflict. He came to terms with the deepest crisis of his emotional life. Fiditi liberated him: freed him from worry, from the anxiety of his social failure, from the careerist obsession, from the lust for power and wealth. Fiditi provided him with creative solitude.

The students were away for Christmas break when Okigbo arrived late in December 1958. He had enough time to make a deep assessment of his choices and settle down, achieving a clear insight into his choices and into the nature of his individual conflict. The growth of the poetic impulse in Okigbo at Fiditi was the consequence of a sober distance from harsher reality. He was reawakened to the possibilities of a recharged, re-examined life. To quote again from 'Debtor's Lane':

No heavenly transports now
Of youthful passion
And the endless succession
Of tempers and moods
In high societies;
No blasts no buffets
Of a mad generation
Nor the sonorous arguments
Of the hollow brass
And the copious cups

Of fraudulent misses
In brothels
Of a mad generation.[6]

The contradictions of living in the fast lane of colonial Lagos of the late 1950s quickly dawned on him. He took the chance to reconsider his priorities and put his life on firm footing. It was in this general moment that Okigbo began to 'take poetry seriously.'[7] He came to understand his failure in terms of the physical and psychical alienation, which he suffered as an individual under colonialism. Colonialism had subjugated his true identity and emphasized his alienation from his primal roots. The consequence of this began to crystallize in Okigbo's imagination and his consciousness; and it soon found expression in the wry bitterness of 'Debtor's Lane' and the moral ambition of 'On the New Year.' Ben Obumselu asserts: 'Okigbo started writing poetry late in life, when he found himself in terrible difficulties; and those difficulties throw a light upon the nature of his poetic aims.'[8]

Okigbo's poetic ambition was to reconstruct his private history, to create a mythos of the self, and to stabilise his sense of identity. He saw himself as the prodigal, returning to the source of origin and myth. He assumed his new role – a creative role – as the priest of Idoto. His sense of alienation had been defined by years of Western, Christian education and his assimilation of an alien cultural value signified by spiritual exile from his ordained duties to Idoto, his family deity, the water goddess whose seasonal visits became symbolic in Okigbo's own creative cycle. It might thus be said that the original aim of Christopher Okigbo's poetic adventure was to find a way to come fully to terms with an identity crisis. His cycles of poetic or creative experience came to symbolize for him a sense of return to the ritual ministrations to the goddess.

Okigbo's generation was young, impatient, idealistic, and primed upon this new, emergent post-colonial society. Their dream was to enter a new history of modern Africa by adapting its resources to an African modernity. Their ambition was for great careers. When he moved to Fiditi, Christopher Okigbo was at the age in which he began to comprehend the nature of the interiorised conflict of the hybrid African, wearing the Fanonian 'white mask' on a black consciousness, derived from a culture in which he had been socialised to mimic an external self. Okigbo's acute, but fragmented consciousness rebelled against that social order. He had grown increasingly aware of the nature of a colonial self, and the imaginative conflict in a dual consciousness – the product of a highly modern European education on one hand, and the new allure of a return to his authentic Igbo ancestral mysteries on the other. His poetic aim was to reconcile these disparate worlds, to find order in the fragmented self. Okigbo perceived the ordinary facts of his individual life as inextricably linked, and inexorably transformed by that gestural performance - the symbolic return to his duties at the Ajani shrine through poetry, after his futile pursuit of the alien gods of Western civilization and the unmediated materialism of modernity. Arriving at Fiditi that lonely December helped him to clarify these questions, and to begin to untangle an existential truth.

Both in terms of its creative significance and in its intellectual sense, Okigbo's apprehension of his critical role soon came to be expressed as the poetry of reconciliation: poetry as a cathartic mode of experience, an act of ablution in that moment of intense self awareness that aided both aesthetic and physical healing. The poet had to move away from the social pressures and entanglements of Lagos high society of that period – from the 'sonorous arguments of the hollow brass' and the 'copious cups' and 'fraudulent misses in brothels of a mad generation;' and sought healing in the primal, pastoral, Virgilian silence of the woods, the breadth of which he first captures in the earliest poem of that period, 'Debtors Lane'. He had also turned to Eliot. Ben Obumselu said in a lecture in 1996:

> Eliot was a particularly appropriate choice for a man in Okigbo's situation. For he spoke about the emptiness of all worldly striving, about the wreckage, which litters the shore of time, about the soundless, withering and wailing of life. It was heart-warming to identify with this distinguished writer who repudiated all the enterprises from which Okigbo had just retired. With its intellectual refinement, its casual references to German, French, Italian, Latin and Greek literatures in the original languages, its acquaintance with the Bhagavad-Gita, Dante, St. Augustine and the chants of Siberian shamans, its unsettling existential wit, its mastery of both expository and lyrical poetic forms, Eliot's poetry both tranquilized the heart and stimulated Okigbo's active emulation... Eliot speaks about the glorious life of the spirit; and this could easily become, for Okigbo, a continuation of the romantic dreaming which vitiated everything he attempted. The change from sport, dream business empires and dream loves to poetry could easily be no change at all. By hindsight we can see that writing poetry changes Okigbo's life by giving a legitimate outlet to the turbulent poetic stream in his nature.... [9]

This sense of coming to terms, of renewal, coinciding with the emergence of a new nation, implied the retrieval of a lost world, and of an innocent and romantic past. A reconnection with that past, Okigbo felt, would sustain the spiritual foundations of a new self, inscribed in the myths of the new nation. By calling upon the power of a mystical past, and by re-inventing himself in the personal sense, there was also an implied sense of collective recovery. The bruised past healed. Its conflict reconciled.

Okigbo's view of his role as a poet in the emerging post-colonial society was transformed by adversity. His conception of the self became linked to the psychic, the imagined, and the spiritual path to Idoto. Although he remained nominally Roman Catholic, his views of his Christianity had evolved over time. By the time he arrived in Fiditi, he had achieved a creative ambivalence to his Catholic faith, although it remained a powerful symbolic influence in his life. Perhaps this explains the circumstance of his poetry, the unique presence of both the Christian Catholic as well as the Igbo ritual symbolism that he integrated into the architecture of his poetry. As he later revealed to Marjory Whitelaw, Okigbo adopted a private, syncretic religion woven into the needs of poetry. He had discarded religious orthodoxy; his conviction became influenced by a need to mediate a creative life, to establish a balance between the pagan impulses of his imagination, and the Christian tensions in his life within a modernist aesthetics. The result was his adoption of a form of moral relativism, a non-absolute view of the world, a form of syncretism, which through poetry revealed – an Okigboan universe, at once secular, epicurean and deeply spiritual. In this manner his life as a poet reordered and recorded his spiritual transformation.

Okigbo's poetry represented a return to his primal space of community and ritual – to mother Idoto. Sunday Anozie affirms this when he writes that Okigbo's poetry '...is born of the conflict between a mythological and religious imagination and a sense of the inorganic and phenomenal in nature.'[10]. Here, Idoto – the watermaid – had found her prodigal, in retreat from a fragile world. His life in ruins. His sense of his place in the new society, uncertain. But having resolved to be 'nothing else but a poet,' late in that December 1958, Okigbo began to assume, in a symbolic sense, his priestly duties, a fact he was to clarify later on in his life:

124

I am believed to be a re-incarnation of my maternal grandfather who used to be the priest of the shrine called 'Ajani,' where Idoto the river goddess is worshiped. This goddess is the earth mother, and also the mother of the whole family. My grandfather was the priest of this shrine, and when I was born, I was believed to be his re-incarnation, that is, I should carry on his duties. And although some one else had to perform his functions, this other person was only, as it were, a regent. And in 1958 when I started taking poetry seriously, it was as though I had felt a sudden call to begin performing my full functions as the chief priest of Idoto.[11]

Here early in January 1959, Okigbo fully establishes the psychological context for his poetry. He also chose to face the truth of his own life. He emerged from introspection towards discovery, from self-doubt towards epiphany: he, in much the same sense as his contemporary, the Congolese poet Felix Tchicaya U Tam'si, who also in seeking a resolution to his own alienation from roots, and the fragmented self, chose 'to be a pagan at the pagan renewal of the world.'[12] Okigbo had turned fully to the imaginative life, 'to assume a fantasy of the other self',[13] as his brother Pius Okigbo put it.

For a more crucial understanding of the origin of Okigbo's poetic life it is thus important to examine the central ideal of his poetry. First, he saw poetry as a means of healing. There is the possibility of an early Freudian influence. There were also other practical considerations, which began to motivate Okigbo towards a vocation in poetry. He had come to Fiditi resolved to begin life anew as an intellectual; he needed to wear a new personal guise, to remold himself in the image of a scholar-poet, and his immediate model was one of those men who had inspired him greatly in his younger days as a schoolboy at Umuahia – the Australian Charles W. Low, whose unorthodox sense of the extraordinary Okigbo had always found enchanting. There are close parallels: like Low, Okigbo had studied the classics, taught Latin, was a passionate cricketer, lived a bohemian life and was fascinated by poetry. Low also had left great prospects in Melbourne after graduating from both the universities of Melbourne and from Cambridge to teach in a boarding school for boys in the 'colonial outback' of rural Umudike ten miles outside Umuahia township. Low had left Umuahia in 1952, while Okigbo was at Ibadan, to become the pioneer principal of the Government College, Afikpo. Similarly, Okigbo had turned his back on cosmopolitan Lagos to live in a rural environment, and teach Latin and Greek in a boarding grammar school for boys. As he told his friend Leslie Harriman who came to visit him, his great motivation in Fiditi was to do something worthwhile with his life to justify every opportunity he had been given. If he could help inspire some younger people – as Charles Low had inspired him in the 1940s – that would be enough for him. It is part in imitation of Low that he abandoned the prospects of a degree in science to study for honors in Classics at Ibadan. Okigbo sometimes struck people, who encountered him less intimately, as over-indulged and spoilt and as even quite intolerably self-regarding; the carefree individual with a scant sense of responsibility. It would have been surprising to those who knew him then that uppermost in Okigbo's mind late in 1958 was the need to be a role model – to justify his own sense of worth.

Okigbo's bohemianism was a revolt against the rat race, the stuffy manners and venality of middle-class society; the false propriety and the fake domesticity of its emergent money grubbing elite. Lagos had been the haunt of affectation and all kinds of scams; Fiditi offered a simple life. It offered above everything else, the solitude necessary for the reflective life and for seducing the muse of memory. It is apparent that Okigbo absorbed the ideas and spirit of the bohemian cult at this stage of his life, as articulated in Malcolm Cowley's summary in 1934 of the bohemian spirit in his book *Exiles Return*: (1) the idea of the child in you, whose recuperation from the suppression of a cruel past saves and re-endows the creative self; (2) the idea of self-expression – each man's, each woman's purpose in life is to express himself, to realize his full individuality through creative work and beautiful living in beautiful surroundings; (3) the idea of paganism – the body is a temple in which there is nothing unclean, a shrine to be adorned for the ritual of love; (4) the idea of living for the moment – it is stupid to pile up treasures that we can enjoy only in old age, when we have lost the capacity for enjoyment. Better to seize the moment as it comes, to dwell in it intensely, even at the cost of future suffering. Better to live extravagantly, gather the rosebuds 'burn my candle at both ends...it gives lovely light;' (5) the idea of liberty – every law, convention or rule of art that prevents self-expression of full enjoyment of the moment must be shattered and abolished. Puritanism is the great enemy. The crusade against Puritanism is the only crusade which free individuals are justified in allying themselves; (6) the idea of the female equality – women should be the economic and moral equals of men. They should have the same pay, the same working conditions, the same opportunity for drinking, smoking, taking and dismissing lovers; (7) the idea of psychological adjustment – we are unhappy because we are maladjusted, and maladjusted because we are repressed, etc.; (8) the idea of changing place...'[14] in Okigbo's particular case, this is reflected in his cosmopolitanism; in his choice to live in Fiditi and be 'wholly free.' Okigbo stood, thus, against the conservative ethic of production and the moral codes of his Judeo-Christian upbringing. He was neither thrifty nor measured in his self-expression. His work ethic at best was spontaneous. His desire for the sensual, immoderate.

Christopher Okigbo had found a kinship with Alex Ajayi when they discovered a common interest in poetry. They were also age mates, having both been born in 1930. In 1958, Ajayi was the youngest principal of a school anywhere in the entire Western region, which gave him great prestige among his peers. As individuals, they could not have been more different. One, impassioned and mercurial; the other, calm and phlegmatic. It was often amusing to see the physical contrast between the principal and the vice-principal: Alex Ajayi, a well groomed gentleman, loose-limbed, standing at over six feet tall and unflappable; while Christopher Okigbo, whom he described as physically small, about 5 feet 4 inches tall, but possessed of 'a raw, boundless energy'[15] which made him formidable. Alex Ajayi was to describe Okigbo as 'a terrible rascal.'[16]

Christopher Okigbo's favorite nickname for his unflappable friend came from a line in Ajayi's poem 'Ode to Death,' in which the poet addressed death as 'inscrutable thou!' Okigbo addressed him thus whenever Alex Ajayi slipped into one of his stubborn moods, calling him 'inscrutable thou!' Sometimes Okigbo sarcastically called him 'principal' in mock formality whenever he felt that Ajayi was acting far more rigidly than was necessary. But they complemented each other in their work at Fiditi, and shared as Ajayi recalls, 'the dream of two highly educated young men, two idealists who wanted to build the best school around and live an intellectual life away from the bustling city...but as I think also, Chris was motivated more by a deep search for a personal form of fulfillment. He wanted to satisfy himself that he could do something with his life, and once convinced he went ahead and challenged his world...'[17]

An important aspect of their friendship is underscored by the fact that Alex Ajayi allowed Okigbo freedom and leeway at the grammar school, never made extraordinary demands on him, and freed him from routine chores. Ajayi allowed him to do much as he liked, to live a fully creative and adventurous life in Fiditi. Their easy friendship came from a mutual awareness and respect for each other. Alex Ajayi understood Okigbo's artistic temperament, his impulse for extravagant self-expression, as well as the depth of his emotional predicament in 1958. As he confessed many years afterwards, Alex Ajayi, when he first met Okigbo in 1956 in Mellanby Hall at the University of Ibadan had been struck by the quick wit and the extraordinary brilliance lurking within so restless a human spirit, and he had immediately realized that he was a 'tortured genius'[18] who had polyvalent abilities that needed nurturing. 'He had a sense of the elegant. The things he chose to do he did superbly...with breathtaking finesse. Chris was a natural scientist. But he was an impulsive scientist – too restless and impatient: he could have taken a science degree at Ibadan. But, as he told me once, he didn't want the Bachelor of Science degree attached to his name, which was the only reason why he did not pursue a degree in the sciences. He wanted to be known as: "Christopher Okigbo, B.A. honors," and that was why he had gone to take an arts degree in the university! But quite aside from all that, he was so well informed about everything. He was a pure genius, non-conformist, and an outlaw to ordinary conventions of morality, with a stubborn mind of his own.'[19]

Alex Ajayi's dream that he shared with Christopher Okigbo was to build Fiditi Grammar School into one of the finest boarding schools in the entire Western region of Nigeria. By the time they both left in 1960, Alex Ajayi's achievement in only two years came to be recorded as the golden moment of Fiditi Grammar School. The first thing they did was to introduce some of the traditions, which marked the unique character of English public schools. Okigbo's Umuahia background was invaluable on that score. Alex Ajayi wrote later in the *Daily Times* of how without Okigbo's contribution much of the achievement associated with the school in his era as principal would have been impossible. Okigbo was full of ideas, full of plans, driven. They spent many evenings discussing their ambitious plans, according to Alex Ajayi. 'Those were some of my best times with Christopher. His eyes, deep-set and passionate, would come alive whenever Christopher discussed any idea or plan that excited him. He would wake me up at very ungodly hours, walk down from his house with only a blanket wrapped around his small frame just to discuss an idea that suddenly occurred in his sleep!'[20]

Christopher Okigbo was a unique presence in Fiditi. His unorthodoxy invited curiosity. Many years later, even after his death, those who encountered him in Fiditi had vivid memories of his life in this small, rural town. An original and eager restlessness distinguished Okigbo's life – a life defined by too many complicated desires, which communicated much energy and turbulent passions. Former students and colleagues at Fiditi remembered his sense of humor, his lack of pretension. He had an easy ability to engage intimately with people at different levels. He remained stylish, cosmopolitan, something of an enigma among the students, as well as in the larger Fiditi community. The poet came across as a liberated intellectual whose eccentric ways became the subject of local lore. Okigbo's legend grew out of a bohemian lifestyle which marked him out prominently in the Fiditi community. Idowu Oshikoya, a Fiditi townsman who once worked in the Grammar School as a gardener, remembered Okigbo. Reflecting candidly upon his life, he concluded: 'the man had the most unusual of ways:'[21]

> We were surprised at how unpretentious and open he was. Here was a man who was the principal's closest friend in Fiditi. Here was a very educated and highly cultured man with a respectable background. But it meant nothing to him. He had no airs or pretensions. Sometimes, we decided that his ways were from too much book – too much awareness of the ordinariness of things. And too much book may have spoiled his head, as far as were concerned. But he was a very likable man. He was free with everyone. He would always come

around and drink palm wine with the ordinary folk in the village. And he will take those silent walks in the evenings alone, smoking his pipe as he went along. What I remember very well was the day he took my bicycle and went away with it for days. I don't remember where, but that man had a car, a red car, and I remember asking why he would want to ride a bicycle when he had a car. But that was his nature – he wanted to experience everything, to know and taste everything, even our women.[22]

Those solitary evening walks along the lonely paths of rural Fiditi would combine to inspire the early poetry of Christopher Okigbo. Experiencing the verdant, pastoral energies of the tropical Fiditi landscape opened him up to a power, from which his first poetic stirring would draw so profoundly. There are familiar strains or elements of the romantic sublime, for from those lonely evening wanderings, in moments invoked among the unspoiled Fiditi countryside are to be recovered, the first impulses of Okigbo's platonic unconscious stirred by the powerful force of nature. It suggests a search for the divine, for something external, and it remains present in all his poetry. The Fiditi ambience animated the genius of a repressed imagination. We hear in the echoes of the Virgilian trope of the *Four Canzones*, a highly modernist conceit in its search for recuperative myth. 'The pastoral cast' of his poetry was searching for an escape, and locating his imagination from the troubled urbanized world 'of bailiffs' and telephones ringing off the hook from creditors in 'Debtor's Lane,' to the clear pastoral locale of 'A Song of the Forest,' collected in the *Four Canzones* written in Fiditi in the middle of 1959:

> *But you, child of the forest*
> loaf beneath an Umbrella,
> teaching the woods to sing a song of the forest.[23]

These lines coming directly from the opening lines of Virgil's *Eclogues*, in the scene of the meeting between the farmer Melibeous, who had just been expelled from his farm, and the Shepherd, Tityrus to whom he laments his fate, reflects a personal narrative of his own 'expulsion' from the metropolis. Sunday Anozie establishes this link in his early biographical study of Okigbo's poetry. Okigbo's evocative personality as a pastoral poet in Fiditi, apparently gained from his sense of ease, 'loafing' under the umbrella of a most fruitful land.

The publication in 1958 of Achebe's novel *Things Fall Apart* in London to international acclaim coincided with Okigbo's difficulties in colonial Lagos. As an event, it was also to prove inspirational, especially for someone like Okigbo looking for a new purpose in his life after the ruin of his career. It is easy to see how the appearance of work by his close personal friend would excite him. The novelist Chukwuemeka Ike placed the significance of the appearance of Achebe's first novel in context:

> When Chinua's book came out in London, it was one of a stimulating, inspiring experience. Suddenly, there was one of us who had become published, a living writer! It was suddenly clear to us that we too could write. It was certainly one of the motivations for Chris. We used to talk about it in one of the frequent times he dropped into my home or C.C. Momah's in Ibadan while he was living in Fiditi. But being Christopher, he chose the lateral option; he chose to be a poet. To be a poet in that period, late in the 1950s, was even more fascinating. Poets were romantic figures. Christopher was a romantic figure![24]

It was a remarkable achievement. Achebe suddenly proved that writers were not dead Englishmen, but were one's peers. The impact was immediate.

Christopher Okigbo's poetry flowered with the invocatory power of the lyric poet: the spontaneous eruption of his poetry in Fiditi revealed one of the finest poetic sensibilities of his generation. Before he arrived in Fiditi he hardly considered himself a poet. The relative isolation of life in Fiditi afforded him the occasion to awaken the enormous depth of his imagination and the desire for creative self-expression. That sense of the solitary in Fiditi – the demons of personal ambition and lust momentarily silenced – freed his ego and saved him from self-doubt. The effect of the Fiditi landscape can be felt in the deep Virgilian echoes of Okigbo's first efforts. Okigbo's original poetic output in the period from late December 1958 to the middle of 1960, collectively published as *Four Canzones*, suggest an early apprenticeship to the muse of renewal. These poems have an evocative pastoral ring.

In an interview with Dennis Duerden at the Transcription Centre in London in 1963, Okigbo identified the moment in Fiditi when he began to take his writing seriously. He had begun to experiment with the Greek and Latin poets. Ben Obumselu suggested that Okigbo had contemplated a translation of Virgil's *Aeneid* into English but had given up the idea in Lagos as too difficult. He had been too distracted by his social commitments to give full attention to the creative urge. According to Alex Ajayi, the need for poetry as a means of expression arrived suddenly to him as a revelation and it surprised him that he had something to say. Alex Ajayi was a close and important witness to Okigbo's first serious attempts at writing poetry. His later accounts equally affirm Okigbo's experiments in composition, by drafting his poetry originally in Latin and Greek, utilizing a great facility afforded him by his wide reading in the classics to refine the rhetoric of his poetry, then translating the work into English. 'I read many of his early drafts in Latin and Greek, and they were elegantly composed,'[25] Ajayi recalled. Indeed, Okigbo's brother, Pius, suggested that Christopher wrote better poetry in Greek than he did in English. Pius Okigbo's comment is notable, for though an economist he could have proceeded to an equally distinguished career in classical scholarship; he also had a wide knowledge of modern poetry. However, it is important to observe that Okigbo's experiments in the Latin and Greek forms at the onset of his career arose from the insecurity of a novice poet who felt a greater comfort in utilizing the classical forms of which he had achieved mastery from his background in the classics. Okigbo's beginnings as a poet were tentative and cautious, a reality which is obscured by the later blossoming. Okigbo's poetry remained incidental, until late in December 1958, when Alex Ajayi had shown him samples of his own poetry. The appearance of Achebe's novel, and Ajayi's manuscript aligned with the stars of Okigbo's quest for a holy grail – a way to communicate his painful experience by aesthetic means. Okigbo evidently always felt the dormant impulse to write. But when Ajayi showed him the poetry manuscripts it inspired the resolution 'to be nothing but a poet.'

Alex Ajayi had been writing poetry, influenced by the English Romantic poets. He had collected the typescripts of poems he had written as an undergraduate at the University of Durham – his Odes to Life, to Death and to Duty. The 'Ode to Death' especially touched Okigbo in a personal way. His initial excitement and response occurred because poetry was a new possibility: it was romantic to be a poet, and it was an extraordinary form of individual expression. There was not yet one outstanding modern Nigerian poet. Azikiwe and Osadebe had published by then, but they wrote in a Victorian form and they were mostly known for their political rather than literary life. Okigbo quickly embraced the poetic option, although with initial caution. He took recourse, like Dryden, in the roots and the structure of classical poetry and his apprenticeship was served under Virgil and Lucretius. But he was still wracked by self-doubt. He needed constant affirmation. Okigbo described his poetic life as 'a calling,' the imperative of which he felt through the close companionship with Ajayi.

Nineteenth-century English Romantic poetry suited the natural condition in which Okigbo existed – the romantic melancholia and the search for the sublime appealed to his artistic consciousness. Shelley, Coleridge and later Hopkins, awakened some dormant pagan force. Alex Ajayi found a parallel between the tortured life of John Keats and the life of Christopher Okigbo and was to comment years later:

> Christopher's life reminds one greatly of the life of John Keats whom we both admired and to whom I introduced him. He was one of those poets whose works we read together, endlessly, many nights in Fiditi. The emotionalism, the intensity of their lives is almost like a twin experience.[26]

From the beginning, Okigbo's poetry came to express the deepest nature of the conflict in the soul of his generation – the hybrid, alienated, and tortured consciousness trapped between two powerful cultures. He aimed to recover the spirit of an age and a cultural experience that was passing rapidly; to represent the nature of the conflicts in that new society struggling to be born – uncertain, individuated but seduced by hope. Perhaps this is the greatest value of Okigbo's poetry: that he was the first of his generation of poets writing out of the experience of the postcolonial to capture the spirit and the conflict. The anguish that marked his own personal life reified the cry of his own generation.

Okigbo's early experiment with the form and structure of Greek and Latin poetry came to bear upon the structure of his own imagination. His ambition was to find a mathematical order in rhythm, something he later called 'the logistics' of poetry. Okigbo was reading widely – Lucretius, Ovid, Virgil – composing and experimenting with the strict rigorous rhythmic structure of hexameters and dactyls; examining and trying to understand the rhythmic elements and the nuances of classical poetry – the syllabic variations and pulses, the spondee and the caesura – all of which afforded him the technical expertise he needed to differentiate and free poetry from the dross of daily speech, and to comprehend its relationship to mythic experience. He was fascinated by the choral complexity of the Odes of Pindar, their stanzas and sets of strophes and anti-strophes and their metrical scheme, the epode. He was also reading Horace and Catullus. He was reading with greater interest at Fiditi the metrical Latin hymnody, especially the fourth century 'Corde natus ex parentis' by Prudentius, the 'Dies Irae' said to have been composed by Thomas of Celano, and the processional 'Vexilla Regis' by Fortunatus. Wipo's Easter sequence, 'Victimae Paschali Laudes' influenced parts of *Heavensgate*. Theocritus celebrated the power and simplicity of rural, life over the corruption and artificiality of the city, which fitted Okigbo's mood at that time.

When Okigbo began work on 'A Song of the Forest,' it seems that the general model was Virgil's pastoral poem, *Eclogues*, with its setting in the imaginary, allegorical arcadia. We also sense the influence of the Odes of Alex Ajayi. There is a possibility, by comparing the classical structure and the tenor of the romantic sublime in Okigbo's early Fiditi poems, that Alex Ajayi's work accounts significantly for the poetic style which Okigbo chose at that time: allusive and metrically ordered. They used to read their poems to each other regularly in the silent Fiditi evenings. After every reading of the poem, 'Ode to Death,' Ajayi recalled, Okigbo used to say, 'Olu,' (he always preferred to address Alex Ajayi in his Yoruba diminutive) 'you know, this is good … fantastic!'[27] And he would dance around in his excitement, and in that distinctively Okigbo manner 'whenever he hailed an extravagance that delighted him.'[28] That creative contact with another poet, in the rural setting of Fiditi, was without doubt important in the evolution of Okigbo's life as a poet; it hastened his quest on the path towards self-discovery.

Okigbo saw the poetic life as a new way of existence, a mystical code for communicating his existential dilemma. It was also something he could share with his friends and laugh about. Self-discovery may have been epiphanic, but Okigbo suffered equally from doubts about his own abilities as a poet. He craved self-affirmation and the validation of his peers. It was a method he developed to gauge reactions and responses to his craft, to test his footing. His close friends were his sounding boards. He was thus very public, very celebratory of each moment and every fruit of his creative labour. He seemed always open and willing to share his work and listen to criticism. He was never, in his method, it seemed, capable of privacy.

Ben Obumselu however pointed out something even more necessary in our understanding of the deep doubts that plagued Okigbo as an artist, when he said, 'All that sharing was a way of arriving at something…it was not Christopher. His real poetry was deeply personal to him; he was in that sense not very public.'[29] That way of publicly sharing his poems before they were finished may have obscured Okigbo's deeper agonies as a writer who suffered from a serious crisis of confidence. But it also opened him up to an awareness of a creative purpose and a community of interest with whom to share, weigh the enchantment of his verse and fathom his creative purpose. Okigbo constantly aspired towards aesthetic wholeness and purity. It was a slow, cautious process. But once he had wrestled with the technical questions, Okigbo came to accept poetry as an important part of his own ritual of reconciliation with Idoto, through which he had to construct an aesthetic and philosophical basis for himself as an artist in a society in rapid transition.

Fiditi's intellectual and social life virtually revolved around Alex Ajayi and Christopher Okigbo. The Grammar School was the major institution in the town, and there was not much else, in terms of cultural life. Okigbo and Ajayi therefore tried to create an ambience conducive to the senses; an idyllic world remote from the rush, the material and social distraction of the city. 'Our own little Bloomsbury,'[30] Alex Ajayi called it. They decided, as part of their efforts to keep in touch with the cultural life evolving rapidly in the metropolis, especially with the University College, Ibadan not too far away, to invite significant intellectual and cultural figures to spend time with them and to give talks to the Fiditi boys. They encouraged visiting writers, scholars, diplomats, and artists, to spend convivial evenings, weekends or even terms at Fiditi. It suited Okigbo and his longing for social intercourse. Alex Ajayi put it quite simply: 'We reckoned that it would be important to stimulate the interests of boys at the Grammar School by exposing them to the makers of current events, and a large breadth of fresh ideas; we thought we could accomplish this by inviting important members of our generation, the new intellectual elite to share with us the splendour of rural Fiditi. We also gained personally from the interaction; were saved from any sense of isolation and social inertia by these regular visits.'[31] In the event they stimulated an exciting process, which connected rural Fiditi to the ferment of the metropolis. They turned a sleepy, rural space into a lively social and intellectual haven which saw the coming and going of exciting and colourful individuals who came to play significant roles in Nigeria's post-colonial state. Much of that interaction planted the seeds of modern Nigerian letters in the last half of the twentieth century. One of those who taught briefly at Fiditi was the petroleum chemist Patrick Amenechi. After graduating with a first class degree in Chemistry at University College, Ibadan, Dr. Amenechi came to teach part-time at Fiditi Grammar in 1959/60 year before proceeding overseas for higher degrees. Patrick Amenechi occasionally stayed over for weekends with Okigbo or Alex Ajayi in their flats. Sometimes, he would spend just an evening or a whole week in their company. Years later, Dr. Amenechi, who had become the Chairman of Unipetrol (formerly Esso Petroleum), recalled of those years with Okigbo:

> Christopher and I had been in the same generation at the University College. He was my senior at the university by a couple of years. He was in the Arts while I was taking my degree in Science, so we never really were in the same groups. But you'd never fail to notice Chris on campus. By the time he went to teach in Fiditi, I had graduated and was sort of, marking off time teaching part-time at the school, you know, never really being what I wanted to do. One thing I knew then was that Chris was teaching and reading Amos Tutuola's book *The Palmwine Drinkard* to his boys. That book really immensely excited him. I think the sheer unconventionality of it – he was endlessly probing the events and the structure of the novel. That was what essentially gripped him. He would often refer to what he called the child-like narration and would say excitedly: 'This is Art! This is very good art!' It was about then that he began his own writing. Things were happening. Achebe's novel had just come out. Chris was certainly moved towards poetry, trying to discover the inner beauty of Tutuola...[32]

From Fiditi, Okigbo was able to maintain regular contact with such close friends as Christian Momah and V. C. Ike, who were also beginning to cultivate the possibility of a literary life. Momah had moved from the Land Department in Enugu to the University College, Ibadan Library in 1958, as Assistant University Librarian, while Chukwuemeka Ike, had been employed since 1957 at the University Registry, as Assistant Registrar in charge of student affairs. Momah would give up on his literary ambition until much later in his life, after he retired as the United Nations librarian and had settled in the United States in Somerset, New Jersey, before writing his first novel; but he had already begun writing short stories in Ibadan. Chukwuemeka Ike was already working on his first novel, *Toads for Supper*, set in the complicated social and ethnic politics of a modern university in Africa. Ibadan provided the narrative canvas of Ike's story. One of the most exciting intellectual figures who came to Fiditi in 1959 was the surgeon Alex Boyo. Alex Boyo and Okigbo's brother, Pius, were friends at Oxford. In Nigeria Dr. Boyo became Professor of Medicine, first at Ibadan, and then at the University of Lagos. He was later appointed a fellow in Cambridge. Alex Boyo was already one of the most inspiring Nigerian scholars at the prestigious University College Hospital, Ibadan. His patrician state loomed in the imagination of the young Fiditi boys many years afterward; young Bode Olajumoke was so struck by Alex Boyo's impressive manners, that he began to imitate him and earned a life-long nickname – his contemporaries at the Fiditi Grammar School still called him 'Boyo', several years after Alex Boyo came and went from Fiditi. As Alex Ajayi recalled, it was Alex Boyo who first introduced him and Okigbo to the West Indian writer George Lamming from Barbados, sometime between late 1959 and early 1960. George Lamming was in Ibadan as a visiting writer at the University College where he was giving a series of lectures in the days preceding independence. George Lamming too was invited to Fiditi as guest.

The poet's brother, Dr. Pius Okigbo was perhaps the most electrifying visitor to Fiditi in 1959. He was invited to talk to the students and he gave a memorable lecture on life as a student in America. After studying with a Fulbright at Northwestern University in Evanston, Illinois in the United States, Pius had briefly been appointed as Assistant Professor of Modern Economic Theory at the University of Wyoming, and from there was invited as a tutor and post-doctoral research fellow at Nuffield College, Oxford. While at Oxford he did some work for John Maynard Keynes. Pius Okigbo was a striking intellectual figure of his time. In 1959, he was offered a substantial grant and installed in comfortable circumstance at the University College, Ibadan, under a commission to study Nigeria's macro-economic systems. He lived on campus in a flat on Saunders Road. The economist Dr. Aboyade, also doing his doctoral research at Cambridge, was his research assistant. It was an enchanted circle. Between 1959 and 1960, Pius Okigbo conducted most of this research at the Henry Carr Library of University College, Ibadan; but he was also traveling all over the country, gathering economic data. This research, using complex mathematical calculations for determining the revenue formula for Nigeria eventually led to his famous mapping of Nigeria's national income, which was later published by Cambridge University Press.

From Ibadan Pius became a regular visitor to his younger brother at Fiditi. For his birthday in August 1959, he gave Christopher Okigbo Walt Whitman's *Leaves of Grass*. On one of Pius Okigbo's visits to Fiditi, Christopher had showed him the first drafts of 'A Song of the Forest.' While they were reading it together, Pius Okigbo suddenly turned and said, 'You know Chris, you would make a great poet, you know? This is really good!'[33] It meant much for Christopher Okigbo that his famous elder brother approved of the progress of his craft. He craved that kind of affirmation from someone whose 'intellectual energy' Christopher Okigbo admired greatly. Pius always brought new books with him – especially of modern American poetry – and new insights, which he shared with him. While studying in the United States, Pius developed a significant interest in nineteenth and twentieth-century American poetry: Robert Frost, Carl Sandburg, e.e. cummings, Malcolm Cowley, Charles Olson, Stephen Crane, Wallace Stevens. Sometimes, Chris Okigbo and Ajayi drove down to Ibadan to spend weekends with Pius on Saunders Road. During such visits they would stay up all night with the economist, reading and discussing poetry, smoking endlessly, drinking strong coffee through the night. Alex Ajayi said of these visits. 'The air in those nights was heavily scented with something joyous and important that was going on. There were times when we talked and read poetry all night long; reading mostly the poets that Pius himself loved – Lowell's *Life Studies* had just come. And Pius often read him aloud. In those times we talked till the morning light met us'.[34] It was Pius who introduced Christopher Okigbo to the range of American poets whose influence can be glimpsed in his later work. We frequently hear the echoes, apparent connections to the black mountain poets, the confessional poets, the sublime madness of Robert Lowell and Ginsberg and the entire spectrum of Beat Poetry. But what fascinated and appealed immensely to Okigbo was the imaginative freedom – the rejection of moral cant, which the Beat poets expressed and symbolized in their rejection of bourgeois morality. It was at this time that Christopher Okigbo's conception of the artist truly crystallized. He conceived of the artist – the poet – as a liberated consciousness; one who lived at the boundaries of social morality, whose expression of moral freedom was limitless. The poet was the priest, the prophet and the outsider.

From thenceforth, Okigbo lived a life that was totally committed to poetry and to pure sensual experience. The artistic consciousness, he increasingly felt, was the product of an irrational beauty. It took possession of the poet even at unusual times. Alex Ajayi and Okigbo elaborately entertained guests who visited Fiditi; sometimes there would be dinners which lasted late into the night. There were 'sonorous debates' after dinner, over coffee or brandy or beer. Okigbo was a formidable raconteur, but sometimes in the midst of these debates, as Alex Ajayi recalled, Okigbo would 'enact his disappearing act' – he would get away, suddenly inspired, disappearing for hours to write undisturbed. He would emerge later with some new poem. It was a way of dramatizing his life as a poet: the muse was always to be wrestled with when it made its quick, brief, capricious appearance. The poet must be ready to receive her. Poetry was never to be taken lightly. It was an experience which Okigbo elevated to the magical.

Ulli Beier was also a constant visitor to Okigbo at Fiditi and in 1959 first introduced him to the German journalist and critic Janheinz Jahn, who was gathering materials for his book *Muntu*. Okigbo also drove down regularly to Oshogbo to visit Ulli and his wife, the artist Suzanne Wenger. Beier was already editing *Black Orpheus* the magazine which he had co-founded with Jahn in 1957 after the International Conference on African literature in Rome in 1956. Such frequent visits not only enlivened Okigbo's intellectual life, but also placed him strategically as a gateway figure among the emergent cultural elite, for such visits widened his experience.

Okigbo and Alex Ajayi also often visited the campus of the University College for cultural stimulation. The public lectures. The literary readings. The dinner parties. The May Havana. The nightclubs. Fiditi was well located, as a crossroads town between the north and the south of Nigeria. For instance, Alex Ekwueme had just returned from his studies in the United States where he had qualified as an architect and had taken a job as the Nigerian representative of Esso, the American oil marketing company. Oil had just been discovered in great commercial quantity in Nigeria, and Esso was trying to establish its presence in the country as an oil distributor. Ekwueme recalled that part of his job as Esso's representative required that he travel up and down the country. He often stopped by Christopher Okigbo's home in Fiditi, usually on each of his trips back and forth from Northern Nigeria. Ekwueme remembered how on each occasion Okigbo would load his car's boot with tropical fruits of all kinds, which were bounteous in Fiditi. 'He lived in a haven of tropical solitude, from that bounteousness of spirit his poetry flowed.'[35] That was how Ekwueme in 1996 described the ambience of the poet's Fiditi.

Okigbo's other numerous friends passed by Fiditi. Emmanuel Ifeajuna, who was teaching science at a secondary school in Abeokuta, came regularly. Sometimes Chinua Achebe would come from Enugu, where he was then working as the regional controller of the Nigerian Broadcasting Service, for meetings in Ibadan. He would use the opportunity to drive down to spend the weekend with Okigbo and Ajayi in Fiditi. When Achebe married his wife, Christie, at the Protestant Chapel of Resurrection on the campus of the University College, Ibadan in 1960, Okigbo and Ajayi were among his small circle of close friends to bear witness. In late 1959, Wole Soyinka returned from England after graduating from Leeds, full of new ideas and brimming with angst. Okigbo was one of the first people that Soyinka visited when he returned to Nigeria from Europe. He had worked briefly as a director at the Royal Court Theatre in London and had ambitious plans to start a theatre company in Ibadan. Soyinka began to stage his early plays, collaborating with Martin Banham whom he had met at Leeds, and Geoffrey Axworthy who was already at the University Theatre in Ibadan. With the pioneering work of Ene Henshaw, Soyinka's drama of that period constitutes the moving spirit of modern Nigerian theatre. Even in those years, Wole Soyinka was constantly in motion, traveling in his Land Rover jeep. He remembered his frequent visits with the poet in Fiditi. Okigbo, he said, was always a charming host:

> As soon as I arrived, Chris would say 'Ah Wole, with what do I entertain you now? Okay, wait!' and then he would go about trying to trap these straying fowls that wandered about his compound; he would catch one and he would make food. He had developed an elaborate system for trapping the fowls, starting by creating a hole on his wall![36]

The poet J. P. Clark also came around regularly. 'They would engage themselves in endless arguments on any topic under the sun,' recalled the sports journalist, Bisi

Lawrence who had been one of Alex Ajayi's student at Christ School, Ado-Ekiti, and had later worked under Chinua Achebe as a broadcaster. He gave a good description of Fiditi: 'It seemed like the place of pilgrimage...you were always sure to drop in on the intellectual superstars of that generation who were lured by Okigbo and Ajayi's presence at Fiditi; they made rural Fiditi tingle with the carefree joy of an enlightened time....'[37] The journalist, Ignatius Atigbi also remembers visiting Okigbo in Fiditi in the middle of 1959 while on vacation from London after reporting the Nigerian constitutional conference in London in 1958. 'I had just moved briefly to Paris from Fleet Street as Reuters correspondent; and when I visited Chris, he had just started writing poetry; and he was also interested in what was happening on the side questions at the constitutional conference in London which I had reported, and on the politics of decolonisation. We talked about such things: about the future of the Nigerian enterprise. Things like that. He was excited and optimistic like many people, but he also frequently expressed cynicism about the emerging political leadership. His role as a poet, he said, was to be a witness.'[38]

A new society peeped over the threshold. Although it held promise, the approach of independence was also a source of concern for many Nigerian intellectuals. The British seemed to be leaving without a fuss, but there was a deep sense of disappointment about the process of decolonization: the whole idea of independence 'on a platter of gold' negated the sense of a final struggle. Wole Soyinka has written about his own cynicism and how he expressed it openly in the theatre in which he became so active. Alex Ajayi himself was a witness to the mood in Fiditi:

> Some of us wanted to fight, to take our independence rather than be given. Endlessly at Fiditi, this was the talk whenever friends, like Emma Ifeajuna came. Okigbo and Emma talked insurrection. Like many other intellectuals, they thought that the British were leaving behind a troubled country. There was a lot of cynicism. In fact, it was possibly in Christopher's home in Fiditi that Emma (Ifeajuna) first decided to go and join the Army. He chose his destiny clearly, prodded and supported by Christopher...it was a revolutionary option.[39]

Okigbo had chosen to be the griot of that change, the poet chronicling from the impulses of his personal experience, the imperishable story of his times. The story of Nigeria echoes perpetually in his Fiditi poetry. Okigbo, the poet-priest of the conflict generation, was always part of this unique story. Idoto had claimed her child, her prodigal once lost to alien gods, had returned by indirection, by the same forest routes.

On a visit to Okigbo in Fiditi in 1959, Leslie Harriman remarked that he had heard that Okigbo was fully engaged in his poetic vocation. 'I'm told you're now a poet!' Harriman said. Okigbo waved it aside, saying: 'Don't mind them. All I did was to change "daffodils fluttering in the breeze" to "plantain leaves dancing in the wind." And now, they say I'm a poet!'[40] The two friends had a good laugh. However, this comment illustrates a remarkable expression of Okigbo's artistic humility. It was in part an acknowledgement of his limitations as a poet. Okigbo was always ready to acknowledge his indebtedness to diverse sources and influences, although the appearance of other great voices in his poetry merely illuminated his imaginative universe. This is what critics of his works have come either to acknowledge as the 'cosmopolitan spirit' of his poetry, or like Michael Echeruo to deride it as 'awkward plagiarism.'[41]

Okigbo's tendency to borrow from other poets, was once described by his brother Pius as 'piratical.' But when he did, Christopher Okigbo stole with genius and originality, and managed to transform each work within his own poetic landscape into one of a universalist reaching for metaphors – his need to domesticate alien idioms and alien landscapes into something memorable and familiar. The 'poplars' for instance that do not grow in tropical Africa find their place suddenly within it. The image of 'the shrub among the poplars needing more roots, more sap to grow to sunlight, thirsting for sunlight...'[42] evokes an impressive ecology of the spirit and the psyche. He had apparently accepted the axiom that, as Ben Obumselu put it, 'what constitutes literary greatness is not a work's cultural authority – the degree to which it sums up, or represents its writer or its moment – but rather, its strangeness, the degree to which it is unlike anything that came before it.'[43] This in an important way sums up Okigbo's entire creative purpose. By weaving metaphors borrowed from other creative founts, and beaten carefully into personal levels of meaning, Okigbo's poetry extends the degree of its own uniqueness.

Okigbo had been at his dramatic best on the occasion of Leslie Harriman's visit to Fiditi, to give a talk to the boys about life in the new diplomatic service. Leslie Harriman had been posted briefly as first secretary in the new legation at Santa Isabella, Equatorial Guinea. Okigbo introduced Leslie with much flourish to the boys saying: 'This is diplomat Leslie Harriman. Today, he's going to talk to you about his sex life in Spain!'[44] Harriman was almost completely bowled out. But he had the presence of mind to keep the talk on the exact course of the topic for which he brought the film slides. After his talk, Okigbo invited him to the principal's house, where he was entertained to a sumptuous lunch. At one stage in the course of the lunch, Harriman asked Okigbo where he got mackerel seeing that Fiditi was dry land, from which there was no possibility that such a species of fish could be obtained. Okigbo replied that he ordered mackerels by some special arrangement for the protein needs of the boys and the development of their brains. At the end of the meal, and after the table had been cleared, Okigbo stood to propose a toast to diplomat Leslie Harriman, at the end of which he congratulated him for devouring his best python steak. Harriman went behind the house to throw up the entire lunch. Okigbo's capacity for mostly innocuous mischief and hearty pranks was legendary.

The long friendship between Okigbo and the poet John Pepper Clark began late in 1959 while Okigbo was in Fiditi. J. P. Clark had long been aware of Okigbo while a junior at the sister Government College, Ughelli and had watched Okigbo earn his caps at the cricket match in Warri in 1948. Just as Christopher Okigbo was leaving the University College, Ibadan in 1956, J. P. Clark was arriving, so they were hardly contemporaries on campus. But Okigbo was slightly senior in the classics department to Clark's elder brother, Blessing Akporede Clark, with whom he was more closely acquainted before he got to know J. P. Clark.

J. P. Clark (who later wrote under the name Bekederemo) was taking the English honours degree by 1959 and was also editing *The Horn,* the poetry journal. This was founded with the help of Martin Banham, then one of the younger lecturers in Ibadan's English department. Banham conceived *The Horn* on the model of a student literary journal that he had known in Leeds in the 1950s. J. P. Clark had already established a controversial reputation as a poet on the Ibadan campus with the poem 'Ivbie'. J. P. Clark took his degree alongside Michael Echeruo, Abiola Irele, Obi Wali and Emmanuel Obiechina, who turned out to be the most important literary theorists and scholars of that generation.

In June 1959, Clark abandoned editorship of *The Horn* following a 'great emotional crisis'[45] in his life – some accounts say, as the result of his failed love affair with the attractive Christine Clinton, who was also in his class at the University College, Ibadan. Christine and Clark were a mismatch from the outset: J. P. was a petulant poet, while Christine was a gentle child of the Lagos aristocracy. She was also 'something of a star'[46] on the University College, Ibadan stage. Clark himself had described the relationship as one between 'beauty and the beast.'[47] It fell apart with devastating consequences for the poet. Christine would later marry another of Okigbo's friends, the critic and literary scholar Ben Obumselu who had by then over-come tragedy in his own love life and was already in Accra, Ghana, moving later to Oxford where they met.

Nevertheless, the failure of J. P. Clark's turbulent love affair apparently affected him so deeply, it was said that his academic life at the university suffered as a result. When it came time to take his finals he was so distraught that under mental stress, he blanked out in the examination room, for which he was briefly hospitalized. He abandoned his degree examination and refused to return to the university for a repeat. Clark then moved on to Lagos where he joined Peter Enahoro, his classmate from Government College, to work at the *Daily Express* newspaper. The conflict in J. P. Clark's life was so intense that he refused all suggestions and reprimands, including incessant prodding from his father to return to the University and to retake his degree examination.

It was in the backdrop of this crisis that J. P. Clark's path crossed with Okigbo's. Clark's brother, Akporede, already employed in the new Nigerian Foreign Service in 1959, apparently intimated to Okigbo on a visit to Fiditi, the troubles of his younger brother, who was also writing poetry. B. A. Clark was familiar with Okigbo's personal crisis. 'I was impressed by how quickly he had gone on with his life; his choice of poetry was therapeutic. In spite of his difficulties at the time, he never lost his lively humour, his adventurous spirit, his love for life and he had gone on to make a successful teaching career after the disappointments of the civil service.'[48] B. A. Clark had apparently also acquainted his younger brother with Okigbo's doings at Fiditi. Okigbo was a great example of stoical re-engagement with life and its purpose. Chris Okigbo and J. P. Clark also had close mutual friends, one of whom was Emma Ifeajuna. For both poets, therefore, meeting for the first time in 1959 on more personal terms and sharing similar experiences, they discovered a unique emotional bond. That was how a great and legendary friendship began. John Pepper Clark was glad for the companionable friendship. Okigbo for his part was impressed to learn that J. P. had already begun writing poetry as an undergraduate at University College.

The deep friendship would last until Okigbo's death and beyond. The title poem of J. P. Clark's post-civil war collection of poems, *Casualties,* was dedicated to the memory of Christopher Okigbo. Idoto's poet, Clark would assert, was that war's most tragic loss. The dramatic tension in J.P. Clark's personality – a visceral need for symbolism and performance, the turbulent ego, even rage – matched Christopher Okigbo's. Both had gone through similar personal crisis and tragedy. Both poets were at the same stage in their writing careers when they first met, 'seeking more roots to grow to sunlight.' There were few people at the time with whom J. P. Clark could share the same sense of disturbance or who would empathise with his personal crisis. Nor were there too many people who could get along as easily with the talented but mercurial Clark. At the time they met, J. P. was adrift. Okigbo, non-judgmental and hedonistic, stepped into his life with laughter and the gift of his open spirit. This was possibly what sustained their friendship. Okigbo offered the kind of sympathy that Clark needed at that moment in his life.

Okigbo drew from a reserve of intimate experience to convince Clark to return to the university. Kayode Jibowu, who had been J. P. Clark's closest friend at University College, Ibadan, observed that Okigbo and J. P. Clark were temperamentally suited.

There was 'an apparent inner tension which flowed in both personalities, the result of the genuineness, and the sensitivities of their artistic temperament.'[49] Kayode Jibowu's comparison of Okigbo and Clark was of two mountains with equal volcanic power, as he said in 1992:

> Chris and J.P. were two physically small people. The same size. Much of J. P.'s so-called aggressiveness was merely a mask for a deeply acute and sensitive soul – J. P. has often been misunderstood, and categorised as difficult. Of course he is difficult, but he is an individual with great sensitivity. I think between the two – Chris and J. P. – there was the equal ability to outrage; and much of that was what I think, they shared together: they both were something of exhibitionists! Aside from this was the absolute tension of their lifestyles: they were both equally intense individuals. Very intense. But where J. P. gathered into a perpetual storm, Chris dissipated with outrageous playfulness. I think they recognized this and perhaps, that was why they were such great friends![50]

Clark became a regular presence in Fiditi from 1959. They began to share their poetry. After he helped to convince Clark to return to the University of Ibadan, Okigbo would drive down to the campus from Fiditi, sometimes spending nights in J. P. Clark's undergraduate lodgings at Tedder Hall. They pollinated the poetic consciousness of each other in ways that are now obvious; this can be seen in the classical timbre of much of J. P. Clark's works, for he had introduced Clark to the 'great classics.' In significant ways the modern strain of Okigbo's poetry gained from Clark, who was influenced by 'the modern greats' Eliot and Pound. The strong Eliot accent in Christopher Okigbo's early poetry would mark a clear departure from the classical influence of poets like Virgil. It signaled the emergence of a new phase in the development of Okigbo's poetics, especially from 'Debtor's Lane,' the second part of the *Four Canzones*, which he completed shortly after he met Clark late in 1959. J. P. Clark returned to editing *The Horn* at University College, and published Okigbo's 'On the New Year' in the 1958–9 issue.

Christopher Okigbo's love life was always turbulent. It was no less chaotic in Fiditi. He was ruled by a passion for sensual experience. His womanizing was legendary. His friend, the novelist Nkem Nwankwo in *Shadow of the Masquerade* tried to justify the roots of Okigbo's sexual appetite.

> We – the two of us – were artists – men of leisure setting out for a debauch. Every perfect debauch calls for perfect leisure, said Baudelaire, in his state of hashish intoxication. But our debauch was innocent of hashish or any hallucinogen. It was entirely sexual. We would simply scout the town for women to sleep with…In retrospect it is possible to put a Freudian spin on these escapades, these sex binges, fornication as a fix, as a sign of ego-deficiency, as a refuge from the stark reality of one's aloneness in a loveless life without even the consolation of religion. We can blame heredity or upbringing – Chris and I were both taken from home at age eleven or twelve and for seven years lived in a hot house of snobbery. Wrenched from our culture at our formative years, we were deprived of the nurture of our relatives…at the crucial point when our hormones were driving us crazy…we were caged within barracks and denied access to females. Unable to profit from what should have been the most profitable lesson of our lives – how to cultivate and love, and become friends with the opposite sex, we made do with homosexual gropings and some masturbation. But none of this could substitute for the real thing. At the university the cultural bias against women ensured that few women of our class would be available to mate and be partners with. Is it any surprise then that when we graduated and became the beneficiaries of the white man's privilege and knew that beautiful women would give their bodies to us for the asking, we would behave like children in a generous toy store? Or that the sexual entropy which had been building up all those years would explode?[51]

The writer of *Danda* points to Ibadan as the city of libertines in which Okigbo had numerous sexual encounters; class or station was no boundary to his desires. As a young, well-educated bachelor, at the prime of his life, he had the advantages and the means to indulge fully in the freedom of an awakened sexuality. The late 1950s, with its weakening strictures on sexual morality provided a great opportunity for Okigbo's life of sexual indulgence. His encounter with the Beat poets and their moral philosophy was also an important stimulus. That was when June came into his life. She was Okigbo's live-in lover from the middle of 1959 to early 1960. She was a beautiful young woman of about twenty-one who had just completed secondary school in Eastern Nigeria when she came to live with Christopher Okigbo.

The poet may have been engaged to marry June – an arrangement which both their families possibly sanctioned – especially after his failed attempts to woo Safinat Attah. June had been sent down from Ojoto, in the hope that she would commit Christopher Okigbo to a regular, responsible family life. According to Alex Ajayi, everyone was anxious for Okigbo to settle into dignified domesticity. But it did not work. He was still obsessed with Safi and was still in pursuit of her. Indeed while he was living with June, Okigbo was still wooing the Igbira princess strenuously. Okigbo drove down frequently to Ilorin to see her. For her part, although she was madly in love with Christopher, Safi could not make a full commitment to the volatile poet.

Moreover Safi Attah was under severe pressure from her illustrious family to find a good man – preferably, a well-bred northern prince with whom she could settle down. Christopher Okigbo was considered too irreverent and risky, too spoilt and over-indulged. He had just made a terrible mess of his civil service career. There was so much tension and uncertainty that marked their love affair. In the middle of 1959, Safi sailed for England again, to the University of Reading for post-graduate studies. The difficulties in their relationship are easily glimpsed in the resigned tone of 'Love Apart,' which appeared in a later variation in 'Lament of the Lavender Mist' which he completed in Nsukka in 1961:

The moon has ascended between us
Between two pines
That bow to each other.

Love with the moon has ascended
Has fed on our solitary stems

And we are now shadows
That cling to each other
But kiss the air only.[52]

With June, Okigbo was non-committal. June for her part had an uneasy, diffident relationship with the poet. 'She was curiously ill-at-ease with Christopher,' recalled Alex Ajayi. 'It bordered on awe.'[53] There was much, Ajayi observed, in the difference both in experience and personality between the worldly, mercurial poet, whose complicated views about sexuality and extremely liberated lifestyle contrasted so fundamentally with the innocence of the young woman with whom he came to live in something of a trial marriage. From some accounts, Okigbo treated June selfishly and without much consideration for her sense of insecurity and inexperience. One day, for instance, Okigbo took her out to party in the company of some of his old University College friends at the Paradise Club in Ibadan. Late into the night, Okigbo abandoned June and disappeared with another woman into the city of Ibadan. June was unnerved, and was rescued by some of Okigbo's friends, who had to drive her home to Fiditi in the morning. There were a number of such incidents with her, in which Okigbo's selfishness, that cruel streak that sometimes manifested itself in his relationships with women, was demonstrated. Such lack of consideration for the feelings of his young lover displayed what his friend the novelist Nkem Nwankwo also described as Okigbo's 'demonic side.'[54]

Okigbo was a complex person, and the contradictions of his life are illustrated in this narrative of cruelty. Yet Okigbo was also capable of extreme acts of compassion. Alex Ajayi rationalized this by positing that his actions in his dealings with June and his other women, were part of Okigbo's unique individualism. Ajayi however also affirmed that Okigbo himself was very fond of June and loved her in his own extravagant and passionate way. There were more moments of joy and rectitude in this relationship with June than the outcome proclaims. Christopher Okigbo's individualism however proved too much for June to endure. Okigbo would be judged harshly under current feminist perspectives, his actions typifying a characteristic patriarchy, an extreme typical of the way men who subject women to the worst forms of indignity. Perhaps that is true. Perhaps this is why his relationship with June, and with other women did not endure. But it must be weighed as an aspect of Okigbo's complex personality. He was a deeply flawed and vulnerable individual.

As the vice-principal at Fiditi, Okigbo was generally required to do some administrative work but he could not stomach the routine – Okigbo was too spontaneous to be bound by an organized way of doing things. His teaching schedule was capricious and disorganized and perhaps this fact is behind Echeruo's description of Okigbo's life as a teacher as 'simply a failure.' One of the things Alex Ajayi recalled was how Okigbo hated waking up early in the morning. He would sleep till mid-day, by which time classes would have been well underway. On many occasions, Ajayi had literally to sit over Okigbo, cajoling, demanding, threatening and coaxing him to wake and come to school. Okigbo would resist all entreaties, but would finally reluctantly wake up and stroll to school. He loved languor and an easy pace of life. Sometimes when he had malaria, Okigbo would refuse to take palliatives preferring to enjoy 'the sweet fever which is better than any medicine.'[55] He curled up under his blanket because he enjoyed the fever.

Nevertheless, when he did show up in school he was an inspiring teacher, and an enthusiastic member of the community, who was much admired by the students. He loved the outdoors, and excelled as Games Master. It is remarkable that many of the Fiditi boys closest to him, and to whom he devoted the most attention, went on to great things in life. Among them, Vincent Demola Dedeke, S. A. Odegbami, Patrick Agbasi, George Ofodile, Bode Olajumoke, Olu Ladipo and Babs Animashaun. These were the students who were most often to be found in the company of the poet at Fiditi because they were, like him, sportsmen. He was especially devoted to Babs Animashaun, a talented but difficult student, who got into frequent brushes with the school authorities. Okigbo adopted him because he saw in the stubborn and turbulent spirit of the young star – a living mirror of his own complicated nature. 'He felt a sense of responsibility for Babs Animashaun and on more than one occasion stood between him and the anger of the principal who was ready to expel him,'[56] reflected Bode Olajumoke. Animashaun's saving grace was in the elegance of his mind and the quality of his performance and he went on to become investor and businessman. The various accomplishments of this crop of Fiditi boys later in their professional life ought to be a vindication of the quality of the poet's talent as a teacher.

The openness and distinctive drama of his personality soon made 'Mister Okigbo' very popular. The Fiditi students found him inspiring, and easy to get along with. Okigbo, with his disdain for form, would break down conventional rules of behavior and morality. Babs Animashaun recollected, 'You could tell that he was different … a genius … a very unconventional man. That was the most interesting [thing] about him. He was such a very easy and accessible [man] in his relationship with people, very open-minded and never had difficulty mingling with both the high in society and the lowliest: his casualness was almost a legend in itself.'[57] He developed a warm relationship with many of the boys, and established a firm but uncomplicated authority. He was approachable because he brought down the difficult barriers of authority and privilege. According to Dr. Patrick Amenechi, it was amusing in those years at Fiditi, to see Christopher Okigbo on the football field with his small physique, drilling the boys, many of whom were physically bigger than their Vice-Principal and games master. Besides, only just in his late twenties, he was not much older than some of the students. But he earned their deep respect and admiration by 'the sheer force of his personality.'[58]

Okigbo's charisma so appealed to the imagination of the young students in the Grammar School that, many years after his death, Bode Olajumoke was still awe-struck by his persona and his bohemian lifestyle. Dr. Olajumoke was to become well-known as a corporate lawyer, public administrator and politician in Nigeria. When he left Fiditi Grammar School, inspired by Okigbo, he went to work briefly in broadcasting. He later studied Law in the Soviet Union and England, rising to be Deputy Permanent Secretary in Nigeria's Ministry of Defence before venturing into the turbulent national politics of the 1990s in Nigeria. He played a prominent role in Nigeria's democratic transition from the Abacha military dictatorship. Bode Olajumoke was in class two at Fiditi when Christopher Okigbo arrived to teach. His account of the poet is vivid:

Mister Okigbo was an extremely impressive figure. A very unique man; he struck everybody immediately as very learned, very cultured, very sophisticated and above all very warm. He was popular with the boys especially those of them who were sportsmen – the footballers. He also loved and related easily with the school's best-known rebels – but you had to be as brilliant as you were rascally before he would indulge you. He encouraged us to be free in our consciousness, he wanted to liberate us from deadening fear and moral repression, and wanted us to aspire to the truest aesthetic and intellectual values. Although everybody knew him as free and casual, he was by no means a frivolous man, because sometimes, of course, he could be quite firm with matters. One of his greatest attributes was this disarming simplicity in the way he related to everybody irrespective of age or station. That is what anyone would mostly remember about Mr. Okigbo. I certainly remember him clearly because he was then living with one of his young cousins, the late Ben Okigbo who was my friend, and whom he had brought to school at Fiditi. Ben always regaled us with stories of mister Okigbo's escapades with women. That was another thing you were bound to remember…he loved women! They also loved him. The man was a gripping and fascinating individual, who affected the life in Fiditi so deeply and who influenced the boys greatly. I would certainly say he was by far the most well liked...I mean you could not but be drawn to him...of all the teachers at the Fiditi Grammar school in the 1950s.[59]

Okigbo introduced cricket at Fiditi early in 1959. Always an assured cricketer, the poet could often be seen in the evenings, wielding the bat and playing the game with the boys. He took them to cricket matches and made them play against schools already famous for cricket in the region, like the Government College, Ibadan and the King's College, Lagos. The Fiditi boys apparently gave a good account of themselves judging by the reports of the 1959/60 session in the Fiditi Grammar School magazine. Okigbo also established the boxing team and became its patron. The magazine reports that the boxing society had 'come to a new era when…Mr. Okigbo stepped in.'[60] Okigbo had also promised to help procure necessary equipment for the boxing team. Table tennis, took 'a turn for good…(with)…the arrival of topnotch players in the person of Mr. Chris Okigbo and Mr. Akinola.'[61] Okigbo was also the motivating force behind football at the school, winning matches among secondary schools in the western region of Nigeria. The school's magazine for 1959/60 reports that:

> At the beginning of this year season(sic), the game has received a climax of encouragements through the commendable efforts of our football master Mr. C. Okigbo BA (Hon) London who during his secondary school days was a very conspicuous school footballer. He induced the school authority to provide the first and second eleven teams with international soccer boots, hoses, knee-caps, goal nets and inexhaustible football cases and bladders. All these ginger up school footballers for this year season (sic) [62]

In that year, they came close to winning the Grier cup, the regional championship for schools in the west, crashing out only in the finals. This was a spectacular feat for a relatively new school like Fiditi playing against other schools with more established reputations. Again, the Fiditi magazine gives an account of Okigbo's inspiring motivation: 'As a gamemaster Mr. Okigbo transformed footballing in the school into an ingenious skill, and our team, into invincible Spartans bullying every other opponent into automatic and unconditional submission.'[63] Then there is the possibly apocryphal story of how sometimes he experimented with marijuana with some of his sportsmen in order to bolster them during football practice. 'It was not beyond him,'[64] said Leslie Harriman.

By the middle of 1960, Okigbo's life in Fiditi was coming to a climax. Sometime in April or May of that year, Alex Olu Ajayi had informed him that he was moving finally to a new position, which had been reserved for him at the West African Examination Council (WAEC). He would soon resign his position as principal of Fiditi Grammar School but delay his move until the first set of boys at the Fiditi Grammar School who had registered for the West African School Certificate Examination for the 1959/60 school year had completed it in June. It was a busy time for both men. Okigbo was giving extra classes to the only boy who had registered for the Greek examination. Okigbo had also responded to an advertisement for the position of Assistant University Librarian at the new University of Nigeria at Nsukka. The Eastern Nigerian government in 1956 had chartered the University at Nsukka as the country's first indigenous university and it was to open later in 1960. (The University College, Ibadan was still affiliated to the University of London and awarded the London degree until 1962.) Alex Ajayi himself wrote a letter recommending Okigbo's position.

During the Easter holiday, Okigbo and Ajayi embarked on a journey to the East. They traveled through Ogbomosho Road to Onitsha, circumventing Benin City. At Onitsha they had been ferried across the bridgehead, from where they headed first to Ojoto. That trip – Okigbo's first trip to Ojoto in two years, since his civil service imbroglio – resulted in the poem 'Lament of the Flute,' with its startling opening and epiphanic mood:

> Tide wash... memories
> fold-over-fold free furrow,
> mingling old tunes with new[65]

and the 'Lament of the Lavender Mist', the 3rd and 4th parts, of the *Four Canzones,* with the nostalgic mood of a reconciled prodigal, leaning back finally to 'where springs the fountain' of the later *Heavensgate.*

Okigbo's last days in Fiditi were socially hectic. There was elaborate preparation for the celebration of Nigeria's independence. Okigbo had been vigorously involved, as were many other people, in those preparations to usher in Nigeria's moment of freedom from British colonialism. There was a celebratory tone in his writing in this period, as independence signified a personal sense of healing. He was excited by the mood of political freedom. On 1 October 1960, the Union Jack was lowered and the Nigerian flag flown. The symbolic moment dawned. Okigbo celebrated independence in Lagos, then federal capital of the new nation. The city was agog with festive bunting. Okigbo had an uproarious day in the company of Leslie Harriman and, J. P. Clark. They drove down to Ibadan, where they watched Wole Soyinka's independence play *A Dance of the Forest* at the University Theatre and went to the post-production party at the University College, Ibadan staff club. Later that night they drove to Lagos where everybody was involved in one way or the other with the rites of celebration: Achebe was busy at the broadcast station. Even Soyinka's foreboding, expressed in his play, did not stop him from being Master of Ceremonies at the state ball hosted by the president, Dr. Nnamdi Azikiwe in Lagos.

Okigbo's sister-in-law Georgette, Pius's Belgian wife, recollected how Christopher and his friends – Clark and Harriman – had stormed her home on Ikoyi Crescent, Lagos in a state of elation. They told her how earlier in the day the three had gone to the Ikoyi Hotel, the best hotel in the city in those years to enact a little drama: they took one look at the menu, and satisfying themselves that no African cuisine had been included, ordered pounded yam and egusi soup. They were regretfully informed that the Ikoyi Hotel did not serve that kind of food under its roof. Okigbo sprang up and yelled: 'You mean you're in Nigeria...an independent Nigeria...and you can't serve a simple thing like pounded yam and egusi? I don't believe this!'[66] Leslie Harriman and J. P. Clark soon joined him. Okigbo berated the hotel for what he called its 'blindness to the moment.' The manager, a European professional unaccustomed to such a scene, apologized profusely and quickly saw the merit of their argument. He promised to rectify the situation in the light of current realities. The Ikoyi Hotel soon afterwards began to include local dishes in its menu. He said to his sister-in-law Georgette: 'Madame, we showed them what it meant to be independent and free!'[67] His great excitement marked what Okigbo and most people of his generation saw as a new age, a sense of rebirth.

It was in this mood of renewal that Okigbo left early that October for his new position as Assistant Librarian, to begin a new life at Nsukka, another cycle of experience. Fiditi had nurtured him unto a path of poetic consciousness: the old tunes had mingled with the new, giving spirit and form, to the evocative quest of Idoto's prodigal: he was led to his homecoming by the spirit of political freedom, by a sense of rebirth. Just before he left Fiditi in 1960, his poem 'Moonglow' appeared in *Reflections,* an anthology edited by Frances Ademola. In acknowledgement of his great debt to his Fiditi experience, Christopher Okigbo dedicated the poems written in this period to his students at Fiditi Grammar School – where he had completed the *Four Canzones,* which would see print in *Black Orpheus.*

One important evidence of Okigbo's achievement as a teacher might certainly be seen in the fact that the single boy who registered to take Greek in the School Certificate Examination passed with distinction. Fiditi had given him purpose. But Okigbo's real work had only just begun. A new power had crept into his voice.

## NOTES

1  Malcolm Cowley, *Exiles Return* (New York: Viking, 1934) p. 50.
2  Ibid.
3  Interview with Alex Ajayi, Lagos, 1992.
4  Ibid.
5  Marjory Whitelaw, Interview with Christopher Okigbo, Ibadan, March 1965.
6  Christopher Okigbo, 'Debtor's Lane' (1958). *The Horn* 3: 2 (1959–60), pp. 6–7. Reprinted in *Black Orpheus* II (1962), p. 6.
7  Marjory Whitelaw, Interview with Christopher Okigbo.
8  Ben Obumselu, 'Christopher Okigbo: Poetic Portrait'. Essay delivered at 'Song for Idoto': A Celebration of Christopher Okigbo, National Museum, Enugu, 2 November 1996.
9  Ibid.
10  Sunday Anozie, *Christopher Okigbo: Creative Rhetoric* (New York: Africana Publishers, 1971).
11  Marjory Whitelaw, Interview with Christopher Okigbo.
12  Tchicaya U Tam'si, *Selected Poems*, trans. Gerald Moore (London: Heinemann, 1970).
13  Interview with Pius Okigbo, Lagos, 1995.
14  Malcolm Cowley, *Exiles Return*, pp. 60–1.
15  Interview with Alex Ajayi.
16  Ibid.
17  Ibid.
18  Ibid.
19  Ibid.
20  Ibid.
21  Interview with Idowu Osikoya, Fiditi, 1993.
22  Ibid.
23  Christopher Okigbo, 'A Song of the Forest', *Four Canzones* (1957–61) *Black Orpheus* 2, 1962.
24  Interview with V.C. Ike, Lagos, 1994.
25  Interview with Alex Ajayi.
26  Ibid.
27  Ibid.
28  Ibid.
29  Interview with Ben Obumselu, Lagos, 1994.
30  Interview with Alex Ajayi.
31  Ibid.
32  Interview with Patrick Amenechi, Lagos, 1992.
33  Interview with Alex Ajayi.
34  Ibid.
35  Alex Ekwueme, 'Remembering the Weaverbird' opening remarks at 'Song for Idoto': A Celebration of Christopher Okigbo, National Museum, Enugu, 2 November, 1996.
36  Interview with Wole Soyinka, Abeokuta, 1994.
37  Interview with Bisi Lawrence, Lagos, 1995.
38  Interview with Ignatius Atigbi, Lagos, 1994.
39  Interview with Alex Ajayi.
40  Interview with Leslie Harriman, Lagos, 1993.
41  Interview with M.J.C. Echeruo, Syracuse, New York, 1998.

42  Christopher Okigbo, 'Siren Limits' 1961, *Limits* I–IV, *Labyrinths.*

43  Interview with Ben Obumselu.

44  Interview with Leslie Harriman.

45  Interview with Alex Ajayi.

46  Robert Wren, *Those Magical Years* (Washington DC: Three Continent Press, 1981).

47  Ibid.

48  Interview with B.A. Clark, Lagos 1997.

49  Interview with Kayode Jibowu, Lagos 1992.

50  Ibid.

51  Nkem Nwankwo, *Shadow of the Masquerade* (Nashville, TN: Niger House Publications 1994) pp. 58-61.

52  Christopher Okigbo, 'Lament of the Lavender Mist' (1961), *Black Orpheus* 2 (1962) pp. 8–9.

53  Interview with Alex Ajayi.

54  Nkem Nwankwo, *Shadow of the Masquerade.*

55  Interview with Alex Ajayi.

56  Interview with Bode Olajumoke, Lagos, 1994.

57  Interview with Babs Animashaun, Mandilas House, Lagos, 1993.

58  Interview with Patrick Amenechi, Lagos, 1992.

59  Interview with Bode Olajumoke, Lagos, 1993.

60  Football Captain's report, *The Fiditian* 2:2 (1959) quoted in Bernth Lindfors, 'Okigbo as Jock', *When the Drumbeat Changes* (eds) Carolyn Parker and Stephen Arnold (Washington DC: Three Continents Press 1981).

61  Ibid.

62  Ibid.

63  Ibid.

64  Interview with Leslie Harriman.

65  Christopher Okigbo, 'Lament of the Flute', *Black Orpheus* 2 (1962) p. 7. Reprinted with 'Two Flutes' in *Poems from Black Africa* (ed.) Langston Hughes (Bloomington, IN: Indiana University Press 1963) pp. 98–9.

66  Interview with Georgette Okigbo, Ilupeju, Lagos 1992.

67  Ibid.

# 6

# *A librarian ravenous for literature & women*

## NSUKKA 1960–62

> So would I to the hills again
> So would I
> to where springs the fountain
> there to draw from
>
> ('Lustra IV', *Heavensgate*)

Nigeria's political independence from Britain in October 1960 was the culmination of years of political struggle by a generation led by Dr. Nnamdi Azikiwe, whose ideas shaped the meaning of the nation in West Africa in the twentieth century. There was also the need to establish a cultural identity and to retrieve the past from a history of colonial domination. When Christopher Okigbo relocated from Fiditi, in the deep heartland of Western Nigeria to the new University of Nigeria at Nsukka in the Eastern region, the fragrance of national celebration still clung to the air. The mood was celebratory:

> Thundering drums and cannons
> in palmgrove:
> the spirit is in ascent.[1]

He wrote of that moment. The 1960s was a remarkable decade in the history of the black race – long held back by years of colonization and despoliation. Independence meant that a new reality had dawned for Okigbo's generation. The colonial child was now a man. Okigbo's poem expressed high hopes for Africa at the threshold of its own historical rebirth. Time had assumed a clearer, more precise order and proportion. The spirit was truly in ascent.

As both witnesses of colonialism and inheritors of the legacies of national liberation, Okigbo's generation felt called to exercise a moral power and to signify the great sense of national awakening. 'There was a lot of hope, a lot dreams – a sense of historic privilege,'[2] the playwright Wole Soyinka recalled of this moment. However, the mood was also tempered by the silent fear that all great changes provoke – a fear of possible failure, the truncation of the soaring hope, which came with liberty. There was some cynicism among the conscious intellectual elite. Many people felt that the great new tide of independence, the evocative and transcendent mood was flawed. Even though the loud drums of celebration drowned out the less timorous signals of danger, Wole Soyinka glimpsed the possibilities of failure; the marred awakening of independence. Soyinka's early play, *A Dance of the Forest*, commissioned for the occasion, foreshadowed the crisis of the new nation.

Okigbo was one of those intellectuals and artists who shared Soyinka's inner disturbance – although he would later tell Soyinka at the opening of his independence play at Ibadan, that its message was 'too cynical, too dark for this occasion!'[3] He preferred to celebrate a buoyant hope. In many of the arguments they had after the play had been staged, Okigbo emphasized this criticism. Okigbo was not alone. The colorful celebration of Nigeria's independence was a moment of sheer joy. Nigerians rode on euphoria. The air that October had a feeling of newness, of the final birth of a new nation in the season of the rains. Okigbo's generation born into two powerful and conflicting worlds – hoped that independence would resolve the conflict of their existence as children of a colonial past. That sense of hope animated Okigbo.

The University of Nigeria, Nsukka was built to express this new hope. As the first Nigerian university to award its own degrees, it was the ultimate symbol of Nigerian nationalism. The university opened its gates that October to one hundred and twenty pioneer students under the romantic motto 'To restore the dignity of man.' It was that vision captured in the wording and spirit of Azikiwe's humanist vision and pan-Africanist agenda, and it emphasized the desires of a new elite of nation builders, poets, scientists, and teachers trained to serve and renew Africa. The nobility of that vision was etched in the coat of arms of the new university: the dignified majesty of the lion, that royal tetrarch of the jungle which symbolized the ambition of the young university. Nsukka also emphasized the dignity of labour. It was conceived as a land grant university, which provided liberal *and* technical education, while the University College at Ibadan emphasized a classical and humanistic curriculum.

According to the novelist Chukwuemeka Ike, who was Deputy University Registrar, the move to Nsukka was an act of faith:

> What Nsukka meant at that time, was something new and indigenous. Something that stimulated the adventurous spirit of our generation. Many of those individuals who wanted to prove that they could run their own society, including their own university. I mean, the idea of a new, indigenous university was a wonderful thing! Going to Nsukka offered us a challenge, something like a reason to prove our abilities, and to engage in the pioneering work required of the new educated men in labor for a new, possibly great country, which we had inherited from colonialism in the middle moments of the twentieth century. That it opened its doors in 1960 endowed it with a remarkably romantic significance.[4]

The new university was thus not only symbolic of the sense of political freedom and liberty gained, it also expressed the awakening of a people from a dark and painful past. The University of Nigeria was conceived as the harbinger of an African renaissance.

Alex Ajayi recalled that Okigbo was inspired by the romanticism of Nsukka's founding. The poet became intimately tied into the beginnings of Nigeria's first indigenous university. The manner by which he got the position of Assistant University Librarian at Nsukka was also quintessential Okigbo. At Fiditi Okigbo had seemed incapable of disciplined and routine employment. But Okigbo was determined, given the general mood of national rebirth, to start afresh. It is possible that he had been inspired by Chike Momah to find a niche in university administration. Momah had taken up a librarianship position at the University College, Ibadan in 1957, after three years as a Land Officer in Enugu, and seemed to be enjoying it. Another influence was Chukwuemeka Ike who had been appointed after graduating as an assistant registrar at the University College, Ibadan in 1956, under Dr. Biobaku, his old school master at Umuahia. When Biobaku moved into state administration as Secretary to the Government of the Western Region, Nath Adamolekun was appointed Registrar. Mr. Adamolekun encouraged Ike to apply for the job as Deputy University Registrar at the new university. Ike was among Okigbo's friends who apparently encouraged him to apply for the librarian's job. He said, 'We had a regular discussion around these subjects, and around the question of his career interest. A number of our friends thought that Christopher did not have the temperament for a career in librarianship.'[5] The fact that Christopher Okigbo had no previous training or experience as a librarian did not deter him. Anyhow, with Alex Ajayi already on his way out of Fiditi Grammar School, Okigbo apparently did not have many options. Alex Ajayi had also encouraged Christopher Okigbo to apply for the Nsukka job and drove Okigbo from Fiditi to Ibadan for the interview in the senate chambers of the University College. The story has been told by Chinua Achebe, of how Okigbo bought a book on librarianship, which he read during the ride between Fiditi and Ibadan. He got the job. There are, however, indications that his brother Pius may have influenced Christopher's appointment. By this time, Pius had become an influential figure in the Eastern regional government, where he had been appointed Economic Adviser to the premier, Dr. Michael Okpara. Pius Okigbo and Dr Okpara were contemporaries early in the 1940s at Yaba Higher College, Lagos, where they played a lot of chess together. The premier also knew Christopher Okigbo. With such a pull in the Eastern regional government, owners of the University of Nigeria, it was not difficult for Pius Okigbo to provide a powerful recommendation for Christopher who needed a fresh start.

It would be unfair, nevertheless, to suggest that this fact alone guaranteed the library job at Nsukka. Okigbo had personal qualities that must have impressed his interviewers, and his personal merit was adequately considered. Apparently, the only other candidate was the critic and poet Michael Echeruo. Echeruo did not get the job in the library but was appointed to teach drama, first at the College of Arts and Science in Enugu, then in the English Department at Nsukka. Michael Echeruo's father was an equally powerful minister in the Eastern regional government at this time.

Christopher Okigbo assumed duties at the university library on Monday 8 October 1960. The two years he spent in Nsukka between October 1960 and August 1962 would prove to be productive years for his writing. *Four Canzones*, although reeking 'too much of Eliot'[6] had just been published by J. P. Clark in *The Horn*. Nsukka in 1960 was in a rural outback, one of the last outposts of traditional Igbo civilization one hour's drive away from Enugu, the Eastern regional capital. It was a beautiful place surrounded by hills, and at an elevation which made the weather temperate. The new university campus was built on a crest of the hill in the midst of a lush pastoral landscape. Okigbo found Nsukka's rustic character most suitable to his temperament. Nsukka had the same pastoral qualities as Fiditi, which afforded the artistic mind the possibility of creative rumination. The happy difference was the cosmopolitan energy and intellectual mood of the people who had gathered in Nsukka. While in Fiditi, Okigbo had to make frequent pilgrimages to the University College, Ibadan, to find intellectual kinship. Nsukka was self-sufficient in that sense. At the founding of the university, many of the qualities of rural Igbo life were still intact and visible. Nsukka pulsated with the charming purity of a virgin place. This sense of the unspoilt nature of the land and its culture touched Okigbo's imagination.

In another important sense, resuming his life in this beautiful hill country, symbolized for the poet in an intimate way, a sense of spiritual homecoming. Settling in Nsukka was the culmination of a transition. It had begun earlier after Easter in May 1960, during the journey he had undertaken with his friend, Alex Ajayi to the East, to visit his ancestral home – Ojoto – after years of self-imposed exile. On that trip, they had visited Okigbo's friends and numerous relations in other places in the East, 'to reassure them on his life,'[7] as Ajayi said. Okigbo felt a new sense of well-being, a final healing that helped him to break with a traumatic past. The lush May mornings heightened the perennial beauty of the countryside. There was a profound sense of peace, of fruition and gathering, of renewal and rebirth.

> I have visited;
> on palm beam imprinted
> my pentagon –
>
> I have visited, the prodigal…[8]

Okigbo's May 1960 visit to Ojoto before settling in Nsukka was thus also atonement following his difficulties in Lagos and the disappointment the scandal of his civil service debacle had caused his friends and relations. It was the completion of a cycle, and a final breaking with the poet's 'cruel past.'[9]

Okigbo had spent considerable time with his father, talking late into the night; the poet smoking his pipe and cracking endless jokes with the old schoolmaster, retired from the Catholic Mission School system. He was always a reassuring figure in his son's life and that trip home, as Alex Ajayi observed, helped rekindle the easy friendship they always shared. James Okigbo's undisguised bond with his last son by Anna was expressed in a tough and grudging admiration for each other. Although Christopher did cause the old man numerous moments of anxiety, James Okigbo kept faith in him, and allowed the full expression of his quixotic personality. By all accounts, the old schoolmaster appreciated, and indeed encouraged, his son's individualism. He was a man of liberal temperament and had taught his children to be independent and free to make their own choices. He had insisted from their childhood on the liberation of their minds. His father's re-statement of faith in him was especially important in helping Okigbo fully reconsider his options.

Making peace with his past involved a final healing of the trauma of his mother Anna's death; it led to a reconsideration of his relationship with his stepmother, Elizabeth, with whom the poet could not get along easily as a child or teenager. Christopher had expressed this defiance in the most extreme of ways. For instance, according to Okigbo's sister Susan, when in his senior year in secondary school, Christopher Okigbo had made a point of separating himself from the laws of the household. He constructed a demarcation from the corridor of the family house in Ojoto to carve a separate space for himself in the corridor. It was both a statement of protest against his stepmother, and an expression of his fierce independence and individualism. Susan recalled. 'Christopher preferred to live in that space in the passage to his room in the family house, even though it was inconvenient for everybody else!'[10] We hear echoes of this in *Heavensgate* in the line about the 'young bird in the passage' standing on one leg at the passage and mourning 'a mother on a spray', Okigbo seems to be referring to those significant elements of his past from which he constructs the central meaning of his poetry. We may read it as Okigbo's figuration of a state of innocence and aesthetic limitations. Those lines however refer to Okigbo's adolescent act of rebellion, his symbolic abdication of his place in the family, in defiance of his father and in rejection of his stepmother, his act of separation or self-exile. Such acts of rebellion were constant in Christopher Okigbo's young life. Thus, in returning to that origin – where springs the fountain – he affirms the desire for reconciliation, through self-awareness, by comprehending the basis of his psychic conflicts.

Okigbo also visited Ire, his maternal home, and spent a reflective time with his maternal uncle, the old priest of the Ajani shrine, whom the poet always thought of as a regent standing in for him as the priest of the goddess. He spent evenings at the groves of the Ajani shrine, contemplating the ancient mysteries of the Igbo religious system. The result of Okigbo's trip was the poem 'Lustra' the fourth sequence in the *Heavensgate* poems. Ojoto was 'where springs the fountain,' the source of Christopher Okigbo's creative experience and identity: the poet had gone 'there to draw from' its spiritual fountains and after a long spiritual and physical absence, the poet symbolically reclaims his heritage in Idoto.

Although it was a brief stay, Okigbo was inspired by nostalgia, and by the charm of his village in that season of fertility, and its significance as the wellspring of his humanity. This Easter journey thus enacts a rite of spiritual return:

I have had my cleansing....
Emigrant with air-borne nose[11]

The spiritual and aesthetic essence of his ancestral land, ensconced in forests and groves only twelve miles from Onitsha, rekindled Okigbo's imagination.

The 'stations of the cross' in the poem represent Okigbo's psychic or symbolic journey, revisiting those silent, repressed parts of his memory and the various turns of his life's journey. *Heavensgate* is the projection of an aesthetic experience through which the poet constructs and explores the fable of man one in which the interpretation of the poet's private life is linked to the terms of a communal myth, and yields the possibility of collective redemption. And redemption is by a return to an experience, which Okigbo enacts, partly by the symbolic offertory to the upkeep of the Ajani shrine through his uncle Nweze Ikejiofor, whom he gave money regularly for that purpose, and partly by the possibility of his poetry. The poet had smelled his native earth again. His pilgrimage was complete. He felt the fragrance of the foliage, the inspired openness of the solitary paths, and the symbolic power in the thrush of vegetation in the heart of the farming season. It was from these that he resolved his sense of alienation. Idoto fed him a new creative impulse. There is this total sense of 'newness and rebirth' in the lines of 'Lustra':

Here is a new laid egg
here a white hen at midterm.[12]

Alex Ajayi illustrates the significance of this May 1960 journey to the East. On returning to Fiditi, he and Okigbo travelled to Ibadan for an evening of socializing at the home of the botanist Richard Akpata. Midway into the conversation, Christopher Okigbo suddenly asked Dr. Akpata, 'Richard, have you been to your village lately?' to which the botanist replied in the negative. Okigbo then said with some gravity, 'I think you should go there more often. You must learn the tunes. You don't know anything yet, you know, until you return!' This encounter encapsulates the general mood of African intellectuals seeking a spiritual return to a mythical past, to retrieve experiences of value.

Alex Ajayi's reason for embarking on the Easter trip was more prosaic: he was committed to research for the University of Durham, studying the emerging literature from Africa. The trip to the East was an opportunity to meet with the new writers living and working in the Eastern region. They spent some time in Enugu where they stayed with Chinua Achebe, who had by then moved to the city of the red hills, as the regional director of the Nigerian Broadcasting Service. During the visit, Achebe had shown them the completed manuscript of his second novel, *No Longer at Ease*, and they had spent time discussing aspects of the new novel. Achebe had plainly fictionalized important elements of Okigbo's life in that novel. Indeed Obi Okonkwo is an Okigbo hybrid. The character Christopher in the novel is also a composite of Okigbo, and the incident in the girls' school, where the white principal chased them out, was an actual incident that involved Okigbo. Alex Ajayi vividly remembered that visit to Achebe in Enugu:

> Christopher had taken more to the first novel, *Things Fall Apart* and I remember that Chinua and he argued on the fine points of his new novel. Chris later rendered quite unforgettably a traditional Ibo folk song on his flute, which he thought Unoka would have done beautifully with his own flute, in the first novel, *Things Fall Apart*. As he did it, Chris danced to all our amusement. He was alive with the flute![13]

They also visited Okigbo's elder sister, Susan, in Onitsha. The poet relished his sister's cooking, which he always generously complimented. Okigbo's old friend and classmate Dr. Ebong Etuk, who they also visited, was senior Medical Officer at the General Hospital in Onitsha. 'When, later, he came to live in Nsukka,' Ebong Etuk remembered, 'Christopher would visit me more regularly at Onitsha. We would still race our cars at high speed. He loved speed. And he tested most of *Heavensgate* and the beginnings of *Limits* with me, in my sitting room, drinking beer.'[14]

Onitsha was then a lively, cosmopolitan city, much more manageable than the ugly urban sprawl which developed, especially after the civil war. In the 1960s it still had beautifully paved roads and a lively middle-class society of educated and cultured residents. A glimpse of the Onitsha of Okigbo's time can be seen in Chinua Achebe's story for children, *Chike and the River,* which Okigbo was to publish a few years later at the Cambridge University Press. Onitsha had an important intellectual tradition, which was still vibrant by the time Okigbo moved to Nsukka: it was a tradition influenced by the literary spirit of the Englishman, Dr. J.M. Stuart-Young, who lived in Onitsha founded the Onitsha literary club early in the twentieth century. Stuart-Young's influence helped to shape the literary and intellectual culture and outlook of the city. Dr. Nnamdi Azikiwe and Dennis Osadebey, the two most important poets of their generation, participated actively in the Onitsha literary club in the 1920s.

There were Onitsha's great schools, its ebullient newspapers and its diverse, cosmopolitan middle-class community that found need for literary and other cultural expression. But most importantly at the height of the Igbo social renaissance, there was the development after the Second World War, when soldiers who had fought in the war began to flow back into the city and influence a new dynamism in the social process. Onitsha witnessed a boom in intellectual and literary activity, reflected in its tradition of political pamphleteering and the rise of the small presses that published the cheap chapbooks. Onitsha thus became for many years the Grub Street of West Africa.

So quite aside from playing an important role in the nationalist struggle, Onitsha sustained an intellectual ferment and a literate culture. By 1960, the University College, Ibadan had set up the Eastern Nigerian office of the Department of Extramural Studies in Onitsha, headed by the literary critic Dr. Obi Wali. As Obi Wali recollected several year later, 'Christopher used to drive down, very regularly, both for professional reasons, as the University Librarian, and for social reasons, if he wanted to hang out at Onitsha. There were the bookshops and the small presses there with whom he did business. I was writing my novel in Igbo at the time, and I would show it to him. Chris was very enthusiastic and encouraging. There were many of his friends and family living in Onitsha, and that back and forth enlivened both the social and imaginative collaboration which was the temper of the 1960s.'[15] It was an exciting time.

Settling in Nsukka therefore on 8 October 1960, a week after Nigeria's independence celebrations, Okigbo equated his mood to the growth of the vegetative life of the planting season around his journey of Easter 1960. The poet chose to recount, within an imaginative dialectic, the story of his life as a product of the process of history. *Heavensgate,* the first sequence of poems written in Nsukka, emerged thus from that experience of restoration and reconciliation. 'Heavensgate', Okigbo had written in his introduction to *Labyrinths,* 'was originally conceived as an Easter sequence. It later grew into a ceremony of innocence, something like a mass, an offering to Idoto, the village stream of which I drank, in which I washed, as a child.'[16] Christopher Okigbo's poetry blossomed in Nsukka, perhaps because it grew from the fascinating cadences of the landscape. The early signals of the harmattan, which had begun to plant kisses of mist over the lushness of the Nsukka forest and its seven hills, were in the air when he arrived in Nsukka that October. For the poet, this landscape was thrilling. It rekindled the exultant feeling of self-renewal. There was beauty in Nsukka both in its sense of solitude and in its buoyant ambience.

Vincent Chukwuemeka Ike also transferred to Nsukka that week. He would write thus, several years later, about the impact of the Nsukka scene on his friend: 'The picturesque Nsukka hills which transformed many of the pioneer Nsukka undergraduates into poets and turned some house wives into painters may have played their part. What the hills failed to provide, Christopher supplied himself.'[17] Okigbo once told Gerald Moore, that Nsukka 'rings with the intensity of silence that provokes us all to minstrelsy.'[18] The hills at Nsukka ran up to embrace the sunlight, with a spread of green vegetation.

When Okigbo assumed duties, the campus was only work in progress. Some new concrete flats and bungalows dotted the campus, a number of prefabricated buildings were just sprouting: it was lean provision. The Welsh poet, Peter Thomas, who later shared a deep friendship with Okigbo, described the new university that October, as 'an unfinished wilderness of mud and concrete.'[19] Nsukka had the sense of a frontier town, a new outpost of the imagination, whose mud and mortar was to be the raw material for the poet. It was immediately an exciting community: the staff was a mix of Nigerian, English and Americans, mostly seconded from Michigan State University and the Peace Corps.

Nsukka was an experiment and everybody involved in it was trying to make it work. Okigbo was astounded, as Chukwuemeka Ike recalls, to discover that he was the most senior member of the new university library staff. He had been designated acting University Librarian. This meant that the university turned to him to establish a functioning university library, until the substantive university librarian arrived. Okigbo worked in this position from October 1960 to 1961. Okigbo's responsibility was to build a new university library from scratch and run an institution that would meet the research needs of faculty and students. Such a vast responsibility was not his original expectation when he applied for the job as Assistant Librarian. He had expected to grow on the job working under experienced, professional librarians. He rose to the occasion.

The new turn of events challenged him, and saw Okigbo perform one of the finest personal feats of his professional life: without any blueprint he almost single-handedly established a distinguished collection for the new university in its early years. He encountered initial difficulties, but those who worked with him in those pioneer years acknowledged his genius for motivating people. He spent time and effort seeking books from any source. He consulted and paid several visits to the regional library at Enugu and was always willing to learn. The University of Nigeria was beset with problems of funding in its early years and the administration had to rely on strict budgetary and financial rules to get the university going. Expenditure was controlled directly from the office of the Vice-Chancellor, the African-American Dr. George Johnson, one of those pioneers sent from from Michigan to help establish the new university. The protocol to get funds allocated to departments was highly bureaucratic. Okigbo was typically impatient with the bureaucracy. A pioneer member of the university library staff of the University of Nigeria staff at Nsukka, Mr. Ugorji, remembers that:

> …Okigbo's amazing informality was legendary. He was known all over the campus for it. He would barge into Dr. Johnson's office to demand anything he wanted and he always got it. He had no time for formalities. He once told Johnson: 'if you don't give me what I want, you can take your library because I'd be gone!' He worked hard – and I could say this because I personally observed him. Everything, including the way he worked was fascinating: this was a man who didn't know the difference between night and day. Most nights the light in his office was on. You could see him there in his office working – writing away with an almost feverish concentration. He was the most senior member of the library staff, and because he wanted to do a good job he would go to the library at Enugu to learn and get tips on how to manage the library. But I think the greatest thing about him was the way he related and affected the people working with him. He was sort of everybody's darling.[20]

Okigbo's disdain for red tape never ceased to amaze, perhaps even startle, the American head of the university. Dr. Johnson was an affable man, with whom Okigbo soon struck a warm friendship. He quickly saw that behind Okigbo's impatient ways there was a more serious purpose: he was committed to building a first class university library. He was busy looking out for books and sourcing journals. He did not seem concerned by the reality of budget constraints, and he did not let that hinder his enthusiasm. He was dismissive of the frequent excuses of the lack of funding that seemed initially to bedevil the university.

The university library started in a little building attached to the faculty of education. Okigbo's influence was imprinted squarely by the range of the books that he was able to acquire in the short time that he was librarian. The work did have a critical effect on his poetry in the sense that this access to books exposed him to the widest selection of the modern literature of his time from every part of the world. Much of this came to influence his own writing.

Okigbo was assigned a bungalow on campus, with two small bedrooms and a living room on Fulton Avenue. He had originally been given one of the flats on Cartwright Avenue, but the Nsukka flats did not suit his social purpose. He ran an open house. He rejected accommodation on the third floor of Cartwright flats on the grounds that walking up the stairs would put enormous strains on his numerous visitors, particularly the young children whom he frequently entertained. Okigbo loved children. He used to go occasionally into the neighboring Nsukka villages to invite groups of children to his house on weekends and get his steward to cook for them. He found much pleasure in their company. He thought it was a needless inconvenience to have the children go up and down a three-storey block of flats. The noise of his active social life was bound to be distracting to his neighbours. The continuous flow of visitors to his house, in short, demanded some place of easier reach and greater convenience. So he demanded accommodation in one of the bungalows.

New social attitudes began to shape the life in the 1960s. A great liberal spirit seized the world, symbolized by the election of the youthful President Kennedy in the United States. It was the decade of counter-culture. The Beat generation was at its height and the hippies had also arrived. The flame of the flower children burned, making statements in arts, culture and politics. This movement came to redefine the world, and affect the spirit of a generation and the way it saw itself, emphasizing alternative lifestyles and morality; and a notion of inexorable cultural transformation in which social rebellion – the crossing of social boundaries which were taboo – marked the creed of the young. This sense of radical individualism also fused with the ideas of shared community. Soon, it was linked to the civil rights movement raging in America, and the post-colonial years of freedom in Africa. This mood appealed to Okigbo. He was affected by its liberating energy. He soon adopted the idiom of Beat poetry, and the alternative morality and lifestyle of the movement, and its sense of the decadent and the contingent.

In Africa especially, cultural regeneration followed the activities of young African intellectuals and artists of the day, who had experienced deep conflicts as colonial subjects, and had become awakened to the task of renegotiating their colonial identity. The novelist Chinua Achebe, one of the most significant figures of that awakening, said in *Morning Yet on Creation Day*: 'that we in Africa did not hear of culture first from Europeans.'[21] Okigbo was not only in the centre of this renaissance, he was among the group of intellectuals who began to stir new currents and thinking about Africa, and its diaspora. Evidence of Christopher Okigbo's acute perception of his role within the events of that history, as well as his clear understanding of the emergent complexity of post-colonial, twentieth century society was indicated in a letter, which he wrote to Chukwuemeka Ike and to the musicologist, William Echezona, on 1 December 1960:

> This is in continuance with what I talked over with you the other day. I think we should now give serious consideration to the formation of a committee on Afro-culture, which should concern itself primarily with the nature of the creative mind and with the part it plays in the maintenance of those values which have always been inseparable from the idea of a civilization. I believe that such values are threatened by the developments variously known as industrialization, mechanisation and mass-communication that together constitute the technological revolution of our time. This revolution has been accompanied by the rise of scientific philosophy which is obviously in harmony with it.
>
> The Arts, too, are in a state of transition that can be revolutionary, and in the general confusion, it is very necessary to reaffirm not so much the values of the past which understandably have little or no appeal to a people already committed to technology, but the psychological forces at work in the creative mind. The forces that give momentum to the technological developments are powerful, and power indeed appear[s] to be the only solution to the many social and economic problems of our troubled world. But the human agents of these forces are often insensitive and blind insensitive to aesthetic values and blind to the consequences of ignoring the subtle springs of creation on which science itself as well as the Arts depends for its vital continuance.
>
> The importance I attach to such factors as image, symbol, myth, and icon is not due to any initial prejudice, but rather to an objective realisation of the controlling influence of these factors in the development of human culture.
>
> If I thought that the world would be saved and happiness of mankind guaranteed by the sacrifice of aesthetic sensibility I would not hesitate to accept the sacrifice, but what I believe is the contrary. It is because I see everywhere the threatening shadow of the catastrophe that overtake [sic] us, that I strive so earnestly to animate the only philosophy that can save us.
>
> In order to provide a platform for crystallising these ideas, we should also project a literary

bulletin perhaps under the title 'KULCHUR.' The major fields of interest could be literary criticism, creative work, and progress reports on various aspects of Afro-culture etc. I am suggesting that we meet sometime over the weekend in my house to get going.[22]

It was to this meeting that Okigbo invited the young scholar Sunday Anozie, a fresh undergraduate at the university. Anozie reports in his book *Christopher Okigbo: Creative Rhetoric* that Okigbo already had his own ideas about a cultural movement that would emerge from the spirit of the new age and within the intellectual community of the new university. Increasingly his voice would animate this disturbing vision of 'the threatening shadow of the catastrophe that overtake[s] us.' He soon found his 'kindred spirits' – the community of artists and intellectuals in Nsukka early in that 1960 – with whom he shared these disturbing questions.

Okigbo's poetry bloomed out of a combination of a sense of freedom, of physical and emotional liberation, and of shared kinship. Living in Nsukka was an energetic group of young, vibrant intellectuals of the new generation, many of them trained at University College, Ibadan. Okigbo's circle helped to sustain his artistic vision. Among his closest peers at Nsukka, were the Deputy Registrar Chukwuemeka Ike, who had just completed work on his first novel, *Toads for Supper* and William Echezona, who taught music theory and was the head of the music department. There was also the poet Michael Echeruo who taught drama; and later Donatus Ibe Nwoga, who returned in 1961 from England to teach modern poetry. One friendship turned to tragedy. The economist Ola Fashola, a Lagos boy, who had returned from the United States of America and was a popular lecturer who was sometimes known as 'Fash' or 'Longus'. Okigbo and he were a regular pair at Okpara Hall, the female hostel on campus. Fashola was a particularly intense and colorful man, who had married an English woman, Barbara. He later came under severe emotional pressure in Nsukka, had a mental breakdown and committed suicide. Fashola's death, tragic and unexpected, towards the end of Okigbo's time at the university late in 1961 was one of the low points of the poet's life at Nsukka.

This group began to enunciate some of the original ideas upon which a theory of modern African literature came later to be developed. Obi Wali, who moved from Onitsha to Nsukka to teach the Romantic poets, was later to cause a stir at the 1962 Kampala conference, with his seminal essay, 'Dead End of African Literature?' This was based on an idea, which had begun to circulate around Nsukka at this time, and which would later form the essential plank of Ngugi wa Thiong'o's argument in *Decolonising the Mind*. The kernel of Obi Wali's idea arose from discussions taking place in Nsukka in the early 1960s; the premise was that no true literature could emerge from post-colonial Africa if writers continued to produce in the languages of colonialism. Sunday Anozie suggests that the seed of that argument originated in his own undergraduate essay in 1960, and found its way into Obi Wali's more polished perspective. Sunday Anozie's recollection of the Nsukka years captures the ambience in which the poet Okigbo lived. As Anozie said 'When those men met, and this was frequent, and argued literature and the new writing, and this was mostly through the night, nothing could compare with the charged atmosphere, from those moments of grace.'[23] This group, convened as a result of Okigbo's letter to Ike and Echezona, eventually transformed into the 'African Authors Association of Nigeria,' inaugurated on 5 August 1961 by the Minister for Education, Aja Wachukwu. The association published a journal called *The African Writer*, edited by M. J. C. Echeruo.

Okigbo's growth as an artist could be accounted for in his Nsukka years by a ferment of literary ideas in which he involved his friends. Often when Okigbo wrote anything new, he would pass it around that circle, and would listen intently to whatever anyone had to say. Always needing 'more roots/More sap to grow to sunlight...' Okigbo sought that kind of kinship. His community of writers and scholars at Nsukka offered insight, guided his inspiration and created an intense bond with those with whom he shared the burden of his imagination. His work routine drew from this literary kinship: he would write something new, he would listen to criticism, and he would rework the poems again and again, until he was personally satisfied with their final shape and tenor. Okigbo strained towards the perfect sound – the refined riff and the subtlest echoes and harmony of deep music.

Chukwuemeka Ike also recalled the ambience of Okigbo's creative world in those early years at Nsukka. He said that Okigbo 'had acquired different kinds of Igbo musical instruments *ekwe, udu, ogene, uyo*...and planted them all over his living room. At one time he hoped to form an African orchestra. Later it appeared he acquired the instruments to create the right atmosphere in which he could invoke the muses to provide him inspiration for creative work.'[24] Christopher Okigbo often claimed that a background of traditional music was essential for an appreciation of his poetry. He experimented by commandeering anybody to contribute a musical accompaniment while he read. It could be his steward, an Efik boy whom he called Ete, who became an impromptu musician when he was free of household chores. It could be any visitor to his home. Once, Christian Momah and his wife Ethel came to visit him briefly at Nsukka. They were visiting from Enugu and needed to return for other appointments. Momah recalled, 'He literally forced us to listen to his early scribbling by the simple technique of locking his front and back doors, and pocketing the keys. "You will not leave my house before you have listened to my poems," he told us with his devil-may-care smile. I do not recall if *Heavensgate* was one of the poems. It might have been because, though I was under duress, I came away thinking what a wonderful poet he could become.'[25] Chukwuemeka Ike's wife, Adebimpe, remembered: 'often it would not matter whether or not you cared for poetry or for traditional music...But you did it because it was Christopher...few people could resist him. He could be importunate and he was charming.'[26]

Adebimpe Ike also remembered that Christopher Okigbo had the habit of turning up at their home late at night in Nsukka to ask for his favorite meal of pounded yam or beans. These calls occurred mostly when the poet had that feverish need to express himself, whenever he had written anything new. He would drive down at those deadly hours to Ike's home on the University of Nigeria campus. Bimpe Ike remembered those times as 'beautiful and innocent...lawless...just like Christopher who had no time for the orthodox or for boundaries.'[27]

> He would bring with him an empty bottle, which he would hand to me. He would then ask me to beat out some tune as a musical accompaniment to his poem and he would read joyously to whatever crazy tune formed in his head. And in the end he would ask me: 'do you like it?' And it was usually so beautiful. I think he relied and trusted on my judgment far more than I should. But his poetry had a wonderful ring that flowed with the sound as I hit those ordered tunes from the bottle.[28]

Soon after, the poet would ask for his dinner, eat it and roar off noisily into the night. It was part of the exciting life of that small, university community, where a new poetic tension was emerging in Okigbo along with a new creative vision from the impulses around him. For the most part, Ike supplied music for the early poems in *Heavensgate*, which Okigbo was working on at that time.

Among the remarkable people in Nsukka that October 1960 was Peter Thomas, the Welsh poet who taught medieval literature, and who soon became Okigbo's friend and collaborator . They became very close friends 'from that day when Chris surprised me with a visit in my little bungalow at Nsukka,'[29] wrote Peter Thomas. Thomas had begun to hold seminars on Milton and the early English Romantic poets in his bachelor's bungalow nearby Okigbo on Fulton. He often met two successive groups of nine or ten students every afternoon. One day, at about dusk, 'a slim, trim, round faced Igbo with close-cropped hair and a quizzical, slightly brooding look, appeared at the door and asked if he might "sit in" on the class, although he was not a student. When the session was over and the others had gone, my silent auditor stayed on for a beer and a chat. He was, he said, the Acting University Librarian, a classics graduate (1956) from Ibadan University, and he hoped, a poet.'[30] This was how Peter Thomas recalled their first meeting.

Okigbo referred to Peter Thomas as his 'kindred spirit'. They began to operate on the principle of what Peter Thomas revealed years later in 1991 as 'Mi Casa Tu Casa.'[31] They spent endless evenings together reading and discussing poetry, drinking beer and smoking their pipes late into the night. Both men shared a deep sense of drama and ritual. In their personalities were the complementary traits that sustained what became a deep intellectual and artistic friendship. Peter Thomas had graduated from Oxford, where he had been a student of C. S. Lewis. At Nsukka he gave his lectures dressed in his Oxford hood and gown; he was an eccentric presence in Nsukka, replicating Oxonian manners in a land grant university. Peter Thomas and Okigbo were the same age, and shared a love of nature and a mystical consciousness. While Okigbo was extrovert, Peter Thomas was more bound to silence and introspection and his exuberance was more intellectual than physical. Okigbo combined both in the expression of his humanity. Like Okigbo, Thomas was also raised Catholic, and still served at the altar at Catholic mass on campus. Both men were drawn to poetry. With this 'kindred spirit' on the campus of the new University of Nigeria who shared his notion of poetry as the lost language of the enlightenment, Okigbo's poetry blossomed. From his association with Thomas he acquired a new idiomatic force. His poetry achieved a quality of startling newness sustained with an inner glow, different from any other poetry written by his peers.

Okigbo's life constantly reached for shared experience – friendship, companionship, comradeship. Okigbo's hunger for friendship was legendary. His exuberance often obscured the poet's moments of deep solitude when he became withdrawn, solitary, indeed melancholic. These moments can be traced to the effects of his childhood in which he learnt to absorb suffering alone and in silence. He never quite resolved his fear of rejection and abandonment, after the loss of his mother. But he subsumed his fear by his vigorous and public pursuit of adventure to stem the dreariness of life. His friendship with Peter Thomas grew because they were both poets, but even more because they were men of intensity; they shared the same sense of insecurity and an awareness of loss and personal tragedy. The Welsh poet's lively humor and active intellect also veiled his own deep personal sense of tragedy and melancholy. Years later, after Okigbo's death, Peter Thomas was to elaborate on the significance of the years spent together with Okigbo at Nsukka. In a letter in 1991 he wrote thus: '…You ask why Chris's poetry blossomed at Nsukka while I was there, and the answer is, because I was there, as (Ulli) Beier graciously agreed the one time I met him.'[32] In an acknowledgment to this fact, Okigbo dedicated a part of *Heavensgate* to Peter Thomas. The Welsh poet helped to clarify the basis of his association with Okigbo in Nsukka hinting at the shared impulses:

There was the matter of his professional work that kept him from his writing far too often; and the worse problem of wanting to write but feeling unready or unable. That was what brought us together over the making of *Heavensgate,* and perhaps lies behind the inscription on a version of *Limits* still in my possession, from which I took the epigram for this chapter: 'I could never have written this if I did not meet you.' Talking with me, or having me read to him, would somehow set him to work again, or temporarily exorcise the paralysis that beset him.[33]

Okigbo's work with Peter Thomas led critics of modern Nigerian literature to talk later of the 'Nsukka School.' Under the critical guidance of Peter Thomas and the kinship of the muse, Okigbo fashioned the myth of the watermaid and the idiom of her adoration. Peter Thomas describes the poet's life at this period, in a memorial poem to Okigbo, titled 'Anagnorisis: for Chris at Heavensgate':

Kindred spirits he called us,
Mad with the madness of the moon
And mine, his neighbour –
Kindled from my hearth, her flame:
Often and unannounced he came
To shape with his laughter my singing house
Or under stars alone
Foster the ashes that aspire
To open Heavensgate with tongues of fire.[34]

Peter Thomas had with him in Nsukka a copy of his own poem, which was titled 'Heaven's Gate,' written about 1955, in which he celebrated the beauty of Bishop Ken's country retreat in Wiltshire, England. Bishop Ken, who lived there between 1637 and 1711 saw 'Heaven's Gate' as an 'Ideal spot for spiritual meditation,' Peter Thomas's poem had begun thus:

Now I can say I've stood at Heaven's Gate
And leaned across the brink of ecstasy:[35]

And it was from this beginning of Peter Thomas's poem that Christopher Okigbo had chosen the title of one of the most remarkable of his Nsukka poems.

From 'silence' they tried to discover greater, newer poetic insights and to draw unique inspiration. They waited upon the muse with the fervour of mystics. Sometimes, those meetings between the two poets even took a dimension of extraordinary drama. The critic and literary scholar Professor Helen Chukwuma was one of the early students of the English department at Nsukka in 1960/61. She remembered both poets and the drama of their lives as artists. Sometimes they dramatized this with fascinating ritual. Okigbo and Thomas formed an impressive and colourful pair, whose activities added variety to life in a new university. Professor Chukwuma in 1993 described the life of the two poets:

They were a very fascinating pair. Sometimes while walking past Peter Thomas's little bungalow in those years, with all the windows thrown wide open and the curtains open we would see Peter Thomas sitting down on a rest chair, and Okigbo lying down on the mat. They would be smoking their pipes and looking up to the ceiling, not uttering a word. All around them, in the silence, there would be the loud contrasting strain of classical music, which wafted in the air from Peter Thomas's gramophone. It always turned out that in their silence, with the accompaniment of the classical music, and looking heavenward, they were waiting for the 'muse' to descend to them. We thought it was very strange, very fascinating![36]

What Helen Chukwuma heard was apparently the invocation of the impressionist composers, especially César Franck and Claude Debussy, under whose spell the watery inspiration of Okigbo's *Limits* took form.

The same period also saw the evolution of Okigbo's poetic vision, or revelation, centering on mother worship or revelation, 'Anagnorisis', and also what he began to articulate as 'the logistics of the poetic form.' Okigbo, an 'impulsive scientist' with a keen interest in mathematics, had developed this view of poetry as 'constant plausible movement'[37] – a theory derived possibly from his reading of the Heraclites. Okigbo believed that poetry was motion, which could attain a mathematical order. He began to demonstrate this architectonically in symbols and diagrams. He claimed that he could sustain a poetic insight by designing a definite poetic structure to a corresponding mathematical form – an ideally matching complex of structures. This matching of geometry to metaphors was an idea that began to grip Okigbo early on in Nsukka, and it yields in both the structure and nuance of parts of *Heavensgate*, especially in 'Initiations'. This is exactly what the poet proposes in the lines:

And I said:
The prophet only the poet
And he said: Logistics
(Which is what poetry is)...[38]

His idea of poetry evolved and was sharpened by his discussions with Peter Thomas: the very idea of poetry containing a wider prophetic, symbolic principle, which yields from the motion of a well-ordered system appealed to Okigbo enormously, and he began to utilize this in the construction and articulation of his poetic strategy. By the time he began work on *Heavensgate*, he had constructed a philosophy of his own poetry. The effect is the high craftsmanship, the deliberate genius of his poetry.

For Peter Thomas, coming from the Celtic world, with its own sense of magic and ritual; where the idea of ghosts, spirits, the hills and the sea and all nature, were as much a valid experience as in Okigbo's Igbo society, there was a match in their apprehension of phenomena. He combined his understanding of the mythology of 'the white goddess' from the works of Robert Graves, whom Peter Thomas admired with the influence of C. S. Lewis, who had been his teacher at Oxford. This was to affect Okigbo's new aesthetic direction. The muse was the source of those incarnate voices, the inspirational element to every lyrical imagination. Thomas linked the 'white goddess' to the lady of the lake in Arthurian legends. 'The lake image,' wrote the critic and literary scholar, Obi Maduakor, while tracing the influence of Peter Thomas on Nigerian poetry, 'links the muses to their natural habitat in water in classical mythology.'[39] The muses also shared a certain kinship with Milton's 'sisters of the sacred well,' Yeat's Maud Gonne or Queen Maeve (as the symbol of Ireland), and Joyce's bird-like girl in *A Portrait of the Artist as a Young Man*. Christopher Okigbo linked the muses to the 'Mammy Wota' legend in Igboland. 'Through Peter Thomas's persuasion, Christopher Okigbo realized that the muse could be slippery, elusive and inconstant. What is generally known as creative paralysis occurs when the muse withholds from the poet a spiritual or a physical manifestation that can be translated into a creative act,'[40] Obi Maduakor wrote in the spring 1980 issue of *Research in African Literatures*.

Because of this 'slippery, elusive and inconstant' nature of the creative muse, Christopher Okigbo and Peter Thomas often waited in silence. One of the results of this constant waiting for the appearance of the muse, was the poem 'Watermaid', the third sequence in *Heavensgate* in which Christopher Okigbo in fact, celebrates her brief epiphany:

Bright
With the armpit-dazzle of a lioness,
She answers,

Wearing white light about her;

and the waves escort her,
My lioness,
crowned with moonlight.

So brief her presence
Matchflare in wind's breath
so brief with mirrors around me.

Downwards
the waves distill her;
gold crop
sinking ungathered.

Watermaid of the salt emptiness,
grown are the ears of the secret.[41]

Okigbo was struggling apparently to synthesize his own creative impulse with the ideas gathering around him. As Peter Thomas explained later:

> ...Behind the matchless moment of 'intuitive pulsion' (in the poem 'Watermaid') lies a short poem of Robert Browning's ('The Meeting at Night') that was a particular favorite of Christopher's. The narrator lands in his boat on a moonlit beach, where waves leap 'in fiery ringlets,' and crosses the fields to a nearby farm for a meeting with his sweetheart. When he arrives outside her window there is 'A tap on the pane, the quick sharp scratch / And blue spurt of a lighted match' and poet Okigbo had his 'match-flare in wind's breath' glimpses of his muse, escorted by waves and wearing white light for a crown as he stood there with mirrors around him.[42]

These were the influences of the *Heavensgate* poems. Okigbo was attempting to make a statement about life and the individual in a society in transition. *Heavensgate* is a sensitive autobiographical testimony of a new poet groping for form and meaning, struggling to understand the nature of his new role in a new society.

New writing from Africa was just beginning to make its impact on the literature of the twentieth century. There was worldwide interest in Africa. By this time also, a more assured voice emerged in Okigbo's poetry, especially with the completion of *Heavensgate* in 1961. Okigbo's poetry, beginning from his Fiditi poems, the *Four Canzones*, was hardening into what seemed to be a private idiom, inspired of course by his closeness to the new university library. While building and stocking, he explored the library ravenously. He was always seeking new rhythms, new influences and fresh insights in the poetry he was acquiring.

He was especially seduced by the Beat poets Ferlinghetti and Allen Ginsberg. For his birthday in August 1960, Dr. Pius Okigbo had given him a copy of Ginsberg's *Howl*. Okigbo described the book to Sunday Anozie as 'very mad!' and said that he was excited 'its attempt to reinvent the pulsion of ordinary language into high poetry.'[43] He began to read Walt Whitman, the American Romantic poet who was the canonized saint of Beat and hippie counter-culture. He thought that Whitman had '...the freedom of language and honesty of spirit.'[44] He devoured Carl Sandburg. He would read aloud, with Peter Thomas, or to Dr Pius Okigbo when he visited him in Nsukka from Enugu. He began to reach for a new idiom accepting much of Crosby's Dadaist manifesto, the view that the artist should strive for pure poetry.[45] For Okigbo this meant that he should write not necessarily to communicate, but to express himself. The startling effect of this on Okigbo's poetry was its experimental breath.

Chukwuemeka Ike witnessed these transformations in Okigbo's poetic voice, as he wrote:

> His poetry, when it began to flow, sounded so unconventional, so unorthodox, so much like Christopher that many of his friends dismissed it as worthless. A more cautious colleague, reluctant to commit himself one way or the other, remarked that the poems were such as would either pitchfork him into prominence as one of Africa's leading poets or dump him into the slough of despond from which he would be unable to scramble out for many years.[46]

Okigbo's lifestyle at Nsukka also expressed this rebellious spirit of the 1960s. Influenced by the 'decadent' mood of that moment, among the crop of new writers expressing a new moral vision of the world, abandoning bourgeois morality – like the Beat poets – Okigbo was thrilled to reject the dominant, traditional social morality of his generation. He already had begun to express this in his open lifestyle. He was avant-garde in every respect.

Okigbo's attraction to the decadent, his reaching for the erotic, for the deeply sensual and for free love are emblematic of his courage; he dared to be unconventional and he chose to live freely in a society in which that kind of freedom was almost unthinkable. Sunday Anozie would note in *Creative Rhetoric* that, 'Okigbo was one of those writers who cared very little about his personal external appearance. While he was Assistant University Librarian at Nsukka he was often seen walking about, even in the middle of the harmattan season, in a pair of khaki shorts and an open-breasted short-sleeved shirt with the button all loose, and roughly shod in an old pair of sandals.'[47] Christopher Okigbo would have been a vivid presence in any environment. His personal aura captivated his audience. He was hedonistic, and his pleasure seeking was open and promiscuous. Part of Okigbo's uniqueness stemmed from his disregard for convention, and the honesty of his personality. He was memorable because he was unambiguous in his pursuits.

Okigbo was active on campus as the coach of the University of Nigeria, Nsukka soccer team and patron of its cricket club. The pioneer generation of students in that university who met Okigbo, and saw him at work as a poet, retained the sense of a remarkable individual, and he inspired a cult following. He soon developed close, personal relationships with some of the undergraduate poets in the seminar group organized by Peter Thomas in his bungalow. Among the poems he read aloud to them were 'Debtor's Lane' and one of the *Four Canzones*, which he had completed at Fiditi. The group included Okogbule Wonodi, Pol Ndu, Sunday Anozie, Romanus Egudu, Nduka Eya, Bona Onyejeli, Uche Okeke and Sam Nwaojigba; all of them were pioneer undergraduates of the Nsukka English Department. It was an odd fellows group of campus poets and artists, who lived the avant-garde lifestyle of the artist modeled by Okigbo. They adopted Okigbo as the icon of the new poetry movement blossoming in Nsukka. This counter-culture sustained the Nsukka mythos of the poet as a social rebel. Okigbo was to the Nsukka poets what Whitman was to the Beat poets or what Ezra Pound was to the poets emerging in England. Helen Chukwuma gives an account of these new campus poets in the early 1960s.

> This was a group of young men, who were all unconventional in their dress and manners. They went about the campus, with the solemnity of their artistic burdens, and made out as though, they had something very new, very profound and different to offer. They really appeared different from the rest of the community. They wore tussled hair, simple clothes, and they walked about with the star in their eyes. You would find them reading aloud on the road, taking no notice of anyone but consumed by their poetry.[48]

The extent of Okigbo's influence on this group would emerge later on, and can be seen in the work written by the most important poets from that group like Okogbule Wonodi and Pol Ndu. Ndu's rise as a significant voice of poetry in Africa was cut short by his tragic death in a car crash in 1979 on returning home after his studies in the United States. His *Songs of Seers* is testimony to the influence of Okigbo on a new generation. Romanus Egudu and Sunday Anozie were to become influential critics who would help define the critical sensibility of postcolonial literature.

Sunday Anozie became especially close to Okigbo in Nsukka. He started out trying to be a poet but he had been dissuaded, he later revealed, by the intensity of the poetic life: he had observed Okigbo closely at work. Anozie described the poet's work routine as 'matched only by idolatry.'[49] The poet's brother Pius indeed recalls that Okigbo 'could at any time, withdraw from the swirl of life around him to concentrate his mind and thought singularly on the work before him. He could, and often did, as occasion demanded, retreat into himself for two, three days with little food but armed with a pen and paper, he would scribble all day and all night until the last drop of verse in him had oozed out unto the pages of the notepaper.'[50] As for Anozie, on one occasion when Okigbo was trying to compose a poem, he was desperately trying to find an elegant way of expressing the experience. Sunday Anozie was in silence watching the poet in his agonized state. After a while he said to Okigbo: 'Look, Chris, are you sure that what you're looking for is not the word, "town-crier"?' Okigbo leapt from his chair, embraced Sunday Anozie and kissed him on both cheeks. 'Sunday, you've got the word! "Town-crier!" That's just the word!'[51] And he set out again to write. Sometimes he wrote furiously, sometimes ponderously. But at all times he conducted a dialogue from within himself, as if from a secret part of him, where only he could reach. Sunday Anozie's greatest memory of Okigbo at Nsukka, was the poet's legendary capacity for kindness and generosity. Anozie would say: 'The most important thing about Chris was the quality of his mind. He was capable of great empathy, of limitless kindness. He was one of those men who could share totally of themselves, and of anything they owned with others. If Chris had only a pair of trousers, for instance, and you wanted it, he was prepared to give it to you. It wouldn't matter that he would have nothing else! He was an extremely generous soul.'[52]

Sunday Anozie was as intense as he was brilliant. He was also indigent. Okigbo took Sunday Anozie to work for him in the university library, mostly to supplement his pocket money, but also to expose his mind to a range of great books. It was a part-time job. Anozie needed it badly, because he was frequently broke. He was constantly in danger of withdrawing from the university. So he applied for the UAC scholarship, early in 1961. He was among the applicants invited for an interview, which was scheduled in Lagos. As the day of the interview approached, Anozie grew more silent and pensive. A brooding, melancholic air hung heavily about him. His trouble was deeply etched on his furrowed countenance. The trouble was that he had no money to travel to Lagos, and he agonized silently about his impecunious state. His chance of a scholarship to continue in the university was slipping.

Okigbo took Sunday Anozie's brooding silences for anxiety, and said to him, 'Come on Sunday, you should be happy for this interview. Are you worried that you're not going to do well? Look, don't worry, there's nothing those chaps would ask you that you wouldn't answer.'[53] Anozie kept quiet. Somehow, Okigbo intuitively found the cause of his worries. On the morning when Anozie was to travel to Lagos, he called at Okigbo's bungalow. The poet was still in bed but at the door Okigbo's steward handed Anozie some money. It was money to transport Anozie to Lagos and back, and to make him comfortable while he was in Lagos. Anozie took the money gratefully and proceeded on his journey. As he would acknowledge years later, but for Okigbo's act of kindness and empathy he would never have gone to Lagos; even that morning, all dressed up for his interview, he had not had the money to undertake the journey.

Sunday Anozie did secure the UAC scholarship, which saw him through the rest of his undergraduate studies. In that way Okigbo was instrumental in shaping the destiny of one of the most brilliant and influential literary critics of his generation. When Anozie returned to Nsukka after the interview, he put the leftover money in an envelope, with an accompanying note thanking the poet for his kindness, and saying that he would come in later to let him know how he fared at the interview. He handed the envelope to Okigbo's steward. Okigbo used the spare money to buy things for Anozie, one of which was a copy of Gilbert Highet's *Poets in a Landscape* which he kept for a lifetime. As one of those who shared intimately in the intensity of Okigbo's life and work he was witness to the great passions which ruled the poet's existence. From this relationship of deep intellectual kinship Okigbo wanted to sharpen Anozie's poetic impulses. But later when he discovered that Anozie had veered into literary criticism, the poet encouraged him greatly. Anozie eventually was to write one of the earliest and most perceptive books on Okigbo's life and poetry.

As he reveals in *Creative Rhetoric,* Okigbo gave him his first insights into the philosophical works of the German materialist, Hegel, and into the Greek tragedies. Anozie's relationship with Okigbo was of 'an admiring acolyte and his master.'[54] They shared, apart from the intellectual life, some exciting adventures at Nsukka. For the younger Sunday Anozie, Okigbo's life was ceaselessly intriguing. It was a tumult of paradoxes. The poet was mercurial: just as he could be easily drawn into open laughter, Okigbo almost in the same breath, could flare into great temper. Anozie witnessed a particular occasion at the university library. One day, Professor Philip Bordinat, one of the American professors in the English Department where Anozie was a student, had come into the library and imperiously gone straight to Okigbo's office. With impatience and scant courtesy to the poet, he said: 'Look here Mr. Okigbo, the books I ordered a few days ago for my literature class, where are they?' Okigbo was trying to offer an explanation to him on the matter, but Professor Bordinat was too irritated to listen, and made some uncomplimentary racist remarks, something about stupid Africans who could never get anything together. Philip Bordinat was a man of impressive build who exuded authority as a professor of the English department. But at that moment, Okigbo rose from his chair, his eyes flashing in great anger as he said to Philip Bordinat: 'Now, you look here Bordinat, you can't come here to the library to tell me what to do! Who in fact told you that you could come to my country and order me about?'[55] Okigbo ordered him out of his office. Philip Bordinat backed away from the poet's potent fury. Anozie was worried that as a witness to that scene he might get in trouble with Bordinat. But Okigbo assured him, 'Oh, don't worry Sunday, I've put him in his place. He won't trouble you.'[56]

Christopher Okigbo detested any form of racism. He always thought of himself in universal terms as a poet unrestricted by the tensions of social or racial boundaries – a cosmopolitan poet. Christopher Okigbo's love life was marked as much by lack of racial or social boundaries as by convention: he lived a bachelor's existence in his Nsukka years. With his friend Peter Thomas, Okigbo would disappear for days in the neighboring Nsukka villages, in search of the freedom of physical experiences. Wole Soyinka traveled frequently to the East and visited Okigbo at Nsukka. At this time

Soyinka was doing his research on the Rockefeller traveling grant, documenting indigenous theatre traditions in Nigeria, which he would later fuse in his dramatic works. Often Okigbo would take him to a home in Nsukka, where two sisters were in love with him. Every time Okigbo visited their home, he was treated with much respect and with great courtesy, 'like royalty,'[57] were Soyinka's exact words. Okigbo always encouraged Soyinka to sleep with one of the sisters. Sometimes, Okigbo and Peter Thomas would drive up to Ede-Obala, which had good palm wine, and spend evenings in the bars with local people.

At this time, Okigbo was also involved in a love affair with an undergraduate, one of the pioneer students in the history class in the university. They had an open relationship. Okigbo insisted on the freedom of sexual intimacy. Indeed for Okigbo, it was a basis for his relationship with all of his lovers. He was extremely casual with matters of physical sex. This idea of free love was inspired by the Euro-American counter-culture which Okigbo absorbed. Okigbo believed that love transcended mere physical experience – it was the totality of experience. Sexuality was to be open and uninhibited, undiminished by moral conventions. At the beginning of their relationship, Okigbo would ask her to make love to any of his friends. At first she felt insulted. She would resist and complain. But soon she discovered that Okigbo didn't mean any insult, and that it was an expression of his peculiar sense of liberty. Frequently Okigbo suggested she should have sex with his friends, just to please him! Sunday Anozie remarked that Okigbo believed in open, liberated sex, uncomplicated by a false morality. It would require a deeper understanding of Okigbo's inner personality to understand the poet's capacity for two extremes, sometimes kind, sometimes cruel, especially in his relationships with women.

Women found Okigbo very attractive and were drawn to him, because of a sense of his emotional fragility: Okigbo's great needs for love and consolation seemed to excite the maternal instincts in many women. This powerful need always drew him to vulnerable women who tried to protect and love him. His amorality made him both exciting and dangerous. His restless needs inspired equal passion. His appetite for the sensual was possibly a sublimated desire for a lost mother, for he once told Sunday Anozie: 'in women, I seek something of my mother.'[58] Okigbo's restless sexual quest can thus be explained as a fundamental lack which drove him from one pair of female arms to another. He demonstrated a complicated relationship with women and sex. One day he came down from the upper room in the Mbari Club, thrusting his fingers in the nose of Isidore Okpewho so that he could 'smell vagina.'[59] Okigbo also once told Anozie how after he made love to a woman, he would not take his bath for many days. 'He said he loved the odor of sex about him.'[60] Okigbo's sexual fantasies could also be seen in the sexual images of his love poems. One example is the sexual 'masochism' of the 'oblong-headed lioness' in 'Siren Limits':

An image insists
From flag pole of heart;
Her image distracts
*With the cruelty of the rose…*

Oblong-headed lioness –
No shield is proof against her –
Wound me, O sea-weed
Face, blinded like strongroom –

Distances of her armpit-fragrance
Turn chloroform enough for my patience –

When you have finished
& done up my stitches,
wake me near the altar,
& this poem will be finished…[61]

These carnal images, sprinkled all over *Labyrinths* reveal Okigbo's sexual allegories, an obsessive conquest of feminity. Nkem Nwankwo has traced this down to a background of sexual repression, which his generation suffered through its experience of missionary education and the restrictions of an English type boarding school. The result was this explosion in adulthood, especially in an age of growing sexual freedom and political liberty, of the repressed desires of childhood. This repressed desire found outlet in the sexual revolution of 1960s society. In Okigbo's world, sexual freedom was *sine qua non* to a creative life. This intense desire both for freedom and for love framed his numerous sexual affairs. There may also have been something potentially perverse in Okigbo's sexual habits.

Aside from his relationship with the undergraduate student, Okigbo carried on an affair with Evelyn, the wife of one of the American professors in the university. Sunday Anozie describes her as a woman of arresting beauty 'who fell hopelessly in love with Chris at Nsukka.'[62] By his account, it was a relationship that demonstrated Okigbo's love of danger and adventure. Living in the narrow social orbit of Nsukka, in those early years was difficult for a socially active American woman. She was also married to a serious-minded scientist who was totally absorbed by his pioneering scientific research. Life for her may have grown rather dull. Okigbo first met her in the new university library when she came to check out some books, and there was an immediate spark. It was not difficult for an affair to develop between this liberated American woman and the equally liberated, strikingly individual poet. She found a willing outlet for her desire for sexual adventure in the exciting personality of the poet of *Labyrinths*, who dared to confront life with flamboyance and a fearlessness that appealed to her imagination.

They soon became lovers and found ways to consummate an affair marked by a deep sexual attraction. Anozie said, 'Their relationship was stimulated by a sense of the dangerous and the forbidden. They had incredible chemistry.'[63] Anozie was a close observer of that love affair. He described the nature of this relationship as 'emotional, dangerously physical and daring.'[64] In those years, her husband came home regularly from his lectures to take a siesta, before driving down again to continue his work in the laboratories on campus. He would then work till late in the evenings. These were the times that Okigbo carried on his sexual affair.

Sometimes, Sunday Anozie accompanied Okigbo to the house and after the signal from her that her husband had gone into his usual nap, they would begin to kiss right in the sitting room in the presence of Sunday Anozie, and they would retire hurriedly into an adjoining bedroom where they would spend half-an-hour of intense love-making while her husband slept in the next room! When the lust was spent, Okigbo would hurry out of the bedroom and would say to Anozie, 'Come on Sunday, let's get out of here. I don't want this man to wake up and break my head!'[65] And they would rush out into the noon.

Sometimes during lecture hours, when the professor was away to school, Okigbo would drive her down to his own home, where they would spend most of the day in bed. The affair lasted until Okigbo left Nsukka. It was such a feature of Okigbo's life at Nsukka that Chukwuemeka Ike drew on this relationship in his novel, *The Naked Gods*, which was set in the 1960s in a university campus like Nsukka.

This affair is echoed in a more fundamental, and personal way in Okigbo's poem, 'Watermaid', for this lover indeed is Okigbo's real 'white queen,' whom he celebrates in the poem. Okigbo attempts to merge two important motifs, of the water goddess, taken from Robert Graves' 'white goddess,' and reinvigorate it with an actual muse, in the person of a 'white queen', his own lover, a 'white woman' in Nsukka, 'whose secrets I have covered up with beachsand.' Okigbo tells the story of this love affair in his poem:

> And I who am here abandoned,
>
> count the sand by wavelash abandoned
> count her blessing, my white queen.
>
> But the spent sea reflects
> from his mirrored visage
> not my queen, a broken shadow.
>
> So I who count in my island the moments,
> count the hour which will bring
>
> my lost queen with angels' ash in the wind[66]

We have the image of the poet, marooned on an island, possibly Nsukka, acknowledging an emotional dependency on his muse, his 'white queen,' the physical alter ego to Idoto, at once lover and at once mother.

Okigbo's serial love affairs did not stop his pursuit of Judith Safinat Attah, whom he later was to marry. The relationship was off and on. As Obumselu suggested, Christopher Okigbo could not love any other woman in the way he loved Safinat. Okigbo once told Peter Thomas about Safi: 'Every time I see her, I fall in love anew.'[67] It was stubborn love. From when Okigbo met Safi at Ibadan, while she was in St. Theresa's, he was in pursuit of her. Their families had come to know each other closely too. Safi's elder brother, Abdulaziz Attah, who was to become one of his generation's most renowned public servants, and Christopher's own elder brother, Pius Okigbo, who was to become the foremost Nigerian economist of his time, close friends when they worked in the colonial civil service as Development Officers in Eastern Nigeria in the 1940s. Abdulaziz had been Pius Okigbo's contemporary at Achimota College in Ghana and had also been educated at Oxford. Both were intellectually sophisticated, cosmopolitan, and of liberal temperament.

Abdulaziz Attah was married at that time to an Efik woman, the artist Afi Ekong. The relationship between Christopher Okigbo and Afi Ekong also became close. She used to visit Okigbo frequently at Nsukka. Afi was to prove important because she helped to influence the eventual outcome of this turbulent relationship with Safinat, when many members of the Attah family were being difficult over Christopher Okigbo's moves to marry her. Many of Safi's relations thought that Okigbo was too much of a 'loose canon', and that put a lot of pressure on her. In any case, Okigbo was a well-known womanizer. Safi was painfully aware of this, yet she was deeply in love with the poet – for all his philandering. Okigbo's relentless wooing of Safi was equally legendary. Put in Pius Okigbo's pithy language: 'Christopher pursued her to the very end of the earth,'[68] an indication of the seriousness that Okigbo put into the matter.

Christopher and Safi's love affair brought together two distinct individuals: Safi was reserved, aristocratic, with quiet steel; Okigbo on the other was intense, exuberant, and rebellious. They found themselves entwined by the power of inexplicable chemistry. Christopher Okigbo's elder sister, Susan, had this to say several years later: 'We all loved Safi. She was a giving soul, demanding nothing from Chris. She was a special woman: and there was no one else of all my brother's women who could understand him so well, and accept him so totally. There was no other woman whom Chris could have lived with as husband and wife, because Safi understood him and gave him whatever space he needed emotionally to exist as a poet.'[69] And Safi herself would confess her true love:

> I loved Chris very much. He was a very cheerful and kind person. Very good man. Our daughter – Obiageli – reminds me so much of him: the same intensity, the same energy, the same mannerisms. Sometimes I tell her: 'why didn't you come as a man, so that we can finish what we started!'[70]

And there was no better way for Okigbo, dramatic to the end, to demonstrate this love than to dedicate his life's work, *Labyrinths*, 'For Safinat and Ibrahimat; mother and child.' Yet it was a relationship that was as complicated and as tumultuous as the poet himself.

Safi had moved from Ilorin to Yola where she served as an education officer in 1960/61. She used to visit the poet occasionally at his bachelor's bungalow in Nsukka. At such times 'they shared sensitive moments together.'[71] As Sunday Anozie has said, there was nothing more pleasing for Safi in those years than sitting down while Okigbo read his poems to her. She listened with 'that rapturous look in her eyes,'[72] sometimes with tears, sometimes with laughter, when Okigbo regaled her with some of his usually lewd, and wildly irreverent jokes.

In spite of Okigbo's complicated serial relationships, there is profound evidence that he reserved a special place for Safi in his heart. Their friends testify that they spent many happy moments together. But it was a relationship in which Safi was always giving, always accommodating. Sometimes, as Susan Okigbo recalled, the poet would turn Safi straight back to Yola, if she came to Nsukka without informing him beforehand. But he would also drive the thousand miles to Yola in the north of Nigeria, whenever he felt the impulsive desire for her. Okigbo had these frequent, sudden epiphanic moments of desire to see Safi recalled Michael Echeruo: 'And everybody on campus would know, because we would start contributing spare tires, money, and all kinds of things for Christopher to travel!'[73]

Their relationship entered a period of uncertainty in 1961. Apparently, Okigbo conceived parts of *Limits* in reflection of this. As he wrote in his introduction to *Labyrinths*, he had traveled to Yola to see her. But going to Yola turned out to be in pursuit of a 'white elephant' – an illusion. Okigbo had in fact written that *Limits* occurred to him 'at the end of a journey of several centuries from Nsukka to Yola in pursuit of what turned out to be an illusion.'[74] Okigbo, still wooing her, continued to encounter resistance from Safi's family who were not yet in support of his proposal of marriage.

Okigbo's metaphor of the illusory captures the sense of frustration he felt in 1961 in the relationship with this Igbira princess. They had planned to elope and get married in July 1961 in a quiet ceremony at the Enugu registry, to be witnessed by a few of Okigbo's friends and a number of his relatives living nearby. For this occasion he invited his brother Pius, then living in Enugu as Economic Adviser to the East, his cousin Bede Okigbo, who was then a professor in the agriculture department at the University at Nsukka, and a handful of his close friends. It was to be followed by a quiet luncheon at Pius Okigbo's home in Enugu. There was then a hitch in the plan and they had to cancel it suddenly as a result of pressure from Safi's family. That disruption, which took Okigbo to Yola, hardened his disappointment and resulted in the angst and the 'masochism' of 'Siren Limits', the fourth sequence of *Limits*. However, Okigbo and Safi were married later on 29 July 1962, by which time he had moved to Ibadan. Safi was already pregnant at that time and they were still calling the banns for a wedding in church when, one afternoon, Okigbo rushed into the house and said, 'Safi, get ready quick! We are going to the registry to get married!'[75] The best man was fellow Sigmite, Ignatius Atigbi, then West African Regional Manager and Correspondent of the Reuters News Service.

The year 1961 was Okigbo's most inspired season at Nsukka. He completed work on *Heavensgate* and began to work on parts of *Limits*. A new and exciting range of cultural activity was on the horizon. At that time, a group of young intellectuals began to meet and come together under the auspices of the Mbari Club which was founded in Ibadan in March 1961. Wole Soyinka, now at the School of Drama at Ibadan after his return from England, already had his own idea of starting a writers and artists centre. The poet John Pepper Clark was at the Institute of African Studies at the University of Ibadan. In the east, Christopher Okigbo and Obi Wali were at Nsukka, and Chinua Achebe was close by in Enugu, at the Nigerian Broadcasting Corporation.

It is significant that the grains of Okigbo's ideas, already contained in the letter of 1 December 1960 he wrote to Ike and Echezona, would grow into the Mbari Club – an idea which he began to share, no doubt, with writers when they visited him at Nsukka. Ulli Beier, 'a great organizer,'[76] who had started the journal *Black Orpheus* in 1957 was the motivator and supporter of the Mbari idea of a writers and artists collective. He visited Okigbo frequently at Nsukka and they apparently discussed Mbari as early as 1960. When writers visited Okigbo at Nsukka, developments in the new literature, and the critical ideas, which began to shape it, were the subject of vigorous discussion. Okigbo was often at the center of those discussions to formalize the process; to define the basis of the new literature coming out Africa, and to connect it to a wider, more international audience. Okigbo's bungalow was often loud with sustained debate, and the discussions often went on sometimes till dawn. Okigbo always loved to entertain. In Anozie's words: 'He was a thorough mythmaker and he loved to shape the hollow night with the ring of his laughter.'[77] This was the beginning of the literary and artistic movement which would define the years that the American literary scholar, Robert Wren would describe in his book *Those Magical Years*.[78]

In May 1961, the poet received news of the birth of Pius and Georgette's first daughter. This happy occasion matched the mood of the ripening season of Isthar, which also symbolized the fertile moment of the creative spirit. Okigbo wrote the poem, 'Newcomer,' perhaps one of his most beautiful poems as part of his Easter sequence. 'Newcomer,' written for Georgette and the new baby, became the fifth sequence of *Heavensgate*. The beauty of the poem derives mainly from the subtle images of life and growth deployed to heighten the mood of fertility. It evokes the completion of a cycle following the changes in the season. The sensitive power of the poem reflects the affection that Okigbo retained for the little baby, who was later christened Anne Uzo Okigbo – named after Okigbo's mother.

Gerald Moore visited Christopher Okigbo at Nsukka in July 1961 when he was touring to establish links with the new writers coming out from newly independent African societies in those exciting years. He was then in the Extramural Department at Uganda's Makerere University and had been in contact with Ulli Beier, who was at the Extramural Department of the University of Ibadan. *Black Orpheus*, Ulli Beier's magazine, had published Okigbo's 'Debtor's Lane' that year. It was from him that

Gerald Moore heard of Okigbo for the first time and thus came to visit him at Nsukka that July. Gerald Moore retained a vivid recollection of his visit to the poet at Nsukka:

> He was writing *Heavensgate* and would often try out bits on me and others. We went together to a village near Nsukka, where we drank palm wine with alligator pepper. He was courting a girl there at the time. I don't remember the name of the village. It was only a forest walk away from the campus.[79]

One of the remarkable high points of Gerald Moore's visit to Okigbo was when the poet took the critic to his home town, Ojoto, near Onitsha, many miles away from Nsukka. As Gerald Moore recollected, at Ojoto they had actually gone and stood beside the sacred stream, Idoto; and they had also driven to Onitsha, where they stood at the bridge crossing to Asaba. Out of that experience had emerged the poem, 'Newcomer' which attempts evoking the mysticism of that shared moment.

> I am standing above the noontide,
> Above the bridgehead;
>
> Listening to the laughter of waters
>     that do not know why:
>
> Listening to incense –
>
> I am standing above the noontide
>     with my head above it;
>
> Under my feet float the waters
> Tide blows them under…[80]

Okigbo, had informed Gerald Moore during this visit that the priesthood of the goddess Idoto was in his family and would have descended to him by incarnation, 'but for his mother's passionate Catholicism,'[81] he felt therefore like a prodigal son to Idoto, alienated because of a historical disruption of the priestly lineage of the water spirit.

On their way to the Ajani shrine at Ire, Ojoto, they crossed a spot where several long, wooden images of human figures had been uprooted and laid on a rock. Okigbo was deeply touched and disturbed by the desecration of traditional holy grounds. 'He was shocked by this flagrant abandonment of old beliefs and practices,'[82] Gerald Moore recalled of that occasion, that he uttered his shock almost in the same words that would recur in the 'Fragments out of the Deluge', the first part of *Limits,* which Okigbo wrote after Gerald Moore's visit to Nsukka:

> And the gods lie in state
> And the gods lie in state
> Without the long drum.
>
> And the gods lie unsung,
> Veiled only with mould,
> Behind the shrinehouse.
>
> Gods grow out,
> Abandoned;
> And so do the…[83]

From Onitsha they crossed over to the cable point at Asaba. There, Okigbo pointed out to the English critic, the word CABLE written on the rocks of the cable point. He also told Moore, the story of how he used to swim across the Niger from Asaba to Onitsha as a boy. On their way back from that trip, Okigbo's car, an old American

Zephyr, broke down – it was generally an exciting time for Moore, as he recollected, because Christopher Okigbo was a most entertaining host.

Gerald Moore later became influential among the new writers in Africa, and was central in shaping the emerging critical tendencies in the literature of Okigbo's generation. One significant impression that Gerald Moore took away about the poet at Nsukka was the simplicity of his world, uncluttered by ceremonies. In his little bungalow on campus, Okigbo had only a bed, which he shared with his constant stream of friends whenever they visited him. He would lie there, and play the oja – the Igbo reed flute – which he loved passionately. Following a long career as a critic and teacher of literature in many African universities, Gerald Moore was still awestruck by the personality of Christopher Okigbo. He captured the essence of the poet in a letter he wrote about his first encounter with Okigbo:

> What I remember is a vivid, intense personality, a person direct and easy to get on with, if you shared his passion for poetry, or music or any other excellence. That's how I remember him now, and every reading of his poetry refreshes that image.[84]

During this visit, Okigbo had given Gerald Moore an early version of his *Heavensgate* which still had a Latin refrain, '*De Profundis Clemari*', at the end of Idoto. Gerald Moore and Ulli Beier were to include that early version in the Penguin *Modern Poetry from Africa* (1963). That anthology was to launch modern African poetry, and the new poets like Okigbo, into international recognition.

Late in 1961, Christopher Okigbo was transferred to the Enugu campus library of the University of Nigeria, which then belonged to the Nigerian College of Arts and Science. Okigbo was involved in the negotiations to take possession of that library for the University of Nigeria. Okigbo had acted until then, as the University Librarian. He specifically asked to be transferred when Dr. Raphael Victor Athaide was appointed substantively as the University Librarian. The university had recommended Okigbo as one of the first recipients of the USAID participant fellowship that would have enabled him to travel for postgraduate work and deepen his professional training and experience in librarianship. His friends were traveling abroad: Chukwuemeka Ike was going to Stanford, M. J. C. Echeruo to Cornell, and Obi Wali to the University of California, Los Angeles. Okigbo did not take up the award. He had realized that there was no future for him as a librarian.

For a while, he became possessed by the idea of going abroad to take a degree in modern letters, preferably at a French Canadian university. However, providence intervened. One of the regular visitors to Okigbo in his Nsukka bungalow was Philip Harris, then Regional Representative of the Cambridge University Press in Ibadan. Harris had met Okigbo through Ulli Beier, who had taken Okigbo to the CUP office in Ibadan, where Okigbo in his usual passionate manner had protested that works of his friend, the poet J. P. Clark, had not been included on the publishing list for that year. Ulli Beier said that Harris was 'bowled.' They interacted closely thereafter through Okigbo's work in the University Library at Nsukka.

Philip Harris was due to go back to England and was looking out for a local representative. Sometime in 1961, Harris came to Nsukka. He later wrote to Peter Thomas asking whether Okigbo would be a suitable recruit to replace him at Cambridge University Press. Although Okigbo was already slated to travel for further studies, the job of a publisher's representative appealed far more to him. Soon after Philip Harris's visit to Nsukka, Cambridge University Press arranged for Okigbo to fly to London to meet his managers. He returned a week later to announce to his friends his plans to join the Press as its West African Regional Manager in Ibadan.

It was a unique time: Ibadan was on the verge of an artistic and cultural ferment, as well as a political explosion. It was a moment which would mark Okigbo's poetry deeply, and shape the character and history of that generation. Okigbo's decision to move to Ibadan enabled him to join up with his other literary and artist friends and to get fully involved in the Mbari Club, which had been founded in 1961. The poet left Enugu for Ibadan in January 1962. Another phase ended with the beginning of a new, exciting life in the West. At Nsukka his poetry had blossomed. Going back to Ibadan, he would begin the most eventful cycle in his career as a poet. He was approaching his final, creative homecoming.

## NOTES

1   Christopher Okigbo, 'Lustra IV', 1960/61, *Heavensgate, Labyrinths with Path of Thunder* (London: Heinemann, 1971).
2   Interview with Wole Soyinka, Abeokuta, 1992.
3   Ibid.
4   Interview with V.C. Ike, Lagos, 1993.
5   Ibid.
6   J.P. Clark's letter to Sunday Anozie quoted in *Christopher Okigbo: Creative Rhetoric* (New York: Africana Publishers 1971).
7   Interview with Alex Ajayi, Lagos, 1992.
8   Christopher Okigbo, 'Lustra IV', 1960/61 *Heavensgate, Labyrinths*.
9   Ben Obumselu, 'Christopher Okigbo: a Poetic Portrait'. Essay delivered at 'Song of Idoto': A Celebration of Christopher Okigbo, National Museum, Enugu, 2 November 1996.
10  Interview with Susan Anakwenze, Nsukka 1994.
11  Christopher Okigbo, 'Limits I–IV', *Heavensgate* 1961.
12  Ibid.
13  Interview with Alex Ajayi.
14  Interview with Ebong Etuk, Uyo, 1996.
15  Interview with Obi Wali, Port Harcourt, 1993.
16  Christopher Okigbo, *Labyrinths*, p. xi.
17  Chukwuemeka Ike, 'Christopher Okigbo: Reminiscences', unpublished essay.
18  Gerald Moore, letter to the author, 1992.
19  Peter Thomas, letter to the author, 1992.
20  Interview with Mr. Ugorji, Zik Library, Nsukka, 1995.
21  Chinua Achebe, 'The Novelist as Teacher', *Morning Yet on Creation Day* (London: Heinemann, 1975).
22  Christopher Okigbo, unpublished letter to V.C. Ike, 1 December 1960, Nsukka.
23  Interview with Sunday Anozie, University of Port Harcourt, 1993.
24  Chukwuemeka Ike, 'Christopher Okigbo: Reminiscences.'
25  Chike C. Momah, letter to the author, July 2003, Somerset, NJ, USA.
26  Interview with Adebimpe Ike, Lagos, 1994.
27  Ibid.
28  Ibid.
29  Peter Thomas, letter to the author, 1991.

30  Peter Thomas, 'Ride me Memories': A Memorial Tribute to Christopher Okigbo (1932–1967), *African Arts* 1, 4 (1968), pp. 68–70.
31  Peter Thomas, letter to the author, 1991.
32  Ibid.
33  Ibid.
34  Peter Thomas, 'Anagnorisis: for Chris at Heavensgate', *Don't Let Him Die* (eds) Chinua Achebe and Dubem Okafor (Enugu: Fourth Dimension, 1978).
35  Peter Thomas, letter to the author, 1991.
36  Interview with Helen Chukwuma, University of Port Harcourt, 1993.
37  Peter Thomas, letter to the author, 1991.
38  Christopher Okigbo, *Heavensgate* 1960/61, *Labyrinths*.
39  Obi Maduakor, 'The Influence of Peter Thomas in Nigerian Poetry', *Research in African Literatures*, spring 1980.
40  Ibid.
41  Christopher Okigbo, 'Watermaid,' *Heavensgate*, 1961, *Labyrinths*.
42  Peter Thomas, unpublished chapter in a book on Christopher Okigbo.
43  Interview with Sunday Anozie.
44  Ibid.
45  Pius Okigbo, 'A Toast of Christopher Okigbo' *Glendora Review* 1 (2) 1995 (34-39) Lagos.
46  Chukwuemeka Ike, 'Christopher Okigbo: Reminiscences'.
47  Sunday Anozie, *Christopher Okigbo: Creative Rhetoric* (New York: Africana Publishers, 1971).
48  Interview with Helen Chukwuma, Port Harcourt, 1993.
49  Interview with Sunday Anozie.
50  Pius Okigbo, 'Toast of Christopher Okigbo'.
51  Interview with Sunday Anozie.
52  Ibid.
53  Ibid.
54  Ibid.
55  Ibid.
56  Ibid.
57  Interview with Wole Soyinka.
58  Interview with Sunday Anozie.
59  Interview with Isidore Okpewho, Port Harcourt, 1993.
60  Interview with Sunday Anozie.
61  Christopher Okigbo, 'Siren Limits', 1961, *Labyrinths* (my emphasis).
62  Interview with Sunday Anozie.
63  Ibid.
64  Ibid.
65  Ibid.
66  Christopher Okigbo, 'Watermaid', *Heavensgate*, 1961, *Labyrinths*.
67  Peter Thomas, letter to the author, 1992.
68  Interview with Pius Okigbo, Lagos 1991.
69  Interview with Susan Anakwenze., Nsukka, 1994.
70  Interview with Judith Safi Attah, Lagos, 1991.
71  Interview with Sunday Anozie.
72  Ibid.
73  Interview with M.J.C. Echeruo, Syracuse NY, 2000.
74  Christopher Okigbo, *Labyrinths with Path of Thunder* (London: Heinemann, 1971).
75  Interview with Judith Safi Attah.

76 Interview with Wole Soyinka.
77 Interview with Sunday Anozie.
78 Robert Wren, *Those Magical Years* (Washington DC: Three Continents Press, 1981).
79 Gerald Moore, letter to the author, Umago Italy, 1992.
80 Christopher Okigbo, 'Newcomer', 1961, *Heavensgate*.
81 Gerald Moore, letter to the author.
82 Ibid.
83 Christopher Okigbo, 'Fragments out of the Deluge', *Limits*, 1961/62, *Labyrinths*.
84 Gerald Moore, letter to the author.

# 7
# *Gentleman,*
# *poet & publisher*

## CAMBRIDGE HOUSE, IBADAN 1962–66

I have lived the sappling sprung from the bed
of the old vegetation;
Have shouldered my way through a mass of ancient
nights to chlorophyll...

('Elegy of the Wind', *Path of Thunder*)

Christopher Okigbo moved in 1962 from the lush, hilly terrains of Nsukka to Ibadan as the West African Regional Manager for Cambridge University Press. According to his friend Sam Nwoye, who later became the Librarian of the University of Nigeria, Nsukka, he discerned no future for himself in pursuit of a career in librarianship at the university. But even more important, Ibadan was in a cultural and political ferment. Okigbo's move to Ibadan coincided with the founding of the Mbari Club, the artists and writers collective whose activities stimulated one of the most important cultural and artistic movements in postcolonial Africa. – 'those magical years' as Robert Wren described them.[1] Okigbo became central in that ferment. Cambridge University Press had a small, but prestigious presence in Ibadan, and Okigbo inherited its symbolic stature.

Cambridge University Press did active business with the new universities in Nigeria. It originally established its office in Nigeria principally to supply the academic needs of the University College of Ibadan when it had been founded in 1948. It quickly established the same relationship with the University of Nigeria when it opened in 1960. Okigbo's duties at the library, which included procuring books and establishing useful contacts with numerous publishers and book suppliers, brought him in close contact with the book industry. He had established an amicable relationship with many of the international publishing companies in the course of his tenure at Nsukka. His entrepreneurial instincts had led him to being a publisher's representative on the side. In that role, Okigbo had represented Cambridge University Press at an unofficial level in the Eastern region, connecting them with book marketers as well as with the academic suppliers to the new University of Nigeria and at the School of Arts and Science in Enugu.

The Cambridge job was tailor-made for him: it had a veneer of luxury and the circumstances that offered adequate comfort. It not only gave him greater social prominence – a wider scope and freedom and a range of new choices to operate socially and politically – but it also afforded him an easier pace of work, and an

174

opportunity to live fully as a poet within a changing intellectual, cultural and historical milieu.

The year 1962 was a time of intense transition. The political and cultural mood of Ibadan was giving form to the most exciting literary and artistic movement in post-colonial Africa. Cambridge House retained its ambience of a cultured manse. Ibadan society was culturally alive in a way with which Okigbo felt an immediate kinship. Things were happening rapidly. On the artistic side, Okigbo had emerged from relative obscurity as a writer to become a poet of growing importance. He made his first important public appearances in that year. Okigbo's *Four Canzones* appeared alongside work by Lenrie Peters in the eleventh issue of *Black Orpheus* in 1962. The Preludes to *Limits* appeared in *Reflections* an anthology edited by Frances Ademola. The Mbari edition of *Heavensgate* also appeared in that year, and so did the early version of 'Lament of the Silent Sisters,' the first part of *Silences*.

Many of Okigbo's close associates were moving into powerful positions in the new nation. In January of that year his elder brother, Pius, was appointed Economic adviser to the Federal government, reporting directly to the Prime Minister. Okigbo's close friend and literary collaborator, the novelist Chinua Achebe was also soon posted from Enugu to Lagos to assume duties as the influential new Director of External Broadcasting at the Nigerian Broadcasting Service. Lagos was close to Ibadan where the cultural scene was in full swing.

Change was sweeping through post-colonial Africa. It held the promise of a new awakening, expressed through the intense visions and actions of a small artistic and cultural elite. The response of that generation expressed itself in two ways. First, the dynamics of post-colonial euphoria required a new idiom in constructing the cultural world – in music, art or literature. It was a gift of the tongue. This generation spoke with utter clarity. Secondly, post-colonialism inspired a new era of conflict, one that would later underscore the ambiguity of the post-colonial state.

The year 1962 was memorable in more than one respect: there was the political upheaval which erupted following the party crisis in the Action Group. The violence and the general mood of political tension in Ibadan early in the 1960s became the watershed of the conflict, which enveloped Okigbo's generation. Okigbo was a quintessential product of the revolutionary spirit of the anti-colonial struggle which shaped his political ideals. Post-colonial politics had become explosive as the new political elite struggled for power. Okigbo lived his most vigorous life as a poet within this intense, highly charged and active political and cultural milieu. In many ways, his work was also vastly influenced by the direction and the philosophical content and amplitude of the emergent movement in art and literature at this time in Ibadan that tended towards creating a nationalist ethic and idiom. The political anxieties of that era soon gave rise to cynicism about the direction of the new society. The rapid and fluid moments of change spawned the psychological condition that produced the great new literature of that age. Always engaged with what was happening around him, Okigbo soon emerged as one of the leading figures that shaped the events of that history. He was deeply conscious of place and time, and of the great changes that accompanied rapid decolonization in Africa.

His apprehension of inexorable change drew him to Ibadan of the 1960s – J.P. Clark's poem 'Ibadan', the city of the 'running splash of rust and gold' – characterized by its complex paradoxes of a modern political and cultural capital – was also steeped in a traditional, ritual consciousness. In the 1960s, Ibadan was Nigeria's equivalent of New York's Greenwich Village in its most active years, and had the magic of

Hemingway's Paris with its open café society of stray artists and philosophers – iconoclasts inspired by a bohemian spirit, which contained the temperament of that breed whom Gertrude Stein called 'the mad generation.' As Nigeria's premier university city, it drew important scholars and artists, romantic figures, dissidents and political exiles from fragile places, intellectual pilgrims who provided a convivial kinship to poets, musicians, painters, critics and all those who were awakened to the imagination. Ibadan was exciting because it was diverse and cosmopolitan. For many years, it remained the largest city in West Africa. Living in Ibadan engendered a compelling sense of freedom and gaiety, and its deep social engagements made it a haven for sybarites.

The novelist Nkem Nwankwo had graduated from the University of Ibadan in 1962, and had just been appointed the writer-in-residence at the University of Ibadan library, where he began working on his novel *Danda*. In *Shadow of the Masquerade* Nwankwo wrote:

> There was something too about Ibadan of our youth that made it the libertine's dream. It was Falstaff or Sir Toby's dream world free of puritans…Ibadan was a huge village and lived at the leisurely pace of the village; avoided the speed and neuroses of the city. That meant that life was easy and everything – especially sexual gratification – was available with minimum effort, at minimum cost. The culture of the people was tolerant of the body and its biological needs. The Yorubas had absorbed Christianity and Islam but not at the expense of their pleasure loving ways, their epicurean *Weltanschauung* or worldview.[2]

The city of Ibadan drew an important part of its character from the decay and poverty of its urban slum – a sprawling inner city that sprouted amidst the surrounding hills from which Ibadan took its name. But there was also a vigour to life which banished the gloom of those slums with the compelling festivals of open laughter on its streets – mixing the carnivalesque of the beggar masks with the intense political campaigns of the 1960s; Ibadan flourished not only as the cultural melting pot of the conflict generation, but as its most politically virile city.

Christopher Okigbo lived among an elegant circle of friends and associates who shared the same intellectual passions as himself. This contributed immensely to his experience of life in Ibadan. In some respect, Ibadan's small, privileged artistic and intellectual community was inbred and incestuous, made up largely of individuals sharing the same kinds of social values and backgrounds. Most of them had been educated at University College, Ibadan and thus formed a small, elite society of peers who knew each other intimately. Perhaps the conflicts, disagreements and dispersion that later affected their relationships had much to do with the intense lives they led in Ibadan, but at that time, this fact of a convenient, compact social network, made social intercourse easy and exciting. Okigbo's Ibadan doubtlessly reflected the same problems prevalent in such closed, socially contained societies: there were the usual vicious gossips, adultery, envy and all the familiar mortal distractions, but life was generally good.

Wole Soyinka was very involved with community theatre, staging plays with the Orisun theatre group, a traveling theatre company which he founded at the time, and the '1960 Masks', a theatre company which had people working with it like Christopher Kolade, Femi Johnson, Ebun Odutola (later Ebun Clark), Joel Adedeji, Dapo Adelugba, Funlayo Sowunmi, (later Funlayo Ajose-Ajayi) and others, like Gaius Anoka, and Ralph Opara. Ulli Beier got Lalage Bown, a colleague in the extramural department, to prepare an edition of J. P. Clark's *Song of a Goat* for publication. Ulli Beier was shuttling between Oshogbo and Ibadan, establishing the Mbari Mbayo Club in Oshogbo with the dramatist, Duro Ladipo and others. The Oshogbo arts movement, which was Ulli Beier's pet project, was ancillary to the Mbari Club in Ibadan. Ulli Beier and Duro Ladipo were emphasizing the folk tradition in Oshogbo while the Mbari Club was more elitist and modernist and centred on the University of Ibadan. The nexus of social interaction in Ibadan among this elite group was the very congenial atmosphere of the University of Ibadan staff club.

In the evenings it was usual to find Okigbo enjoying the congenial atmosphere of the University staff club where he often met friends who were teaching at the University: among others was James Ezeilo, a senior Lecturer in Mathematics with a Cambridge doctorate; Louis Ekpechi (to whom he dedicated 'Siren Limits') and D. C. Nwafor, both Professors at the University College Hospital; Ben Obumselu who taught English. Okigbo and his friends also loved the Ibadan palmwine bars, quite unusual places like Osumare, and the Seven Sisters located where the Femi Johnson building now stands in Ibadan. There was also Risikatu's bar on the old Oyo road, towards Ibadan Boys' High School. Sometimes, they met at the open air bar near the Ogunpa Motor Park, patronized by Ibadan's ordinary folk. When there was not much to do in Ibadan, they would drive down to Lagos, ninety miles away, to Bobby Benson's Caban Bamboo club, to listen to Bobby himself, or Roy Chicago or Victor Olaiya, whose tunes were part of the rage of the highlife renaissance of the 1960s. It was for instance, at Caban Bamboo one evening, on one such visit, that Wole Soyinka was inspired to compose spontaneously 'Taxi Driver I Don't Care,' to the musical accompaniment of Bobby Benson with whom he jammed on that occasion. The song became famous when Bobby Benson, to whom it has since been ascribed, recorded it as a single LP. It was testimony to the spontaneous energy of the imagination that made Ibadan and Lagos fecund and alive in the 1960s.

There were the nightclubs at Lafia Hotel, which frequently featured Agu Norris or Chris Ajilo; there was also *Paradise*, behind Kingsway and CMS bookshop at Okebola. It was the haunt of the city's fashionable young. The scene of the pub in which metal on concrete jars the drink lobes of the protagonist in Wole Soyinka's experimental novel, *The Interpreters,* is possibly set in the bar of the Paradise Club in Ibadan. The characters that populate the novel derive from figures in this close-knit circle of friends in Ibadan. In many ways *The Interpreters* is Soyinka's allegory of their lives in Ibadan and the existential questions that they hotly debated in Cambridge House are reflected in the lives of the characters that Soyinka brought to life. Ibadan drew them all.

John Pepper Clark had established himself at the Institute of African Studies of the University of Ibadan, and the poet and playwright Wole Soyinka doing pioneering work in modern African theatre, was at the University's Institute of Drama as a Rockefeller Fellow. Later on in 1963, Soyinka moved to the new University of Ife, which had its campus temporarily at Ibadan where the current Ibadan polytechnic is located. However, at the time Okigbo came back to Ibadan from Nsukka, Soyinka was involved with the University of Ibadan theatre, working closely with people like Geoffrey Axworthy and Martin Banham.

The University of Ibadan theatre was active, with the Festival Players run by Professor Ferguson, who ran the Classics department, staging numerous plays. There were such memorable productions as *Toussaint l'Ouverture*, a play based on the struggle to liberate the black people in Haiti in which Professor Adeleye played the lead role. There was also the equally memorable performance of T. S. Eliot's, *Murder in the Cathedral*. When Soyinka's *Kongi's Harvest* had its debut in Lagos, for instance, Okigbo and his friends drove down to watch it. General Ironsi, who later became Nigeria's first military head of government, was in the audience for that production, which took place at the new Federal Palace Hotel. There was such constant reaching out for the plenitude of life. But cultural life in Ibadan mostly revolved around the Mbari Club. The Mbari production of the popular Yoruba opera actor, Duro Ladipo and his theatre group was active. The production of Ladipo's famous operatic work, *Oba Koso* had a premier at Mbari. The clubhouse had a good restaurant. Okigbo often dined there with his friends, or went there for a lunch of his favourite dish of pounded yam and bitter leaf soup.

Torch Taire, the businessman and art collector, also lived in Ibadan and moved around Ibadan's circle of artists and intellectuals. He recalled that early in the 1960s Ibadan society was especially conducive for a socially active individual like Okigbo. 'Everything was charged with a sense of newness, of creativity and of participation. People were moving in and out of Ibadan, because it was the place to be at this time; life was not serious, even though serious work was going on.'[3] The pace of that society was very important for Christopher Okigbo's poetry. He was a man of leisure. The city sustained his emotional needs. Cambridge University Press provided the material ambience necessary for his art to flow. In terms of the moral and aesthetic questions that he had to confront in his creative life at Ibadan, early in the 1960s, his kinship with the central artistic figures helped his perspective. In short, Okigbo flourished in the unique moment of that city. His social encounters in Ibadan helped to sharpen his apprehension of his role as a poet. These factors are important in his growth as an artist in the post-colonial moment.

The Mbari Club offered a focal point of entertainment to Ibadan's city elite, especially those living outside the University campus. The Mbari movement was the result of discussions that began to take place among a few of the writers and artists who began to meet on the platform of the Mbari Club, to interact and stimulate ideas among themselves, to project the ideals that eventually became central to the Mbari movement. Late in December 1961 they had acquired their original site at the Adamasigba area of town, close to the famous Dugbe market in Ibadan's central district. Mbari was conceived as a writers' and artists' club with the purpose of stimulating a meeting point for what was then new and valuable in Nigerian art and literature. It was the culmination of many meetings at Nsukka, Enugu, Ibadan, London, and even in Paris. They first began to meet in a Lebanese restaurant upstairs. The Mbari center soon had an exhibition salon. It hosted the first exhibitions of the experimental Oshogbo artists championed by Ulli Beier and his Austrian wife Suzanne Wenger. Malcolm and Georgiana Betts also exhibited at Mbari. They were both teaching at the School of Arts in Zaria and were regular visitors to Ibadan. Georgiana later married Ulli Beier at the end of his marriage with Suzanne Wenger, and apparently after Georgiana's with Malcolm ended. The Mbari exhibitions also featured the works of some of Africa's leading modernist artists, Ben Enwonwu, Uche Okeke and Bruce Onabrakpeya. The center soon became the rallying point of the new art movement, bringing together many Nigerians and other diaspora African artists whose works were exhibited at the Mbari Salon. Among the most prominent was the African-American painter Jacob Lawrence, the Ghanaian modernist Vincent Kofi, the Sudanese Ibrahim Salahi, the Mozambiquan Malagatana Valente Ngweya, and Ethiopia's Skunder Boghossian. Okigbo was involved in organizing the activities of the Mbari Club, of which he soon became Secretary. He was also editor of the Mbari publications.

Among the founding members of Mbari was the novelist Chinua Achebe: it was he, who is said to have suggested the name Mbari – in reference to the Igbo shrine of the goddess *Ala* or mother earth, 'whose walls are often flooded with murals depicting all man's preoccupation in peace and war.'[4] Chinua Achebe occasionally drove to Ibadan from Lagos to join the meetings of the club. Ulli Beier recalled that, although Achebe was inevitably infrequent in the Mbari meetings because of the distance, he was nevertheless very involved in its affairs. The novelist Cyprian Ekwensi was also living and working in Lagos as the Federal Director of Information, and was a regular visitor to Ibadan. Although Ekwensi was not a member, he nevertheless was a frequent guest of the Mbari Club. Ulli Beier, its prime promoter, had put the resources of the Extra-mural Department of the University College of Ibadan to good use. Robert Gardiner from Ghana and Lalage Bown from Scotland, with Ayo Ogunsheye a Director of the department, continued that tradition. Among many contributions Lalage Bown took the publishing programme in hand and as a result of her detailed work the seventeen books had a pioneering effect on publishing in Africa. The department she headed was known in Ibadan for the space it provided artists and writers, outside the stuffy, conceited ambience of the academy. As Nkem Nwankwo recollects, 'For us the creative people, the most hospitable unit on campus was the Extra-Mural Studies program.'[5] And of Lalage Bown he wrote '...She became a fixture at Mbari, with her unusual neo-classic name – Lalage was the name of the mistress of Horace – and her head-cheerleader persona. One never figured out what she did as director of EMS except throw elegant parties and appear everywhere with elegance and panache. She was really quite a sweetheart with her cheerful ways and wit and indomitable spirit.'[6] Okigbo and Lalage Bown became firm friends after he rescued her and her two foster-daughters from a bad car accident near Ibadan airport, and she often joined in the informal beer-and-poetry evenings which he held at Cambridge House in Eleyele. He remained in touch, after she had moved to Zambia, until his death.

Among the artists, Demas Nwoko and Uche Okeke were the most active in the Mbari movement. They had graduated from the Zaria Art School in 1960, alongside artists like Simon Okeke, Felix Ekeada and Bruce Onabrakpeya, and had established a counter movement to classical aesthetic pedagogy at Zaria. They soon became known as the 'Zaria rebels' because they began to practice the use of the indigenous idiom in the expression of modern Nigerian art. They also became active in the explosive cultural scene of the early post-colonial years. Onabrakepya was teaching arts at St. Gregory's college, a Catholic boarding school for boys in Lagos, and sometimes exhibited at Mbari, while Simon Okeke was making important works alongside being employed as curator at the National Museum in Lagos. Demas Nwoko, a gifted builder and architect, painted elaborate murals in the Mbari center in Ibadan, as well as at the University of Ibadan. After studying art in Zaria, he went to Paris on a fellowship for further studies in Art and Architecture. Spare, passionate and innovative, Demas was very active at the University of Ibadan theatre – as choreographer, and set designer for many of the famous theatre productions of that period – especially of Soyinka's early dramatic works. The novelist Nkem Nwankwo described him as 'a Renaissance man very much in the spirit of Leonardo da Vinci. In his slim frame was stored enough energy for four men...'[7] The actor, theatre director and broadcaster, John Ekwere had established a branch of the Mbari Club in the Eastern Nigerian capital, Enugu. At the time, Ekwere was working as Head of Talks in the Eastern Nigerian Broadcasting Corporation. The painter, Uche Okeke later joined him in Enugu, but came to Ibadan from time to time. Uche Okeke had returned from a German scholarship to Enugu in

1963, and soon after became active in the movement. He in fact did the illustrations of so many of the works published at the time, like Chinua Achebe's *Things Fall Apart*, for instance. Demas Nwoko did the illustrations of Christopher Okigbo's *Labyrinths*, while Bruce Onabrakpeya illustrated Chinua Achebe's *Arrow of God*.

In the early days of Mbari, the South African writer and exile, Ezekiel Mphahlele was the chairman of the meetings. Frances Ademola, a Ghanaian broadcaster married to a Nigerian, was the secretary of the club. The writers D.O. Fagunwa and Amos Tutuola were also both living in the city at this period; although they identified with its principles, but they did not become part of the Mbari circle, as they always found the ambience too elitist. However, Mbari honoured Fagunwa and Tutuola on different occasions. D. O. Fagunwa especially, then working at the Nigerian Council, would render invaluable service to the Mbari Club in his time when he helped solve the publishing constraints on *Black Orpheus*. Mbari had by then adopted the *Black Orpheus* as its official publication, edited by Ulli Beier with Wole Soyinka as co-editor and O. R. Dathorne, then a senior Lecturer in the Ibadan English Department, as its reviews editor.

There was not much in those years to point to a canon of work called 'African Literature' in English. But the Mbari movement was from the first committed to inspiring the consciousness, to placing new African writing in the center of international discourse and attention. Ulli Beier found outlets and funds and nurtured the emergence of what became the most significant body of modern African literature in the immediate post-colonial years written in the English language. The best description of Ulli Beier in that period comes from Nkem Nwankwo who later became active in Mbari while living in Ibadan. He wrote that Beier 'was often seen at the club house brooding over the establishment like a hen over her hatching eggs. The fortunes of Mbari seemed to mirror his physical outlook. At the beginning in the early sixties, he was a miracle worker, garnering funding from several sources, discovering new talent and quietly but effectively expanding the membership. His Leonine head with a cap of thick salt and pepper hair sharply contrasted with his tie and dye, symbolized the resurgent youth of the club…'[8]

By 1963, the West Indian Oscar R. Dathorne and the Nigerian, Ben Obumselu, alongside scholars like John Ramsaran were beginning to establish the early theoretical framework for the systematic study of African Literature at the University of Ibadan. Their pioneering work in the English Department led to the development of a curriculum based on the works of the emergent writers in Ibadan. Molly Mahood convinced Ben Obumselu to return to Ibadan from Oxford in 1963 after his doctoral work, rather than go to Ghana with some of his friends, like Adu Boahen; they had both been recruited to join W. E. B. Dubois to publish the *Encyclopedia Africana* – modeled after the *Encyclopedia Britannica*. At his return, Obumselu began to investigate the emerging literature written by writers of his generation at Ibadan. Much of his pioneering work in this period with Ibadan colleagues and the Sierra Leonean Eldred Durosimi Jones helped to establish a critical direction and a discursive idiom for the post-colonial literature. Obumselu particularly recalled the cynicism among traditional critics and scholars, mostly European, when Dathorne and he began to design and teach the first experimental courses in new African literature at Ibadan. It was a tentative start with the study of the works of the new writers – Achebe, Okigbo, Clark and Soyinka. The Ibadan English Department was an unlikely place for it to begin, steeped as it was then in the classical English tradition. 'Many people actually didn't think much of it. African literature, especially the new writing did not exist by any stretch of most imaginations,'[9] Obumselu had said in an interview with a chuckle.

There were other people however, who began to take the new writing seriously. Aside from the pioneering work done by Janheinz Jahn, an early collaborator with Ulli Beier on *Black Orpheus*, there was also Gerald Moore, at Makerere University in Uganda, who too was helping in the establishment of a body of critical thinking from East Africa. Modern African writing is the result of the need to engage and chronicle the new realities in Africa. But in 1962, the central question was: What was African writing and who, truly, was an African writer? A significant move towards answering these questions was made at the first conference of African writers, at Makerere University, between Wednesday 8 June and Saturday 18 June 1962.

The Makerere conference was sponsored by the Congress for Cultural Freedom, and the Mbari Club in association with the Extra-Mural department of Makerere University whose director, Gerald Moore, was already well acquainted with Christopher Okigbo and other figures in Nigerian writing. Writers came from all over Africa and the diaspora. Christopher Okigbo was invited and he traveled with other Nigerian writers via London and Kigali – Achebe, Clark, Soyinka, Okara, Obi Wali, Donatus Nwoga, and the West Indian Arthur Drayton who was working for the University of Ibadan Department of Extra-Mural studies in Jos.

The writers arrived in Kampala on Thursday 9 June 1962 and, as Obi Wali recalled, spent most of the weekend in 'the active search to discover the joys of Kampala'[10] Christopher Okigbo thought it was 'a literary desert'[11] and hoped that the conference would do for the city, 'what irrigation does to the Sudan.' He nevertheless felt, like most of the writers, that Kampala was a great venue for the writers conference. 'It was cool,' Okigbo had said, 'and offered...more than adequate outlets at Top Life and White Nile.'[12] The American writer Paul Theroux, who lived and worked at Makerere in the late 1960s, remembers it as a 'drowsy place' set in a provocative landscape: 'Kampala was a prosperous place,' he wrote, 'busy on weekdays, full of picnickers on weekends, strolling Africans, promenading Indians. It was a town not of dinner parties and social functions but of nightclubs, restaurants, and brothels. It was a green town of friendly faces and natural wonder – roads carpeted with white butterflies, trees full of bats, crested cranes in the parks, and in the low-lying watery places, masses of papyrus that had somehow crept up the White Nile from Egypt.'[13]

During the conference Okigbo was always to be found in the company of the Ugandan playwright and journalist Robert Serumaga and he struck up easy friendship with the South African writers and exiles, Bloke Modisane and Lewis Nkosi. Okigbo first made the acquaintance of the renowned African-American poet, Langston Hughes, who read from his book of poems, *Ask Your Mama,* 'from the name calling game'[14] of the Black vernacular mode, and had caused general mirth when he said, 'Governor Eastland doesn't like me too well and calls me names; so...I have included him in *Ask Your Mama*.'[15] Okigbo also became friends with J. Saunders Redding, the African-American writer and critic, who taught at Hampton, then at Duke and Cornell. Okigbo and Dr. Redding shared many views, especially on the meaning of international blackness, and against racial essentialism in cultural production. He gave Okigbo an autographed copy of *To Make a Poet Black*. Okigbo and Robie Macauley, Editor of the *Kenyon Review*, discussed the possibility of publishing *Limits* and the early version of 'Laments of the Silent Sisters,' but nothing came of it.

On the Monday after the hectic weekend, the conference took off in earnest, with Okigbo leading the discussions on the conference theme: 'What is African literature?' By the end of the day Okigbo had succeeded in stirring up one of the most enduring controversies in modern African literature. There had been a serious argument among the writers about a true definition for new African writing. Was there any such thing as 'African writing'? Okigbo had declared, 'There is no such thing as African writing. There is only good or bad writing.' Obi Wali argued in his seminal paper, 'Dead End of African literature?' that African writing would remain inauthentic if African writers continued to produce in foreign colonial languages. It is still an unresolved question and was just one of the many controversies and high points of the Makerere conference. The conference was characterized by such literary controversies and memorable dramas. For instance a hilarious dimension to the proceedings occurred when the Jamaican playwright, Barry Reckord, described the routine talk of the conference as tending towards an over elaboration of 'stock issues.' By the end of the day there was a referential rash of 'stock literature,' 'stock phrases,' and 'stock characters' and by Wednesday 15 June, the word 'stock' had gone out of fashion, terribly over-used! Okigbo himself had caused another mild controversy in the middle of the panel on Language and African Literature. The poet had thrown many of the writers into guffaws when he wondered aloud about the kind of Pidgin English Nigerian prostitutes spoke in Lagos.

It was during the reading sessions that Okigbo declared in one of his 'impish' moments his now famous words: 'I don't read my poems to non poets!' Apparently this retort was directed at the Cameroonian writer Bernard Fonlon. The writers were scandalized by the Nigerian poet, and Okigbo would live up to this image of impulsive, passionate arrogance of aesthetic elitism. The Kenyan writer Ali Mazrui described him 'an enormously talented but eccentric poet.'[16] But what exactly did Okigbo wish to communicate by his outrageous action? Drawn to drama, was Okigbo simply acting out a well-thought script? Was he thumbing his nose at his peers? Was he just being 'contrary'[17] as his friend the poet J. P. Clark suggested? Was it just playful mischief? Was he being ironic? But he was also shy – that bashful side that he successfully masked with his public image of the eccentric. Ben Obumselu recalled that, although Okigbo was the best reader of T. S. Eliot's poems he knew, he avoided reading his own poems aloud. 'He had no voice for it; his voice was too high-pitched, and he was almost always embarrassed by this inability.'[18] It was thus possible that Okigbo was just too embarrassed to read, and chose rather to be 'contrary.' He succeeded, at Kampala, in creating the personal myth of a restless, volatile poet.

Ali Mazrui does not capture in his book, *The Trial of Christopher Okigbo*, the bohemian, carefree, impulsive personality of the poet, but rather the image of the spare, intense poet, whose intellectual arrogance was declared at Kampala. Scholars of African literature of the twentieth century have tended to frame his poetry with this sense of a rebellious spirit. He was certainly that, but in truth, Okigbo was a myth-maker, driven by a sense of play and amusement. The need to arouse, to seek attention, to be the ultimate impresario – were all part of his sense of fun. Obumselu's view must be taken seriously. It may indeed explain another aspect of Okigbo's nature and personality: under the extravagance of his actions was a bashful Christopher Okigbo who was occasionally withdrawn in company, and who sometimes secluded himself in search of solitude. The effervescent mask that he wore in his dealings with the public hid a deep, psychological insecurity, and successfully veiled his complex life. His longing for love and affirmation led Okigbo to adopt extravagant drama so as to be noticed.

The conference, after ten days of fun and argument, launched the movement for modern African literature as a distinct discipline. But there were other scenes. Wole Soyinka recalled the easy conviviality, and there were also always beautiful Ugandan women with whom to dance the nights away at the bars and clubs in Kampala. The Top Life and White Nile hotels were the regular haunts of the writers. Soyinka particularly recalled Okigbo going out every night in Kampala, escorting a different woman. He maintains that some of Okigbo's 'Queen(s) of the night' were the wives in the harem of the Kabaka of Buganda, Edward 'King Freddie' Mutesa II, who evidently had their trysts outside the royal gaze. The Nigerian actor and broadcaster Segun Olusola shares Soyinka's recollection of events in Kampala:

> We all took part in the active partying during the Makerere conference. Okigbo, always, was the soul of it. I remember vividly. We would go out in the nights, to the White Nile, and Okigbo would have the company of a different girl for each occasion, whom he would introduce as 'Queen of the night.' And they were real queens! They would spend the evening with us, have dinner, and Okigbo would drop her off the next morning. Each night had its own 'Queen of the night' – beautiful girls; and they just loved his sense of fun! Okigbo was one of those people around whom you always had a sense of the party whose presence at the Makerere enlivened the conference, and made it more memorable.[19]

Segun Olusola was already producing the hit TV series 'Village Headmaster' for the Western Nigerian Television Service in Ibadan and was very active in the Ibadan theatre circles. He knew Okigbo well in Ibadan and described him as a 'magnificent impresario.'[20] Years later, when Olusola had retired as Nigeria's ambassador to the OAU in Addis Ababa, he still remembered Okigbo's prominent part in making possible the 'intense social intercourse in Kampala'.[21]

Many of those writers were meeting each other for the first time and in many cases a long relationship began, as between Okigbo and the Ugandan playwright and novelist Robert Serumaga. At the Kampala conference Okigbo met and became friends with Rajat Neogy, the young Ugandan-Indian intellectual, who was editor of the magazine *Transition*. Both men immediately took to one another and by the time the conference ended, Okigbo had accepted to work with Rajat Neogy on *Transition* as the West African Editor. In a letter which Rajat Neogy wrote in 1992, shortly before his death in the United States, he said about Okigbo:

> We first met in Makerere in 1962, and it was instant friendship. Christopher had an irresistible charm and enthusiasm for many things for which I was enthusiastic. He was friendly, intense, amusing and dramatic. I was his 'Indian-African half brother', and when we discussed *Transition*, a magazine that I had set up at the time, after I came back from Europe, Christopher jumped on to it. He had his own ideas, his own conception of the direction of African literature. He did not believe in the boundaries of ideas, he was cosmopolitan. We decided to work on *Transition* together, drawn by the same dream. We dreamed of making that magazine, the defining space, and the greatest medium for canvassing the new ideas streaming out of Africa ... it was Africa which replenished, which represented the greatest inspiration of the poetry which Christopher wrote...[22]

The Ghanaian poet, Kofi Awoonor was also appointed to be Okigbo's assistant, thus beginning another life long friendship. Okigbo's *Limits* – which he had then only just completed – was also read for the first time at the conference in Makerere in spite of his claims that he did not read to 'non-poets.' The Makerere conference offered the great opportunity for African writers to socialize and become acquainted with each other's work and to connect with those trends that, as Wole Soyinka later said in an interview, were 'streaming into the nature of new writing in Africa.'[23]

Okigbo returned to Cambridge House on 20 June 1962 through London. His life in Ibadan remained characterized by an active social engagement, and the intense intellectual stimulation of his peers. Cambridge University Press had established generous, well-appointed conditions for Philip Harris, their last English representative in Ibadan. Cambridge House had the perfect ambience for creative solitude. The poet lived and worked in this house located on number 7 U.A.C. Crescent – the business section of the Onireke G.R.A., in the Eleyele area of Ibadan. Torch Taire remembered Cambridge House as impressive: 'The girls loved it!'[24] he said. It was a beautiful, white house set regally on a knoll at the end of a drive way overlooking a valley. The Ogunpa River separated its grounds from the Ibadan racecourse. There were two bedrooms upstairs, split by a bathroom in the middle, which descended into the sunken lodge downstairs, overlooking a beautiful valley. At the side was the dining room, which led to the garage. Visitors coming into the house would often use the back door, walking through the garage, through Okigbo's study downstairs, and into the lounge. That study served a dual purpose as both the office of the Cambridge University Press and as the poet's private workspace. At one end of the lounge was a wall covered with a stone surface. Okigbo often sat in his desk looking towards it – the 'stone surface' of 'Siren Limits.' A fluffy rug, which was kept immaculately white, was on the floor facing the fireplace at the centre of Okigbo's lounge. The room also had wide Italian windows which admitted light and wind.

Cambridge House was tailor-made for Christopher Okigbo's epicurean temperament. He loved to entertain. Wole Soyinka had nostalgic recollections of those occasions when Okigbo's close friends gathered around the fireplace, roasting game, and discussing until the small hours life's philosophies under the glow of light and wine. Cambridge House rang with loud and vigorous debate. It was a life of ease. As Nkem Nwankwo recollects, Okigbo had inherited the affluence and manners of Cambridge House, including a fine cook and steward. The poet had truly achieved a convenient synthesis of his life and work which related in a seamless way to each other without conflict. 'Being able to work from the house meant that Chris didn't have to get up early and go to work like everybody else. It was perfect for him at a point in his life when he was constitutionally incapable of a regular, well-appointed life style,'[25] writes Nkem Nwankwo. Okigbo's Ibadan was socially serene. The serenity sustained his need for creative solitude. The poet was able to live an active social life within this close-knit circle of friends. Cambridge House became a great rallying ground for Ibadan's cultured society – it had the atmosphere of a literary salon. It was the bastion of the poet's hedonistic pursuits. The business of Cambridge University Press occupied only a part of his life.

Cars infinitely fascinated the poet, and he loved to collect them. Okigbo indeed had an impressive collection of cars in the Cambridge House garage, which included a small Jaguar, a rather sporty Wolseley, and one of the MG models of the time. Later on, he bought Professor Chike Edozien's impressive Armstrong Siddeley, which imitated the Rolls Royce Phantom. In those years the poet would ask a first time visitor to Cambridge House; 'Have you seen my Rolls Royce?'[26] He would conduct a 'grand tour' of the car, parked gracefully in his garage. Okigbo was infinitely proud of that car. The Armstrong 'Sydney', as everybody called it, was a rather conservative looking car with a big bonnet and long hood in the fashion of the 1930s. It was such a big car for the poet and so cavernous, that it was indeed often a source of amusement to see Okigbo's smallish figure, almost hidden behind the steering wheel, as he drove impetuously along the streets of Ibadan. It was amusing to think that the big Armstrong 'Sydney' had been driven by two such small people. Professor Edozien also was a man of diminutive physical stature. He was at that time a professor at the University of Ibadan Medical School and later professor of Nutrition at the University of North Carolina at Chapel Hill, in the United States. He then became the Asagba of Asaba.

The Armstrong Siddeley was only one of the charming accoutrements to Okigbo's socially active time at Ibadan. Cambridge University Press was taking good care of him in other ways. He cut an image in those years of a dashing, young and successful man-about-town. A true city cat, young and upwardly mobile. Okigbo's exuberant lifestyle made him socially prominent in the city. 'He was a very visible figure in Ibadan society; everybody knew Christopher,'[27] his friend Torch Taire remembered. This penumbra of affluence, which hung about the poet, sustained his image of success and dissipation. Okigbo was nevertheless not as rich as it seemed at the time. Although this apparent comfort was just enough to allow him the psychological stability to create and mature in his work, he was perpetually in debt. He lived in style; he loved his collection of fine wine, his exquisite women and he entertained lavishly. This life of leisure and extravagance always told on his finances. Torch Taire described it as Okigbo's 'disdain for money'.[28] 'Christopher lived by the hour … a true prodigal … he had not much because he spent the money as he got it. I think it was because he had also a certain disdain for money, it didn't mean much to him and this was ironic because he was also quite fascinated by the millions. Nevertheless, money meant really nothing to him, strictly; as he would also spend it, if it came, with lavish.'[29]

Okigbo became great friends with Torch Taire who lived next door on Oba Akenzua Avenue, Onireke, and was the regional Sales Manager of the pharmaceutical group, Parke Davis. Onireke was an elegant and affluent neighborhood in Ibadan. Okigbo had prominent neighbours with whom he socialized frequently, including the Deputy High Commissioner of Britain in Ibadan, two Lebanese brothers who were in the transport business, and some ministers of the Western regional government. Kayode Jibowu was then the Western Regional Manager for Shell and lived on Shell close. The actor and insurance magnate, Femi Johnson also lived nearby with his English wife, and worked as the Regional Manager for the Law Union and Rock. He later founded the brokerage firm, Femi Johnson and Co. in Ibadan. There was also Godwin Adokpaye who was regional manager for Mobil Oil who had been Okigbo's junior in the Classics department at the University College, Ibadan.

Also nearby was the Eleyele barracks of the Third Brigade of the Nigerian Army quartered then in Ibadan. Okigbo moved among the top brass of the army, and had friends like Colonel George Kurubo, Okigbo's junior at the Government College, Umuahia who had been commander of the Third Brigade. Colonel Macaulay Nzefili, Colonel Sotomi, and Captain Cyprian Iweanya were among many others in the army of those years with whom Okigbo was very closely acquainted. They often came to the poet's home at Cambridge House to socialize. Colonel Kur Mohammed, the commander of the Third Brigade who was later killed in the January 1966 coup, was also an occasional guest at Cambridge House.

In the immediate post-independence era, Ibadan was the hub of international publishing in West Africa. In the 1960s, international publishing houses were expanding their African operations and encouraging the new writers from both within and outside the university. Ibadan gained especially from the presence of the university in the city. With political independence Nigerians began to replace the expatriate agents of these publishing houses. At Oxford University Press there was T.T. Solarun, who later became a Bishop of the Methodist church. Elderly and experienced at the time, he was the doyen of the Ibadan publishing scene. His office was at the impressive Oxford House, close then to the Nigerian Broadcasting Corporation at Ibadan city centre. Tani

Solarun also joined in with some of the roaring evenings at Cambridge House.

Aigboje Higo was at Heinemann from 1965. When he returned from Leeds in 1962 with an M.A, he became headmaster of the Anglican Grammar School at Otuo. One day Aig Higo visited Okigbo at Cambridge House and told him of his plans to buy a second hand car, as he did not want to waste money buying a new one. Okigbo, Higo recalled, just snapped his fingers and said, 'I think I've got something you might just need!' He showed Aigboje Higo the Zephyr 20, which he had been using at Nsukka. He still owed the University of Nsukka five hundred pounds of the loan he took to buy the car. If Higo could provide that, he could take the car! It was a generous offer and Higo agreed. Okigbo asked to be given the next day to change the old tires, before he handed the car to Higo, who remarked. 'He didn't have to do it'.[32] This was but one of Okigbo's gestures of kindness and friendship which would cement their relationship. It was thus not surprising that when Heinemann offered to appoint Higo as its Nigerian manager, to replace D. O. Fagunwa, he had gone to Okigbo for advice. As Higo recalled, Okigbo had been very excited about it and encouraged him to take the job. Years later, Higo was to become the chairman of Heinemann Educational Books, Nigeria, but he never forgot Okigbo's gesture. With a slight quiver in his voice he said: 'Chris taught me all the first things I had to know about this publishing business,'[33] as he ruminated on their close friendship, many years later in 1991 in his office at Heinemann in Ibadan.

Isidore Okpewho, who had graduated first class in Classics at Ibadan, had gone to work for Longman in 1964 as Publishers Representative under the English manager, Julian Rea. Okpewho, who published so many of the outstanding Nigerian historians and later became a fine novelist and scholar, also enjoyed a close friendship with Okigbo in Ibadan in that close network of intellectuals, professionals and businessmen.

In the social and cultural life in Ibadan of the 1960s Okigbo's personality was interlocked with the importance of Cambridge House. It was a bachelor's home. It suited Okigbo's pursuit of leisure. But much more important is the sense of community which it fostered as a gathering place for artists and scholars. Okigbo delighted in the company of people. His complete informality made friendship with him easy. People came to relax, to play and to feel unburdened in the free, easy ambience of the poet's home in Ibadan. Dr. Pius Okigbo came frequently to visit him there. In his recollection of the Ibadan years he said, 'Chris was the only person I knew, who could hire taxis on credit in Ibadan! Sometimes when I visited him, I would find all sorts of people sitting around ... ordinary folk really, with whom he apparently enjoyed great friendship judging by the informality and ease with which they took to his comforts. Chris had an incredible way with people, and he was not uppity about it!'[34] People turned up at Cambridge House, as Torch Taire said, like patrons to an English cinema house. Taire's poetic description of Cambridge House when Okigbo lived there is insightful:

> A tilted shrine
> Silhouetted against
> A fading sky at dusk
> Protecting treasurable knowledge
> Except for her own nakedness
> Open always
> to all
> And sundry.[35]

The poet Gabriel Okara stayed at Cambridge House during his visits to Ibadan from Enugu. It was from there that he left for the 1963 conference on 'African literature and the University Curriculum', held between March and April in Dakar. Okigbo did not attend the Dakar conference. As Okara recalled 'Okigbo's home in Ibadan had the quality of motion which could never be found anywhere else. It had a continuous sense of joy…'[36] Strikingly, also this 'quality of motion' best describes the movement of Okigbo's poetry.

Cambridge House thus became the hub of Ibadan café culture. It was in that sense very much like Harry Crosby's home in Paris, with its lingering sense of bacchanalia and serious artistic discussion. Okigbo had kept an open house at Nsukka. It was no less legendary in Cambridge House. A constant stream of people of all classes came without formality in and out of his home: university professors, writers, artists, students, army officers, housemaids, craftsmen, soldiers, diplomats, mechanics and drivers. All kinds of people came to visit, including Okigbo's special vintner Ojo, the palm-wine tapper from Ede, who regularly brought down his special order of the frothing drink. In the 1960s, the actor Jimmy Johnson and the musician Tunji Oyelana were members of Soyinka's theatre company and active in the Mbari scene in Ibadan. Jimmy Johnson worked for a long time as Soyinka's assistant at the Orisun Theatre Company, while the musician and actor, Tunji Oyelana worked closely with Okigbo as his secretary at the Mbari Club. As Jimmy Johnson testified, 'I was among those who frequented Cambridge House. In those days you could come around, and lying down quietly on the cushion, reading or just taking a nap, would be Christopher Kolade or any of Okigbo's intellectual friends. It did not matter whether Okigbo was around or not. Anyone could stroll in, make himself comfortable, especially those who were close to him.'[37] Christopher Kolade had moved from his teaching job as Education Officer at the Government College, Ughelli in 1962, into broadcasting in Ibadan. Kolade, who rose to prominence years later as Chairman of the Nigerian Broadcasting Corporation, Chairman of Cadbury Nigeria, and later Nigeria's High Commissioner to London, had been Soyinka's classmate at the Government College, Ibadan. He spent many evenings at Cambridge House disputing the classics with Okigbo, and reading Christopher's early poems aloud. Rather than the University College, Ibadan, Kolade went to Fourah Bay College, Sierra Leone. He was one of those who had been involved earlier on with Soyinka with the 1960 Masks. He too would add to the ambience of Cambridge House with his deeply reasoned arguments. It was not unusual to find Ulli Beier visiting from Oshogbo. 'Whether he was there or not, I just went to Cambridge House whenever I was in Ibadan. I will have a bed and I will be fed,'[38] Ulli Beier recalled many years later.

There were much younger friends of Christopher Okigbo who were among the regular visitors to Cambridge House and to Mbari: people like Femi Osofisan who became the leading playwright of his generation, and the novelist Kole Omotoso, freshmen at the university in the later part of Okigbo's life in Ibadan. They were in awe of Okigbo, who nevertheless adopted them 'for what he saw as our great promise'[39] said Femi Osofisan. He was just completing his A-levels at the Government College, Ibadan when he first met Okigbo, and he continued to maintain contact with the poet even when he left and joined the war in Biafra. Also among Okigbo's younger friends were young men like Safi's brother Ado Ibrahim, who later became the Atta of Igbira, and Ibrahim Tahir, the politician and novelist of *The Last Imam*, who had been a student at Cambridge University. He often came to Cambridge House in the company of the brilliant jazz critic and broadcaster, Aminu Abdullahi, who had taken over the radio program, *Africa Abroad* from Lewis Nkosi, and was working with Dennis Duerden at the Transcription Centre in London. Wole Awolowo, who was always quiet and unobtrusive, especially after his brother Segun's sudden death, found emotional refuge in Cambridge House, and a warm friend and mentor in Okigbo. Okigbo's personal relationships reflected his cosmopolitan spirit: they cut across ethnic, racial, political, class, gender, or boundaries of age or experience. He found great joy in people's company.

Philip Asiodu was Okigbo's contemporary alongside the likes of Leslie Harriman, Alison Ayida, Peter Chigbo, Godfrey Eneli and a few others, who had joined the Nigerian colonial civil service as administrative officers in 1957. By 1963 Asiodu had become the Permanent Secretary of the Federal Ministry of Health. His official duties brought him frequently to Ibadan to chair the meetings of the board of governors of the University College Hospital, (UCH) Ibadan. Although accommodation would be reserved for him in the University's guesthouse, Asiodu preferred to stay with his friend, the poet. There were such colorful visitors such as the painter Ben Enwonwu, then Federal adviser on the Arts, who was at the height of his career as a modernist artist. They spent many long hours of congenial dispute in the loud, open manner of Cambridge House. Enwonwu's short fuse was legendary, but he found Okigbo amusing and sympathetic. They both loved wine. Ben Obumselu remained within the closest circle of Okigbo's friends at Ibadan, and an important member of Ibadan's intellectual circles. He observed: 'In Christopher's life there was no dull moment. It was always excitement. He continuously reached deep inside of him, to find fun; to break down the seriousness of life into simple follies. Life was a big laugh.'[40] He described the life around Okigbo as 'intoxicating':

> His hospitality at. … Cambridge House Ibadan was unstinting up until the middle of the month. When beer could no longer be paid for, the very air of the house was still intoxicating enough. His conversation was loud and extravagant. It was the delight of utterance that moved him rather than the need to communicate. Eager to please, he chose invariably the most outrageous way to do so.[41]

Okigbo's extravagant generosity sometimes went to eccentric limits. Taire said he would go to great lengths, 'Just to make others happy even if sometimes at great personal discomfort'.[42] One particular habit of Okigbo's, which used to infuriate his eldest brother Lawrence, was to write cheques that bounced. On numerous occasions, Okigbo had issued cheques to people on a whim. On getting to the bank, the cheques would be dishonored because Okigbo's account would have been overdrawn. Okigbo would storm into the office of the manager of Barclays Bank in Ibadan to protest. They were often patient with him – the distracted genius – and he would soon find to his great dismay or chagrin, the true state of his accounts.

Obumselu's retrospective account of Okigbo's life suggests that the poet moulded his life on openness in which he gave totally and unstintingly of himself – reserving no moral judgment, demanding none. His apparent amorality obscured a deeply private side, his intense spiritual being, which only found expression through his poetry. Because he chose the most extravagant ways to communicate, Obumselu also observes, that 'It was easy, perhaps correct, to dislike him.'[43] And a few actually did. The Canadian scholar and novelist, David Knight was one of those who visited Okigbo at Cambridge House and found him unbearable. In a commemorative poem, which he had written for Okigbo soon after his death, David Knight recalled Okigbo at Cambridge House:

> I remember you sprawled in a deep wooden armchair, with beer
> On the flat arm, bickering with your wife, not nicely, nastily
> I didn't like you…[44]

David Knight apparently witnessed Okigbo's complicated domestic foibles and his petulant and disagreeable moods. Okigbo preferred the bachelor's life. Safi did not live with him at Cambridge House. She visited and stayed for long stretches, especially during the school vacations. He regarded marriage to Safi both as a symbolic act of healing – it was to Safi he ran for 'cleansing' – and an obligation. He and Safi had a long, courtship full of conflict. The marriage ceremony, botched earlier in Enugu, and for so long deferred by the pressures of family obligations, had finally taken place late in 1962. Love and circumstance had triumphed. They virtually eloped. In 1962, Safi had become pregnant, and Okigbo was under pressure 'to protect her honor.'[45] One afternoon, in a very private ceremony in Ibadan in 1962, they were married at the Ibadan registry. The best man for that occasion was Okigbo's old friend in the University and fellow Sigmite, the journalist Ignatius Atigbi. In any case Safi, the first Northern Nigerian woman to earn a University education, was still bonded to the Government of the Northern region whose scholarship she had held. In 1962, Safi, as principal of Yola Provincial Girls' School, had been transferred to Government Girls' School, Dala in Kano. Okigbo believed in the independence and equality of women, and accepted the challenge of his wife's busy professional life and responsibilities. He encouraged her pursuits and was very proud of her accomplishment. Okigbo did not feel threatened by Safi's career choice, her independence, or the reality of their lives lived separately and in distant abodes. Okigbo was in those terms, an extremely modern and liberated man, clearly ahead of his time in a generation when the modern feminist movement was still to take off, and women's rights were not even an issue, and the professional lives of many women were stultified by the demands of domesticity. Okigbo encouraged Safi's independence, perhaps because it also suited him. Their marriage was based on shared intersections, like the birth of a child; or their frequent visits back and forth. They managed to maintain a tolerable marriage. Her professional life meant that she and Okigbo lived separately. They had thus evolved a relationship which Safi understood perfectly. She did not find Okigbo's need for domestic freedom intolerable. His relationship with all women was always complicated, and Safi understood this too.

Sunday Anozie recalled how in 1963 the poet drove him from Ibadan to the airport, when he was leaving for Paris to study under Roland Barthes and other key figures of the structuralist movement at the Sorbonne. The journey from Ibadan was memorable. Safi came with him, and they argued and quarreled all the way to Lagos. Furious and often choking on his words, Okigbo was passionate and demonstrative. Safi, on the other hand, with a gentler voice was more controlled. She would try to calm him down although she would also forcefully convey her point of view. She would say, for instance, whenever the poet became distracted by his own intense passion: 'Chris, look out. Try driving on your own lane!'[46] or she would warn him about driving too fast. Okigbo would say something nasty, like 'You were still a virgin when I began driving.'[47] At some point when the argument became too intense, the poet said to his wife: 'Listen Safi, I will drive into this bridge and we will all die! It's just that Sunday is here, and I don't want him to die with us!'[48] Sunday Anozie sat in quiet trepidation in the back of the car. He knew how impulsive Okigbo truly was. Anozie was wary that he might actually take the plunge and kill all of them. So he too tried calming him down. It was not beyond Okigbo to carry out the threat. However, at the airport, a much calmer Okigbo told Anozie that if there was anything he needed, he should go to Brussels, where Pius then resided as Nigeria's ambassador to the EEC. He told him that he had some good clothes, which he left behind on his last trip, which Anozie should go and take. Okigbo had also given Sunday Anozie his personal suitcase with which he traveled to Europe. For many years Anozie kept that suitcase as a most treasured souvenir, a memento to a life of true friendship with the poet. Christopher Okigbo's final words to Sunday Anozie at the Ikeja Airport were that he should study the French symbolists very well.

The poet's domestic life was complicated. There was no doubt that he loved Safi deeply. His friends remembered that Okigbo was much too restrained and sober whenever Safi was around. He put on his best behaviour. 'He respected her very much', said Torch Taire. 'It was amusing watching Christopher playing the good husband whenever Safi came.'[49] Safi herself confirmed this: 'Chris became very serious when we were alone. And in photographs he looked much too sober!'[50] Safi Attah understood her boundaries or limits with Christopher Okigbo. Ben Obumselu described her as 'a quiet, self-respecting girl from a highly aristocratic family; she never expected much from a man. For instance, she was most likely not to pick the phone if she was in the house. She did not consider it her business.'[51] Their marriage worked on such a mutual understanding – Safi gave him a wide berth to live his life fully. But he honored his relationship with his Safi by devoting an important part of his emotional life to her. It was paradoxical. Okigbo was always fascinated by women, and driven to serial infidelities, and could not be reined into orthodox domesticity. Bachelorhood suited him enormously. Indeed the younger writer Kole Omotoso, from observing Okigbo's domestic life closely, for a long time lived with the impression that all true artists could never live successfully in conjugal bliss. He came to believe that absence was absolutely necessary for true artistic consciousness to be attainable. He thought that the ambience of Cambridge House was a sacred shrine of bachelorhood. Okigbo himself told Omotoso, during one of his numerous visits to Cambridge House, that he felt distracted by continuous feminine presence in his space and could not perform his artistic and creative functions. He preferred a 'going and coming' – a cycle of adoration. It was like that in his marriage. The anguish of literary craftsmanship forbade domesticity: the swing of moods, the eccentricities of the moments of inspiration, were far too severe for a conventional marriage to endure. It was in a sense, Okigbo's affirmation of the transcendence of the imagination. This frame of mind provides a glimpse into some of the reasons behind Okigbo's complicated relationship with women. They were goddesses to be worshipped and discarded. Torch Taire recollected that no woman, aside from Safi, stayed the night at Cambridge House. Okigbo could not tolerate that. His affairs were far too casual, and so his women would come and go. Permanence was intolerable. We probably glimpse in Okigbo's attitude, the psychology of a child orphaned too early, and unable to reconcile or heal, or to trust the presence of the absent mother whom all women might have represented in his mythic unconscious. Afraid of loss or haunting goodbyes, he became an 'emotional grasshopper'[52] incapable of attachment, because attachment was too painful. And of his numerous relationships, Pius Okigbo said 'Christopher soon learnt that to get on with his work he had to forget the faces and the names after the momentary pleasure or thrill was over.'[53]

The casualness of Okigbo's numerous affairs with women thus illuminates an important aspect of his character. Okigbo 'fell in love' easily and openly; and each new relationship was a moment to be celebrated – he let everyone know about it – that he was in love. His emotions were public. Okigbo's relationships were democratic, determined by neither class nor status: his affairs ranged from the undistinguished to the celebrated, from the married to the unmarried. From the beautiful Hausa girl Ramatu, who lived at the Hausa quarters near the Ibadan Polo club and helped her mother sell beans cake, to the housemaid Bisi, an irreverent and raunchy girl whose uninhibited ways he found liberating. From the beautiful wife of a European publisher with whom he had a whirlwind affair, to the 1963 Beauty Queen of Western Nigeria, Rosemary Anieze. Okigbo's sexual interests were diverse. Torch Taire recalled that for Okigbo beauty enchanted him greatly, character fascinated him endlessly. Olu Akaraogun said. 'We often marveled at Okigbo's choice of women. He could just pick an ordinary girl off the streets and groom her. After a few changes they almost certainly turned out to be stunningly beautiful. Chris had an uncommon knack to spot beauty in ordinary places, nurture them and transform them eventually.'[54]

Okigbo's elegant dinners and soirées at Cambridge House were grand affairs which used to attract many in Ibadan's small, cultivated society. It was usual at such dinners to run into Mr. Bell, the Deputy High Commissioner and head of the British Consulate in Ibadan and his wife, close neighbors at Eleyele; or Doig Simmons, the artist and medical illustrator at UCH. On more than one occasion Okigbo had invited Professor Kenneth Dike, the distinguished historian and legendary Vice-Chancellor of the University of Ibadan. Many other notables often found Cambridge House a place of refuge. The representative for André Deutsch in Nigeria and his young, elegant wife Zelda were frequent dinner guests of the poets. André Deutsch had opened its Nigerian office in Lagos soon after the Makerere conference. They had embarked on an ambitious publishing venture in Nigeria, and published Wole Soyinka's *The Interpreters* and some of the early works of the novelist Nkem Nwankwo.

When Okigbo entertained at Cambridge House, he was at his theatrical best: he loved the part of the perfect host – the ultimate impresario, dressed sometimes in his impressive white tuxedo suit and black bow tie, and laughing, 'haw-haw-haw' in the restrained, deep-throated manner of the gentry. It was, in part, theatre. The poet often saw his part as mere play – like play-acting on a stage! But he enjoyed it thoroughly and loved the impression he made as a socialite. Okigbo himself was well entertained elsewhere. He was a constant guest at the home of the Bells, and Mrs Bell especially visited the poet at Cambridge House quite often – probably drawn by a mutual interest in poetry. They also found each other attractive. Okigbo spent many evenings reading poems aloud, talking literature and exploring great political and philosophical questions of the moment.

Ben Obumselu tells the story of how the power of poetry was made manifest when Okigbo and he were at dinner with the Bells. While Okigbo was reading one of Robert Graves's poems aloud, the Bells' six-year old daughter was moved by the poem to tears. Her spontaneous reaction confirmed to Okigbo that great poetry could provoke emotion in a physical way. It was one of Okigbo's aspirations as an artist, that his poems should affect people, not so much by the meaning but by the tension invoked by the poetry. Robert Graves's poetry had achieved that in a little girl. He savoured the experience for a long time. He indeed revealed this aspect of his artistic ambition in an interview with Dennis Duerden in London in 1965.

Sometimes, Okigbo's sexual exploits took the form of intrigue, some of which Nkem Nwankwo has highlighted in his memoir, *Shadow of a Masquerade*. Okigbo was excited by life at the dangerous edge. He loved to play jokes on his friends and was known for his 'volatile good humour'[55] as Peter Thomas put it. Sam Okudu recalled with amusement the occasion when Okigbo had surprised him with a visit 'with a car full of beautiful girls.'[56] Okudu was then the Assistant Registrar of the University of Ibadan. Two other couples were visiting the Okudu's campus home with their spouses when Okigbo arrived breathlessly in the living room. He feigned great annoyance, and said to the men, within the hearing of their spouses: 'Look here fellows, why are you all wasting my time?' Turning to their wives he said: 'Why are you ladies keeping your husbands? We agreed earlier to meet these Hausa girls. I've brought them and I've been waiting. I couldn't wait any longer, so I decided to drive over to Sam's house! Now they're outside waiting. Come on let's get out!'[57] Sam Okudu's wife said to Okigbo: 'You have come again with your jokes, Chris!'[58] and the poet said to her very seriously: 'It's no joke. Look, have I told you a lie before?'[59] The women were still incredulous and their husbands were having a good laugh. Okigbo then said, 'Okay, if you think I'm joking let's go outside and you will see.' The men agreed as they had made no such arrangement with Okigbo. They went outside and sure enough, there were three beautiful Hausa girls in the poet's car. After a few lighthearted chats, Okigbo sped off with the women leaving Sam Okudu and his other friends in the hands of three irate women. It was even more dire for Okudu whose wife believed that 'Chris does not lie.'[60]

In spite of his lifestyle, and his womanizing, Okigbo loved Safi in his unique and passionate, even if distracted, way. He deeply respected her. 'I fall in love with her anew every time I see her,'[61] the poet told his friend Peter Thomas, one solemn evening at Cambridge House. Okigbo had found his soul mate, and his innate being responded. She was the muse whose 'image insists from flag pole of the heart.'[62] Kayode Jibowu remembered Okigbo's 'sudden bouts of longing for Safi,' as he wrote in 'Siren Limits'[63] which happened like the descent of the muse. 'There were times when Chris was gripped by this sudden desire to see Safi very much, when he just wanted to see her very much and be with her. He would just feel the spontaneous urge and enter his car and drive down to Ilorin.'[64]

In 1963 Safi was again transferred to Ilorin as the Principal of the Queen's School. Ilorin was an easier commute to Ibadan than Yola. Jibowu remembered one such weekend in 1962, when he and J. P. Clark accompanied Okigbo on the road trip to Ilorin to visit Safi. It was a typical Okigbo unplanned trip. He just felt a sudden need to see Safi and he decided to travel to Ilorin on an impulse that morning. So Jibowu drove them to Ilorin in Okigbo's Wolseley. They were engaged in a long conversation about poetry and politics, when Okigbo suddenly said: 'Look at Jibs driving … just like in the books!'[65] Okigbo always drove casually, with his index finger on the wheel. Obumselu recounts that Okigbo often defied the laws of mechanics by trying to change his gears without de-clutching. Jibowu's careful, straight-from-the manual driving did not suit him. Okigbo preferred a more radical form of self-expression. He thought Jibowu's driving too conventional and cautious, reflecting his character. They spent the day in Ilorin where Safi, as always, entertained them lavishly. Such frequent, inspired visits stoked the fire of their marriage and reduced the tedium of distance. Okigbo nevertheless preferred the distance. Her presence was the brief transfiguration of the watermaid of his poems. Okigbo disdained the dreariness of conventional existence as 'life without sin.' He lived in constant rebellion against conventional morality. Life meant more to him than could be expressed in the easily defined rules of social conduct.

Okigbo disdained convention. This fact is significant in understanding his personality. He was always an outsider, resisting the disciplinary supervision of a step-mother, an act which hardened into social rebellion and a demand for personal freedom from moral responsibility. Ironically, it made him enormously attractive in a society long structured by the demands of stringent moral codes. Okigbo seemed totally freed of the burden of responsibility; he was liberated and incapable of cant. In 1987 Wole

Soyinka, not long after he won the Nobel Prize for Literature, answering a question at the University of Jos, said: 'Christopher is one memory I always am incapable of reliving without some pain. We shared everything together, the same passion, interests, the same kind of women, wine, music, poetry ... everything. He was also one of the greatest sources of strength for me at the hour of my personal crisis during the Radio hijack fantasy in Ibadan in 1965.'[66] Soyinka and Okigbo shared a deep friendship fuelled by the same mercurial impulses, the same epicurean temperament, and an equally heightened sense of justice. They admired each other's work enormously. Among the recovered fragments of Okigbo's papers in Enugu was a manuscript of the 'invocation dance,' an early foolscap draft of the dialogue in Soyinka's play, *A Dance of the Forest*, apparently sent to Okigbo for comments. This mutual offering was regular practice. They recognized in each other's work the same moral values and the same urgency.

Just before the rains in February 1963, Wole Soyinka's daughter Moremi was born. At the naming ceremony, Okigbo was the only one of Soyinka's literary friends who was present at Soyinka's Felele residence. Wole Soyinka's brother-in-law, the newspaper columnist Olu Akaraogun recalled that, just as every one was suitably gone on food, wine and tobacco, Christopher Okigbo, 'a prolific and recondite raconteur,'[67] and always in the mood for friendly mischief loudly called everyone to attention, saying: 'Just look at the little angel!' The new baby, Okigbo said, was much too beautiful and did not inherit Soyinka's 'dreadful' face. In any case, Wole was too footloose and too absent from home, the wonder was when he had time to make a baby with Laide. And turning to Soyinka, Okigbo said, 'So Wole, you're telling us you're having your daughter's naming ceremony today. Are you sure you're the father of this baby?'[68] Everyone laughed. Soyinka reacted in mock horror, and said, 'Now Chris, get out of my house!'[69] Many years later, Olu Akaraogun, Laide's elder brother, said with a chuckle, 'Chris was a gypsy.'[70] He could enjoy himself and partake fully of pleasure without self-consciousness. The novelist Nkem Nwankwo writes thus about his relationship with the poet:

> ...*joie de vivre* ... that was the secret of my friendship with Chris. Chris and I made a formidable team. We had a lot in common; we were natural outlaws, free spirits caught in a world of routine and conformity; we were clever, gifted people who were put through the cruel mill of a rigid, unimaginative educational system. Our soaring spirits were clipped by that experience...our impoverished, zero-culture society had even less use for us than it had for other useless elite ... we spent our lives butting our heads against an indifferent universe, seeking fulfillment from nullity... [71]

Okigbo's entire life, framed in that context of an existential paradox of 'seeking fulfillment from nullity', led him to excess. But it was not extravagance, in the way that Bloke Modisane accounts for it, which denied his inner will to live or which led to self-abnegation. It was more an extravagance of spirit. It was a life marked, as Ben Obumselu says, 'By his freedom from practical anxieties, his willingness to try anything, and his intolerance of the hypocrisies of good form.'[72]

The American writer Paul Theroux was introduced to Okigbo in 1963 when he spent three weeks with the poet in Ibadan. Theroux was starting out then on his own illustrious and controversial literary career. But at the time he visited Okigbo in Ibadan, he was a young unknown American with literary ambitions doing a tour of Africa. He was only twenty-three, and serving in the American Peace Corps as an English teacher in Malawi. He was swept up into the enchantment of Okigbo's circle of libertines and intellectuals. He fell in love with the 'intoxicating' mood of Cambridge House: its life without inhibition or protocol, its open doors, and the social mix of the guests. Okigbo introduced him to the other haunts of the Ibadan poets – its women, its bars, its dance halls, its theatre, and the sense of timelessness which characterized the city in the 1960s.

Theroux became a regular visitor to Queen Elizabeth Hall, the female hostel of the University of Ibadan, where he soon fell in love with one of the undergraduates. He came to Ibadan with the manuscript of an experimental poem, which he had titled 'Bitches Murderous Beauty.' Torch Taire recollected that Theroux read it aloud to Okigbo and his Ibadan friends. Theroux also read the beginning of a novel which would later be published under the title, *Waldo*. After this visit to Ibadan, Theroux wrote one of the early reviews of *Heavensgate* in issue number 22 of the magazine *Transition* in 1965.

In Cambridge House Theroux observed piles of unopened mail that kept growing on Okigbo's table, an indication of how the poet conducted the business at Cambridge House. His accounts were disorganized. As his wife Safi, would say, 'Chris was not cut out for business. He trusted people too much and too easily; and gave them books which they never paid for.'[73] He ran the whole operation capriciously, extending credits, which he was unable to collect or for which he was ultimately unable to account properly. It was in much the same way that he conducted the affairs of his life: loose, disordered, spontaneous.

Ben Obumselu reflects upon the socially restless life of the poet: '… with all his contradictions, Okigbo remained for his innumerable friends the finest example of that abundant indiscriminating love which Baudelaire called "the holy prostitution of a soul that gives itself utterly with all its poetry and charity…to the passing unknown". His one perfect and unforgettable poem was himself.'[74] Because he was in search of the finest poetic idiom, he became aesthetically promiscuous.

One must look behind his ornate mask. There was a serious side to the Okigbo personality totally obscured by his need to amuse. In expressing himself by the way he chose to live, Christopher Okigbo wrote his own rules: he existed in a sublime state of the mind in which he saw clearly the hypocrisy and contradiction of the human moral condition. This was an important reason for the poetry he wrote. It gained poignancy from Okigbo's own basic dialogical conception of the human condition. Okigbo's moral ideology significantly echoes his critique of Christian morality in *Heavensgate* in 'Initiations:'

> At confluence of planes, the angle:
> man loses man, loses vision;
>
> So comes John the Baptist
> with bowl of salt water
> preaching the gambit:
> life without sin, without
>
> life; which accepted,
> way leads downward
> down orthocenter
> avoiding decisions…[75]

Okigbo, who grew up under strong Roman Catholic influence, would reject the absolute prescriptions of Christian morality. The conduct of his adult life was completely in rebellion against those teachings of the church that repressed the expression of his full humanity. He did not hold tightly to any strong religious or doctrinal sentiments. Yet his poetry was a highly spiritually charged composition with its sense of the spiritual quest. Okigbo remained a nominal Roman Catholic all his life and indeed hung a bold white cross on the walls of Cambridge House.

He had stopped going to church. He had become agnostic, or at best a syncretic humanist. Okigbo's perennial search for meaning also indicates that he suffered greatly from a haunting feeling of alienation and unfulfillment and its anxieties, which he expressed as a form of quest towards self-awareness. The result is what Anozie describes as 'a dynamic ritualistic rhythm' which empowers the mystic essence in his poetry. In sum, Okigbo had adopted the alternative morality and worldview of the Beat movement, and was fascinated by the counter-culture of that era, when he emerged as an artist in the 1950s and the 1960s. He was reading the new American poetry at this time. He was moved by the alternative lifestyles of key figures of the Beat movement, like Kerouac and Ginsberg. He experimented with the idea of free love and the sexual freedom of the movement. He ultimately came to take the metaphysical refuge of his Igbo spiritual identity. The English critic Gerald Moore perceptively wrote, 'Okigbo also spoke interestingly about his relationship to his poems, his sense of being no more than a mouthpiece (perhaps a chosen one) for a force beyond his full knowledge or comprehension. The attitude is typical of traditional African poet-seers, and Okigbo was always acutely conscious of his heritage in Igbo religion and the need to make poetic amends for deserting the hereditary priesthood of Idoto, which was his by right.'[76] Okigbo said, in the 1965 interview with the Canadian Marjory Whitelaw, that when he discovered poetry he felt no longer a need for religion. He was working towards a new spiritual synthesis based upon his fascination with both the Christian elements in his life and his lost connection with his indigenous Igbo religion.

Kayode Jibowu who lived in the close orbit of Okigbo's social world in those years at Cambridge House notes that: 'Chris was a person who was too much in search of the truth... the truth of everything. I believe that was why he saw the extreme of things always. And reached for the extreme.'[77] There was no middle ground in his search for unique or fulfilling experiences. Later in his life Jibowu was to become a born-again Pentecostal Christian. But he said 'Chris was a very spiritual person in his own very unique way.'[78] Okigbo, the poet, sought to express his spiritual quest through poetry. He was in that sense in perpetual quest. This does explain the religious imagery that pervades Okigbo's poetry right through to 'Path of Thunder.'

J.P. Clark had introduced Kayode Jibowu to Okigbo, long after their UCI years. They were three small and tempestuous men who felt things passionately, and expressed themselves extravagantly. Jibowu recalled how, as undergraduates at Ibadan in the middle of the 1950s, he and Clark shared the same passion for classical music. On one occasion, after a long argument about an interpretation of Beethoven's piano concerto No.5, they both broke down and wept. There was a rerun of this dramatic argument with Okigbo and Kayode Jibowu in Torch Taire's house. Okigbo preferred the William Backhaus 1920s recording of the concerto and Jibowu preferred another. At some point Okigbo got fed up and went and put a jazz number on the record player. Anyway, Okigbo loved jazz more than he cared for classical music. Jibowu stood up and changed the jazz number. Okigbo was infuriated, and said in annoyance: 'Look, what's all this pretension about? You don't even understand Beethoven!'[79] A scuffle developed between the two as Torch Taire walked in. Torch remembers the incongruousness of the small and wiry Christopher Okigbo matched in a physical struggle with the stocky and heavier Jibowu. Okigbo picked up a cricket bat which was lying around the room and lunged at Kayode Jibowu. Torch tried to restrain him and

Okigbo kept saying, 'Let go Torch, let me break this foolish man's head!'[80] Kayode Jibowu had said something to the effect that Okigbo wrote 'mere ditties' and dared call himself a poet. Okigbo shot back saying, 'Oh, I wish I could write ditties. They are lovely things to write. But I don't write ditties! Go and ask Wole, ask J.P, who the poet is in this country ... you block head, you never could write anything!'[81]

Cambridge House also offered Okigbo refuge from the chaos outside. There is a sense of the distinct, personal disturbance fused with magical sensuality always present in the poems written in Ibadan. This was to become the purpose of Okigbo's writing: 'to bring out the sense of an inner disturbance,'[82] as he confessed to the Canadian journalist and writer Marjory Whitelaw. His growth as a poet was against a background of political transition and change, exploding with extreme violence in post-colonial Africa. Silence indeed was necessary in the life and work of the poet. It was as important to him as tumult, as the sense of motion. People who knew him often pondered these contradictions in Okigbo's personality; these silences and withdrawals in which he relapsed into deep melancholy and during which visitors to Cambridge House felt its gaunt and awkward stillness.

He tried various forms of escape in order to write: he would sometimes go to Torch Taire's home nearby when he could no longer stand the human motion of Cambridge House. Or, as Taire recalled, when as was sometimes the case, the Electricity Corporation disconnected the power in Cambridge House, because Okigbo had not have paid his light bills, being either too broke or too distracted by other pursuits to do so. Even after Torch Taire got married to his wife Oluremi, Okigbo would appropriate their house. At such times, Torch and his wife would be forced to go over to Cambridge House because they could not sleep with the lights on in their house while Okigbo worked on his poems all through the night. Taire was close enough to observe Okigbo's working routine. He recalls that poetry was neither instant nor easy for Okigbo – 'he worked hard on his poems...he struggled for words'.[83] Okigbo's poetry was thus, not wakened merely by a flash of inspiration. The goddess was often far more slippery than is imagined. Okigbo combined craft – something to which he committed an intense mental energy, perhaps all his humanity – with a careful reaching for the highest form of music in his poetry.

It was usual to find Okigbo exhausted early in the morning, after the labour with the muse, with crumpled balls of paper scattered about his study, the result of an effort to arrive at some creative satisfaction or clarity. Observing Okigbo at work was an unforgettable experience for the playwright and poet Femi Osofisan. He spent a night in Cambridge House with the poet which proved to be a startling introduction for the young Osofisan to the ways of the muse at the feet of a master poet. About this time in 1965, Femi Osofisan was only a senior at the Government College, Ibadan. He was planning to enter the University of Ibadan in that year, and he had discovered the salon-like atmosphere of the Mbari Club. 'There were always all these famous writers and artists hanging around Mbari. It was intensely fascinating,' he recalled. He found Christopher Okigbo 'the most intriguing of them all ... He went about in this white robe.'[84] Osofisan had begun to read Okigbo's poetry at about this time and became deeply engrossed by it. 'It was so different from everything else that I had read.'[85] It was at that point that his interest in the literary life was kindled, heightened by the enchantment of the life around Okigbo and his crowd of bohemian friends – the famous writers, artists, musicians, actors and intellectuals of all shades, in Ibadan.

Osofisan resolved to become a writer principally because of Okigbo. He wanted to discover the process of writing – to learn the poet's craft and routine. He let Okigbo know of his interest, and thought nothing more of it until one evening when Okigbo drove down to the Government College, Ibadan and invited the young Osofisan to Cambridge House. He could stay overnight in Cambridge House and observe him at work. They stayed up and worked all night. That encounter remained vivid for Osofisan many years afterwards: 'It was instructive. Okigbo would write and tear up his effort. Each time he did this I was shocked. At the end of that ordeal in the morning, he had only four lines from all that staying awake with numerous pieces of paper lying around him. He showed me the poem and asked for my comment. I thought it was great. But he was not satisfied with his work. He tore that up too. That further shocked me!'[86] This was just one example of those nights when Okigbo spent long hours crafting a poem, wrestling with the muse, only to emerge the next day not satisfied. Okigbo would show the result of his midnight labour. The poem would attract acclaim and admiration, and he would destroy it. He was never totally satisfied with his craft. He apparently destroyed what would have formed a considerable body of his poems. Literary scholars and readers of poetry are today the poorer for it doubtlessly. But it also demonstrates Okigbo's artistic quest, his reaching for the purity of the poetic line, and for perfection in craft. He told Robert Serumaga who interviewed him in London in 1965 that he considered poetry 'technical …a form of craftsmanship.'[87]

Okigbo imposed strict standards on himself as an artist. This reaching for the purity of art also powerfully demonstrates that aspect of his personality, the innate, ordered universe, which Chinua Achebe referred to as the 'in-born finesse'[88] with which Christopher Okigbo did things. It also reflects his artistic honesty and purpose. He was his own greatest and most demanding critic. The night in Cambridge House was Okigbo's dramatic way of giving Osofisan, the young, aspirant oblate to the muse, lessons in the Olympian labour of artistic creation. He was instructing him in a practical way about something, which he knew deeply as a poet, that the muse was never to be taken for granted. Okigbo also loved to read his poems aloud to his friends to hear the echo and movement of his poetry, to test the notes from 'the scansion he carried in his head.'[89] 'I hear sounds as they say a worshipper hears the flutes,'[90] he writes in the final sequence of his poems, 'Lament of the Silent Sisters'. Out of this process the poet grew. He was humble with his work in the way that writers often are not. He recognized his limitations as a poet and in his striving towards mastery he shared his deepest poetic experiences with others. He valued that kind of shared intercourse with poetry. Ben Obumselu however suggests that this tendency for Okigbo to be public with his poems may be an indication of 'his initial uncertainty about his abilities as a poet. He was tentative because he did not feel sure about himself as a poet until he arrived at *Distances*.'[91]

Okigbo thus worked and reworked his poems till they glittered like fine crystal. As Ben Obumselu said, he was 'a connoisseur of the poetic line.'[92] He relied enormously on the measured judgment of Obumselu. Often in the evenings, Okigbo visited Obumselu 'with poetry in his head.'[93] He would drive down at ungodly hours to Obumselu's home at the University of Ibadan, just to discuss a line or two of the poems brewing in his mind, or sometimes, to hand him a draft piece of his latest poem for his opinion. He noted that Okigbo had 'a feverish need to communicate at such moments when new ideas worked like those scansions in his head.'[94] Okigbo had enormous respect for Obumselu who had consistently played the role of his editor and critic, at various times from their undergraduate years at Ibadan onwards.

Obumselu remained Okigbo's closest intellectual collaborator and confidante; he it was who swept the minefields of the poet's imaginative endeavour with care and empathy, and thus fostered what is beautiful and sublime in Okigbo's poetry. The poet came to rely as much on Obumselu's 'clinical editorial skills'[95] in this phase of his life as in his calm friendship. They shared a close literary fellowship, the result of which transformed the poetic landscape and style of one of the twentieth century's most talented poets. Obumselu in short meant to Okigbo what Pound meant to Eliot, he polished the dreariness from Okigbo's invocations. Thus, Okigbo offers a touching acknowledgment to Obumselu in the final version of his collection, *Labyrinths with Path of Thunder* later on, 'for criticisms that continue to guide me along the paths of greater clarity.'[96]

Ben Obumselu's return from Oxford to the University of Ibadan in 1963 coincided with important transformations in Okigbo's life and letters. It was fortuitous for Okigbo. His poetry was beginning to evolve; and he was beginning to publish in *Transition* and *Black Orpheus,* two of the leading literary journals in Africa in that period. A product of the New Critical School of Northrop Frye, Obumselu's intellectual and social relationship with Okigbo is reflected from 1963 in the difference in tone and in the formal variety and texture of the poetry. Of their relationship, Obumselu himself said, 'There would be no logic or fairness in saying that I reconstructed one line or the other in Christopher's poetry. But I could say perhaps, the only thing... the only influence I had on Okigbo was that I showed him the possibility in the principle of the continuity of the poetic image.'[97] This is what the critic Anozie later discerned as the organic relatedness in his poetry. Obumselu's influence on Okigbo's methods was the result of his own fascination with the form of the continuous image in poetry. Okigbo's routine – the ongoing, rigourous process of poetic construction and refinement – gained from this principle. Obumselu always forced Okigbo to work and rework his poetry in that continuous reaching for a state of creative perfection – or what Anozie calls 'aesthetic grace'[98] – when poetry yields its own meaning and purity by its own internal coherent logic or movement.

Okigbo was excited by Obumselu's doctoral dissertation submitted to Oxford in 1963 on 'The myth of the Artist in James Joyce'. Obumselu's ideas matched his own conception of the artist and the creative process – the idea of the sublime vision, the romantic ideal that charges and transforms the imaginative mode, and the idea of the connection between madness and creativity in the artistic unconscious. Okigbo soon adopted the paradigms of Obumselu's modernist thesis and its deeply existentialist backbone. In 1964, Obumselu had lent Okigbo a copy of Jacques Maritain's book *Creative Intuition in Art and Poetry* for an understanding of what Maritain called the 'intuitive pulsion' or that 'musical stir', without sound or word, formless and only audible to the soul. Okigbo read the book overnight. The next day, he drove to Ben Obumselu's house on Saunders Road very late in the night, very excited. He said to Obumselu: 'You know Ben, I love it! But I don't understand a word of it!'[99] Only Christopher Okigbo perhaps, Obumselu noted in characteristic laconic humour, would love a book, without a care for what it was saying! But we can still hear the echo of Maritain call back to us in Okigbo's poem, in the fifth sequence of 'Lament of the Silent Sisters':

I hear sound as, they say
A worshipper hears the flutes –

The music sounds so in the soul
It can hear nothing else –

I hear painted harmonies

From the mushroom of the sky –

Silences are melodies
Heard in retrospect…[10]

These lines truly echo Maritain's conception of poetry as '…unformulated song, with no words, no sounds, absolutely inaudible to the ear, audible only to the heart.'[101] Okigbo was a poet indeed inspired by 'the charm of utterance.'[102]

He maintained the habit of sounding out his poems first on his circle of close friends. He basically 'commandeered' his audience – anybody around him who showed any interest in poetry – to listen. He wanted to let poetry stir or provoke, and seduce. Many times, he had knocked at the doors of his friends in the Onireke neighbourhood, particularly Torch Taire, Kayode Jibowu, Femi Johnson or Godwin Adokpaye, when they might well have retired to bed with their wives. 'Christopher will wake anyone up just so that you would listen to him read a new poem which he would just have written.'[103] He was oblivious to the fact that his nocturnal appearance may have disrupted or interrupted some private conjugal activity. He was powerfully gripped by the desire for utterance. Sometimes during his numerous nocturnal visits to Adokpaye's house nearby, Okigbo would come clutching manuscripts of his poems. Adokpaye recalled many such times when Okigbo woke him up very late in the night, screaming excitedly in the dead of night: 'Godwin, open the door … you must listen to this!'[104] He would start reading. It often turned out to be a new poem, which he had just finished writing.

At some point, he would stop suddenly and start making corrections feverishly and silently, disregarding Adokpaye, and oblivious of any other of his immediate audience, whom he would have woken up in the first place to listen to his poem. Okigbo would get so engrossed in his work that sometimes he would fall asleep on the warm carpet in Adokpaye's lounge. Preferring not to disturb him, Godwin Adokpaye would climb upstairs to his restless wife, and would often leave Okigbo alone there, where the muse had caught and wrestled him to sleep. It was usual for Okigbo to wake in the middle of the night, gather his paper and walk out of the house, leaving all the doors wide open! Cambridge House was separated from Adokpaye's home by two streets. A low stone wall rounded Adokpaye's home, which Okigbo preferred to scale rather than walk through the gate. Okigbo was absent-minded and carefree. Sometimes they would be at the dining table in Adokpaye's home to which Okigbo was a regular and honoured guest. Half way through, he would suddenly get up from his chair, abandoning his half-eaten food, and hurry out of the house on a sudden impulse or flash of inspiration. Sometimes he would be gone for days. On many occasions he abandoned his manuscripts on Godwin Adokpaye's dining table for days, until he would be reminded to come and pick them. He lived life with such sense of freedom and cultivated the image of the renegade and unconventional poet. Okigbo played by his own unique rules. On occasions, he would insist on having Mrs Adokpaye prepare his favorite dish of pounded yam, no matter how late. He would eat quickly and speed off again in search of other adventures. Godwin knew the poet as 'a restless spirit in a hurry to complete this cycle of his life. He was always in a hurry, always up to some new adventure.'[105]

His friends loved him for his unique individuality and tolerated his eccentricities as the gift of genius, honored him in a society where the modern artist, especially the published poet, was increasingly considered the embodiment of national cultural genius. Okigbo's rising stature as a poet in post-colonial Nigeria of the 1960s, made many of his personal lapses tolerable. But most people also indulged him because he was so easy to like; his charm was effortless; his pranks mostly harmless and entertaining. 'He was like a child. You could never really get very angry with him,'[106] said Mabel Segun. Okigbo's extravagant generosity was equally legendary. 'Most people knew that he meant no harm. His open, generous spirit was infectious. He lived freely and he insisted on this individuality. He took fully of his friends. He had no barriers to friendship really – everybody was his friend! – and he gave as much of himself and his resources without bounds. He had no respect for time and was quite indisciplined to its demands. If you got angry with Christopher, it was only just for a moment,'[107] recalled Torch Taire. Godwin Adokpaye himself also remembered Christopher Okigbo's deep and genuine love for children, reflected in the poet's unique relationship with Adokpaye's first daughter, Annie.

Okigbo had been extremely fond of little Annie, with whom he had become genuine friends. He would usually come round specifically to take Annie riding on his horse in the evenings at the Ibadan polo club. Sometimes on bringing Annie home after the horse ride with her, the poet would tether his horse the tree which stood in front of Godwin Adokpaye's house and would walk out, through the back door, scaling the low wall, to his own house. On many occasions he left his horse, which would be retrieved, sometimes days later. 'He did this to let Annie feel that the horse belonged to her!'[108] recalled Godwin Adokpaye.

The birth of Okigbo's own daughter in 1964 was a joyous moment, which he celebrated loudly. Annabelle Obiageli Ibrahimat was born at the University College Hospital, Ibadan, and as Safi said: 'From the beginning, Obiageli was a charming little baby and was her father's little angel. It was love at first sight with those two. They had too much in common and there was no question about it!'[109] Christopher Okigbo was very excited about fatherhood. He had gone about town, proclaiming the birth of his daughter. His friend Peter Thomas recalled Okigbo's proud announcements of the birth of his daughter, something which the Welsh poet considered quite unusual among the Igbo whom he thought preferred male children. But Okigbo thought of the birth his daughter as the completion of a cycle. It was the return of his mother. He wrote 'Dance of the Painted Maidens' to celebrate her:

> For you return to us
> From a forgotten farewell
> From the settled abyss
> Where the twilights cross.[110]

Obiageli's birth was one of the most concrete events in his marriage:

> For it is you, shower of rain after drought
> That we have waited
> Menses after menses, without antimony without
> Bracelets; while you swam
> Diver of centuries, your longest journey, the sea
> Of ten thousand leagues…[111]

The birth of their child also brought another important dimension to Okigbo's life: it improved the poet's relationship and standing with his mother-in-law. Safi's mother came to stay at Cambridge House during Safi's maternity break. It was a period of domesticity for Okigbo, without the clang of dizzying parties at Cambridge House. The poet and his visiting mother-in-law struck up a famously redoubtable relationship, and became increasingly fond of each other. 'They were great friends, those two,'[112] Safi recalled many years later at her home on Glover Road home in Ikoyi, Lagos, on the eve of her departure to Italy where she had just been appointed Nigeria's Ambassador to Rome and the Holy See.

Safi's mother retained her fond memory of Okigbo. She became very excited at the mention of the late poet. Perhaps, it was a reflection of the friendship they both enjoyed, that her face brightened and she uttered the lone cry of memory: 'Oh Christopher!' Safi's mother came to know her son-in-law apparently more closely, beyond the veneer of the public image of the irresponsible and occasionally improvident poet; one who could say to an interviewer: 'I have no future plan.'[113] During this visit to Cambridge House at the birth of Obiageli, she found him not only lovable, but sensitive and entertaining. Okigbo devoted a lot of attention to her. He basked in the privilege, not having known his own mother, of adopting Safi's mother. He found ways to be intelligible to her. Safi's mother didn't speak much English and Okigbo couldn't speak Yoruba very well. So, it was endlessly amusing to Safi just watching both of them trying to communicate with each other. 'They would always crumble in laughter at their own failed efforts,' Safi remembered. He frequently took her driving around Ibadan, visiting his friends, treating her to the Ibadan social scenes and the cultured life of the city in which he was a denizen.

Okigbo's Ibadan was in turmoil: the euphoria of independence had waned, replaced by a deep gloom of disappointment. The illusion of political freedom thus shattered, replaced by political violence and social chaos, events in Western Nigeria heightened the apocalyptic temperament of the intellectuals and artists of the sixties. In an important sense, the force of the liberation and the civil rights movements around the world in the 1960s also framed the mood of emerging politics in Nigeria. It had a revolutionary spirit. The growing disenchantment with the political situation in the country, especially following the party crisis in which Action Group had been splintered, was palpable among Okigbo's circle of friends; it was the subject of some of most vigorous debates in Cambridge House. Okigbo's home soon became the centre of the serious political debates, and even intrigues, of the period.

Bola Ige had made a name for himself as one of the leaders in the radical faction of the Action Group, and as the National Publicity Secretary of the party. In that role, he had become one of the most visible opponents of the Akintola regime in Ibadan. His friends called him Cicero. As a leading figure of one faction of the party, which had been forced into opposition in Ibadan, Bola Ige had been under constant threat of physical harm or detention. One of the places in the city that Bola Ige found refuge was in Okigbo's Cambridge House: 'Behind the ambience of perpetual partying was a more serious purpose. It was the place we dropped in to replenish after a night out in town: to argue literature, or for some of us, to engage in illicit consolations. The next place was Femi Johnson's house close by Okigbo's, especially when his English wife was away. Their homes were not only shrines of pleasure and places of memory, of deep friendship, they were also the refuge for progressive politics; and they were so convenient and nearby each other.'[114]

Following the 1959 election in Nigeria, the leader of the Action Group Obafemi Awolowo abdicated his position as premier of the Western region to become the leader of the opposition in Lagos. The negotiations had collapsed to work out an alliance with the NCNC, with the proposals for Nnamdi Azikiwe to assume the premiership with Awolowo as the Deputy Prime Minister and Minister of Finance. Intra-party intrigues in both parties had frustrated that move with the result that the NCNC had chosen to form an alliance between the Northern Peoples Congress, with Nnamdi

Azikiwe as the president and Commander-in-Chief, and Balewa, the NPC candidate as Prime Minister. As leader of opposition in the Federal Parliament – the House of Representative – Awolowo left the position of Premier of the Western region to the deputy leader of the Action Group, the redoubtable Samuel Akintola in Ibadan. Awolowo nevertheless retained his place as the leader of the party. It was an agreeable relationship until the smoldering underbelly of politics revealed a conflict.

The Action Group reeled from the failed alliance. Forced thus into opposition, key leaders of the Action Group felt isolated from the central government. Although Awolowo had resigned as Premier he nevertheless tried to interfere in the regional government under Akintola, which the premier resisted. Soon a rift had developed within the party. The historian, Michael Crowder writes about this in his book, *The Story of Nigeria*.[115]

The mood was as intoxicating as it was foreboding. Christopher Okigbo was too close to the major actors in the crisis to be merely an observer.

By June 1962, Ibadan was engulfed in political tension, a prelude to the great violence that followed. This serious ideological conflict instigated the leadership crisis in the party, and ultimately led to a serious breach of peace. A state of emergency was soon declared in the Western Region following the subsequent eruptions in the Western Regional Parliament. Ibadan was placed under curfew. In the upshot, twenty nine leaders of the Action Group, accused of planning to overthrow the Balewa government in the centre, were arrested and charged with treasonable felony. Among those charged with the Action Group leader Obafemi Awolowo in 1963 was Okigbo's old friend, the eccentric mathematician Dr Chike Obi of the Dynamic Party. Chike Obi had smuggled Anthony Enahoro, one of the wanted politicians in that incident, across the border to Dahomey, from where he escaped first to Ghana, and then to England.

What followed was the long legal battled to extradite him in the celebrated 'fugitive offender' case. Chike Obi, meanwhile, was locked up at the Kirikiri prisons in Lagos. Bola Ige was not charged but had been arrested and locked up at the Lekki interdiction site. With all the memorable drama of his appearance in the celebrated case, the Sowemimo Court subsequently jailed Awolowo for ten years. Obafemi Awolowo's imprisonment suddenly transformed him into something of a national hero – he came to symbolise the true voice of opposition against the conservative post-colonial leadership at the centre of government in Nigeria. Awolowo's political stance began increasingly to reflect the ideal for the younger generation of post-colonial nationalist intellectuals of Okigbo's mould, for whom the political condition of the new federation was a constant issue of disputation.

With this background, Okigbo developed the most acute visions of his society, something which in time would significantly mark the tenor of his final output, and signify his ultimate creative testament. He had also begun his experiments with the oral, declarative form evident in his last poems. The situation in Western Nigeria invoked in a sublime way, the tragedy of the new nation. It was emblematic of its future and deeply disappointing, because the emergence of the new nation in 1960 had been deeply symbolic for Okigbo's generation. It was this sense of rebirth and newness that had empowered the sentiments of *Heavensgate*. But there he was in Ibadan at the onset of a new phase in Nigeria's post-colonial history – the political crisis that had erupted in western Nigeria, the result of the factional rupture within the Action Group, the ruling party in the west. It also signified the rupture of the new nation.

Elsewhere in Africa, many of the newly independent nations were also erupting in the violence of post-colonial transition. In the Congo, the charismatic Patrice Lumumba was murdered, and the Congo was thrown into strife. Patrice Lumumba's death in 1961 infuriated many people in Africa – especially young, progressive intellectuals like Okigbo. Lumumba was one of the African politicians of that era, in the mould of Nigeria's Nnamdi Azikiwe and Ghana's Kwame Nkrumah, who affected the imagination of that generation of Africans. By his death, there was the sudden apprehension of the crisis of the new nations. Lumumba's death also signified a form of martyrdom, of the heroic individual as communal carrier in a conflict society – a theme which Soyinka explored fully in his play *The Strong Breed*, conceived and written at that time. The first sequence of *Silences*, which Okigbo wrote in that period, also explores the idea of martyrdom and of turbulence signified in the fate of the drowning Franciscan nuns. Seen in the context of his struggles against imperialism, Lumumba's death would implicate, for a highly conscious poet of Okigbo's romantic imagination, the sense of ritual self-sacrifice. Coming almost in tandem, the Western Nigerian crisis invoked a similar vision of disorder, threatening the fabric of post-colonial Nigeria. It is important to note that these transformations of the political landscape were taking place just as the poet was arriving and settling to a new life in Ibadan – that centre of political intrigue and violence in the 1960s. Christopher Okigbo responded in typical extravagant emotion, poetically. The lofty idealism of *Limits* gave way to the haunting tragedy, the deep anger and apocalyptic prophecy of the 'Lament of the Silent Sisters', the first sequence in *Silences*. This part of his long poetic sequence, Okigbo said, was influenced partly by Lumumba's earlier death and partly by the events in Western Nigeria just beginning to crystallize in 1962.

Okigbo finished the original draft of 'Lament of the Silent Sisters' in November 1962. The poem also marked a major break in Okigbo's artistic phase, beginning as it were the period of the poet's career in which the modernism of Eliot and Hopkins would begin to tend towards a creative mix with other 'disparate' sources in Okigbo's poetry. Sources like Malcolm Cowley, Raja Ratnam, Stephane Mallarmé, Rabindrinath Tagore, García Lorca – all of whom Okigbo acknowledged in Volume 3, Number 3, Issue 8 of *Transition* in 1962, where 'Lament of the Silent Sisters' was first published, and there was also acknowledgement in the final collection of his poetry. For some reason, he did not acknowledge Hart Crane, whose influence is also obvious in Okigbo's poetry. Okigbo's cosmopolitanism would sustain the character of his later poetry, in which he chronicled the conflict of that society within which he lived: the political crisis and the mood of turbulence charged the idiom of Okigbo's poetry in this period because he was a close and perceptive witness. He began to envision Nigeria as a 'storm tossed ship' – a variation of the theme of Hopkins's *Wreck of the Deutschland* – especially in the prophetic theme implicated by the crier's 'Lament' in *Silences*, and the response of the chorus:

Crier: They struck him in the ear they struck him in the eye;
They picked his bones for scavenging:

Chorus: And there would be a continual going to the well,
Until they smash their calabashes.[116]

This sequence of poems demonstrates Okigbo's acute awareness, his intense vision and sensitivity to the human predicament, much in the same terms as Tennessee Williams' world conscious of evil. Okigbo's deep concern for that society provokes the anguish of the silent sisters. The image of the 'storm tossed ship' must have been one that dominated the mood and the talk around Okigbo's circle of writers and friends at this period, because it is a theme that recurs in the writings of some of his closest peers in the same period. We see this especially in J.P Clark's play *The Raft*.

Okigbo was attuned to his society and was deeply aware of it. He was aware of its irreconcilable contradictions. He often laughed at life and mocked death, the terror of existence. His vision of art had evolved into what Anozie locates and describes as 'A common and healthy conflict between art and society'[117] and which interacts 'between pure aesthetic and common place human concerns.'[118] Something else that emerges from Okigbo is his 'unique versatility,'[119] that ability to integrate dissonant airs into an organic poetic experience; the woven mythologic complex, the universal aesthetic principle, which transcended, as in his life, cultural and racial boundaries. Okigbo recognized always, something vigorous and dynamic and robust in every human experience and in every culture. He could share deeply of it. He believed in the universal sense of the world, and rejected the notion of narrow aesthetic categories. He refused the tag of 'an African poet' preferring to be simply a poet.

By 1961 Okigbo began to read Senghor's poetry more seriously. Senghor was one of the leading political and intellectual figures of the black world, and was a founding member of the committee for *Black Orpheus*. *Black Orpheus* frequently featured Senghor's poetry. In the June 1961 issue of the magazine there were ten of Senghor's poems taken from his new work *Nocturnes*. The poems excited Okigbo. They had a powerful oral pulsion that was spontaneous and attractive. Obumselu confirms the impact of Senghor on Okigbo when he first read Ulli Beier's English translation of those poems. Senghor's poetry connected him immediately to what he already admired in poetry: he felt that it not only had the sustained eloquence of T. S. Eliot's but more. As Obumselu notes:

> But the structure and the rhetoric of Senghor's poetry are radically different from the American poet's. Senghor does not use the same symphonic form; and his imagery is a shower of brilliant sparks which dazzle the reader by their variety of color and trajectory. Moreover, Senghor's verbal tropes are not the foci of his meaning in the same way that Eliot's rivers, fires, and mythical thunderclaps focus his Christian concerns. Senghor's images are truly incidental, exaggerated in tone, and sensual although the sensuality is modified by the subtleties of a style which, as Senghor's French biographer Armand Guibert pointed out, 'sustain the posture and illusion of chastity'. Without substance. Instead, they widen the connections and associations to create a shadowy zone of unstated meanings round the subject matter of the poem. This is the so-called surrealistic imagery which, in Senghor's own account, is an African thing not deriving from Andre Breton and the French surrealists but from the Wollof and Serer griots of Senegal from whom he learnt his trade. Senghor's *Nocturnes* (which contained five 'elegies') introduced Okigbo to the 'elegies' and 'laments' which would dominate his subsequent work. They taught him to 'score' his poems for traditional musical instruments. Above all, they demonstrated the 'surrealistic' image which is capable of raising any and every poem to the pitch of art without mythological or philosophical props.[120]

In 'Elegy of the Wind' for instance, Obumselu again points out the strong strain and allusion to Senghor's 'Elégie de Circonsis,' especially its connection with the image of sexual mutilation in the circumcision ceremony, and the theme of the creative disruption of the social order, 'the demolition of home and country in order to rebuild them.'[121] There is also the disruption, and mutilation of language, in the search for new forms of poetic expression. In fact from 1962, Okigbo's work began to reflect this influence of Senghor, and a tapestry of themes, which Obumselu says 'surveys the poet's past life, admits his failures and looks forward exultantly to future creative possibilities.'[122] Okigbo had arrived at that stage, where he could adopt and 'use all the resources of the various traditions he inherited in speaking about his own life, his convictions and dreams.'[123] And in that, Obumselu believes, anyone really looking for Okigbo's originality and an understanding of the great value of his poetry, can find them.

Okigbo was working feverishly between 1964 and 1965. He had started work on a proposed large prose work, which he had apparently discussed with J.P. Clark. There is no evidence that he got beyond the ideas stage. His poetry appeared in a number of prestigious magazines and anthologies in Africa. As he wrote on 20 May 1963 to Henry Rago, the editor of the magazine *Poetry* in Chicago, 'I have been heard in Africa and Europe, and would want, if possible to have an audience in America.'[124] He was deeply involved with the artistic questions and the critical issues of the day; he traveled frequently. In August 1963, Dennis Duerden interviewed Okigbo at the Transcription Centre's Dover Street studios in the West End of London. Okigbo's anti-negritude outburst of the previous year at the Kampala conference was still topical. By this time he had agreed to be the West African Editor of Rajat Neogy's *Transition*. Duerden tried to establish from Okigbo, in the interview, what was the focus of *Transition* as a cultural journal based in Africa. Okigbo gave a reply which echoed his cosmopolitan vision of art. He said:

> ...we believe, you see, that time has come to question some of our old prejudices, to ask ourselves, for instance, whether there is such a thing as African literature, what characteristic a body of work may exhibit that will entitle that body of work to be classified as African literature? What is a good African novel, for instance, what is an African painting, what is African art? These are broad issues which we hope to tackle, and what is a good poem in fact, what do we consider good poetry? What is a good play, I mean what constitutes African drama? These are issues we think we ought to clear before we can prepare the ground for literary authorship. And this is what we want to do in the critical supplement.[125]

These were major concerns of African literature in its emergent years. Articulating some of those views in the way he did provides an insight into Okigbo's conception of his own poetry as the product of a boundless, universal energy and vision. Some of Okigbo's ideas would reverberate much later in the critical content of African literature, and in the foundational discourse on post-colonialism. Okigbo had asked the question: 'Is there any such thing as African literature?' He believed literature, or any work of the imagination to be the product of a humane, refined and autonomous consciousness.

Not long after, Sunday Anozie published a methodological critique of Okigbo's *Heavensgate* in the journal *Ibadan* under the title: 'A Study of Art as Ritual.' By 1963 in fact, Okigbo had established his reputation as an increasingly prominent and indeed lyrical voice in a generation of brilliant poets in Africa, such as Soyinka, Clark, U Tam'si, Rive, Brutus. He received the adulation of his peers, and this growing importance of Okigbo's poetry is reflected in the appearance of his 'Lament of the Flutes' among the selection in that year collected in Langston Hughes's anthology *Poems from Black Africa,* and in the Penguin anthology compiled and edited by Gerald Moore and Ulli Beier.

When he finished the early draft of 'Lament of the Silent Sisters' he invited Torch Taire and George Kurubo to hear him read, over good French wine early in January 1963. They sat and listened as Okigbo read the poem, enthralled by its contemplative, invocative, and strange power. Torch Taire was particularly intrigued by the mystery of those opening lines: 'Is there... is certainly there...' and, drawn inexorably inward till the fall of the last refrain. They were possibly the first audience for the *'Laments.'* 'I immediately felt something new emerging in Okigbo's poetry,'[126] said George Kurubo years later on a balmy day at the Island Club in Lagos. The haunting testament of the poem and the gaiety of Okigbo's delivery also echoed in Torch Taire's memory for a long time too. 'It was magical. Chris was testing for a new voice, a new kind of eloquence. You could feel a sense of creative triumph in the lilt of his voice as he read. He said he was looking for something extraordinarily new. We were just his witnesses,'[127] Taire said of his experience. From May 1962 Okigbo began working on 'Lament of the Silent Sisters' and completed the early draft in November 1962. It is not certain which version he was testing on Torch Taire and George Kurubo, but what is certain is that when he visited Nsukka early in 1963 he showed a complete draft of the poem to the critic Donatus Nwoga. Another version of the poem also appeared in volume 8 of *Transition* in 1963. He told the American critic Bernth Lindfors who visited him in Ibadan in May 1963, that he was not quite satisfied with the early versions of the poem published in *Transition*. He was doing elaborate revisions for the version, which he later submitted to *Poetry* magazine that May. *Poetry* magazine did not publish Okigbo, but as the poet and critic Michael J. C. Echeruo wrote, 'In the fifties and sixties, *Poetry* had published poets who later distinguished themselves…in submitting to *Poetry*, Okigbo was staking out for himself a place of recognition among the great Anglo-American modernists. Okigbo wanted to step beyond the appreciative but limited world of *Black Orpheus* or *Transition* to the elite (and esteemed) circle of new, even experimental, poets.'[128]

Written in the backdrop of the political disturbances in Ibadan in 1964, 'Lament of the Drums,' the second part of the sequence, the story of Palinurus, mourns the tragic death of Segun Awolowo. His death in a fatal motor accident on 10 July 1963 on his way to Lagos for his father's trial touched Okigbo in a personal way. Torch Taire, an even closer friend of the late Segun recalled that his death inspired a communal grief in Ibadan, and became linked even more symbolically to the wider tragedy playing out in Western Nigeria at the time. These events happening at the same time – the Action Group crisis, the imprisonment of Obafemi Awolowo and the tragic death of his first son – had a profound emotional effect on Okigbo. Segun Awolowo was a promising young man; a dashing socialite with whom Okigbo was socially connected in Ibadan.

This mood of personal and communal grief resonates in the 'Laments.' Awolowo had been jailed for his alleged role as leader of opposition seeking violently to overthrow the government of Nigeria's first republic. Evidence, adduced by Dr. Maja a key leader of Awo's faction of the Action Group, deposed on a plea bargain, substantiated the elaborate plot of the Action Group inspired coup plot. Noting the 'various discordant features' between the poem originally titled 'Lament of the Mariner', and the 'Lament of the Drums' as it finally became, Sunday Anozie writes that:

'Lament of the Mariner', with its quiet elegiac mood and resigned structure, seem not to belong intrinsically to the series which make up *Lament of the Drums*, analogically it is an ode addressed to a statesman or an important public figure, namely Chief Obafemi Awolowo, who for the poet merits comparison with Palinirus. The date of the poem's composition is also revelatory: it shows how early in 1964 Okigbo became aware of the possibilities of a new 'Lament'. Darkening signs are read in the skies, a ship without a mariner (Nigeria without Chief Awolowo, then in prison?) can be seen careering towards a rock, the seasons have turned full cycle and Isthar Laments for Tammuz.[129]

The two 'Laments' had apparently been composed originally as separate poems. Torch Taire who had witnessed the 'birth' of the poems, observed that Okigbo wrote 'Lament of the Drums' first, later on adding, 'Lament of the Silent Sisters' to form a long sequence which he finally titled *Silences*. He had in mind a design for an even longer sequence of poems using a particularized logic of juxtapositions and improvisations. This mode of composition explains the 'discordant features' that Anozie observes. The tragic elegiac quality of *Silences*, which was finally completed early in 1965 captures the terrible mood of the political crisis of the 1960s and Okigbo's perceptions of the era. Taire noted that, by 1962, Okigbo had voted for NCNC.

Between 1964 and 1965 when 'Lament of the Drums' was written, the political realities had shifted dramatically and so had Okigbo's political allegiances. NCNC was no longer a rival to the AG whose fortunes had dwindled dramatically, but had forged an alliance with the Action Group as UPGA. Increasingly the symbolism of Awolowo's imprisonment became the rallying cause of the key progressive intellectuals of that generation. The lull due to the state of emergency declared by the Federal government in Western Nigeria in 1962 was shattered by the federal census in 1964. This followed by the equally controversial federal election in December 1964, and the constitutional crisis which followed the president Dr. Nnamdi Azikiwe's refusal to re-appoint the Federal Prime Minister on account of the widespread electoral irregularities of that period.

The political events of the 1960s signaled the great tension of the post-colonial state: starting with the political crisis in Western Nigeria and the imprisonment of Awolowo in 1962, the wage crisis and the workers' strike in 1963 which nearly halted the performance of government leading to the establishment of the Morgan commission of enquiry, and the result of the census conducted in 1962. Michael Crowder reports the situation vividly in his book *The Story of Nigeria:*

> In December 1962 unofficial results of the census taken the previous May had indicated that the North had a larger population than the three Southern regions combined. This implied that the South would forever be at the mercy of a Northern majority, whereas Southern politicians had been convinced that the census would reveal that the South was in fact more populous than the North. As a result of wide-spread doubts about the accuracy of the census the prime minister decided on a new one. This was held on 5th November 1963 and the preliminary results, announced on 24th February 1964, gave Nigeria a population of 55 million against 31 million for the 1952-53 census: the majority was still in the North.[130]

The census results released in 1964 had their own dramatic consequences: the Eastern and Midwest regional governments rejected them outright. But the Northern government and the Western region under Akintola, who was the NPC's political ally, accepted them. But the Eastern government and the Action Group in the West, through the Solicitor General of the Eastern Nigerian government, took the Federal government to court, and the Supreme Court rejected their writ. The census controversy was still raging when the federal elections took place. The massive rigging of the census which took place in 1964, and the second wave of workers' strikes called in June 1964, in protest against the federal government's delay in implementing the recommendations of the Morgan wages commission, set the tone of a national crisis. Crowder reports that by 1964, as Nigeria prepared for the general elections of that year, the situation was degenerating rapidly:

> In the South there was general discontent with the census results. Workers were still disgruntled over their economic situation, and the educated elite was still exasperated by its government's pro-western policies. In November for instance the federal government had not only failed to condemn the joint American-Belgian Operation in Stanleyville (now Kisangani) to rescue their nationals, Jaja Wachukwu, the Nigerian representative at the UN, had argued that as the operation had been authorized by the legal government of the Congo, 'it could not be regarded as foreign intervention'. Generally the tone of politics took a serious turn for the worse.[131]

The federal elections took place followed by another wave of massive discontent. The president of the Federal Republic, Dr. Nnamdi Azikwe, convinced of the massive electoral malpractices that had taken place, refused to call upon the prime minister to form a government. For two days, Nigeria was without government, and the country seemed to be on the verge of disintegration. There were talks of a military take-over and of Northern secession. Young educated officers in the army, like Chukwuemeka Odumegwu-Ojukwu who would later lead the secessionist state of Biafra, backed the president to take over full powers and administer the federation under a state of emergency. While it seemed the negotiations were going on, the British General Officer Commanding the Nigerian Army, Major-General Welby Everard secured the President in the state lodge for two days and reminded him forcefully that, though he was the commander-in-chief, the military took orders only directly from the Prime Minister.

President Azikiwe, Head of State and Commander-in-Chief of the Armed Forces took legal counsel, from his personal lawyer, Mr. Dan Ibekwe, the federal Attorney-General, Dr. Taslim Elias, the respected Chief Justice of the Eastern Region, Justice Louis Mbanefo and his friend, the Chief Justice of Nigeria, Justice Adetokunbo Ademola, and knew that the limits of his power were apparent. So he relented, and invited the Premier, Tafawa Balewa to form 'a broad-based government' of national unity to allow tempers to cool down. It was this conciliatory action by President Azikiwe, his refusal to take full control of government, which was deemed cowardly and which disappointed the young, idealistic and educated elite, among them Christopher Okigbo. It seemed that the groundwork for subsequent action, including the coup of 15 January 1966 was laid by these events. In fact, the memoirs of Emmanuel Ifeajuna, the true leader of the January 1966 coup, unpublished up to the time, paints the succinct picture of this disappointment with Azikiwe, and his handling of the events of 1964. By this time also, Obafemi Awolowo, already two years in jail in Calabar, had become the cult figure of resistance, among the radical, idealistic and educated people.

And so Okigbo wrote 'Laments of the Drum' both as tribute and as elegy. As Obumselu notes about this poem, there is no explicit reference made to these historical events. 'No anecdotes or statement of any kind is envisaged…The object is song, or as Stephane Mallarmé would put it "to point, not to the thing, but the effect it produces"…we are dealing instead with poetry of mood, evoking regret and sympathy through suggestions of desolation, abandonment, grief without redress, despair and death.'[132] The setting of this poem, Obumselu suggests is all of human history in every culture and every period. With its references to the 'high buskin' of Greek tragic actors whose ordeal refers to the passions of the god Dionysus, the 'chaliced vintage' of Christ's last supper (suggesting betrayal) and to the fourteenth century 'Babylonian' captivity of the papacy in Avignon. The substance of the poem is also drawn from the story in Virgil's *Aeneid V* of Aeneas's sleeping helmsman who is swept overboard and drowns. Obumselu also points to the reference to Celaeno in *Aeneid III*, with the swarm of harpies descending upon the sailor's dinner, as directly alluding to the Nigerian government in 1964 '…they are not just classical monsters, but also like the beggar masquerades of Ibadan streets.'[133]

Okigbo had constructed an abstract parable in which he conceives a personal tragedy in its universal context. There was a new and more terrifying mood of violence in the air in Ibadan by 1964. At that time a feeling of hopelessness had gripped the country. The political leadership had failed to stem or contain the political crisis that had threatened the country from 1962. Okigbo worked feverishly under this mood – 'the smell of blood' was in the air. What Philip Asiodu read to be 'new and opaque'[134] in Okigbo's poetic idiom at the time, was indeed Okigbo's discovery, and a growing reliance on the resources of the traditional oral forms of Yoruba poetry. These aspects of Yoruba praise poetry and ritual chants began to influence the work he was doing significantly from 1964. The dawning of Yoruba poetic revival in the early sixties revealed the new possibilities from which Okigbo began to draw into an original poetic utterance.

Meanwhile, the political furore lingered till the 1964 federal elections were held. Reports of massive rigging dominated the air waves. Although President Azikiwe later relented and invited Balewa after much pressure, to form a broad based government of 'national unity,' the rigging of the federal elections of 1964 was in many ways the last turning point in the fate of the first republic in Nigeria. This event was followed by the bloody regional election in the Western Region late in 1965. The political crisis had spiraled into violence. Anomie not only marked daily life in Ibadan but the sense of instability also took a national significance. All these moods are redolent in the mood of Okigbo's poems composed in that period. Rioting, political intrigue, and public lynching of political opponents in the city was regular fare in Ibadan. Okigbo himself was a victim of this violence in Ibadan. Once at Oke-Bola, at the height of the violence in the west, Okigbo and the poet J.P. Clark were driving together through the streets one evening when they ran into a political mob. They escaped by a whisker. Such experiences made violence an immediate reality, and heightened the mood of failure and disappointment. The soldier-memoirist, Alex Madiebo wrote a poignant account summarizing the events of that era in his book *The Nigerian Revolution and the Biafran War*.[135]

These events signaled for conscious intellectuals like Okigbo, the futility of the political process, especially with the Eastern Region boycotting the general elections in 1965. There were riots in the North, which had led to massacres of the Tiv. General Madiebo, who was Okigbo's junior in secondary school, aptly captures the parlous state of affairs in the Nigerian federation by 1964, and gives a general insight into the conditions under which Okigbo wrote *Distances*.

The new nation states in Africa at the time were characterized by the growing conflict and uncertainty of the post-colonial era. Okigbo wrote *Distances* in part as a continuation of the theme of 'Lament of the Drums', the last sequence of *Silences*, which he was reworking at the same time under this mood of political crisis. The growing uncertainty of national life was disturbing to a perceptive poet acutely aware of his society. The political elite had squandered the heady hopes of independence. Okigbo's anxieties in fact, are deeply echoed in the last poem of the 'Lament of the Drums':

For the far *removed there is wailing:*

For the far removed;
For the Distant...

*The wailing is for the fields of crop:*

The drums' lament is:
They grow not...

*The wailing is for the fields of men:*

For the barren wedded ones;
For perishing children...

*The wailing is for the Great River:*

> Her pot-bellied watchers
> Despoil her...[1346]

This was only a foreshadow to the apocalyptic tension in *Distances,* in which Death, the chief celebrant, appears at that important moment of Nigeria's post-colonial history:

> It was an evening without flesh or skeleton;
> an evening with no silver bells to its tale;
> without lanterns, an evening without buntings;
> and it was an evening without age or memory –
>
> for we are talking of such commonplaces,
> and on the brink of such great events...[137]

In 1964, he began and finished a sequence of the poems published under the title *Distances.* This sequence of poems first appeared in *Transition,* and was immediately remarkable for its new rhetorical style. *Distances* is a projection of the poet's personal experience transformed into a large ritual and religious quest. It demonstrates an urgency, a particular evocation of a personal and public conflict which the poet was experiencing within the particular milieu. Okigbo wrote thus in the introduction to *Labyrinths:*

> *Distances* is, on the other hand, a poem of homecomings but of homecoming, its spiritual and psychic aspect. The quest broken off after '*Siren Limits*' is resumed, this time in the unconscious. The self that suffers, that experiences, ultimately finds fulfilment in a form of psychic union with the supreme spirit that is both destructive and creative. The process is one of sensual anaesthesia, of total liberation from all physical and emotional tension; the end result, a state of aesthetic grace. (*Distances* was written after my first experience of surgery under general anesthesia.)[138]

Christopher Okigbo had suffered from sinusitis for which Mr. Martinson, a Sierra Leonean consultant surgeon of ENT at the University College Hospital, Ibadan, operated upon him. The surgery, the cudwell lock operation, was painful and involved total anesthesia. *Distances* is primarily, a description of his recollection of events from being wheeled into the theatre, under anesthesia, and a description of what he remembered from pre-surgery to the time he woke up after the operation:

> From flesh into phantom on the horizontal stone
> I was the sole witness to my homecoming...
>
> Serene lights on the other balcony:
> redolent fountains bristling with signs –
>
> But what does my divine rejoicing hold?
> A bowl of incense, a nest of fireflies?
>
> I was the sole witness to my homecoming....[139]

Okigbo goes further to describe the cavern-like ambience of his state, 'the inflorescence of the white chamber'[140] in which he hears the distended voice of his subconscious – the miner into his solitude – until it becomes the 'incarnate voice of the dream.'[141] There is, in the attempt to resolve that fantasy of the inward journey which the poet erects in *Distances,* a disturbing, fatalistic vision with the prophetic mystery of his own final experience:

And in the freezing tuberoses of the white
chamber, eyes that had lost their animal
colour, havoc of eyes of incandescent rays,
pinned me, cold, to the marble stretcher,

until my eyes lost their blood
and the blood lost its odour....[142]

The tragic tenor of *Distances* can be explained: Okigbo wrote the poem at a most critical period in Nigerian history, in the shadow of the disturbing signals of the violence and anomie in the final phases of Nigeria's first republic. Okigbo foresaw the tragic consequences of the political crisis, and it appears that the poet inserts himself as a potential martyr in his observation from the process of history, a trend towards a final, catastrophic dissolution of the republic.

For many people living in Ibadan at this period events were moving too quickly. Living within that milieu of uncertainty, Okigbo was profoundly horrified by the tragic flux of history. By July 1964 his friends had started to contemplate 'revolutionary strategies.' 'Lament of the Drums,' composed in 1964, reflects some of the tendencies at play in this period, and testifies to Okigbo's state of mind. We sense futility in his attempts to reconcile both the public and the personal elements of the unfolding national tragedy.

The year 1964 was a watershed year for Okigbo: aside from the birth of his daughter, Obiageli, he had consolidated his claims as Nigeria's national poet. For his thirty-fourth birthday in August, Safi had given him a symbolic present – a horse which Okigbo promptly named Satan. He often went horse riding in the evenings at the Ibadan polo club, just behind his house, separated merely by the languid flow of the Ogunpa river. Okigbo had started badly with horse riding. The first day he tried to mount Satan, he had invited Ben Obumselu and other friends to the polo field to watch. Okigbo wanted to impress his friends by putting on a show as proof of his equestrian prowess. It was typical Okigbo showmanship. Small in frame, Okigbo had tried in vain to mount Satan, and had to be lifted unto the horse. But he eventually reined in the horse and was trotting up and down the polo field.

In the end, Okigbo had to be lifted down from the horse, and borne aloft and groaning to Cambridge House by his friends, because the horse had shivered his waist badly. 'He could not get off his bed the morning after the frolic,'[143] Professor Obumselu recalled with amusement. For a long time, he did not attempt to ride the horse again.

His book *Limits* had been published in 1964 by Mbari Publications to limited circulation. 1965 began on a plain enough note for the poet. Early in January, he was with a group of friends who flew to Port Harcourt to attend Colonel George Kurubo's wedding at which Godwin Adokpaye was best man, and Brigadier Zakari Maimalari had chaired the reception. On 15 January 1965, (exactly a year to the day before the first coup), Christopher Okigbo was best man at Torch Taire's wedding at the Courts in Ibadan. 'Lament of the Drums' finally appeared in *Transition* in 1965. Later in June 1965 it also appeared with some revision in the *Black Orpheus*. In 1965 also, Okigbo and his friends got involved in the organization of the centenary of the Irish poet W.B. Yeats, for which Okigbo wrote 'Lament of the Mask' which appeared later on in a collection of Yeats' centenary essays edited by D.E.S. Maxwell and S.B Bushrui, published by the Ibadan University Press and re-issued by Nelson in 1966. An important feature of this poem written for Yeats is that it foreshadows the direction of Okigbo's aesthetic. He was exhibiting an incantatory style and adopting a range of new idioms.

The new utterance of Okigbo's poetry, Obumselu has pointed out, became noticeable with his 'Lament of the Lavender Mist' influenced principally by the poetry of Léopold Sédar Senghor. Okigbo was also discovering and infusing the tonal elements of the African chant into his poetry. As Obumselu notes, by 1964, a large corpus of *oriki – oriki orile, ijala, ewi, odu ifa, ege*, the *rara* chants and the poetic plays became generally available as a result of the work done by Ulli Beier, Professor S.O Babalola, Kola Ogunmola, the Timi of Ede and the dramatist Duro Ladipo. Duro Ladipo was one of the prominent figures of the cultural revival of the 1960s and was deeply involved in the Mbari Mbayo movement in Oshogbo with his popular Yoruba drama which also appeared in English with the help of Ulli Beier. He had been very influential in the Oshogbo area. Ladipo's important work was in political drama, especially at the height of the Action Group crisis in the west. He was a frequent guest of the Mbari Club in Ibadan. Obumselu observed that as one of the earliest of the leading figures in the Yoruba cultural revival of that period to give systematic study to traditional Yoruba poetic technique, Ladipo demonstrated its viability for contemporary creative use. Ladipo's play *Oba Koso*, first presented in Oshogbo in 1962, was later shown also at the Mbari Club in Ibadan. In 1965, Ladipo's play was taken to the Commonwealth Arts Festival in London. As a result of Ladipo's work, there 'was a revelation to every Nigerian poet of the new possibilities of indigenous tradition.'[144]

Obumselu suggests that this search for a viable indigenous idiom led Okigbo to begin a close and serious study of the *oriki* collections of Ulli Beier, Bakare Gbadamosi and the Timi of Ede. 'So impressed was he by what he read that when Professor Desmond Maxwell invited him to write a centenary poem in honor of W.B. Yeats, he based his tribute very closely on the praises of Oba Olunloye of Ede. From that moment on the technique of the *oriki* became part of his poetic resource…Okigbo found his own love of irrational imaginative leaps re-enforced and legitimized by Yoruba poetry. He also felt free at last, liberated, to give up the lofty pose of T.S. Eliot's ascetic verse and come close to collective idiom.'[145] Of Yeats Okigbo wrote in 'Lament of the Mask':

You who converted a jungle into marble palaces who watered
a dry valley and weeded its banks –
For we have almost forgotten your praise names –
You who transformed a desert into green pasture,
You who commanded highways to pass through the forest –
And will remain mountain even in your sleep.[146]

Okigbo's experiment with this form of traditional chant could be observed in the poetry he began to write from 1964. 'Lament of the Drums,' written in 1964 to commemorate the imprisonment of Obafemi Awolowo, and the death of Segun Awolowo in the car crash, was constructed using the method of the chant. Professor Ben Obumselu reveals that the first section of the poem, conceived on the tonalities of African funeral drumming, is in fact an adaptation of the Ghanaian musicologist Professor J.H. Nketia's translation of the prelude of an Akan drum dirge. 'Its purpose is to introduce the elements which make up a drum orchestra: the wood of the drum heads, the antelope skin of the tympanum, the cane drumsticks, and the ensemble of elephant ivory trumpets. In making this roll call, the poem uses, at least in Okigbo's reading of it, spondaic line endings to imitate the sound of drumming…'[147] This was essentially the poet's response to the use of the traditional resources that were revealed to him in that period.

The most significant international cultural event of 1965 was the Commonwealth Arts Festival, which took place in Edinburgh and several other cities from 20 September to 2 December. Okigbo's newly completed poem, 'Lament of the Drums' was performed at the event. His 'Dance of the Painted Maidens' was also selected in the anthology *Verse and Voice: A Festival of Commonwealth Poetry*, edited by D. Cleverdon, and published by the Poetry Book Society in London.

It was during the Festival in London that Okigbo was re-united with the Nigerian sculptor Ben Osawe. Okigbo immediately recognized him. He had known Ben in their younger days at Onitsha, and Okigbo let out his famous yell, went over, and hugged Osawe. 'Gab! What're you doing here?'[148] Okigbo had asked him in Igbo. Okigbo knew him as 'Gabriel' while they were growing up. Osawe had later changed his name to 'Ben' in honor of his father, a palace artist in the courts of the Oba of Benin when he died. The sculptor's work was beginning to attract some attention in London. The two writers ended up spending the day in Osawe's flat and were excited with his work. Okigbo said to him: 'You have to come back home Gabriel. Exciting things are happening!'[149] Ben Osawe thus came back to Nigeria late in 1965, to join the fray of the Mbari cultural revival. Mbari organized an exhibition of Osawe's work in 1965 at Ibadan. He thus arrived home in time also to witness the first political crisis which had threatened the balance of the Nigerian federation.

During the Commonwealth Festival, Okigbo was the guest of Dennis Duerden in the elegant guest house of the Transcription Centre. Duerden was to arrange lawyers and friends when Wole Soyinka went on trial. Not long after they returned from the Commonwealth Festival, events spiraled out of control, prefacing the onset of the final days of Nigeria's first republic. The Western regional elections were held with massive fraud reported, and the controversial premier S.L. Akintola of the NNDP returned to the premier's lodge. Riots soon broke out in protest. That October, Wole Soyinka was arrested over the 'mystery gun-man' episode at the Broadcasting House at Ibadan. He was accused of hijacking the radio station at gunpoint. An unidentified man, in a hood, it was said, had entered the WNBC studio and forced the duty announcer at gun-point to play a recorded tape which declared a different result in the election. That announcement reversed the results approved by the incumbent Akintola government. Wole Soyinka's arrest and controversial trial became a *cause célèbre*, although Justice Kayode Eso acquitted him when he was finally brought to court. While Soyinka was in detention at the Queen's Barracks at Iyagankun, Okigbo was a regular visitor often coming to cheer him up. Each time he came he stayed and cracked jokes and generally lifted the atmosphere of the place. He would assure Soyinka not to worry as he would be out very soon to pursue his favorite pastime of the game of all sorts. Okigbo kept faith with Soyinka in those difficult and trying days. Soyinka indeed writes thus in acknowledgement 'Christopher Okigbo…would bring his latest verses in typescript, scribbled over in his neat, tiny handwriting, and read them aloud to me, sometimes with Femi (Johnson) as his only other audience. Armed with a hamper of food and drinks we might even have lunch or dinner together…'[150] At his place of incarceration, Okigbo would say to him: 'It is a pity Wole that they don't allow co-habitation here. You would be missing nothing outside.'[151] He may have been part, with Doig Simmons, of an underground plot to spring Soyinka, and smuggle him out to exile through the Dahomey borders if the verdict had been different.

Following the result of the regional elections in 1965, riots broke out in Ibadan and by December 1965 had spread throughout Western region. Life became even more uncertain in the city. Ibadan's intellectuals became restless and increasingly disappointed with the situation of new nationhood. Whenever any of Okigbo's soldier friends visited Cambridge House, the discussions often centred on the state of the nation and the political crisis. One such regular military visitor was the charismatic Major Emmanuel Ifeajuna. After taking a science degree at the University College, Ibadan and teaching briefly at the Ebenezer Anglican Grammar School in Abeokuta, Ifeajuna joined the army in 1961. He was one of the first five Nigerians to join the army as university graduates, so naturally belonged to the army elite. He personified the radical intellectual soldier. By 1965, he was the Brigade Major of the Lagos Garrison Command. But Ifeajuna maintained his contacts with the Ibadan intellectuals and remained as close to Okigbo as in their days as students at the University College, Ibadan. They also had a mutual friend in the poet, J.P. Clark. While 'Emma' Ifeajuna had led the students movement in the university, Clark had been the editor of the Students' Union magazine as well as *The Horn*, the students' literary magazine; and they worked closely on the anti-colonial protests which Ifeajuna organized on campus.

Ifeajuna had other close friends and contemporaries at Ibadan – people like Godwin Adokpaye and Kayode Jibowu all of whom lived in the close and convenient cluster of Eleyele near Cambridge House. Ifeajuna was thus very much at home in their company at Cambridge House, and he naturally enjoyed political debates about the state of Nigeria and the intellectual company of the poet and his circle of University College, Ibadan friends. Torch Taire recalled Major Ifeajuna's last visit on 12 December 1965 to Cambridge House before the 15 January coup. In tune with the mood of the day, most of the talk circled on the state of the nation, and the political crisis which was growing more ferocious by the day. A new phenomenon had been added – 'Wetie' – in which people were tortured to death by political mobs, who regularly set fire to their victims after they had been drenched with petrol. The violence had crept rapidly towards Lagos, the Federal capital, by the new year of 1966. The air was tense with violence, which was both fascinating and horrifying. 'The smell of blood' Okigbo wrote was already floating in the 'lavender-mist of the afternoon.'[152] As the talk progressed that December evening in 1965, somebody just said: 'Look Emma, what are you military chaps waiting for? Why can't the Army take over the government?'[153] Quite unlike him, for he was by no means a man of few words, Ifeajuna said simply: 'We'll see.'[154]

Safi had come to Ibadan with little Obiageli to spend the Christmas holidays. Obiageli had only turned one year in October 1965. The Okigbo family spent a relatively quiet Christmas at Cambridge House. As Safi recalled, Okigbo was characteristically busy and restless in that period. But he also made an effort to spend as much time as he could with his wife and their daughter. He had a splendid time playing with the baby. He would throw her up; make faces at her, at which Obiageli would laugh heartily. He also took Obiageli horse riding, and laughed at Safi's protests. Things seemed normal enough. But she also felt a sense of trepidation in the edgy and muted atmosphere of fear and violence in Ibadan.

Meanwhile, his work as a publisher's representative had dominated an important part of his professional life in Ibadan. Okigbo was involved in negotiating some important publishing contracts for the Cambridge University Press. For instance one publishing scoop was securing the rights to the autobiography of the powerful premier of Northern Nigeria, Ahmadu Bello, and an important book on Nigeria's public finance by his own brother, Pius Okigbo. He also got Achebe to publish *Chike and the River*, a story set in Onitsha for the young. The job of West African regional manager of the Cambridge University Press was nevertheless very routine. Okigbo was basically a publisher's agent. His job mostly involved scouting out good manuscripts and, if he judged them worth publishing, would establish contact with the office in London. He took orders for books for individuals as well as for institutions, and forwarded such requests to London. He was a natural salesman, and the job suited him because it had an easy, undemanding pace.

His home was his office. Cambridge gave him great latitude, allowed him frequent travel, which exposed him to the key political and intellectual figures of the day in Nigeria. Powerful men courted him. He enjoyed the image of affluence that Cambridge provided. He had strong, solid personal contacts that made access to the political elite and his work easy: he had members of family in influential positions in government – his brother Pius Okigbo and brother-in-law Abdulaziz Atta, were powerful figures in the Federal government. He had close personal friends and former schoolmates in powerful positions in business and government. He had to boot, immense personal charm, and knew how to work the establishment. As Torch Taire said: 'Christopher knew anybody worth knowing.'[155] Okigbo's other brother-in-law, Safi's half brother, Mahmoud Attah was Ahmadu Bello's private secretary.

This family connection in the Northern political establishment certainly was a great help in his work. But in truth, although his job at Cambridge provided apparent perquisites, it was nonetheless not a big job. Its West African office was small, without elaborate structures. Cambridge University Press in Nigeria basically revolved around the life and personality of the poet, aided by a retinue of personal staff – his uniformed chauffeur, a great steward and a personal secretary – all paid for by Cambridge. Okigbo's role as representative for the Cambridge University Press in Ibadan was indeed largely a public relations role in a post-colonial outpost. Soon it grew tiresome. By 1965, Okigbo had grown restless and was seeking new fields to explore.

A week before the coup on 15 January 1966, Okigbo had been away in Lagos and had stayed at the guest house of the Cocoa Company, in which Pius Okigbo had some interest at the time. The guest house was located in the Maryland Estate on the road to Ikeja Airport. In those years it was still a low density development, isolated from the restless city, and so it was a convenient place for the kind of solitude Okigbo needed for both his work, and the role he chose to play in the unfolding drama of the days ahead. He had a cluster of friends in the neighbourhood. Ifeajuna was nearby at the Ikeja Garrison. Not too far away from him, at the then newly developing Anthony village layout, the journalist Peter Enahoro (Peter Pan), the editor and columnist of the *Daily Times* lived. The poet J.P. Clark was Enahoro's classmate at the Government College, Ughelli. Okigbo and Clark spent a lot of time together in this period. Clark had moved to teach in the English Department of the University of Lagos in 1965, from his position as Research Fellow at the Institute of African Studies of the University of Ibadan. But he had time to accompany Okigbo to his meetings with representatives of Bozotti, the Italian company, dealing in arms in which Okigbo was developing an interest. They had also been both present at the launching by Heinemann of Chinua Achebe's fourth novel *A Man of the People* at Glover Hall.

There are indications also that Christopher Okigbo was present at some meetings in Lagos, possibly around the coup, held in the Ikoyi Crescent home of the poet's elder brother, Dr. Pius Okigbo. Pius Okigbo was the powerful Federal Economic Adviser to Nigeria and was also on assignment in the period as Nigeria's Representative at the European Economic Community in Brussels, where he was negotiating terms of trade between Nigeria and the European states. As a result he was mostly away in Brussels during this period. The economist might well have been thoroughly scandalized, were he to know at that time, that his brother was borrowing his home to enact one of the most dramatic political conspiracies in post-colonial Africa. These meetings often lasted into the nights in Ikoyi. But sometimes they took place at the Crystal Palace Hotel, Yaba.

One of Okigbo's closest friends, the diplomat Leslie Harriman had learnt about the meetings at Crystal Palace Hotel and confronted the poet about them. Harriman, who confirmed attending the meeting at the hotel in Yaba in January 1966, noted that it was probably one of the last strategic meetings that wrapped up the plan for the 15 January 1966 coup. Harriman had persuaded Okigbo to let him come with him. 'It was a very secret meeting, and I had the impression that Christopher didn't even want me to know about it. He actually made me swear not to say a word about this meeting to one of our closest friends because he did not trust that he would keep quiet about it.'[156] It was indeed a busy period for everybody; but especially for Okigbo, who had also to find a little time to visit his family in Ibadan, as well as for his apparently serious political commitments. He returned to Ibadan on the evening of Friday, 14 January 1966 from Lagos. Then came the 15 January 1966 coup led by Major Emmanuel Ifeajuna. And the seasons turned full cycle.

Okigbo was living close enough to the Eleyele Barracks in Ibadan and was thus able to observe the movement of troops. Great rejoicing followed the coup. Sam Okudu recalled, Okigbo's excitement on that day. On the morning of 15 January Okigbo drove to Okudu's house at the University of Ibadan and said 'Chei! It has happened!'[157] Okigbo and his friends, touched by the euphoria of change, drove round Ibadan and joined the street celebrations. People were blaring the horns of their cars. Okigbo and his friends ended up at Risikatu's bar where they drank several toasts to the army boys. But things were still unsettled. Nothing was certain. The only certain thing was that the army had struck. Everybody tensely awaited the outcome of that adventure. Godwin Adokpaye also remembered the mood in Cambridge House in the evening of that day:

> By this time, there was general tension in the country. Christopher called me into his house and there were people lying around – and they turned out to be some ministers of the displaced Western regional government. They lay there in the parlor; with their guns. There were about six radios in the room, each of them tuned to a different station; monitoring reports – the BBC, the VOA, the Northern stations – everybody was interested in monitoring what was clearly a confused situation. Christopher kept saying that he was expecting to hear one voice. There was a long drawn wait, then came Nzeogwu's announcement. By the 18th of January it was certain that the coup had failed in Lagos and that the Federal prime minister had been killed; as well as Chief Akintola in the West and the Sarduana of Sokoto in the North. On 19 January Emma (Ifeajuna) drove into Cambridge House, the loose concrete had made so much noise. That day in Okigbo's house, there was Peter Enahoro, Emma Ifeajuna and a few others. Emma conferred briefly with Chris and drove out again. He had apparently returned from the East. From then on nothing was the same…[158]

When Ifeajuna returned from Enugu in his red Mercedes Benz car, he came to Ibadan and straight to Cambridge House. There was already a red alert sent out to apprehend him, as the leader of the 1966 coup. Quick, but furtive arrangement was made. Okigbo organized the escape of Ifeajuna to Ghana, through the Dahomey borders, smuggling him 'in a relay of cars' dressed like a woman, through Idi-Iroko to Cotonou, and from thence to Ghana where he stayed with S.G. Ikoku. Christopher Okigbo's involvement in the events of the coup was again typical of his love for dangerous adventure. But more implicit in his action was his commitment – the moral obligation of the artist to his society – in the choices that faced the man of imagination in the disturbing history of the post-colonial society.

In Okigbo's growing investment in the political process was the very acknowledgement that poetry no longer could mediate in that historical context of national crisis. His actions in the period capture the acute sensitivity of his temperament as an intellectual activist. The coup failed and its leader fled to Ghana, although many of the coup leaders were arrested and clamped into detention. When the count of casualties was taken, the Prime Minister, Sir Abubakar Tafawa Balewa, and two regional premiers were dead: the Northern Premier, Ahmadu Bello, and the Premier of the Western Region, Ladoke Akintola. Among the dead were also the colourful Federal Minister of Finance, Festus Okotie-Eboh, and some top army brass including Brigadier Sam Ademulegun, Brigadier Zakari Maimalari, Colonel Abogo Largema, Colonel James Yakubu Pam, Colonel Arthur C. Unegbe, and Colonel Ralph Sodeinde. Following the killing of the Prime Minister, a rump of the cabinet met with the acting president of the federation Dr. Nwafor Orizu, acting in the absence of the President of the Republic, Dr. Nnamdi Azikiwe, who was away from the country. After consultations with the remnants of the Federal Executive Council, Dr. Orizu ceded formal authority of the state to the GOC of the Nigerian Army, Major-General J.T.U. Aguiyi-Ironsi, who had escaped by a whisker from the coup makers, mobilized resistance, and quelled the coup. Ironsi took over the reins of government and assumed full emergency powers. Thus did the coup plan fail. The aims of the January coup plotters have been summarized in Emmanuel Ifeajuna's unpublished account of the incident.

Having smuggled Ifeajuna out to Ghana, Okigbo returned to Ibadan and from all accounts became busy in the new dispensation, working very actively in the subterranean, post-coup negotiations, trying to help stabilize the situation and make Nigeria run. Okigbo returned to Ibadan from his 'smuggling mission' on 20 January 1966. By then Safi had returned with their daughter to Kaduna where she had just been appointed chief women education officer – a strategic position, which required that she tour girls schools and plan policies for the development of female education in the Northern region. She would never see her husband alive again. Things remained unsettled after the coup, except that calm had returned to Ibadan for the first time since 1962. But another crisis loomed on the horizon, and its aftermath would affect Okigbo's life profoundly, as events would later prove. In the euphoria of the coup, however, the poet had continued to work on the last sequence of the poems *Path of Thunder*.

By 17 January 1966 Okigbo completed 'Hurrah For Thunder,' the first section of *Path of Thunder*, which he had planned as a separate and longer piece, completely independent of the poems in the *Labyrinth* collection. This poem, as all of the other parts of the *Path of Thunder* sequence indeed, was deeply influenced, on one hand, by the work of the Congolese poet, Felix Tchicaya U Tam'si whose poems *Brushfire*, Okigbo was reading at the time, and on the other hand by Ulli Beier's book on Yoruba poetry.

Between the end of 1965 and early January 1966, from evidence of his output, he seemed to be absorbing the details of the national drama, writing non-stop, chronicling the events of the new iron dawn in the scope of his new poetry. From all indications, he had started work on the early parts of his last poems, *Path of Thunder*, late in 1965. Ulli Beier was among the first people to whom he read it when he completed it. He had also left a copy of the new poems with the poet J.P. Clark and with Aig Higo at Heinemann. The new tension in Okigbo's voice had grown from *Distances*, and had become clearer and more acute in *Path of Thunder*. It was the voice of prophecy which had marked the third, and as it would prove, the final progression in his poetic quest and in his experiment with poetic form. Philip Asiodu, who came to visit him regularly in this period in Cambridge House, remembers Okigbo reading parts of the poem to him in November 1965: 'It sounded so new and opaque' Asiodu said. 'I could never make sense of the images. It only became clear later on to me, when the events had taken place, that Chris was aware of the conspiracies that led to the January coup and he was writing about it.'[159] Okigbo had also embarked on reworking his poems late in 1964 for publication, introducing interesting variations. Of these variations the poet had in fact firmly declared in the introduction to *Labyrinths*: 'Although these poems were written and published separately, they are in fact, organically related ... the versions here preserved are, however, somewhat different and are final.'[160] He finished revision on the manuscript in October 1965, and sent it off to Faber in London, which considered it for publication. In a letter he wrote to Dennis Duerden of the Transcription Centre on 4 January 1966, only two weeks before the January coup, Okigbo sounded upbeat and confident:

> I have now sent *Labyrinths* off to Peter de Souton [du Sautoy] at Faber. He has written to say he will be glad to consider it. *Labyrinths* has a note in its preface acknowledging my debt to you. For it was in your office that I first saw quite clearly the thematic line between *Heavensgate, Limits, Silences,* and *Distances.*[161]

He also gave a set to Aig Higo, the Manager of Heinemann in Nigeria, who was active in Mbari. Heinemann later published Okigbo's collection under the title *Labyrinths with Path of Thunder* after the war in 1971. It became impossible to get agreement during the civil war as to whether the royalties should be paid to the daughter through the Mbari Club in the West or through Pius Okigbo in the East.

The increasing clarity of Okigbo's poetic style was undoubtedly inspired by the events between January and May 1966, when the last part of *Path of Thunder* ('Elegy for Alto') was written. This impulse, which began to grow and strengthen into Okigbo's poetic style, was also to mark his creative homecoming, his final artistic statement. The poet in search of his own authentic voice, and artistic vision recognized his own transformation in 'Elegy of the Wind':

> For I have lived the sapling sprung from the bed
> of the old vegetation;
> Have shouldered my way through a mass of ancient
> nights to chlorophyll...[162]

The poet had glimpsed the significance of the great event of which he had been part, and which he had witnessed, in the context of that society in rapid transition. The progression of the mood of *Path of Thunder* from euphoria and jubilation to wary, disillusioned prophecy anticipating an iron dawn aptly records both the collective mood of that period and Okigbo's intense individual perception of events. The moments of change, and the elements of that change, Okigbo felt, would not easily resolve themselves, for as he already saw:

> And a great fearful thing already tugs at the cables of the open air,
>
> A nebula immense and immeasurable, a night of deep waters –
> An iron dream unnamed and unprintable, a path of stone.[163]

These were the acute reflections of a now mature poet, beginning to evolve a new poetic idiom, excited by the extraordinary events of change, and wishing to communicate it starkly – in the voice of the public poet. Okigbo's active life in that period, and his closeness to the key political actors of the day, gave him an authoritative insight into the unfolding character of that history. His imagination had become epic.

Dr. Pius Okigbo had re-emerged as one of the powerful men of the new regime. He was one of those whom Aguiyi-Ironsi, the new military Head of State retained in the powerful position of Federal Economic Adviser, and Ambassador to the European Economic Council in Brussels. Abdulaziz Attah, the poet's erudite brother-in-law, Safi's elder brother, also emerged as one of the most powerful Permanent Secretaries in the new government, and so were a number of Christopher Okigbo's close friends, who became especially well positioned in the new order, and began to run the bureaucracy, and shape the activities and policies of government during this period. It was a tense time. Everybody hoped that the nation could be salvaged from the crisis. Many Igbo intellectuals rallied round Ironsi, to ensure that his government worked. His army background had not prepared him for his new role as Head of State. Christopher Okigbo threw himself actively into this regime at an unofficial level. He was often in Lagos at this time, and stayed either in Leslie Harriman's home at Ikoyi, or at J.P. Clark's home at Yaba. Sometimes Okigbo also stayed in Philip Asiodu's house, or, at the guest house on Maryland, which belonged to the Cocoa Company. Although the turn of national events seemed to be distracting, Okigbo nevertheless was actively pursuing his personal business interests too. He met frequently with his European partners in Lagos. Pius Okigbo described Christopher's business plan to install a kernel cracking plant at Enugu, to extract oil. It does seem however that Okigbo was possibly interested in the arms trade, and was negotiating a partnership as the West African representative of the Italian interests who were exploring arms supply contracts with the Nigerian government. Okigbo thus had ample reasons, both of a private and public nature, to be frequently in Lagos during this time of high national drama.

Okigbo's closeness with key figures on the corridors of power of the day could be seen in the roles he played in that period – mostly of mediation. Leslie Harriman tells the story of the day, sometime in March 1966, when Okigbo had turned up at his office at the Foreign Ministry in Lagos. He used Harriman's phone and called Francis Nwokedi, one of the most powerful mandarins of the service, whom Ironsi had appointed Permanent Secretary at Foreign Affairs. Nwokedi had been a career civil servant of the old cloth, who had risen through the ranks in the colonial service, and was one of the few Nigerians to be appointed Permanent Secretary by the colonial administration. He had been Permanent Secretary in the Ministry of Labour for many years, and indeed had designed some of the key labour policies like the establishment of the Federal Provident Fund in Nigeria. Nwokedi had retired in 1965, and was promptly seconded to a United Nations assignment from which Ironsi recalled him to help stabilize the fluid situation after the January coup. Francis Nwokedi's office was only next door to Ambassador Harriman's who was by then deputy Permanent Secretary in the External Affairs Ministry. Okigbo had said to Nwokedi, speaking both in Igbo and English, so that Leslie Harriman would understand: 'I see you want to take over from Wey as the secretary to the Government. But I would advise you, to move into the Head of State's office, find a niche for yourself and show your paces. Find something else...'[164] Francis Nwokedi, Harriman recalled, was clearly angling for Stanley Wey's office and Okigbo did not like it. Harriman believed that Okigbo was worried at the increasing feeling that the coup was an Igbo coup, which had been carried out by mostly ethnic Igbo military officers to entrench Igbo domination of Nigerian affairs. Okigbo chose to call Nwokedi from Harriman's office so that his friend would know where he stood in the matter. He felt that Nwokedi's aspirations, legitimate as it would seem, would sustain an unnecessary fallacy. But above all, Christopher Okigbo wanted to demonstrate to his friend, his true feelings of loyalty 'It was Christopher's gesture of friendship and the open spirit,'[165] Harriman said.

It was about this time that General Ironsi, the new military Head of State, sent words to Okigbo who came to meet him at the State House at the Marina. There was apparently some urgency in the request as it concerned a proposed secret mission. Okigbo had driven one windy evening to the Marina, to meet Aguiyi Ironsi who welcomed him in his study where they held a long private discussion. As it turned out, the meeting was arranged for the Supreme Commander to put forth a request to the poet: he wanted Okigbo to help bring his friend Major Emmanuel Ifeajuna back to the country. 'The only thing which I request from you Chris' he had told Okigbo 'is to bring Emma (Ifeajuna) back. You are the only one he could trust. And I repose much confidence in you.'[166] Ironsi was seeking a process of political closure to the events of the coup, with an eye especially to mollify the Northern Region who wanted the coup plotters tried for mutiny. Okigbo had asked for guarantees for Ifeajuna's safety and freedom. He had told the supreme commander 'I would hate to lure a man to his death.'[167] Okigbo secured Ironsi's word that the leader of the 15 January 1966 coup, would not be maltreated, in the light of the popularity of the coup among the Nigerian public particularly in Southern Nigeria who felt, in those early years, that the plotters had acted with patriotic zeal, and considered them heroes. One of the guarantees for Ifeajuna's safety was that he would be kept in a safe place, preferably in the East. Okigbo set forth to Ghana, along with the poet J.P. Clark, the only two people whom Emmanuel Ifeajuna could trust in the circumstance. He agreed with them to return to Nigeria.

It was such an urgent assignment that Okigbo had no time in fact to return to Ibadan. He hurried in that day to Philip Asiodu's home and stayed briefly before the trip. As Asiodu recalled, 'Christopher came in a hurry, borrowed a suit jacket and left for Ghana. That was the last I saw him.'[168] There were a few indications that Ifeajuna's escape to Ghana was strategic; he considered it a tactical withdrawal in the face of overwhelming odds in Lagos on the night of the coup. When he had arrived in Ghana, Kwame Nkrumah gave him a hero's reception. Ifeajuna requested logistics and men with which to attack Lagos from outside and complete the aborted coup. This was of course not feasible in the circumstance. Besides, Ghana was getting embarrassed by the implication of Ifeajuna's presence there, as it was giving the impression that Nkrumah's government in Ghana had masterminded and supported the coup in Nigeria. Nkrumah was also having his own problems at home, which eventually saw him ousted by a military coup later on organized by the CIA, only a month after the putsch in Nigeria. When Okigbo and Clark arrived in Accra, they met both Dr. Akpata, and S.G Iroku, both of whom were teaching at the Kwame Nkrumah ideological institute at Winneba at the time. Ikoku himself was in exile, having been on the run since 1962 for the sedition trials in which Awolowo was jailed. A meeting was quickly arranged with the Nigerian High Commissioner in Ghana at the time. After some negotiation they managed to secure Ifeajuna's release. Thereafter, they set off from Ghana, and on arriving in Lagos, Emma Ifeajuna was promptly arrested and put into detention with the rest of the coup plotters. But not before he handed his memoirs of the coup to both Okigbo and Clark for safekeeping.

Ifeajuna's arrest at the airport was apparently not part of the negotiations. Okigbo felt betrayed and agonized throughout the period about his friend's safety. He was one of those who prevailed on the governor of the Eastern region Chukwuemeka Odumegwu-Ojukwu, to demand that the prisoners be brought to the prisons in the Eastern region where they would be assured of their safety. In the meantime, Aguiyi-Ironsi himself was under severe pressure to try the coup plotters. Ironsi was torn between two delicate situations – for there were many who regarded the January boys as national heroes. But the feeling in the North ran high in important circles against Ifeajuna and his cohorts. One of the excuses for the murder of Ironsi not too long after was that he dawdled fatally in taking a decision on the coup plotters. It is now speculative, but the course of Nigerian history may well have been different, were the soldiers who had actually staged the coup tried and sentenced. But Ironsi's biographer, Chuks Iloegbunam, argues pointedly in his account that the decision to put the men through a court-martial had already been approved by Ironsi's Supreme Military Council before Ironsi himself was murdered leading to a radical shift in national events.

Meanwhile a crisis was brewing at this time on the cultural scene with disagreements that permeated the Mbari Club involving the four principal figures of the Mbari Club – Ulli Beier, Christopher Okigbo, Wole Soyinka and J.P. Clark – over the issue of the relocation of the Mbari clubhouse from its old place near the Adamasigba roundabout. Okigbo and Clark wanted to move into more spacious accommodation at the Central Hotel which Mbari had acquired, while Ulli Bier and Soyinka did not quite agree to the idea. In the end however Okigbo and Clark had their way and moved Mbari Club to the Central Hotel. The Mbari Club never survived this drift. Soon the forces of history converged in such a way that the writers gradually were drawn apart. As a result of the Nigerian crisis in which the three writers – Okigbo, Soyinka and Clark – became inextricably emotionally and physically involved, they were further scattered in various directions. By the time the cycle of anarchy that engulfed Nigeria exhausted itself, the Mbari Club was moribund. Mbari was challenged by a series of internal conflicts, which later climaxed in the scandal of its funding by a CIA front institution. What appears to have been the prelude to the decline of the Mbari movement was when Beier decided to get the publishers Longman to print and distribute *Black Orpheus*, by then the official journal of the Mbari Club, on the suggestion of its manager in Ibadan, Julian Rea. This started with its thirteenth edition in November 1963. The benefits of such an arrangement were clear to Ulli Beier, but Denis Williams, the brilliant Guyanese critic and art historian objected seriously and threatened to resign from the editorial committee of *Black Orpheus*. Denis Williams's strong objection was on the grounds that 'Longman's was a colonial profiteer getting fat selling bad school text books throughout the former empire.'[169] Ulli Beier nevertheless thought that Julian Rea, a great lover of Nigerian writing and friend of Soyinka had unimpeachable bona fides. 'His sincere interest overshadowed the thing he actually represented,'[170] noted Ulli Beier, and so he supported the proposition by Longman against Denis Williams's strong objection. 'Okigbo and Clark leaned his way, but not with sufficient conviction... Wole (Soyinka) being pragmatic on such issues supported me. Denis Williams felt so strongly that he resigned over it from Mbari. That was a very high price.'[171] These internal conflicts set the tone for the storm created by the Mbari funding situation. The scandal had something to do with the source of its finances. Ulli Beier, who had done much of the work organizing the Club, was at the center of the scandal in Ibadan. The Mbari Club's finances, which came through Ulli Beier, Ezekiel Mphahlele and Dennis Duerden of the Transcription Centre in London, were suddenly traced to the American secret service, the central intelligence agency (CIA). At the time it all appeared to be very complicated. But the origin of Mbari Club itself, it came to appear, was part of an international cultural linkage effort to counter the communist infiltration of intellectual groups worldwide. The idea began with Captain Melvin Lasky, who was an OSS officer during the liberation of Germany at the end of the Second World War and the onset of the cold war. Russian cultural and political interests were spread through the communist sponsorship of cultural and intellectual groups, especially those in the nationalist movements struggling for self-determination. Captain Lasky, sensing the 'communist danger,' suggested to the American government to fund counter groups and publications of its own. That led to the establishment of the Congress for Cultural Freedom, which was launched in Berlin in the early 1950s and which attracted a lot of the world's foremost intellectuals. The main speaker at the event was the African American activist, Martin Luther King, Jr.

The fundamental plan of the Congress for Cultural Freedom was to establish a basis for what it saw as the intellectual freedom for the world – to create a non-ideological free market of ideas, internationally. The Ford Foundation was used as a front for the CIA, through which the Congress for Cultural Freedom got its money. The Ford Foundation had for instance funneled the funds, which began the magazine, *Encounter* in Britain which had people like the poet Stephen Spender running it. Essentially money was provided to run magazines which propagated diverse views, some extremely radical and even anti-American. One of the magazines established in this way was the *Quadrant* in Australia, which supported communism while the *Soledad* in Philippines for instance, also funded by the same method, was anti-communist. Both got their funding through the Ford Foundation. The Congress for Cultural Freedom funded the Fairfield Foundation, which supported the Transcription Centre, headed by Dennis Duerden. Mbari's finances came from through complex channels and when the links were finally revealed there was uproar among intellectual circles in Africa who felt compromised. By the time the story of this elaborate scheme broke in the *Encounter* magazine in 1967, Okigbo was already in the East, swept from Ibadan by the tide of events that prefaced the civil war.

It was under this rising tide in the affairs of Nigeria that the first Negro Festival of Arts was held in Dakar, Senegal between March and April 1966. Okigbo's *Limits* was awarded the first prize for poetry. As it turned out, Derek Walcott, who won the Nobel Prize many years later in 1992, came second. But once again, in his most dramatic manner of reacting to events, the poet Okigbo wrote back to the organizers of the festival, rejecting the prize awarded to *Limits*. This probably was Christopher Okigbo, taking a cue from Jean-Paul Sartre's rejection of the Nobel Prize, an action which Okigbo commended often for 'the sheer principle of it!'[172] Sartre was one of the twentieth-century intellectuals whom Okigbo admired enormously. Okigbo's letter to Sunday Anozie on 5 May 1966, later published in *Creative Rhetoric*, captures his reaction to the matter vividly:

> About Dakar, I did not go. Did you? I found the whole idea of a Negro arts festival based on color quite absurd. I did not enter any work either for the competition, and was most surprised when I heard a prize had been awarded to *Limits*. I have written to reject it.[173]

Okigbo had also questioned why they did not award the prize to the Congolese poet, Tchicaya U Tam'si, whom he felt was a better poet. Okigbo's admiration for this poet is reflected in the echoes of U Tam'si's *Brushfire* in Okigbo's *Path of Thunder* written at that period. As a poet, Okigbo believed in the primacy of individual talent and the transcendence of the imagination over personal, political or national lines. Artistic humility allowed him to recognize the greatness in other poets of his generation whom he respected and admired. It is this aspect of his character, which Anozie describes as Okigbo's 'revolt against all forms of injustice and his defense of individual merit however small it may be.'[174]

Okigbo's rejection of the prize awarded to *Limits* is a reflection on one hand of Okigbo's artistic integrity, and an acknowledgement of his cosmopolitan temperament with regard to the poets he admired and respected. Okigbo's cosmopolitanism explains the variety of the influences in his own poetry. This willingness to range far and beyond his immediate cultural locale, and to respond to his influences with profound honesty, made his poetry very different from the poetry of his generation. As Ulli Beier said, 'he was contemporary.' He infused his own poetry with the purest forms of beauty, and gave back to the world one of the finest poetic statements of the twentieth century. On the other hand, in spite of the gestures of artistic humility which he made over the Dakar prize in 1966, Okigbo took himself seriously as a poet. His action can equally be interpreted as a poet's disdain of the narrow definition of his work – his sense that he belongs to a wider constellation of modernist poets of the twentieth among whom he wished to stake his claim.

Meanwhile, the events of 1966 began to take far more dramatic turns. By May, when Okigbo finished *Path of Thunder*, there was already a rumour of an impending counter-coup by Northern officers in the army. The first wave of the killing of the Igbo and exodus from Northern Nigeria began. Following the organized pogrom of that period, Okigbo began to sense an even more profound turn in the affairs of the nation. He conveys the urgency of his apprehension brilliantly in *Path of Thunder*. By May 1966, there were a series of clandestine meetings held by Eastern Nigerian intellectuals in Ibadan, following intelligence reports of the massive arms' build up, and plans by Northerners to launch further attacks on the Igbo, especially prominent Igbo. There were also rumours of Northern secession plans. These Eastern Nigerian intellectuals began to meet in Professor Kenneth Dike's house at the University of Ibadan on matters of their own safety and to draw up contingency plans. The talks of the possibility of Eastern secession from the Nigerian federation, given the precarious safety of the federation, apparently began to gather moss from these meetings. There are indications that Okigbo was, if not fully involved in these meetings, not unaware of them. By this time he had completely lost interest in the Cambridge University Press job. Okigbo was ready to move on to new things. He had arrived at a reassessment of his options and began to take a different measure of his life. He began to think more in terms of organizing his own business. Moreover, he felt he had no more stake in Cambridge University Press. The company was not growing in the direction in which he was trying to nurture it. Unlike other publishing houses in Ibadan, like Heinemann, Longman and the Oxford University Press, who were expanding their operations, Cambridge chose to maintain a very small operation. As Torch Taire said, Okigbo had envisioned a Cambridge University Press with an elaborate administrative structure, with him in the centre as chief executive. But that was not to be.

On 29 July 1966, came the 'retaliation' coup, in which the military head of state, General Ironsi, and the military governor of the Western region Colonel Fajuyi, were killed in Ibadan. Okigbo was in Lagos on that particular day. There had apparently been a final effort to save Ironsi's government and this had failed. The sense of insecurity, and the rash of violence that took place at this time, appalled Okigbo. Several Igbo military officers had been massacred. He returned to Ibadan on Monday 1 August 1966. He had just escaped from Lagos where he had been nearly killed on the road to the Ikeja Airport, by soldiers led by Corporal Paul Dickson.

The cold-blooded murder of army officers, especially from the Eastern region, broke a deep resolve in him. The agony of the crisis touched off the most intense emotional event in Okigbo's life in this period. The case of Captain Iweanya, one of Okigbo's younger army friends, who was murdered in Ibadan at the Eleyele barracks close to Cambridge House, was particularly heart-rending. Captain Iweanya's young pregnant wife was brought to Godwin Adopkaye's house for safety, and Okigbo could not endure her daily weeping. All these events shaped the mood of *Path of Thunder*.

Christopher Okigbo's escape from Lagos, somehow, also marked his final break with the Nigerian federation. He was no longer safe in Ibadan or Lagos. Okigbo's name was on the wanted list of intellectuals who were closely associated with Major Ifeajuna, the leader of the January coup of 1966. The novelist Chinua Achebe, who was the Director of External Broadcasting in Lagos, was also on the wanted list and had apparently gone into hiding in the home of the Director of the British Council in Lagos, before finding his way eventually to the East. Okigbo's consideration for his personal safety was grounds enough to inspire his escape to the East. Okigbo finally left Ibadan for the East one week and four days after Ironsi was murdered in Ibadan. The original plan was for the poet to travel with Torch Taire's mother, who had come to visit Ibadan at those dangerous moments, but Torch had thought better of it. Knowing Okigbo's volatile and unpredictable temperament, it suddenly did not seem safe to entrust his mother to him in the circumstance. 'He was not the sort of man who would back off, who would be cautious in the face of apparent danger! If Christopher for instance, saw Northern Officers manning a roadblock, and if they stopped him, the tendency would be for him to alight from his car and furiously demand to know what right any one of them had to stop him. He would engage them in words and argue to no end, at grave personal risk!'[175] All the same, Christopher Okigbo, only his suitcase in his car and with the keys to Cambridge House entrusted to his friends, drove away finally from Ibadan, where he had lived his intense artistic life, to his ultimate destiny. The date: 9 August 1966. He arrived in the East exactly one week before his thirty-sixth birthday.

## NOTES

1  Robert Wren, *Those Magical Years* (Washington DC: Three Continents Press 1981).
2  Nkem Nwankwo, *Shadow of the Masquerade* (Nashville, TN: Niger House Publications 1994) p. 63.
3  Interview with Torch Taire, Anthony Village, Lagos, 1992.
4  Chinua Achebe, in *Igbo Art: Community and Cosmos* (eds) Herbert Cole and Chike Aniakor (Los Angeles: University of California Museum, 1984).
5  Nkem Nwankwo, *Shadow of the Masquerade*.
6  Ibid. Lalage Bown was in fact Acting Director and then Deputy Director.
7  Ibid.
8  Ibid.
9  Interview with Ben Obumselu, Lagos, 1992.
10  Interview with Obi Wali, Port Harcourt, 1993.
11  Christopher Okigbo, Transition Conference Questionnaire, *Transition* 5 (July 30–August 29, 1962) pp. 11–12.
12  Ibid.

13  Paul Theroux 'Sir Vidia's Shadow', *New Yorker Magazine* (7 August 1995).

14  John Nagenda, 'Conference Notes', *Transition* 5 (30 July–29 August 1962) pp. 8–9.

15  Ibid.

16  Interview with Ali Mazrui, Sheraton, Lagos, 1992. See also Ali Mazrui, *The Trial of Christopher Okigbo* (London: Heinemann, 1971).

17  Robert Serumaga, interview with J.P. Clark, *African Writers Talking* (eds) Dennis Duerden and Cosmo Pieterse (London: Heinemann, 1972).

18  Interview with Ben Obumselu.

19  Interview with Segun Olusola, Surulere, Lagos, 1995.

20  Ibid.

21  Ibid.

22  Rajat Neogy, Letter to the author 1992.

23  Interview with Wole Soyinka, Abeokuta, 1992.

24  Interview with Torch Taire, Lagos, 1992.

25  Nkem Nwankwo, *Shadow of the Masquerade*.

26  Interview with Torch Taire.

27  Ibid.

28  Ibid.

29  Ibid.

30  Interview with Godwin Adokpaye, Lagos, 1993.

31  Ibid.

32  Interview with Aigboje Higo, Heinemann, Ibadan, 1993.

33  Ibid.

34  Interview with Pius Okigbo, Lagos, 1992.

35  Torch Taire 'Cambridge House,' unpublished.

36  Interview with Gabriel Okara, Elekahia Estate, PH, 1992.

37  Interview with Jimmy Johnson, National Theatre, Iganmu, Lagos, 1992.

38  Interview with Ulli Beier, Victoria Island, Lagos, 1994.

39  Interview with Femi Osofisan, Ibadan, 1992.

40  Interview with Ben Obumselu.

41  Ben Obumselu, 'Christopher Okigbo: A Poetic Portrait'. Essay delivered at 'Song for Idoto': A Celebration of Christopher Okigbo, National Museum, Enugu, 2 November 1996.

42  Interview with Torch Taire.

43  Ben Obumselu, 'Christopher Okigbo: A Poetic Portrait'.

44  David Knight in *Don't Let Him Die* (eds) Chinua Achebe and Dubem Okafor (Enugu: Fourth Dimension, 1978).

45  Interview with Ignatius Atigbi, Lagos, 1994.

46  Interview with Sunday Anozie, Port Harcourt, 1993.

47  Ibid.

48  Ibid.

49  Interview with Torch Taire.

50  Interview with Judith Safi Attah, Lagos, 1992.

51  Interview with Ben Obumselu.

52  Pius Okigbo 'A Toast of Christopher Okigbo', *Glendora Review* 1 (2) 1995 (34–39) Lagos.

53  Ibid.

54  Interview with Olu Akaraogun, Lagos, 1992.

55  Peter Thomas, '"Ride Me Memories": A Memorial Tribute to Christopher Okigbo (1932-1967)', *African Arts*, 1, 4 (1968) pp. 68–70.

56  Interview with Sam Okudu, Lagos, 1992.

57  Ibid.
58  Ibid.
59  Ibid.
60  Ibid.
61  Peter Thomas, Letter to the author, 1992.
62  Christopher Okigbo, 'Siren Limits', *Limits* 1961/2, *Labyrinths with Path of Thunder* (London: Heinemann, 1971).
63  Interview with Kayode Jibowu, Lagos, 1992.
64  Ibid.
65  Ibid.
66  Wole Soyinka's talk at the University of Jos Law Auditorium, 1987.
67  Pius Okigbo, 'A Toast of Christopher Okigbo'.
68  Interview with Olu Akaraogun, 1993.
69  Ibid.
70  Ibid.
70  Ibid.
71  Nkem Nwankwo, *Shadow of the Masquerade* (Nashville, TN: Niger House Publications, 1994).
72  Ben Obumselu, 'Christopher Okigbo: A Poetic Portrait'.
73  Interview with Judith Safi Attah.
74  Ibid.
75  Christopher Okigbo, 'Initiations', *Heavensgate* 1960/61, *Labyrinths*.
76  Gerald Moore, 'The Transcription Centre in the Sixties: Navigating in Narrow Seas', *Research in African Literatures*, 33:3, Fall, 2002.
77  Interview with Kayode Jibowu.
78  Ibid.
79  Interview with Torch Taire.
80  Ibid.
81  Ibid.
82  Marjory Whitelaw, interview with Christopher Okigbo, Ibadan, March 1965.
83  Interview with Torch Taire.
84  Interview with Femi Osofisan.
85  Ibid.
86  Ibid.
87  Robert Serumaga, interview with Christopher Okigbo, London, 1965.
88  Chinua Achebe, *Don't Let Him Die* (Enugu: Fourth Dimension, 1978).
89  Interview with Ben Obumselu.
90  Christopher Okigbo, 'Lament of the Silent Sisters', 1962, *Silences*, *Labyrinths*.
91  Interview with Ben Obumselu.
92  Interview with Ben Obumselu.
93  Ibid.
94  Ibid.
95  Interview with Lalage Bown, email exchange 2001.
96  Christopher Okigbo, *Labyrinths with Path of Thunder*, p. viii.
97  Interview with Ben Obumselu.
98  Sunday O. Anozie, *Christopher Okigbo: Creative Rhetoric* (New York: Africana Publishers 1971).
99  Interview with Ben Obumselu.
100  Christopher Okigbo, 'Lament of the Silent Sisters', 1962, *Silences*, *Labyrinths*.
101  Jacques Maritain, *Creative Intuition in Art and Poetry* (New York: Pantheon, 1953).
102  Interview with Ben Obumselu.

103  Interview with Torch Taire.

104  Interview with Godwin Adokpaye, Lagos, 1992.

105  Ibid.

106  Interview with Mabel Segun, Ibadan, 1994.

107  Interview with Torch Taire.

108  Interview with Godwin Adokpaye.

109  Interview with Judith Safi Attah.

110  Christopher Okigbo, 'Dance of the Painted Maidens', 1964.

111  Ibid.

112  Interview with Judith Safi Attah.

113  Christopher Okigbo, Transition Conference Questionnaire, *Transition* 5 (30 July–29 August 1962) pp. 11–12.

114  Interview with Bola Ige, Ibadan, 1994.

115  Michael Crowder, *The Story of Nigeria* (London: Faber, 1978).

116  Christopher Okigbo, 'Lament of the Silent Sisters', 1962, *Silences, Labyrinths*.

117  Sunday Anozie, *Christopher Okigbo: Creative Rhetoric*.

118  Ibid.

119  Ibid.

120  Ben Obumselu, 'Christopher Okigbo: A Poetic Portrait'.

121  Ibid.

122  Ibid.

123  Ibid.

124  Christopher Okigbo, letter to Henry Rago, Editor, *Poetry Chicago*, 20 May 1963.

125  Dennis Duerden, Interview with Christopher Okigbo, 1963 in *African Writers Talking* (eds) Dennis Duerden and Cosmo Pieterse (London: Heinemann, 1972).

126  Interview with George Kurubo, Island Club, Lagos.

127  Interview with Torch Taire.

128  Michael J.C. Echeruo, 'Christopher Okigbo, *Poetry Magazine* and the "Lament of the Silent Sisters"', *Research in African Literatures*, 35:3 (2004) pp. 8–25.

129  Sunday Anozie, *Christopher Okigbo: Creative Rhetoric*.

130  Michael Crowder, *The Story of Nigeria*.

131  Ibid.

132  Ben Obumselu, 'Christopher Okigbo: Poetic Portrait'.

133  Ibid.

134  Interview with Philip Asiodu, Lagos, 1993.

135  Alex Madiebo, *The Nigerian Revolution and the Biafran War* (Enugu: Fourth Dimension, 1980).

136  Christopher Okigbo, 'Lament of the Drums', 1964, *Silences, Labyrinths*.

137  Christopher Okigbo *Distances*, 1964, *Labyrinths*.

138  Christopher Okigbo, *Labyrinths*, pp. xi–xii.

139  Christopher Okigbo, *Distances*, 1964.

140  Ibid.

141  Ibid.

142  Ibid.

143  Interview with Ben Obumselu.

144  Ben Obumselu, 'Christopher Okigbo: A Poetic Portrait'.

145  Ibid.

146  Christopher Okigbo, 'Lament of the Mask', *Centenary Poems for W.B. Yeats* (eds) D.E.S Maxwell and S.B. Bushrui (Ibadan: University Press, 1965).

147  Ben Obumselu, 'Christopher Okigbo: A Poetic Portrait'.

148 Interview with Ben Osawe, Lagos, 1993.

149 Ibid.

150 Wole Soyinka, *You Must Set Forth at Dawn* (New York: Random House, 2006).

151 Interview with Wole Soyinka, Abeokuta, 1993.

152 Christopher Okigbo, 'Come Thunder', *Path of Thunder,* 1966.

153 Interview with Torch Taire.

154 Ibid.

155 Ibid.

156 Interview with Leslie Harriman, Lagos, 1992.

157 Interview with Sam Okudu.

158 Interview with Godwin Adokpaye.

159 Interview with Philip Asiodu.

160 Christopher Okigbo, *Labyrinths*, p. xi.

161 Christopher Okigbo, Letter to Dennis Duerden, 1966.

162 Christopher Okigbo 'Elegy of the Wind', *Path of Thunder,* 1966.

163 Christopher Okigbo 'Come Thunder', *Path of Thunder,* 1966.

164 Interview with Leslie Harriman.

165 Ibid.

166 Interview with Pius Okigbo.

167 Ibid.

168 Interview with Philip Asiodu.

169 Peter Benson, *Black Orpheus, Transition and Modern Cultural Awakening in Africa* (Berkeley: University of California Press, 1986).

170 Ulli Beier's letter to Peter Benson, 1981.

171 Ibid.

172 Interview with Ben Obumselu.

173 Christopher Okigbo, Letter to Sunday Anozie, 5 May 1966.

174 Sunday Anozie, *Christopher Okigbo: Creative Rhetoric.*

175 Interview with Torch Taire.

# 8

# *Aftermath of a coup, running arms & advancing to death*

## BIAFRA 1966–67

O Mother mother Earth, unbind me; let this be
my last testament; let this be
The ram's hidden wish to the sword the sword's
secret prayer to the scabbard –

('Elegy for Alto', *Path of Thunder*)

Dramatic events led to the secession from the Federation of Nigeria of the Eastern region, which declared itself the Republic of Biafra. This soon led to the civil war in which an estimated three million people died. Among the early casualties was the poet of *Labyrinths*. The exodus of the people of Eastern region from the rest of Nigeria became a flood. There was much anger also in people who had lost relations or friends in the senseless killings following the 29 July counter-coup. The pogrom against ethnic Igbo across the country forced many to the conclusion that for safety they must return eastwards to the region secured by Colonel Chukwuemeka Odumegwu-Ojukwu (whose name became shortened in the overseas press as Emeka Ojukwu). Shocked crowds of displaced people poured into the East, heightening the mood of discontent. Many managed to escape death, but there were many who returned limbless, bitterly scarred, emotionally broken. Death seemed too easy. Families were separated. Every day at the railway station in Enugu, there were gory spectacles: disemboweled women; beheaded corpses; people with eyes gouged from their sockets; children maimed forever by the poisonous anger of their generation; mothers wailing for their dead children; men relapsing into the restless embrace of madness, unable to withstand the devastation of their homes. Each new day, as the victims of the crisis arrived home, the anger rose in the East and, with it, the resolve of the people to protect themselves from the siege.

Christopher Okigbo settled early in August 1966 in Enugu in this dark and ominous time. He found reasonably comfortable lodgings at the Catering Rest House in the Eastern regional capital, and quickly set about more serious personal business. Safi recollects that Christopher Okigbo kept in regular touch with her as events unfolded. He had in fact called her first from Ibadan as soon as Colonel Gowon had taken over power on 2 August 1966. He had admonished her seriously to be careful on how she conducted herself in Kaduna and mind whom she talked to. 'He was very apprehensive of the turn of events and said so.'[1] Safi recalled how worried he was about his wife and child living in Kaduna, the Northern regional capital. He was careful to protect them from the fall out of events. The poet was apparently worried that Safi might suffer the backlash of his personal involvement in the Ifeajuna affair and in the unfolding events in the East.

He called Safi again from Enugu on 15 August, the day before his birthday, to find out how she and their daughter Obiageli were faring. Safi recalled that her husband again implored her repeatedly to take adequate care. Safi also sensed nervousness, which Okigbo tried to mask with his usual exuberance and jokes. He had told of his fortunate escape on the road to Lagos airport between Maryland and Ikeja. The poet was on the Special Branch's list soon after the 29 July 1966 coup which had toppled General Ironsi. Those who had killed Ironsi were on the lookout for Okigbo for his role in the events soon after the January 1966 coup. Okigbo's connection with Major Emmanuel Ifeajuna was enough to put him among the list of Eastern Nigerian intellectuals marked for liquidation. Chinua Achebe's biographer Ezenwa-Ohaeto told how his friends in Lagos hid the novelist in the Ikoyi home of the Director of the British Council in Lagos. Achebe's *A Man of the People* predicted the coup accurately. The novel had coincidentally been published on the eve of the 15 January 1966 coup. As Achebe himself explained years later, that coincidence signaled to the Northern coup plotters the complicity of Igbo intellectuals in the conception and execution of the Ifeajuna coup.

When Okigbo settled down in Enugu he called Safi again to warn her about the potential turn of events. In Okigbo's last telephone call to Safi they talked about her plans to join him in Enugu at the safest chance. Not too long after, direct telephone communication between the North and the East was cut off. These were trying times for Safi who apparently came under intense observation by security agents. Safi had also been operating at great risk in the underground which organized protection and escape for remaining Easterners who were trying to flee the slaughter in Kaduna. She herself had adequate protection. According to Pius Okigbo, Safi's connections with powerful figures in Gowon's government, like her brother Abdulaziz, may have saved her. He was one of the few people from whom he could get regular news about Safi after the disconnection of normal communication lines.

There was speculation that, as a symbolic act of renouncement of his bonds with Nigeria, the poet had divorced his wife by declaring, 'I divorce you,' three times over the phone. It seems that Christopher Okigbo himself may indeed have promoted this myth in Biafra. However Safi Attah's account of those turbulent moments is different:

> It would be just like Chris to say that he divorced me over the phone to impress his friends as the war became certain. But it is not true that he divorced me over the phone. How could he have done that when at some point, we were discussing about how I could join him in Enugu? Those were dangerous times, and Chris was very active, very involved in things. He was very worried about my safety. That was what we discussed the last time I spoke to him. My safety! He asked me to be careful how I conducted myself, and to take very good care of our child and myself. I made a promise to him that I'd be careful. There was no divorce...but you know Chris could joke about such things and if you did not know him at all you'd take him very seriously.[2]

By late August 1966 Okigbo's friends began to arrive in Enugu. The novelists Chinua Achebe and Cyprian Ekwensi had both been displaced from their jobs in the public media – Achebe as the Director of External Broadcasting at the Nigerian Broadcasting Corporation, and Ekwensi as Federal Director of Information in Lagos. Achebe found suitable accommodation in Uwani, close to the Catering Rest House where Okigbo lodged.

Not long after, Ben Obumselu also arrived in Enugu from the University of Ibadan. Obumselu had been caught up in July 1966 in Enugu when he had been completing research for his Oxford degree. Worried about his academic commitments in Ibadan, Dr. Obumselu decided to risk the trip to Ibadan. But it had become too dangerous to travel by road. So he took a flight first from Calabar to the Cameroons where he boarded a TWA flight to Paris, and then to Lagos for Ibadan. Events went out of control and and so he took that same circular route back to Enugu. It was in similar fashion that other displaced Eastern intellectuals and civil servants arrived in the East from their former homes in the old federation.

Pius Okigbo had returned by a tortuous route to Enugu late in August 1966 from Brussels, where he was at the time doubling as the Nigerian government's Ambassador to the then European Economic Community, the EEC, as well as Economic Adviser to the Federal Government. As one of the most prominent Igbo figures in the Ironsi government, Pius Okigbo was one of the targets of the coup in which Ironsi had been killed. But he had been away to Brussels at the time of the coup negotiating the terms of Nigeria's trade with the EEC. He decided to finish his mandate, and tie up his official business in Brussels – 'tidy his table' – and once that was done, he flew home to the East, through the Cameroon. From the East he called Georgette, whose expatriate status gave her some protection in Lagos, to prepare to return to the East.

Many of these displaced persons took temporary accommodation at the Catering Rest House and it was soon booked to capacity. The scarcity of accommodation in the Eastern Regional Capital became acute and people had to share spaces and make do with whatever was available. Christopher Okigbo and Ben Obumselu had to share the comforts of Okigbo's room at the Rest House for a while, because Obumselu could not find immediate accommodation.

Much of the discussion at the Catering Rest House bar in Enugu was all about the tragedy and failure of the old Nigerian Republic. There was a lot of anger about the gruesome killings and it was compounded by the sense of rejection which Easterners suffered, especially the Igbo people who were the main targets of the killings, following the northern officers' coup of July 1966. The bar of the Catering Rest House assumed the easy conviviality of a Club House. Okigbo loved it there. There was not much else to do except drink, trade news and gossip, seek gratuitous pleasure.

By the end of August 1966 the Eastern regional capital was brimming with the active energy of these displaced senior civil servants, distinguished professionals, intellectuals, businessmen, petty traders, artisans and clerks. This exodus to the East, ironically, brought an almost carnival air. The mood in the Eastern regional capital was heady with drama. Colin Legum, the South African journalist, wrote in the London *Observer* of 16 October 1966 that the Igbo return was '... reminiscent of the ingathering of exiles into Israel after the end of the last war....'[3] This great influx of people prefaced the mood of war – 'the path of thunder....'

Among the powerful Eastern Nigerian intellectuals and bureaucrats were men who had been prominent in the deposed government of General Ironsi. Most of them had fled to the East under pain of death. They began to meet regularly in the country home at Awka of Professor Kenneth Dike, the historian who had been Vice-Chancellor of the University of Ibadan.

Pius Okigbo became prominent in early informal discussions at Professor Dike's country home in Awka in those years, and was apparently part of the early strategy sessions of this group which often centered on the imminence of war. Their deliberations became crucial in the final emergence of Biafra.

There was also the group of displaced professors from universities such as Ibadan and Zaria. They began to meet frequently at the Onitsha home of Professor C.C. Modebe to discuss how to absorb these displaced intellectuals within the existing infrastructure in the East. There have been numerous claims about the central role which the University of Nigeria, Nsukka, played in instigating the Biafran resistance. There was a unique convergence of some of the most brilliant men and women of their generation driven by the fear of extermination, who began to start discussions with Eastern intellectuals already living in Nsukka and Enugu. Eni Njoku, who had been Vice-chancellor of the University of Lagos was promptly appointed Vice-Chancellor of the University at Nsukka.

Research scientists returned like the mathematician Professor James Ezeilo. Gordan Ezekwe returned from the Ahmadu Bello University in Zaria, where he had been Professor of Mechanical Engineering, and was working on a design model for an automobile. Chinua Achebe and Christopher Okigbo, were also soon appointed, alongside Kalu Ezera, as Senior Research Fellows at Nsukka's Institute of African Studies. Nsukka thus became the ideological base for Biafra. The novelist Chukwuemeka Ike was already Registrar of the University. The poet Gabriel Okara, working in Enugu was the press Chief Information Officer of Eastern Nigeria, and John Ekwere was at the Eastern Broadcasting Service. Literary figures like Dr Michael Echeruo and Obi Wali had returned from the United States with doctorates from Cornell and Northwestern. By the middle of September 1966, these intellectuals began to meet in various discussion groups at the University town of Nsukka. There were numerous nocturnal meetings and these inspired the strong secessionist passion, which soon flared into street protests in the East.

The second round in the killing spree of Easterners in northern Nigeria, late in September 1966, inspired further resentment. These prominent intellectuals began to articulate the basis for secession more seriously. The idea for a separate Biafran nation hardened in this period. Again Colin Legum, one of the more perceptive commentators on the Nigerian crisis wrote:

> Visitors to Enugu in late October and the following March noticed the remarkable change in mood: from shocked yet resigned acceptance to an electrifying militancy, which had already passed the point of rational compromise. The September massacres were the clinching factor which transformed secession from a contingency plan – one of the several alternatives into an inevitability.[4]

The Eastern region's governor, Colonel Chukwuemeka Odumegwu-Ojukwu, was under intense pressure to take decisive action on the killings and destruction of property and to make clear the status of the East within a common Nigeria. Okigbo, was deeply angered by the violence against Easterners – especially the civilians. Okigbo's involvement with Biafra was provoked by his witnessing the wounded, maimed, and the headless dead, who were brought to the East even in October 1966. He felt his humanity deeply violated. Many times in Enugu in those days of unbridled violence, the poet sat in gloomy contemplation. This was perhaps the most traumatic period of his life. That he chose to fight on the side of his 'beleaguered people'[5] was a demonstration both of his own humanity and outrage. He had to cut his allegiances with old acquaintances although he maintained contact by phone with friends in Ibadan and Lagos. As he told Wole Soyinka, during his controversial visit to Biafra, 'I have no choice but to do this!'[6]

Christopher Okigbo was very active in the meetings and various discussions that went on at Nsukka. He was among those who argued eloquently for vigilance and preparation, in the face of the difficult options left for Eastern Nigerians in the crumbling federation. Passionate nationalism inspired the young radical undergraduates of the University of Nigeria to mobilize for action. Soon the storm gathered in the streets. Preparations for war began in earnest.

However a glimmer of hope was produced by the ad hoc constitutional conference, which Yakubu Gowon had convened on 12 September 1966. Leaders were sent from the four regions to re-establish the basis of a Nigerian nation and to bring peace back to the union. One of the suggestions was the adoption of a loose federation like that in East Africa which would make the regions more autonomous and weaken the center. This meant that each of the regions would have its own police, army, judiciary and civil service, autonomous completely from the other regions. This suggestion made by the high-powered northern delegation was received happily in the East. It was to serve as the fulcrum of all future discussions and agreements when the delegates broke up for consultations with their respective regions. However, by the time the conference reconvened on 20 September 1966 there was a deadlock. The Northern delegation completely renounced its former position. Their new position now was the maintenance of a strong central government, with more states created. The Eastern delegation led by scientist Professor Eni Njoku and Dr. Akanu Ibiam, former governor of the Eastern region, would have none of that. And so the ad hoc constitutional conference broke up. The Eastern delegation returned hurriedly to the East. The failure of the ad hoc constitutional conference was also precipitated by the second pogrom in the north.

The mood indeed changed considerably late that September. Okigbo was very busy. He had access to the corridors of power through his personal friendship with the governor, Chukwuemeka Odumegwu-Ojukwu. He also had personal relationships with individuals in the top echelons of Ojukwu's government, like C.C. Mojekwu and Francis Nwokedi. His own brother, Pius Okigbo, soon emerged as one of the most powerful figures in the government in Enugu. Francis Nwokedi had chaired the commission, which had recommended the unification of services in Nigeria, and it was purportedly on account of the potential implementation of this unification decree that General Ironsi was assassinated. Okigbo's friends in the Foreign Service, like G.I.C. Eneli, were abandoning their posts. Late into the war Godfrey Eneli defected to the Nigerian side, but at the onset of hostilities he was among those top Igbo functionaries compelled by those circumstances to return to the East. Eneli came in from Rome where he was serving as Deputy Nigerian Ambassador. He would help to lead some of Biafra's diplomatic offensives. The diplomat Bernard Odogwu, serving in the Nigerian delegation at the United Nations in New York, flew directly back to Enugu and soon became Biafra's Chief of Intelligence. There were people like George Nwanze and Peter Chigbo, who were Okigbo's contemporaries at the Government College, Umuahia and at the University College, Ibadan. They all became influential public servants, playing strategic roles in Biafra.

Peter Chigbo had been Executive Director of the African Development Bank in Ivory Coast. He surfaced in Enugu to become Permanent Secretary of the formidable Biafran Ministry of Information and Propaganda. George Nwanze was to play a crucial role in the Biafran bureaucracy as Ojukwu's cabinet secretary. Ben Obumselu was soon appointed Biafra's official historian and ombudsman, a position from which he had access to the innermost sanctum of Ojukwu's government. Okigbo's Umuahia classmate, Austin Ugwumba, was appointed as Head of the Biafran Civil Service.

Among the important arrivals in Enugu, early that August of 1966, were more of the soldiers of Eastern Nigerian origin who had survived the coup. There were military officers: Colonel Tony Eze, who had been commander of the Lagos Garrison, and Patrick Anwunah, Chief Staff Officer to the slain military Head of State in Lagos, George Kurubo, who had been the Chief of Air Staff and a member of Ironsi's Supreme Military Council, Hillary Njoku, commander of the 3 Brigade who had been in Ironsi's entourage in Ibadan on 29 July 1966 and had miraculously escaped death. Many of the key officers had been Christopher Okigbo's juniors at school in Government College, Umuahia, which supplied a disproportionate number of young men for the elite Sandhurst Military Academy in Britain, placing them in the elite cadre of the old Nigerian Armed Forces.

The old school tie alone was sufficient to give Okigbo access to the Biafran high command. Many of the officers had found hospitality in Cambridge House, Ibadan. He was in all, a privileged visitor to the State Lodge in Enugu. He played his own part in the Biafran struggle with the same passion that ruled all his life. At the height of the secessionist debate, Christopher Okigbo stormed loudly into Ojukwu's office one afternoon, dismissing all the protocol and saying, 'Where is Emeka? What is going on here? If you don't declare Biafra today, I'm going to do it myself!'[7] He had to be calmed down. After Ojukwu had given some explanation about the difficulty of the situation, the poet went away, though still adamant. He resolved to give the Governor time to make the declaration; or he would do it himself over the Eastern Radio! Such was the mood in the East. Okigbo's actions only dramatized the urgency of the situation. Soon enough, events took an irreversible course, as each side in the conflict began to arm.

One of Okigbo's closest friends and confidantes in the early days in Enugu was Colonel Louis Chude Sokei from the Nigerian Air Force who had been drafted in to organize Biafran Military Intelligence. Handsome, brilliant, cultured and capable, Colonel Sokei was one of Odumegwu-Ojukwu's closest confidantes. He was the same age as Okigbo, and they had known one another as schoolboys in Onitsha in the 1940s. Sokei had started in military intelligence in the Nigerian Army in 1962 but was drafted from the army to organize the Nigerian Air Force. Early in the conflict, Sokei began running a number of secret missions for the new Republic of Biafra. These missions were risky, of the highest classification, and demanded courage and real discretion. Sokei quickly co-opted Christopher Okigbo into these early hushed activities for Biafra. The two were quite inseparable and socialized regularly, participating in the intriguing adventures of Enugu in the early, exciting days of the 'ingathering'.

Together they planned, and embarked, on some dangerous secret missions for the nascent republic. All indications are that, Christopher Okigbo was deeply involved in the cloak and dagger scenarios that presaged the full declaration of the republic of Biafra. By September 1967, before the war commenced, Okigbo had been recruited into one of the most dangerous missions of his life. This was the arms running episode which became widely publicized, revealing a web of events which underscored the complexity of the Okigbo persona. The gun running incident further established the mystique of the poet of *Labyrinths* as a man of action, willing to take enormous risks. This mission on behalf of Biafra had all the marks of Okigbo's love for play, for intrigue and subterfuge. High drama fascinated him. Nkem Nwankwo indeed writes thus of Okigbo:

> He had this Byzantine streak: a keen eye and ear for anything that sounded like plotting. Mostly his plots centered on hoodwinking and luring women to bed, and bragging about his

exploits. But he was also into delicate, complex business deals and political wheeling and dealing of unimaginably intricate detail. You were always aware that something deep was in the offing when you visited his house and saw a strange visitor. Chris's demeanor would be transformed; from the manner of a high-spirited schoolboy, yelling like an Indian, he would grow circumspect, displaying no more than a deadpan poker face yielding nothing more than a shrewd smile and a sense of not giving [anything] away.[8]

The prospects for war grew after the failure of the ad hoc constitutional conference. The need to begin to acquire arms and train young Biafran men as soldiers for the new republic became inevitable. Francis Nwokedi, the top Biafran government adviser, embarked on a tour of Israel and France to explain the East's position on the Nigerian crisis and to appeal for assistance. During one of those visits to Paris, Nwokedi requested arms and personnel to train Biafran soldiers. With Charles de Gaulle in power, France proved to be Biafra's truest western ally. The Nigerian crisis and Biafra's bid for secession matched de Gaulle's policy of supporting nationalist movements, and the principle of self-determination. Following Nwokedi's mission, Paris got involved in the Biafran struggle, quite early at an official level. The man in the centre of this initiative was Jacques Foccart, de Gaulle's secret service chief and adviser on African affairs.

Foccart played a major part in securing the first shipment of arms for the Biafrans. It was Foccart who linked Ojukwu's emissaries to the Foreign legion officer, Roger Faulques, the veteran mercenary, who had worked for the French secret service chief in Katanga for another mercenary Rolf Steiner, who became well-known in Biafra as the war went on. The poet Okigbo and his friend Chude Sokei were specially assigned by Odumegwu-Ojukwu to procure the arms. Okigbo went to Paris late in September 1966, on a secret and complex mission. Okigbo was already interested in the arms trade through his Italian contacts in Lagos, and that may have figured in his recruitment. It was on this trip that he first met Jacques Foccart who would put him into touch with the merchant princes of the arms business in Paris.

The French were the truly great arms merchants of the period, according to John de St. Jorre.[9] The French dominance in the secret arms trade arose mainly from maintaining much of the old stock and the residual channels created by French resistance during the Second World War. With the cold war conflicts in the third world, France became the arms trading center of the world; it sold arms without ideology if the price was right. Okigbo flew to Paris through Cameroon and arrived on 30 September 1966. They had arranged to meet Jacques Foccart later that evening with two of his contacts in the underground arms trade business in France – Paul Favier and Pierre Lopez. The logistics of the poet's stay in Paris were coordinated by Ralph Uwechue and Okechukwu Mezu. Okigbo stayed with Ralph Uwechue, who was up till then the First Secretary at the Nigerian Embassy in Paris. Uwechue would later become Biafra's Ambassador to France, and would also subsequently resign in the course of events later in 1968. But in the heady early days presaging Biafra, he helped to coordinate very crucial international aspects of the build up of the Igbo and Biafran resistance.

Okigbo's brief was to arrange the procurement of arms, their airlifting to Biafra, with payment through the Biafran hard currency account in Paris. The poet finally did business with Paul Favier and together they made arrangements with one of the most experienced runners in the trade, the German-American Hank Wharton. Wharton was contracted to run the arms from Europe to Eastern Nigeria, and everything seemed all set. During the visit to Paris, Christopher Okigbo also had time to visit his old friend, the scholar and literary critic, Sunday Anozie, who was just then completing his Doctorate at the University of Paris under Roland Barthes. Okigbo called at Anozie's lodgings in Paris on 2 October 1966 and, apparently in a hurry, left a note in his usual neat cursive hand: 'Sunday, Stay inside. I'll be back'.[10]

Sunday Anozie missed the poet only by a few minutes and thus just missed a last chance of seeing his friend and mentor alive. He stayed inside his apartment the whole day waiting for Christopher Okigbo to show up. They had a lot to discuss. Earlier in a letter to Sunday Anozie at about the same period, Okigbo had warned Sunday Anozie who was thinking seriously of coming back home to take up a position at Nsukka, to reconsider his decision because of the mood in Nigeria. He wanted to discuss his work with the likes of Derrida, Barthes, Foucault and the structuralists who were beginning to make an impact on the French Academy. Okigbo never returned. Anozie was shocked to read, a month later, about Okigbo's arms running venture in Europe.

After Okigbo's meeting with Paul Favier, they left on the late train to Amsterdam to meet the pilot Hank Wharton, who was to fly the arms consignment to Eastern Nigeria. They had procured and transported the consignment, the large load of arms, to Zestienhoven airport in Rotterdam where the American pilot would pick it up and fly it in a DC-4. At the airport a small problem cropped up. The Dutch authorities recognized the plane, which had been used for many other gun running assignments, and it aroused their suspicion. The DC-4 had been impounded, following an earlier gun running episode, which had caused its demobilization for ten months at Schipol Airport in Amsterdam. John de St. Jorre graphically describes in his book *The Brother's War* how the Dutch authorities watched in fascination as the rain washed away the Panama number on the aircraft revealing, in its place, the old Canadian registration. This trouble at the Zestienhoven airport apparently caused a small delay, after the aircraft had been fully loaded with the arms. Christopher Okigbo in the first place was not satisfied with the loading of the guns in the aircraft and suspected danger. Secondly, as the delay was taking too long, he travelled to London and on to Birmingham where, staying with some Eastern Nigerian students, he monitored the arrangements for the airlifting of the arms to Eastern Nigeria.

Working through his Dutch contacts, Paul Favier quickly arranged papers which Hank Wharton showed the Dutch authorities that he was contracted to deliver arms to Birmingham airport. His papers were correct to that effect, and so they released him. Meanwhile Christopher Okigbo's suitcase and some of his manuscripts were already packed in the DC-4 with the arms. The aircraft was ten thousands pounds overweight. Hank Wharton was to pick the poet up at Birmingham airport and fly on. But Okigbo, also suspecting the safety of the overloaded plane, decided to stay a bit longer in Birmingham and make his own private arrangements to return to Eastern Nigeria. His decision proved prescient. On 6 October 1966, Hank Wharton flew out from Zestienhoven Airport.

Midway on his flight to Birmingham he received instructions to divert his course, possibly because the British did not want Biafran arms in its air space. After radioing the airport in Birmingham, he flew on with his arms consignment to Palma in Mallorca, where he refueled, took some rest and proceeded to fly to Eastern Nigeria, passing over the Cameroons. However, on coming close to Garoa near Cameroon Mountain, the plane ran out of fuel and crashed, near the riverbank, on a marshy plain onto which Hank Wharton had manoeuvred the DC-4. The aircraft broke into four parts and the arms scattered in different directions. Wharton was found to be unbruised 'except for a mild concussion,'[11] and his co-pilot only broke a leg. They were subsequently arrested and charged in Cameroon for illegal arms running by the government of Ahmadou Ahidjo. At the site of the crash Okigbo's suitcase, manuscripts and other personal effects were discovered. The discovery of his suitcase and some of his manuscripts in the crashed plane was reported in the Nigerian papers and by the BBC and other European media, which was how Sunday Anozie heard about it in Paris.

But for a long time, the event passed unnoticed in Nigeria, until the Cameroon President Ahmadou Ahidjo started making noises about it. Okigbo was to heighten the mystery of this adventure by his own dramatic, exaggerated replay of its details. Okigbo told different versions to different people about his involvement and escape from the ill-fated plane carrying Biafran arms. For instance, Ben Obumselu asked him how he escaped. The poet told an elaborate fib about how he crawled into a cassava farm after the crash and found his way home, by trekking through Cameroon to Eastern Nigeria. 'Chris was capable of great fiction'.[12] Obumselu noted. The incident put Okigbo in the spotlight in Biafra; in the public imagination he had become a true hero of the resistance – a truly complex man of action. He went to battle on such an awesome reputation. But in Nigeria, the news caught many of his friends off guard: 'That was when I thought Chris had died,'[13] reminisced Torch Taire. The reality of war and the elaborate separation from the old federation was becoming clearer.

After the arms running and plane crash episode, Okigbo settled for a while into private life, organizing his own business. From late in October 1966, he was trying to establish Citadel Press, the publishing house which he founded with Chinua Achebe and V.C. Ike. Christopher Okigbo and Chinua Achebe went into this publishing venture not merely to escape the tedium of life in Enugu but, as Achebe said '…to really help build a body of African and black literature. It got to the point where we began to think that we could not leave the fate of such a venture to other foreign interests.'[14] One aim of Citadel Press was to publish children's books. Okigbo had been particularly enthusiastic. *How the Leopard Got his Claws* was written by John Iroaganachi and Chinua Achebe in Biafra, based on an Igbo folktale. Okigbo contributed the poetic interpretation of the folksong in the book, and it was illustrated by Kevin Echeruo, a young poet and painter and brother of Michael, who had been deeply influenced by Okigbo's poetry. Among the other major works already selected for the list of the new publishing house was the poetry of Gabriel Okara, of the Ghanaian Kofi Awoonor, and of the young South African exile poet Keorapetse Kgositsile. A critical work by Ben Obumselu was planned. Also slated for publication were Okigbo's own book of essays on 'Modern Poetry and the Imagination.' (These manuscripts were among those lost as a result of Okigbo's death in Biafra, the later bombing of both Okigbo's home at the hilltop in Enugu and the offices of Citadel Press, which were also further gutted by federal soldiers when Enugu fell to the federal forces in 1967.) Citadel Press also planned to publish Emmanuel Ifeajuna's account of the January 1966 coup. There are accounts which indicate that Achebe and Okigbo had disagreed over this manuscript when Chukwuma Nzeogwu, one of the principal leaders of the 15 January 1966 coup, came to them and said 'I heard you are going to publish Ifeajuna's lies.'[15]

The launching of the publishing house in Enugu was planned, not only to mark a major departure from the dependence on foreign publishers by local authors, but also to register a new phase in Okigbo's life. He was determined to settle down. The offices of Citadel Press were located in a small bungalow, at the junction of Zik Avenue and Bank Road. The opening of the Citadel Press offices was inaugurated with some fanfare, attracting the well-heeled of Enugu society; and it helped to lift the social mood in Enugu in those dark and tragic days of the ingathering. There was an elaborate cocktail party to announce the publishing house late in November 1966. The novelist and broadcaster Nkem Nwankwo, who had also escaped from Lagos where he was a broadcaster to Enugu about this time, writes about visiting Okigbo:

> When I got to their offices I first went to see Chinua Achebe. Although we hadn't seen each other for a while our exchange was correct and formal, as always. It was different with Chris. We hugged and howled, and Chris did an impromptu jig. He couldn't be happier to see me, the magnificent bastard! We were reunited, two of a kind, two deeply flawed human beings who desperately needed each other and the world's charity or amnesia.
>
> Greetings over, Chris set about joshing and flirting with the office girls. They seemed all to be his mistresses and you wondered how it was possible to enforce office discipline under the circumstances. I recognized one of the girls as a notorious gold-digger who had tried to enlist me in her book of sugar daddies. But although I was the one for frank speaking, her frank avowal of her mercenary motives stunned me. I may have been intimidated by a worldly manner that put my provincial scruples in the shade. Not surprisingly Chris had no scruples, it seemed. I saw at once that he and the girl were already into what we young people euphemistically referred to as 'fucker friendship'. That was my first visit to the famous publishing firm which never survived the war. When I visited, it was surprisingly functioning with corporate smoothness: vouchers, coffee or tea at regular intervals for the ogas – bosses – office flirtation with one of the ogas etc. Life appeared to be normal again, on the surface at least: the dust from the huge population uprooting appeared to have settled. It was a measure of the adaptability of humans.... In the case of Chinua and Chris, their publishing business with its elaborate corporate set up was one way they kept their sanity on an even keel; one way they could simulate their former executive potency.[16]

Achebe's recollection of Okigbo in this period was, however, quite different from that of Nkem Nwankwo. Okigbo put his soul in the publishing venture, was very involved, and was spending more time with Chinua Achebe's family in their home on Ogui road in Enugu. The friendship between the novelist and the poet apparently deepened during this phase of their lives together in Biafra. Okigbo became close friends with his first son, Ikechukwu. As far as Achebe could see, there was a sober aspect of Okigbo which came to the fore in this period. Okigbo was also writing frequently, experimenting with new forms, listening for echoes that might be incorporated into his poetry. Achebe recalled the day Okigbo had hurried to his home to invite him to listen to some Ikwerre griots. Okigbo was apparently experimenting with the traditional nuances of Igbo indigenous poetic forms. He had specially invited the Ikwerre griots, who had come to record one day at the Eastern Nigerian Broadcasting Service, to his room at the Catering Rest House to perform. He was so excited by his discovery that he wanted Achebe to listen and see for himself. At the end of the performance Okigbo had declared both in wonder and admiration to Achebe 'We are just wasting our time. These are the real poets!'[17] What new kind of poetry would Okigbo's fascination and experiments with the rhythm of traditional Ikwerre poetry have grown into? How deeply might it have affected his own writing? We cannot be certain, although it was quite clear from *Path of Thunder* that he was taking a new turn. But there is at least an account by his eldest brother Lawrence that Christopher was doing a lot of writing, working feverishly in his quiet times at his hilltop home on his manuscripts. Most of these manuscripts are it seems permanently lost or damaged. Some of the recovered papers of Christopher Okigbo were preserved by Dr. Pius Okigbo, and released to Okigbo's daughter Obiageli in 2000. However, various parts were either damaged or missing following subsequent exposure to the elements. Professor Chukwuma Azuonye is currently organizing, in collaboration with Okigbo's daughter, some of the recovered manuscripts from the

Okigbo papers into a comprehensive collection. These have also been registered with the UNESCO heritage commission.

Okigbo had indeed acquired a beautiful, quiet place to live near the Colliery Mines, on the road to Nsukka at the end of Park Lane in the Enugu Government Reservation Area. Approached through the Enugu Forest Reserves, where Lawrence worked, it was meant to be a refuge from all the anxieties of the time. It was a beautiful, colonial style bungalow on the hilltop from where the city unfolded in panoramic splendor. The view always left visitors gasping with pleasure according to the writer Ken Saro-Wiwa who visited Okigbo there in this period. It provided an ambience of refined solitude. Okigbo was naturally proud of his home, and would often show his visitors round his beautiful garden, and sometimes inform them glibly that the whole place was full of lovely snakes.[18] The house on the hill was a lonely place, however. Okigbo only went there to contemplate and write. He still spent much of his time at the Government Rest House, on the account of the government for whom he was running all kinds of special missions. On many occasions, the poet had been thrown out of his room at the Rest House for not paying his mounting bills, but would always be reinstated following directives from Government Lodge. Even when Okigbo went off to the war fronts, he kept his room at the Rest House but often returned to the solitude of the hilltop house, to relax, detoxify, and escape from the conflict outside - he called it 'my hilltop haven.'[19]

From all indications Okigbo spent whatever time he could afford in the solace of his hilltop house writing. Occasionally, he invited guests to whom he would read some of his new work. He maintained an apparent picture of buoyancy even against the background of uncertainty. Thus was the observation of Lewis Nkosi, the South African novelist and journalist, who had been dispatched early in 1967 to Enugu from London, by the *Daily Mail*, to report the mood in Eastern Nigeria. Nkosi spent much of his time in Nsukka at the home of the literary critic Donatus Nwoga and his Irish wife, Patricia. Nkosi had been best man at their wedding in London in 1961. He visited Okigbo and Achebe at their Citadel Press office, and was a guest of the poet at his hilltop home. Okigbo, Nkosi noted, spent a lot of time participating in the pleasures of Enugu's pre-war high society. It was an indulgent time. Fatal uncertainty on the horizon seemed to have loosened the spirit of the time. There were numerous parties, and women, and Rex Lawson's highlife music. People clung to life desperately, and found consolation in the warmth of the human spirit in anticipation of the war that followed.

It was in this context that Okigbo became emotionally involved with Chinyere, 'a young woman from a very good family'[20] as Georgette Okigbo later described her. Chinyere was a much younger woman, only then about eighteen years old, who had finished at Queen's School in Enugu just before the hostilities. The love affair developed and ripened, fed by the mood of desperation and the search for consolation. Chinyere had been impressed as much by the poet's intense wooing as by his apparent erudition. She was also drawn immediately by the compassionate part of his personality. Georgette Okigbo believed that Christopher Okigbo had fallen genuinely in love with the girl. Chinyere often came to Okigbo's hilltop home to spend her day, but was never allowed to sleep over. Okigbo would read his poetry, delighting her immensely by his performance. Okigbo's greatest fear was loneliness – companionship quelled much of the poet's insecurities during this period when personal lives were thrown together by tragic events. Individuals sought emotional anchor through close relationships with people. Strong family ties also became a shield from the violent drama playing out at the time.

Although it was an increasingly difficult and uncertain time, one happy outcome of this phase of Okigbo's life was a healing of the filial distance between the poet and his eldest brother. Lawrence Okigbo was living in Enugu at this time as the Head of the Forestry department. The two brothers seemed to have discerned a new value in their personal relationship, and developed a more tolerant view of each other. Wary in the past of his stern elder brother, Okigbo had begun to spend more time in Enugu in his company. It was a new phase in their relationship. The poet would go over more often to have his meals in Lawrence's home at the Abakiliki Road flats. Lawrence felt that Christopher had come more into himself, and had taken greater control of the life around him. His deep involvement with the Biafran resistance convinced Lawrence that there was certainly stronger fiber in his younger brother, whose life hitherto had been characterized by a deep libertinian impulse that absolved him of duty and obligation. Christopher's sense of moral outrage over Biafra changed all that. He undertook difficult tasks and was driven by the pain he had witnessed. By all accounts, Lawrence, usually impatient with what he always felt was Christopher's profligacy and irresponsibility, became more appreciative of other dimensions of the poet's individuality and character. 'They got closer and began to know and understand more of each other,' their sister, Susan Anakwenze recalled of this time, 'because Lawrence sensed a more serious side of Chris than he knew previously... the way he rose to the occasion when it mattered most.'[21]

This transformation in Okigbo was apparent also to the poet's sister-in-law Georgette, Pius Okigbo's bi-racial Belgian wife who arrived in Enugu much later with the children. She had been working in the Nigerian Broadcasting Corporation in Lagos and had a certain amount of protection from the massacres guaranteed by her European status. Georgette indeed was one of the last people to leave Lagos for the East before the closure of the boundaries. Late in August 1966, when Pius Okigbo returned to Enugu from Brussels through the Cameroon, he had sent urgent messages across to Georgette in Lagos. She was initially worried about the situation and felt that her children would be better protected living with her in Lagos, since her expatriate status gave her some immunity. Nevertheless she relented, after much pressure from Pius, and decided finally to return to the East. As soon as she arrived in Enugu however she was confronted by the stark reality, the pain of the wounded Easterners. She set to work. 'It was a moment of reckoning for anyone with any conscience. The wound was palpable. It moved you into action'[22] she remembered. She was soon drawn into the whirlwind of events. For a brief period however, she was not certain which role she could play in the Biafran struggle. Her husband was busy with the preparations and was hardly around. To relieve her of boredom, Professor Anezi Okoro, dermatologist and novelist, one of the closest family friends of the Okigbos, undertook to look after her. He constantly invited her to his home, where his family offered Georgette the traditional *ngwo-ngwo*, a spicy soup made from goat tripe, which she came to like very much. Georgette also came under the care of Christopher Okigbo in this period, who devoted a lot of time and attention to her, just to make her happy and comfortable. Georgette was grateful for those moments. Soon, she began to visit the hospitals in Enugu with Christopher, where she saw the wounded people, many of whom had lost limbs. These scenes touched a profoundly sensitive core in Georgette. From then on she threw herself deeply into the service of the struggle. She could no longer afford to be distant from the conflict. The Biafran resistance became her war too.

There was a sudden vacancy for a French translator for the Biafran radio to broadcast its programmes and propaganda internationally and Georgette, being fluent in French, volunteered. She began translating most of the early Biafran propaganda materials for the outside world. Georgette's personal experience of war previously, as a teenager, during the Second World War in Europe became useful. She had been part of the underground resistance during the German occupation of Belgium. With the imminence of civil war, the emerging scenario in Enugu was not completely strange to her and it gave her an opportunity to find something to do and contribute personally to the war effort. She became much closer to the poet in this period. Before the crisis, Georgette never really felt close to Christopher, whom she had regarded as extremely 'spoilt, too indulged and selfish'.[23] But, as events in Biafra drew them closer, she too began to reappraise her understanding of the personality of the poet:

> It was strange. But something truly came over Chris. The Christopher I knew was a changed person in Biafra. He had matured with the experience: Chris was always spoilt, too indulged and selfish, but he had begun to show a different complexion. For instance, the Chris I knew was always too undisciplined with time: he would tell me that he would come at a certain time for his lunch in Ikoyi, and I would prepare lunch for him with so much effort, and he wouldn't show up until one week after! He would not even apologize. That always infuriated me. It was inconsiderate. He was selfish in his relationship with his women and he would lie! But Biafra changed all that. There was a spiritual transformation which I noticed, there was the very considerate Christopher. The suffering of the many he saw pained him physically. I'll tell you this: Christopher didn't get involved in Biafra for any ideological reason, no, he fought to protect his land, the desecration of the land which he felt was his root as a person and he was prepared to die for that! He didn't fight because he hated anybody. He was incapable of hate.[24]

Georgette became one of the people with whom Okigbo related most closely in a meaningful way during this emotionally draining period of his life. By February 1967, as events unraveled, everybody seemed too busy, too involved with the gathering conflict. Even his closest friends with whom he would normally socialize became too occupied in the affairs of state.

Even his own relations were too drawn into the events to be socially available. His brother Pius, with whom before there was always time to talk, was at this hectic period always too busy; he was traveling for Biafra and designing new fiscal strategies and economic policies for the new republic. As Georgette remembered, Pius organized what later became Biafra's formidable war bureaucracy, and was far too engrossed with his task to have much time to spend outside of the issues of state. Although their relationship had got warmer in this period, Lawrence did not share the same interests as Christopher – the same need for intellectual stimulation, or passion for the artistic life or for utterance. Bede, Okigbo's favourite cousin, was also very busy at Nsukka, deeply involved in his important research on food production for the imminent war, and could hardly be distracted from that venture. Moreover, when Babs Fafunwa left suddenly, Bede had been saddled with another brief responsibility as acting Vice-Chancellor of the University of Nigeria, Nsukka. It was a truly nightmarish time for the socially active poet who had grown to realize the historic nature of the struggle in which he was personally involved, and in which he was poised to play so dramatic a part. He kept active with the affairs of the Citadel Press.

Attempts to mediate in the Nigerian crisis fell apart finally. There seemed no other choice for the Biafrans than to secede. At the Aburi talks the East felt increasing pressure to define its place in the Nigerian federation or leave. One particularly sore point was the issue of paying the salaries of several displaced civil servants and military officers on which the Gowon government in Lagos had reneged. The other fundamental agreements touched on the issue of regional autonomy. But by 27 May 1966, as a way of establishing federal authority and pre-empting the leadership of Eastern Nigeria, General Gowon announced the creation of the twelve states, breaking the Eastern region into three states. There had been no consultation and no referendum. There had been several other deliberate actions which overturned the Aburi agreements. Following these, the Eastern Nigerian Consultative Assembly, after their meeting in Enugu decided to declare a Republic of Biafra 'at the soonest possible time.' So on 29 May 1967, Colonel Emeka Odumegwu-Ojukwu announced the Republic of Biafra. Fervent Biafran nationalism touched the spirit of everyone, including the poet's. That day, when the Republic of Biafra was declared in Enugu, the poet went out to the bars, drinking many toasts to the new republic with such friends as Chude Sokei and Bernard Odogwu.

By June it became obvious that something was going to happen soon. There was a restless energy in the air. Brisk troop movements in Enugu signaled Biafra's preparation for war. Ironically the sense of flux in the Biafran capital inspired a sense of exhilaration and purpose for the new Republic of Biafra. On 6 July 1966 the first shots of the war were fired in Nsukka and Garkem, beginning the bloodiest event of Nigerian history in the twentieth century. The next day, on 7 July 1966, Christopher Okigbo signed in for combat. Bernard Odogwu knew Okigbo very well. They had remained friends from their younger days growing up together in Onitsha, where they had both been young altar boys and served mass at St. Joseph's Onitsha in the 1940s. In his memoir about Biafra, Odogwu gives an account of Okigbo's impetuous involvement in the war. By this time Bernard Odogwu had been appointed Biafra's Director of Military Intelligence, a position in which he remained until 1970:

> Exactly a day after the commencement of hostilities, Chris stormed into my office fuming and furious. With him were Colonel Ojukwu's younger brother Tom and Mr. Justin Onwudiwe (later Lt. Colonel), and before I could offer them seats, Chris as was typical of him had already barked out an order to me. 'I give you exactly five minutes flat to write out three passes, one in my name and the other two for Tom and Justin.' He then explained that they had gone to the Nsukka front and offered their services, but that some 'silly brats' up there wouldn't allow them to participate in the fighting for the simple reason that they hadn't been to Sandhurst. At first I refused issuing them the passes because I felt the fighting should be left to the professionals, but with strong pressures from Chris I was forced to issue them. Once out there the trio joined Major Nzeogwu and his select group and operated as a guerrilla unit. Soon reports of their exploits and acts of bravery reached all corners of Biafra.[25]

The Biafran Northern axis from Nsukka was an important strategic sector. The Federal forces attacked the new republic from Ogoja and from Nsukka. For three days, heavy fighting went on in Nsukka, until the university town fell into the hands of the Federal army on 9 July 1966.

The loss of Nsukka was painful. One, it was the centre of the new nation's intellectual life. It meant disruption and dislocation of the flow of ideas from that direction. Nsukka had been the hotbed of the agitation, led by students and many of of the intellectuals, which brought about the declaration of Biafra. Many of those intellectuals, a lot of them Okigbo's closest friends who had found refuge in Nsukka, were thus once more dislocated, driven away from their homes by the arrival of the Federal army. Many of them left their most important possessions, their libraries, to the rampaging army. For Okigbo, the fall of the university into Federal hands was, in a personal sense, the profanation of hallowed grounds. The violation of a university to him was anathema. It was deeply symbolic for him because he had been part of the founding of the University at Nsukka. The destruction of its libraries, which he had laboured to establish, was to him the height of barbarity. He also lived some of his most intense poetic life at Nsukka, and had a personal connection to its mythos. Okigbo felt personally compelled to 'chase the vandals out of the university.'[26] This became the slogan of their guerrilla campaigns. Their major strategic objective was to recapture Nsukka and create a military buffer around it.

The Federal army's penetration of the northern boundary of Biafra was quick and surprising. The Biafran capital, Enugu, was only one hour away and a major Federal push could have capsized the city. Fighting their way through Okutu and Okuje, the Federal army rounded off at the peripheries of Enugu-Ezike north of Nsukka. According to Alex Madiebo, a frontline commander in that theatre, the Federal forces concentrated at Obollo-Afor, from where they planned to launch the final onslaught. Thanks to efficient Biafran intelligence, the Biafran forces quickly re-organized 51 and 53 Brigades. The 51 Brigade moved its headquarters under Colonel Alex Madiebo who later became the Commander of the Biafran army, up to Eha-Amufu, while the 53 Brigade under Colonel Anthony Eze, slipped down to Ukehe. Why did Okigbo go to war? It was typical of Christopher Okigbo, poet and man of action, to fight on his own terms. He was passionate and idealistic, and gave little thought to the danger. Okigbo had also apparently become bored with the routine of civilian life in Enugu. He could not bear to be on the sidelines. The unfolding events also challenged his thinking, about the role of the new African writer or intellectual in his post-colonial society. It was also a period shaped by the writings of Cabral and Fanon who had been deeply involved in the movements for self-determination in Africa. Okigbo was not only a man of action but he was also a romantic. On several occasions he openly confessed his admiration for the man of both intellect and action, typified essentially for him by the exploits of Fanon in Algeria. The Spanish poet, Garcia Lorca and the Chilean poet Pablo Neruda had been involved in the Spanish civil war. It was impossible, under the circumstance of war, to restrict Okigbo's adventurous spirit because he was tuned into its romantic significance. Okigbo's decision to go to battle caught Ben Obumselu off-guard. Okigbo, he said, gave no hints that he was volunteering for active military service. 'Christopher simply went off to the war front just as thousands of students flocked to the Balkan wars of 1912/13 and to the Spanish civil war of 1936/39… He was determined to match his untutored military instincts, not against Federal troops, but against Sandhurst-trained Biafran officers. 'I am going to disprove Sandhurst,' he said.[27]

Throughout the re-organization of the Biafran defenses, Christopher Okigbo was heavily involved in a number of daring guerrilla operations which confined the Federal forces at Nsukka town. They were brazenly accomplished with a rag-tag army of civilian volunteers. Major Nzeogwu, the charismatic officer who had led the 15 January 1966 coup in the north, had gained the respect of a lot of the radical student volunteers who surrounded him in Biafra and mostly formed his guerrilla group. Nzeogwu had personally led the assault on the Premier's Lodge in Kaduna where the Sarduana of Sokoto and Premier of the Northern region had been killed. He had achieved legendary status based on a superstition about his invincibility. Ojukwu released from jail Nzeogwu, Ifeajuna and the other military officers detained in Eastern region for plotting the 15 January coup. Nzeogwu, like everyone else, was compelled to establish defensive positions. He had no command; he just led a group of volunteers at Nsukka in guerrilla activities. The Nzeogwu group operated mostly in the area of the 53 Brigade, commanded by Colonel Anthony Eze. Tony Eze was not only the poet's junior at the Government College, Umuahia, but was one of the 'silly brats' from Sandhurst whom Okigbo wanted so eagerly to disprove. Colonel Eze retained his respect and admiration for Okigbo, nonetheless. There were others who Okigbo knew who joined up to fight with Nzeogwu's guerrilla group. Gaius Anoka later became a diplomat and Sam Ukpabi and William Uzoaga later became academics. There were also Ojukwu's brother Tom Bigger and Justin Onwudiwe.

Major Tim Onwuatuegwu, Nzeogwu's second-in-command during the 15 January coup in Kaduna, was also operating at the 53 Brigade. Georgette Okigbo became particularly close to Onwuatuegwu in this period and recalled that this brave and very disciplined mustachioed officer was Okigbo's idea of a fine soldier. Onwuatuegwu was also an old Umuahian all-rounder. 'With the old school tie and all that, Tim struck it up with Chris'[28] remembered Colonel Anthony Eze, the Commanding Officer of Biafra's 53 Brigade, under whom Tim Onwuatuegwu served as the commander of Biafra's crack 'C' Company at Leja. Ben Gbulie was commander of the 7th Battalion of the 53 Brigade. In the early days of the war, Emma Ifeajuna was a staff officer at army headquarters, but he came in frequently to the battlefronts at Nsukka. All these men had been actively involved in the 15 January putsch. There were considerable arguments and personal disagreements about the rules of engagement and the strategies that the Biafran forces must adopt to counter the Federal advance. Nzeogwu and Ifeajuna, with whom the poet identified, favored the mosquito sting attack. Nzeogwu's position was that, with Biafra's limited military strength, the Federal forces would completely rout the Biafran forces in a direct confrontation. The alternative, he felt, was to adopt guerrilla operations to harass the Federal army consistently until they quit. So usually his group of volunteers would go out on irregular operations, where they often dealt surprise attacks on the Federal soldiers and in that way successfully confined them to Nsukka.

The Biafran forces were also having a successful operation at the Eha-Ndiagu and the Eha Amufu axes. It was on that front, that Domkat Bali, who later became Nigeria's chief of defence staff in the Babangida dictatorship, then a young lieutenant fighting on the Federal side, was seriously wounded during the operations in Obollo-Afor. As a result of this particular battle, it became necessary to move Colonel Eze's 53 Brigade headquarters from Ukehe to the Opi junction. The men were quartered at the Opi central primary school, close to the Health Centre. Okigbo and his guerrilla volunteers were also there. Colonel Anthony Eze, the brigade commander, confirmed that Christopher Okigbo was not under any command structure. 'He simply joined the ops with Nzeogwu's guerrilla group.'[29] Because the poet was technically a civilian volunteer, and because he did not come under any direct military command, it was impossible to exercise any meaningful control on him. He was virtually independent. This ambiguity made Eze reluctant to regulate or control some of his actions. As Ben Gbulie recalled, throughout the operations in the Isienu area of the Nsukka battlefront, Christopher Okigbo was always quick to volunteer and assist in any task, however difficult. He would say, 'Look, let's get on with it.'[30] Gbulie, who later wrote one of the most gripping accounts of the conflict in his book *The Five Majors*, acknowledged that Okigbo brought ebullience and a sense of daring into the war trenches in the Biafran Northern sector. But he also recalled the poet's lack of care about the possibility of danger, which would prove fatal:

He was a bit reckless, because throughout the operations in the area of Isienu and Eha-Alumona, he didn't care whether he lived or died. In the military there are rules or forms of immediate action: certain things that guide the operation of trained officers. He didn't abide by those rules. For instance, he almost always sat on the bonnet of the jeep whilst an operation is on – he would sit there with his rifle, his leg thrown wide apart. Although that was not military, it never bothered Christopher. When you reprimanded him, he would just burst out into his loud laughter![31]

He ventured beyond the rules, and operated in exploits for which hardy veterans would have thought twice before volunteering. 'He fought with his soul'[32] to quote Gaius Anoka. Okigbo was among the band of guerrilla soldiers whose daring penetration of the enemy lines was so frequent, that it spawned some of the memorable legends of the war. During many of such operations, he would simply borrow a military fatigue from any of the boys in the regular army, and head off. He would just put himself ahead of Biafran soldiers and fight, harassing the Federal positions endlessly along the Nsukka axis. He soon gained the respect of the trained fighters.

Okigbo had no rank in Biafra, in spite of all the usual reference to him as a Major in the Biafran army. The truth is a bit different, but typifies Okigbo's style. Gaius Anoka recalled that Okigbo decided to take the rank of Major to ensure that rank-conscious Biafran soldiers would take his orders. 'He just cut the pips one day and sewed it to his shoulder'.[33] He chose the rank of Major because the Brigade commander was a Colonel, and by military regulations he could not choose an equal rank. He would not go down to the rank of captain. In his judgment, the Major's pip was fitting enough, perhaps even more because of the mystique which had been endowed on it by the Majors' coup of 15 January. Such was the popularity of the January boys that the stature of the Major's rank had been enhanced significantly in the public imagination. He became known among the boys as Major Okigbo.

Gaius Anoka maintained a close friendship in the trenches with Okigbo. They were both poets and shared similar interests in the theatre. Anoka had attended King's College, Lagos and Caius College, Cambridge. He returned to teach at his Alma Mater, and became involved in the cultural life of Ibadan and Lagos in the Mbari years. Anoka was a formidable member of Wole Soyinka's 1960 Masks, acting alongside other of Okigbo's friends such as Ralph Opara, Christopher Kolade and Femi Johnson. While at King's College, Gaius Anoka had been master in charge of the cadet unit. In that role, he had got the Fourth Battalion in Lagos to take the boys in the cadet group on routine weapons handling and basic military training. That experience later served him well when he got involved, first in Biafran army's intelligence unit, but later on with Nzeogwu's guerrillas as the war broke out. It was quite a relief for Okigbo to have a kindred spirit among the fighting men. They would read long passages of poetry to each other just to pass the time.

Okigbo read frequently to his friends – Gaius Anoka, Sam Ukpabi and William Uzoaga – his high-pitched voice forming deep echoes in the nights at the war camp, carrying the tones of his vision. He tried to prove that reading poems had the power of tranquilization. It was his theory that the best poetry should affect its audience physically; that of all the forms of aesthetic expression, poetry transmitted the most potent rhetorical energy. He would try to demonstrate it, and at such times, William Uzoaga would tell Gaius Anoka, in a mix of Igbo and English: '*But, Nwata a bu kwanu brain!*' (But, this young man is brilliant!).[34] The force of his personality and the luminosity of his imagination often impressed those who met Okigbo. In the dreariness of battle, among falling soldiers, his spirit never failed; he did not allow the melancholy of war to stifle his spirit and natural enthusiasm for life. Okigbo found occasions to make jokes and created laughter to relieve the harshness of the situation. He intrepidly maintained his sense of humor. Gaius Anoka came to conclude, years later, on the two fundamental elements, based on the Greek concepts of the *suki* and the *phillia*: one representing the abstractions of the virtuous soul embodied in the psyche and the gut and, the other reflecting the Aristotelian virtue of love and loyalty to friends, family and community, that Okigbo's life enacted an absolute union of each notion. Many times Okigbo read in the dim light of their camp at the Opi primary school from long sequences of a version of his *Path of Thunder,* which had then not been published anywhere. Gaius Anoka also confirmed that Okigbo had written many wartime poems, fragments wrought in the heat of events, and that he carried them always with him in a pouch. Often he said to Anoka, 'Wherever they find me it would be with my poems. I'd have something to say.'[35] The poems Okigbo wrote in this period, it seems now, are permanently lost. They probably have been interred with him or otherwise destroyed.

Okigbo, in his last days in Biafra, it seems, often talked casually about death. He went to war in part to keep his sanity and to escape from the inertia of humdrum life in Enugu. When he went off to the Nsukka front he had left the work at Citadel Press to Chinua Achebe. He still managed to keep in touch with the novelist, although this he did less regularly as he got more involved in the fighting round Nsukka. He had not let Achebe know that he was going off to fight. According to Achebe 'Christopher had designed all possible manners of deception to throw me off the scent of the fact that he had joined the army and had gone off to fight. He tried to keep it a secret from me, although the hints were quite strong.'[36] Achebe himself suggested that Okigbo did not want to let him into the secret because he might have tried to convince him to stay out of the battlefront. But Christopher Okigbo apparently did not think the war would last for long. His idea on going off to the war front was to keep harassing the enemy by constant raids, and finally drive them out of Nsukka and from Biafran territory so things could then return to normal. From his vigorous involvement in the fighting, Okigbo discovered a redeeming sense of self and a final coming to terms with the purpose of his life; a meaning which eluded him at earlier points of his life. Obumselu recalls that Okigbo planned to write a sequence of poems that would be a memorial for the war. 'Like Xenophon during the Persian invasion of Greece (499-449 BC), he wanted to write his *Anabasis.* But he did not merely wish to report the historical struggle.'[37] He wanted to experience it. War still held some romance for him. The early excitement and fascination for Okigbo came from a sense of the dramatic action and the exhilaration of battle. Its more tragic implications were still far off.

Occasionally, Okigbo's band of guerrillas would go deep into enemy held territory for the usual midnight raids, and they would be repulsed, after which the poet would be seriously reprimanded, and warned against certain actions during combat – especially those actions which made him particularly vulnerable. Ben Gbulie believed that Okigbo's enthusiasm came from a naive understanding of the rules of war. But it was also, more importantly, a reflection of the bold and intrepid aspect of Okigbo's individuality. Okigbo was naturally selfless and, when committed to a cause, became enthusiastic and passionate and could push this to the dramatic limits. He was one of those who felt that the Biafran military top brass was too slow and bureaucratic and that it was too theoretical in matters of warfare and strategy. He felt that war should not be conducted according to the textbooks – it was, in his view, a drearier reality, far removed from the forms of engagement taught at Sandhurst.

Okigbo regularly argued with Anthony Eze about these matters. Always anxious for Okigbo's safety, Colonel Eze was reluctant to include him in any major operation and this infuriated the headstrong poet. In the end, Okigbo always had his way by his almost wilful disregard of the rules of military hierarchy. He was already a popular figure among the fighting men. A cult following had developed around him: the image of the artist, the bold intellectual man, the easy-going, humorous poet, finding laughter in the ruins of his world, creating humour to save the spirit from failure. The image of the poet-soldier loomed large in the consciousness of those fighting men, many of them young, radical undergraduate volunteers, who longed to recapture Nsukka, Biafra's intellectual bastion. Chukwuemeka Ike has described how, at the end of every successful operation, Okigbo would be hoisted up and carried shoulder high by the combatants. Sometimes, at such moments of heady victory, he would sit on the bonnet of his Peugeot 404 wagon, and the guerrillas would ride slowly back to camp, singing the songs of victory. It seems that the drama of war was as strong an impetus as the idealism behind Okigbo's involvement in the battles. Okigbo, with no military training, was apparently too naive about the real nature of a shooting war.

On a few occasions however, he was confronted by the reality of the war and the potential for fatalities. For instance, Gaius Anoka wrote a humorous poem in the war, using the phallic image of a pipe. He described the dreary moments of battles and the booming guns, which were like those pipes out of which death came like the water that dissolved the will of fighting men. The final refrain to Anoka's poem was something like: 'And the enemy pissed all over our heads!'[38] Gaius Anoka remembered that he had read it one evening to Okigbo who had laughed heartily. Okigbo said to Anoka, 'You know Gaius, you might just make a great war poet yet!'[39] Two days after reading the poem to Okigbo, the Federal forces attacked Biafran positions with 106 RR guns at noon. It was one of those sporadic actions which threw everything into confusion. People scampered under cover, with the Federal soldiers bombarding. Death missed Gaius Anoka by inches. Only an impulsive shift of the body had saved his life. The force of the shell lifted him physically off the ground and hurled him meters away into the bush. Then everything calmed down and there was deathly silence. Christopher Okigbo was the first to rise from where he had taken cover, and ran to Gaius Anoka, who was lying still there on the ground, covered with dust. Okigbo quickly examined Anoka and found that he was alive, just dazed. He then burst out in great mirth, saying 'Kai! What a near miss! Where is that your piss poem? … you see, the enemy has truly pissed over all our heads!'[40] Okigbo had made so much of a joke out of it that the incident lost much of its deadly significance. Everybody, including Gaius Anoka, laughed. They all knew how lucky indeed they were to be alive. Okigbo said to Anoka: 'Don't worry Gaius, we shall read this poem after the war!'[41] The poet's great humour lightened the burden of the war.

Okigbo had found two displaced boys at Ukehe, uncertain about where to run to. He had taken them under his wing. He came with them one afternoon to the Opi camp, and had said to Gaius Anoka, 'Let's keep them. You keep one, I keep the other.'[42] They were very young boys between twelve and fourteen years – boy soldiers. Emma Oti, who became the poet's batman, had been a student at a Catholic junior seminary in Nsukka before the war, and had moved into Ukehe when the Federal forces occupied Nsukka. Gaius Anoka took Paul Ene who came originally from Ukehe.

According to Gaius Anoka, Christopher Okigbo had in his search for adventure opened the Isienu road by default. He often took the two young boys on reconnaissance, at great risk, along with him from Opi through the Isienu road leading on to the university farm. Many times they passed the night at the abandoned Isienu

Grammar School. They would usually return to base early in the morning. Gaius Anoka would warn Okigbo about the danger of his constant adventurous trips. There had been one incident in which he would certainly have died, but for Anoka's persuasion. Anoka remembered a particular incident, which made Christopher Okigbo a little more cautious in his adventurous forays and his incessant penetration deep into the Federal positions at Nsukka. His default opening of the Isienu road, which cut right through strategic Federal positions, allowed Okigbo occasionally to go up to the university farm for stores. He would bring back fruits, meat and such things. One day, the poet gathered a few of his young volunteers for an attack on the Federal positions. His plan was to move straight through the Isienu road, attack and then withdraw quickly back to base. Gaius Anoka disagreed seriously with Okigbo because Isienu road had become very dangerous. The Federal forces had taken vantage positions around the hills, from which snipers could easily pick off Okigbo and his group. It was suicide, Gaius Anoka said, to attempt any attack through that route. But Okigbo had argued relentlessly in defence of what he thought to be a formidable plan, until Anoka brought out a prismatic glass and a survey map, which had been supplied to 53 battalion by the land department in Enugu for a practical demonstration. He was able to show Okigbo that the Isienu road was a valley of death. Okigbo had been startled by what now became obvious. Anoka's practical knowledge of the geography and landscape of that axis, helped to convince Okigbo of the potential consequence of his adventure. As Anoka remembered, Okigbo stood up and said to him in great relief, 'Kai! I would have been finished!'[43] This demonstration also convinced him to have more regard for Gaius Anoka's superior views on strategy. In any case, Okigbo was always bad at geography. But he learnt to be a little more cautious, and to take orders from the professionals slightly more seriously. The implications of the war and the situation of the battlefield were gradually sinking in.

On 21 July 1967 Christopher Okigbo drove down to Enugu from the Opi base. The Biafran forces were planning a major operation, and Okigbo came to Enugu urgently on the errand to procure stores for his band of guerrilla fighters. By coincidence the playwright Wole Soyinka had that day arrived in Enugu for a meeting with Ojukwu. It was part of Soyinka's efforts as an emissary to find a resolution to the conflict. It was on his return from this trip to Biafra that Gowon's government arrested and incarcerated him for the duration of the war. Soyinka's presence had raised the suspicions of Biafran military intelligence and he was being held for interrogation at their headquarters when Okigbo arrived from the war front. The poet had first called on Bernard Odogwu at his office but was told to look for him at the military police headquarters on Abakiliki road. Bernard Odogwu has given an account of what transpired in his book *No Place to Hide*:

> I was just about saying to Soyinka, that I did not think he had answered my questions, when he interrupted and asked, 'Where is Chris Okigbo? Is it possible that I could see him?' I told him Chris was at the war front, but then if there was anything like an invocation as claimed by magicians, I was to witness one that day, for no sooner had Soyinka and I finished mentioning Chris Okigbo's name than Chris in person fully arrayed in battle gear, appeared through the door. Chris had been to my office to see me and when told where I was decided to track me down. What happened between the two friends Okigbo and Soyinka, cannot be adequately described in words. Even till this day, I still relive that scene with some amount of relish and nostalgia. The two geniuses went into an automatic embrace and while still in that position, went into a jig dance round the room with the two military policemen in the room and myself watching in profound admiration. They made so much noise that some of

the military policemen standing guard outside the office came dashing in, thinking that something had probably gone amiss inside. In the process the rifle of one of them was 'accidentally' discharged and yet both writers were still in their act oblivious of the pandemonium they had caused. Finally when the jigging ended, both went into a long argument on the merits and demerits of the on-going war. I remember Soyinka asking Okigbo, why he was fighting when he should have used his personality and influence in preventing it. At the end of the debate, Soyinka apologized for being carried away: 'I recognise the fact that you people had gone through hell in the last one year and that most of us in Nigeria were guilty because not many people had the guts to speak up while damage was being done'. 'I hope' he continued, that pretty soon we shall be able to find some sort of peace formula to unite the country once again'. We all laughed when Wole Soyinka, concluding his remarks said that he hoped it would not happen in his lifetime when he would come to Enugu with a passport in hand and through an immigration post. The parting when it was time for Chris to go was a sentimental one, reminiscent of a typical Shakespearean scene 'Well dear Wole,' Chris said, 'I hope we meet again, but if not, I hope this parting was well made. Keep the flag flying high as always.'[44]

Soyinka had two possible intentions behind his visit: he wanted to meet personally with Ojukwu, and secondly he hoped to make contact with his old Ibadan friends who had escaped to Enugu. His meeting with Ojukwu and the Biafran leadership was connected with some agreements to an alternative course of action, which would involve a possible alliance with the leadership of Western Nigeria to forge a Southern solidarity, in which case he was bearing important messages to that effect. It was also at this point that the elaborate alternative which Soyinka represented hardened into what was then to become the idea of 'the third force,' which in fact was anchored on the completion of the motives of the failed coup of January 1966.

In the event, Biafra had planned two strategic moves which would have consequences for the eventual outcome of the war. One was the massive Nsukka operation to dislodge the Federal forces and halt their advance into Enugu. The other was a midwest operation, to link with a possible Western Nigerian initiative and take Lagos. There was excitement in the air.

Bernard Odogwu saw Christopher Okigbo out, and they arranged to meet at the Hotel Presidential where Soyinka was lodged. The Biafran intelligence chief also observed that the poet was not looking too good, and that the war had taken a physical and emotional toll on him. Odogwu and Okigbo had discussed the war and talked about Okigbo's future plans. From Odogwu's account, Okigbo had planned to take a break from the fighting after the operation which was to be Biafra's major push to dislodge the Federal troops from Nsukka. During this last visit to Enugu from the war front, the poet had also paid social visits to other people. It was almost as if he knew that he might never have another chance for farewells. He wanted to see as many people as he could before heading back. He went to see Chinua Achebe in the office of the publishing house, and it was to prove to be for the last time. Achebe recalls that he had rushed back to Enugu from his country home in Ogidi, after his mother's funeral, to meet Okigbo at the Citadel Press office. They were having their meeting when suddenly there was an air raid and they dived under tables to take cover. The novelist Nkem Nwankwo was in the office with them on that day and gives a vivid account of that scene:

> … the tocsin of war jarred those of us at the home front out of our mid-day lethargy. It came in the form of an unaccustomed air-raid siren. We all tumbled out of the offices to two major construction ditches nearby. Under the direction of Major Okigbo, we split into two groups: officers, meaning Chinua, Chris and me in one ditch, and the rest in the other. The cause of

the alarm appeared immediately: a cargo plane converted into a bomber, sailing across the horizon like an old, abandoned Goodyear blimp. We watched this huge bird of terror nosing its way blindly in the manner of a whale caught in a dark, becalmed sea. Half a dozen puffs of white smoke had been directed towards the monster from Biafra's homemade air defence guns, but were pitiably short of target…[45]

At the end of the air raid, they rose from their hiding place to see the thick white smoke of a bombed house rising in the horizon, in an area which then seemed close to Chinua Achebe's neighbourhood. They had concluded their business hurriedly and left. Nkem Nwankwo remembered having a sense of premonition as Okigbo drove off. Achebe soon arrived home to discover that the bombed house was indeed his home. There were no casualties, because his wife had gone with their children to Awka to visit Achebe's mother-in-law who was ill at the time; a journey that possibly saved his family. But the bomb scene soon attracted sympathizers. Achebe said: 'And there was Chris lurking around with those sympathisers. I still remember him clearly, in his white buba, mingling with everybody else, and soon he left.'[46]

On this same visit, Christopher Okigbo, accompanied by Emma Oti his batman, called at the office of the poet Gabriel Okara at the Biafra Ministry of Information, to discuss the manuscript of his book of poems which Citadel Press was planning to publish. Gabriel Okara recalled that afternoon when they met – for the last time, as it turned out – they filled the day with tales of the war. Okigbo had talked about the fighting in Nsukka. Okara said of this visit. 'Christopher was very optimistic, very charged by the war.'[47] Okigbo was deeply involved in the battles. He painted the scenes of war, and propounded theories of war and strategies in combat. He regaled Okara with the tales of his numerous exploits on the battlefield, such as when he led an attack on an armoured tank. He even propounded his theory for stopping a military tank in its course of destruction, describing in elaborate detail, the routine of the combatant, He said to Okara, 'When you're attacking a tank, don't go very near … just keep at a distance and aim…'[48] There was something about tanks that fascinated Okigbo. It possibly had to do with his enduring fascination with the clang of iron. As he told his stories to Okara, it was all too obvious that Okigbo was in a state of elation. He relished those moments in battle and the exhilarating sense of danger and drama.

For Okigbo, the Nsukka battles were truly emblematic – 'when true men showed their paces'.[49] He was optimistic about the outcome of the war with the liberation of the East from the mad violence. At one point Gabriel Okara asked Christopher Okigbo to confirm the rumours about his gun running activities into Biafra on behalf of the Eastern government early in the conflict. As Okara recalled, Christopher Okigbo had paused and somewhat ponderously answered: 'You don't really know me Gabriel; I can do many things you know…'[50]

Christopher Okigbo had also called briefly next-door to see his friend Peter Chigbo, the Permanent Secretary of the Ministry of Information and Propaganda. They had also discussed the war. Chigbo remembered of their meeting. 'Chris said he would take some time off to rest after the operations which they were planning. But as far as I could see, he was in great spirits.'[51] He apparently also went to the cabinet office where he visited George Nwanze, and his own secondary school classmate, Austin Ugwumba, who was then Permanent Secretary in the Cabinet office. Finally, Okigbo visited his elder brother, Pius in his office and later at his home on independence layout, where he asked for a quick lunch. He was famished. He wanted pounded yam and egusi soup. His nephew, Dubem Okafor, went quickly to the kitchen, and made lunch for him. The poet ate hurriedly, all the while complaining, as Okafor recalled, that the pounded yam was 'as hard as stone.'[52] Dubem Okafor had been living with Okigbo in Cambridge House in Ibadan before university and was now staying in Pius Okigbo's house on that day when Chris came from the war front, 'complaining of hunger.'[53] Okigbo ate quickly, and 'thereafter he read some of my poems and promised to help squeeze out the water in one of them, the patriotic one I did on Biafra, when, correcting himself said, "If" he came back from war. He never did.'[54] Pius Okigbo recalled years later his impressions of that visit: 'Somehow I feared that Chris was going to die. That day when he visited me, he looked battle drunk.'[55] It does seem that the poet used the opportunity to reassure Pius, who had security reports and was worried about the poet's activities in Nsukka. Everybody worried about his safety. Their father was constantly inquiring about Christopher. Pius used the opportunity to extract a promise from the poet to visit their father the next time he had the opportunity, just as a way of reassuring the old man. Okigbo made a solemn promise. That evening Okigbo rushed back to the base at Opi.

The Biafran Northern sector had stabilized with the 51 Brigade operating successfully on its axis. However two deaths touched the poet Christopher Okigbo in a deep and personal way. Chukwuma Kaduna Nzeogwu was ambushed deep in the Nsukka axis; Tom Bigger, Ojukwu's half-brother, ran into federal troops who opened fire on him in a bend on the Eha-Alumona road. Both were men with whom Okigbo had found deep friendship in Biafra. These deaths opened the poet's eyes further to the harsh reality of war. Up to that time, it had been mostly an adventure. Death was abstract and distant. When Nzeogwu died on 26 July 1967, it reverberated round Biafra. It also coincided with the loss of Bonny Island, Biafra's outlet to the sea. Christopher Okigbo was thrown into one of those few profoundly gloomy moments of his life. War had gradually assumed a deeper, more terrifying guise: from that moment he brooded and seemed more preoccupied. The deaths ignited the quest for heroism among the fighting men in Nsukka. The fallen were celebrated in popular songs. New legends were born about the exploits of the Biafran forces. Nzeogwu's death had also brought about a major, strategic reorganization of the Biafran army. Mosquito sting operations came to a halt and from that moment it was straight warfare. Although Chukwuma Nzeogwu had died without holding any formal command of troops at that time in Biafra, he was deeply involved in the Biafran war plans. He had led increasingly effective bands of guerrillas, including Okigbo's band, which operated independently and with freedom in the Nsukka area.

From highly secret discussions going on at the time in the Biafran high command, Nzeogwu was preparing to assume the strategic command of the Brigade and proposed to lead the Midwestern campaign, or Liberation Army as it was called. With his untimely death it became necessary to change the plan and tactics. Colonel Victor Banjo was then brought in to lead the operations into the Midwest. Okigbo was apparently aware of these plans and started to make arrangements to join the campaign whenever it took off. Okigbo's friend Emma Ifeajuna had joined Victor Banjo. There was a lot of troop movement; by 1 August 1967 the 12th Battalion had moved from the Biafran Northern sector at Nsukka to Onitsha to form the nucleus of the Midwest operation. During the night of 6 August 1967, Christopher Okigbo received a note from Ifeajuna, written with red ink on the torn card of a cigarette pack, inviting the poet to join him at Onitsha. Okigbo had been very excited and was raring to go, '"Yes" he said to Gaius Anoka "let's get there and teach the vandals a lesson!"'[56] He was prepared to drive down to Onitsha the following day to join the Biafran forces, but Gaius Anoka called him aside and dissuaded him. After a long argument, he was able to persuade Okigbo about the folly of his plan to join the operations. 'Chris could most certainly have died in that operation,'[57] Anoka reminisced.

The possibility of death in the Midwest was the trump card that Anoka played with him. He said to Okigbo: 'Chris, think about it, where would you wish most to be remembered to have died fighting?'[58] Okigbo thought deeply about it for a while, and said, 'You know Gaius, you're right. I'd love to be remembered fighting and dying here!' Okigbo's attachment and commitment to Nsukka proved more profound. It was the land of intimate memory, a place that once nurtured and healed him, and allowed his poetry to flourish. This largely informed the poet's will to fight and, if need be, die fighting to liberate Nsukka. It was a decision that was purely nostalgic and senti- mental, as well as underscoring the romantic idealism that drove the poet to war. Anoka insists that it was not the fear of death that stopped Okigbo from joining Emma Ifeajuna and Victor Banjo at Onitsha that day. The poet's complete disdain for death was remarkable. Death held no terror for him. He was rather, sometimes fascinated by the phenomenon of death, and the nature of mortality. Anoka remembered one of those evenings at the Opi Health Centre, when, with Chris Okigbo, Sam Ukpabi and William Uzoaga, he sat down to a peaceful interlude of entertainment, by having Okigbo read his poems. After reading they talked. The subject of mortality crept in, especially after Okigbo read this portion of his 'Elegy for Alto,' which evoked the death wish:

> O mother mother Earth, unbind me; let this be
> my last testament; let this be
> The ram's hidden wish to the sword the sword's
> secret prayer to the scabbard – [59]

Anoka retained a vivid memory of their conversation that evening, one of the last times when they were to have such intimate discussion with the poet. He remembered Okigbo saying: 'You know Gaius, I have enjoyed myself thoroughly. I have seen the world. I have stayed in the best hotels in the world … eaten the best food and drank the best wine. I have lived in the most fantastic houses. What is it? Women? I have loved beautiful women … the best! I have enjoyed myself. And so, if I die now, what does it matter?'[60]

'So, you mean you want to die now. Is that what you're saying?'[61] Anoka had asked him, convinced of Okigbo's reckless sense of destiny.

'No, no … that's not what I mean. What I'm saying is, perhaps it's a lovely thing to die. After all, who knows?'[62] the poet replied. The answer hung in the air, in the silence of the bold night. Meanwhile the battle in the Nsukka sector got fiercer. There were reports by 14 August 1967 of a surging attack by the Federal forces heading towards Ikem. The crack 'C' company led by Tim Onwuatuegwu spearheaded the counter- offensive. In that attack, Anoka had penetrated close to Orba, where he met the British journalist and writer Frederick Forsyth, reporting from the Biafran war for the BBC, who wanted to prove that the Biafran soldiers were still at Nsukka. The battle for Nsukka was bloody.

Georgette Okigbo had volunteered for the International Red Cross and she had organized its camp at Okpatu, only a few kilometers from the Opi Junction to help the early refugees displaced by the sacking of Nsukka. When the war began, with the help and permission of Ojukwu, Georgette Okigbo organized the Red Cross Society and established the first worthwhile links with other Dutch and the French charity groups. She was one of the motivators in Biafra that led to the founding of Médécins Sans

Frontières by a group of French doctors with whom she came into contact. In the early part of the war, she had become deeply involved in caring for the wounded soldiers, and had established the camp at Okpatu to help the early refugees displaced by the sacking of Nsukka. She worked relentlessly and gained the trust and admiration of the soldiers. So it was easy for her to move back and forth from the military camps. The Okpatu camp not only catered for the displaced refugees waiting in the camp, but also cooked for the Biafran soldiers at the war front. Georgette often personally brought Okigbo's food to the Opi base where she had become especially popular with the men. Tim Onwuatuegwu, commander of the 'C' company, where Okigbo sometimes operated, became close to her too.

One of the things Okigbo did in this period was hand into Georgette's care, Chinyere, the girl he had fallen in love with in Biafra. He had told Georgette, 'I want her to stay with you and learn some courage. Take good care of her for me.'[63] Having ensured that Chinyere was in the good hands of his sister-in-law, Christopher Okigbo felt less guilty about going to the war front. Arrangements were made for Chinyere to come and visit the poet occasionally at Opi. Sometimes she brought his food in the company of Georgette. If Okigbo wanted anything at the Okpatu camp, he often sent his young batman Emma Oti. 'I was very proud of Chris. He was very popular with the boys. He fought like a man,'[64] said Georgette twenty-five years afterwards, long after the poet's death at the battlefront. On 16 August 1967, Okigbo's thirty-seventh birthday, Georgette arranged a little birthday party for him with cakes and a birthday card. It was one of her most cherished memories of the poet's last days. Okigbo had appeared in the company of some of his closest friends that night at Okpatu. Georgette recalled that he had been in an unusually pensive mood and seemed preoccupied, almost abrupt. Earlier in the day, he had argued violently with Gaius Anoka, who had seriously reprimanded him on his reckless courting of danger by the way he operated at the war front during the battle at Ikem the previous day. Okigbo was furious and impatient and quite irritated by Gaius. He said to Anoka: 'You do not run, my life for me Gaius. You don't!'[65] And they had argued. So, for most of the day on his birthday, and through the party which Georgette Okigbo organized for him, Okigbo avoided Gaius Anoka. He was remarkably less expressive, given his normal sunny and breezy nature. Georgette made a mental note of that.

However, Okigbo had also been deeply touched by Georgette's gesture which had been planned as a surprise event. Georgette recollected that although pensive he also tried to enjoy himself. As a birthday present, Georgette gave him a collection of his favorite Stan Getz jazz records. It is doubtful that he had time to play those records before his death. Okigbo cut the cake, took a mouthful and afterwards they sang the birthday song. In the end, Okigbo had looked intently at the candle burning out and said 'You have all made me happy today. And I am glad. I hope I have another chance to celebrate another birthday next year at this time … under more peaceful times. Thank you Georgette.'[66] Georgette recalled that the whole event had been very brisk lasting only about thirty minutes. Okigbo did not even sit down during the entire affair. They did not stay too long, for soon Okigbo went off into the night again with his friends, back to Opi and the battlefront.

There was pressure on the Biafran military commander, Brigadier Hillary Njoku to do something spectacular very soon to boost the dwindling morale in Biafra. His command was threatened. Biafra was losing ground. The Federal forces were just miles away from the Biafran capital, and with a resolute push it would capitulate. So on 14 September 1967, Brigadier Njoku held a war conference at Ukehe, in which he outlined his plans, and issued his final directives on a massive military operation which the Biafrans had been planning. One of the objectives was to push the Federal forces out of Nsukka and recapture other Biafran positions in that sector and dig in. It was based on an ambitious operational plan but tragically inadequate tools. For that operation, the Biafran high command was prepared to throw in everything, including the newly formed Armoured Brigade, consisting of the four Biafran 'Red Devils' under the command of Major Kevin Megwa, another of Okigbo's close friends in Biafra. There was excitement in the air, as 'Operation Torch' or 'Op Torch' took shape. The date was fixed for 16 September 1967. This operation would prove to be Christopher Ifekandu Okigbo's last.

At the commencement of the operation, 53 Brigade shelled Federal locations, throwing them into some disarray. The shelling continued till about 9 o'clock in the morning. The objective was for Tim Onwuatuegwu's 15th battalion of the 53 Brigade to move through the Opi-Eha Alumona Road and clear that axis, supported by Kevin Megwa's 'Red Devils,' giving room for Ben Gbulie's 7th battalion to move through the Opi-Nsukka Road and clear it, on the right of Nsukka and re-organize at a little place called Ofoko. When the shelling stopped, the Armoured Brigade led by Kevin Megwa moved out towards its objective. The mood was highly charged. Before Kevin Megwa moved, Gaius Anoka had called him aside and warned him to be in the rear, so that he could be able to control operations and take adequate command in the event of any accident. Gaius Anoka told Major Megwa, that a dead commander was useless in such an operation. Anoka's gesture had infuriated Christopher Okigbo who quickly reprimanded him and told him off angrily: 'Why do you talk of death to a fighting man? Do you want to discourage him!?'[67] Major Megwa had taken the advice, but apparently also put it down to 'cowardice and idleness.' He proceeded in high spirit, leading the column of 'Red Devils' out to war.

Earlier, Colonel Okafor had harassed the Federal Forces with the 'Red Devils' and, as it turned out, the Federal forces were expecting them. Outside Eha-Alumona, Kevin Megwa's column ran into a Federal anti-tank unit which opened fire. The first 'Red Devil' at the head, carrying Kevin Megwa, was hit and set ablaze with the column commander inside. Only one of the 'Red Devils' escaped. Kevin Megwa's death touched Christopher Okigbo profoundly. He began to experience increasing anxiety. Death suddenly lurked with all its menace everywhere. In the evening of 17 September 1967, Christopher Okigbo sent for Georgette to come to him at Opi. When she arrived, the poet was lying on his camp bed with his AK 47 automatic gun beside him. Georgette had brought a bowl of rice and chicken and encouraged him to eat. Georgette had the following recollection about the poet: 'Chris couldn't eat much. He called his boy Emma to take the food and eat. Emma couldn't eat either and Chris suddenly pulled his gun and said fiercely, "Eat that food or I'll shoot you!" It was clear to me that something was disturbing him.'[68] Georgette sat down beside Okigbo who was looking worn and tired. But he still had spirit left in him. He told her that he was feeling ill. Georgette felt his pulse and his temperature and said, 'Ah, but Chris you're not running fever, my darling.'[69] And Okigbo remained silent awhile, with a distant look, caressing his gun lying on the ground beside him. And then suddenly he said to Georgette, 'Madam, I think I'm going to die.'[70] But Georgette discouraged such talk and asked him to take a lot of rest. She assured him that when he had rested he would just be all right in the morning. 'I think you're strained,'[71] she told the poet.

Later that day, in the company of Gaius Anoka and Georgette, Chris Okigbo went over to Colonel Anthony Eze's house, where they chatted over drinks and talked about the operations the following day and other matters. Then they returned to the camp. Apparently Okigbo had gone to discuss his own role in the operations the next day. At the Opi barracks, Georgette asked Okigbo and Anoka what they would like brought for them to eat in the morning. Gaius Anoka asked for Quaker oats and balls of *akara* (bean cake). Okigbo wanted to know what Anoka wanted that kind of food for, which had become a luxury in Biafra since the war began, and mocked him endlessly for being too soft and spoilt. The next day, early in the morning however, Georgette sent somebody from the Okpatu camp to take to Opi a flask of Quaker oats and the balls of *akara*. That day, 18 September 1967, was Okigbo's truly first involvement in any military campaign under direct orders. He was to be part of a reserve unit, left at the Opi Junction to man the rear, while the forward battalions in the 51 and 53 Brigades under Madiebo and Eze fought farther afield. A Biafran bunker had been built at the Opi Junction by Colonel Udeaja, the tough army engineer who was another Umuahian. It was in that bunker that Okigbo and Anoka were sitting over their breakfast of Quaker oats and *akara* when they heard distant shelling. They ran out to verify the situation from their position. They were still trying to get a clear picture of the situation, when Gaius Anoka's batman, Paul Ene, suddenly opened sporadic fire, shouting: 'Enemies! Enemies!' Gaius Anoka slapped him in anger, but mostly to make him quiet, and he asked him if he wanted to kill Biafran men. But the boy swore that he saw a movement of soldiers in the bushes which was not of their own men.

There was sudden confusion in the camp. Men were fleeing from all directions. Anoka advised that they take cover. Okigbo and he began to fire low so as not accidentally to kill their own men. But soon Biafran soldiers began to run and scatter in all directions. Ben Gbulie described those last moments: 'The federal troops were pressing from Ede-Obala and Eha-Alumona simultaneously – a two pronged attack. Chris wanted to get into the bunker. But I tried to stop him with Major Gaius Anoka. The bunker was an obvious deathtrap: there was only one entrance for the bunker, one slate or aperture to the front, facing Ede-Obala. Thus, one could not see the 'enemy' coming from Eha-Alumona. This I explained to him, would be foolhardy; to go into that bunker was suicide. In fact I told him in plain terms that anybody who entered that bunker could regard himself as dead. We both pleaded to Chris not to go there. It hadn't the makings of an adequate military bunker. But he was resolved: he would hear none of it. He was tired of running backwards, tired of hasty withdrawals. Tired of rout against Biafran troops and did not mind if he died defending Biafra from that bunker.'[72]

Biafran troops of the 16th Battalion under Colonel Okon had already pulled out of Ede-Obala, where they had been flushed out. The B Company of the Biafra 53 Brigade had been shelling Abangwu's hotel and while this was going on the Federal forces had assaulted Ede-Obala, burning the market. Just in time, Captain Ananaba had rushed breathlessly to convey this news. Meanwhile, the Biafran troops on the Eha-Alumona axis had been routed and thrown completely into disarray, while the Federal forces were surging forward, towards Opi, firing heavily. Opi was bombarded with a miscellany of weapons and was in fact not defended at all, mostly because the Biafran main forces were forward of the location. As Ben Gbulie said, although it was strategic, Opi was not an ideal place to locate a defensive position, mostly because of its position in the valley. But the poet Okigbo was trying bravely to stop men from running. He wanted quickly to form a defensive position with Ben Gbulie and Gaius Anoka. He had said to Gbulie, 'Ben, we will die here. Let us finish it here!'[73]

Gaius Anoka had sent his batman Paul Ene and Okigbo's batman Emma Oti, back to the base at the Opi Health Centre to get reinforcements to defend Opi. But Okigbo had advised Anoka to go by himself, knowing that the Biafran soldiers were rank-conscious and would listen more readily to him. Gbulie himself with his troop had flanked off to the rear to defend their positions. Okigbo told Gaius Anoka to hurry. Anoka was reluctant but after a while he agreed to go and said to Okigbo: 'Look here Chris, be careful, I know you've been very erratic these past three days. Please don't do any thing foolish.'

'It's okay. I promise...' Okigbo said.

'Promise?'

'Cross my heart,'[74] Anoka recalled him saying as he waved him off. Okigbo had been taking some medication which had made him sleepless, restless and erratic for three days. Just before Anoka left Okigbo at the bunker, he asked him if he had his bullets. Okigbo touched his front pocket and smiled and said he had three left. He always kept five bullets in his pocket. His point was that rather than being caught alive, without ammunition, he would finish himself off with his last reserve.

Gaius Anoka had only walked some yards away, when the shelling became more intense, growing in its iron voice. He looked back at his friend, and saw him standing in the distance. Okigbo waved him on impatiently with his white handkerchief. Anoka indeed only just managed to continue amidst the hail of bullets and intense gunfire. And that was the last he saw of the poet: his recollection of Okigbo remained that shadowy silhouette, of the lone figure standing, waving him on, fearless and resolved to finish it where it all started. For only a few meters away and standing in its menacing ugliness, was an armoured tank belonging to the Federal army, with its turret raised menacingly high, facing Opi, ready to enact its iron testament. Alex Madiebo also gives an account of this final battle in his book *The Nigerian Revolution and the Biafran War*:

> The situation at Nsukka was getting out of hand and further offensives in my sector became meaningless unless that sector was stabilized. The enemy was bull-dozing his way on two axes from Nsukka through Ekwegbe and Ukehe and the resistance being offered by 53 Brigade was no longer effective or impressive. Army Headquarters ordered the despatch of a battalion reinforcement to assist from my Brigade and I moved the First Battalion immediately. A few days later, another battalion was demanded from me. I withdrew the troops around Igumale and despatched them to Enugu. The situation improved but remained far from being stabilized after the Igumale force tried to re-take Opi from the left flanks through Leja. The enemy suffered heavy casualties but retained the initiative. We tried another desperate right-flanking move through Uguozo to Idi south of Opi aimed at cutting the enemy's main line of communication. The operation was initially successful until an immediate armour counter attack by the enemy pushed out our troops. A special task force was armed with grenades, mines and explosives and other incendiaries in addition to their personal weapons. They displayed such gallantry and bravery and inflicted so much casualty to men and equipment that the enemy punitive bombardments, as a result of that offensive, went on throughout the following day, directed against all towns and villages within range of their guns and mortars. The greatest disaster of that operation was the well-known poet, Major Christopher Okigbo, one of the bravest fighters on that sector, who died trying to lob a grenade into a ferret armoured car.[75]

It was the same armoured tank which Gaius Anoka had seen earlier. Ironically, armoured tanks fascinated Christopher Okigbo. He associated them with extreme violence. Okigbo's 'Lament of the Drums' resonates with this absolute fascination with tanks, which Okigbo believed had such tremendous prowess in war:

Thunder of tanks of giant iron steps of detonators.
Fail safe from the clearing we implore you:[76]

Okigbo had a far too simple, perhaps even romantic knowledge of military tanks. He was awed by their efficacy. He believed, as he used to tell his friend, Torch Taire, that with just one armoured tank anyone could sack an entire country or take over a government. He probably took that belief too far into consideration when he made his final gambit: when he mounted that tank to lob his grenade it was to prevent the possibility of the Saladin tank from taking its 'giant iron steps' and making its fatal 'iron testament' on Biafran positions. He died fighting. It was during the rainy season. And the rains were particularly heavy that September.

## NOTES

1  Interview with Judith Safi Attah, Lagos, 1992.
2  Ibid.
3  Colin Legum, 'The Massacre of the Proud Ibos', *Observer* London, 16 October 1966.
4  Ibid.
5  Ibid.
6  Interview with Wole Soyinka, Abeokuta, 1992.
7  Interview with Susan Anakwenze, Nsukka, 1994.
8  Nkem Nwankwo, *Shadow of the Masquerade* (Nashville, TN: Niger House Publications, 1994).
9  John de St. Jorre, *The Brother's War* (Boston: Houghton Mifflin, 1972).
10  Interview with Sunday Anozie, Port Harcourt, 1992.
11  John de St. Jorre, *The Brother's War*.
12  Interview with Ben Obumselu, Lagos, 1992.
13  Interview with Torch Taire, Lagos, 1992.
14  Interview with Chinua Achebe, Ogidi, 1998.
15  Interview with Ben Obumselu.
16  Nkem Nwankwo, *Shadow of the Masquerade*.
17  Interview with Chinua Achebe.
18  Interview with Ken Saro-Wiwa, Lagos, 1992.
19  Ibid.
20  Interview with Georgette Okigbo, Ilupeju, Lagos, 1992.
21  Interview with Susan Anakwenze, Nsukka, 1994.
22  Interview with Georgette Okigbo.
23  Ibid.
24  Ibid.
25  Bernard Odogwu, *No Place to Hide: Crises and Conflicts Inside Biafra* (Enugu: Fourth Dimension, 1985).
26  Interview with Georgette Okigbo.
27  Ben Obumselu, 'Christopher Okigbo: A Poetic Portrait'. Essay delivered at 'Song for Idoto': A Celebration of Christopher Okigbo, National Museum, Enugu, 2 November 1996.
28  Interview with Tony (Anthony) Eze, Surulere, Lagos, 1992.
29  Ibid.
30  Interview with Ben Gbulie, Queen's School, Enugu, 1992.
31  Ibid.
32  Interview with Gaius Anoka, Owerri, 1992.

33  Ibid.
34  Ibid.
35  Ibid.
36  Ezenwa-Ohaeto, *Chinua Achebe: A Biography* (Oxford: James Currey, 1997).
37  Ben Obumselu, 'Christopher Okigbo: A Poetic Portrait'.
38  Interview with Gaius Anoka.
39  Ibid.
40  Ibid.
41  Ibid.
42  Ibid.
43  Ibid.
44  Bernard Odogwu, *No Place to Hide.*
45  Nkem Nwankwo, *Shadow of a Masquerade.*
46  Interview with Chinua Achebe.
47  Interview with Gabriel Okara, Port Harcourt, 1993.
48  Ibid.
49  Ibid.
50  Ibid.
51  Interview with Peter Chigbo, Umuoji, 1993.
52  Dubem Okafor, e-mail to the author, 25 Feb. 2002.
53  Ibid.
54  Interview with Pius Okigbo, Lagos, 1992.
55  Ibid.
56  Interview with Gaius Anoka.
57  Ibid.
58  Ibid.
59  Christopher Okigbo, *Path of Thunder, Labyrinths with Path of Thunder* (London: Heinemann, 1971).
60  Interview with Gaius Anoka.
61  Ibid.
62  Ibid.
63  Interview with Georgette Okigbo.
64  Ibid.
65  Ibid.
66  Interview with Georgette Okigbo.
67  Interview with Gaius Anoka.
68  Interview with Georgette Okigbo.
69  Ibid.
70  Ibid.
71  Ibid.
72  Interview with Ben Gbulie, Enugu, 1992.
73  Ibid.
74  Interview with Gaius Anoka.
75  Alexander A. Madiebo, *The Nigerian Revolution and the Biafran War* (Enugu: Fourth Dimension, 1980) pp. 165–166.
76  Christopher Okigbo. 'Lament of the Drums', *Silences, Labyrinths.*

# Epilogue

An old star departs, leaves us here on the shore
Gazing heavenward for a new star approaching;
The new star appears, foreshadows its going
Before a going and coming that goes on forever

('Elegy for Alto', *Path of Thunder*)

The cloud was darkening by 7 o'clock in the evening of 18 September 1967. Things were moving at a frenetic pace. There was much activity as stray soldiers, running away from the heat of battle, wounded and shell-shocked soldiers, poured into the camp at Okpatu where Georgette was working, overwhelmed by the casualties. She tended the numerous wounded, some of whom had been evacuated from the scenes of the carnage barely in one piece. She was keeping an eye on the road nevertheless, waiting for when Christopher Okigbo would storm into the camp in his loud and boisterous manner.[1]

The confusion at the war front had seeped gradually into the Red Cross camp as friends, relations, colleagues and lovers of the soldiers besieged the camp to assure themselves of the safety of their own. Sometimes she would hear a piercing wail joining the echo of the voices of mourners. Someone would have discovered a close relation among the dead. Christopher Okigbo's body was not among the dead recovered that day. The night wore on. Just about a few minutes past 8 o'clock that evening, it had grown eerily dark, and something unusual happened to Georgette. She related the incident: 'At about 8 o'clock when they brought in this young man, I was still busy. There were many injured men. But I recognized him instantly, because I knew him as one of those young, medical students who sometimes helped us at the camp. He was saying: "help me, I'm going to die" – now, I'm a Catholic, I swear to God, I'm not superstitious – but that was Christopher's voice! It came through clearly to me. Something strange happened to me instantly: and I have never been able to explain it to myself, but it was in that moment somehow, that I knew that Chris was dead.'[2]

Then she felt a strange, gnawing fear. But in spite of her premonition she kept hoping – a futile hope as it turned out that he would emerge from somewhere in his usual sudden manner, still full of enthusiasm and, as usual, bearing his numerous tales of adventure. For Gaius Anoka, it never once crossed his mind that day that the poet might have been killed. 'For two days,' Anoka said, 'no one really looked for him. We just thought Chris would appear, somehow.'[3] Gaius Anoka thought that Okigbo would take one of the detours through Enugu-Ezike which Biafran soldiers often used to escape from enemy territory.

On 20 September 1967, two days later, the shocking news of Okigbo's death came through the radio. Georgette was already drained of all emotions and could not cry. She stared blearily into the distance, the fleeting image of the poet becoming suddenly lost in the instant opaqueness of memory. She shed no tears; she only piled up an emotional dam, which would burst later on. But Chinyere, his young lover whom Okigbo had entrusted to Georgette for 'safe keep,' was inconsolable: she mourned Okigbo, bursting into a loud wail at the news of his death. She remained dazed for days. The tragedy was a mortal wound for Gaius Anoka who was shocked beyond words. Tim Onwuatuegwu had met Georgette and said, in a voice choked with emotion: 'Madam, with Chris dead, something in Biafra is dead.'⁴ William Uzoaga was too deeply affected by Christopher Okigbo's death, so much that he just could not take it any more. He had watched in a a few short weeks, how the war led to the deaths of such remarkable men as C.K. Nzeogwu, Tom Bigger and Kevin Megwa. Christopher Okigbo's death was the limit. It was William Uzoaga's last time at the war front. Sam Ukpabi also moved on, after the death of one with whom he had found companionship in the trenches – whose burgeoning laughter, ceaseless energy and poetry stole the moments away from the darkness, the curious fatalism of the war front where death, ever constant, sapped the will of men. The novelist Chinua Achebe himself had given an account of his own reaction to Okigbo's death in his introduction to *Don't Let Him Die*, a collection of memorial poetry to Christopher Okigbo, published in 1978 and edited with Dubem Okafor. (This also, was Achebe's son's profound, but innocent wish to his father, who alas, had no such powers, as children often think their fathers do, of reversing mortality).

Achebe was driving to his country home at Ogidi when he heard the news of Okigbo's death on his car radio. Numbed by the announcement, he quickly pulled off the road to allow the reality of his friend's death to sink in. All over Biafra, the death of the poet had settled heavily on the public consciousness. He became the folk hero, in so many of those songs which inspired Biafran young men to great heroic acts. One of the most memorable has been quoted in the edition of collected essays on Okigbo edited by Donatus Nwoga:

| | |
|---|---|
| *Enyi o, enyi o o –* | Elephants, O Elephants - |
| *Enyi Biafra alala* | Biafra's Elephant is gone |
| | |
| *Enyi o, enyi o o –* | Elephants, O Elephants - |
| *Enyi Biafra alala* | Biafra's Elephant is gone |
| | |
| *Chetakwanu Chris Okigbo –* | O Remember Chris Okigbo |
| *Chris Okigbo bu enyi Biafra* | Chris Okigbo is Biafra's Elephant |
| | |
| *Chetakwanu Aguiyi-Ironsi –* | O Remember Aguiyi-Ironsi |
| *Aguiyi-Ironsi bu enyi Biafr* | Aguiyi-Ironsi is Biafra's Elephant |
| | |
| *Chetakwanu C.K. Nzeogwu* | O Remember C. K. Nzeogwu |
| *C. K. Nzeogwu bu enyi Biafra* | C. K. Nzeogwu is Biafra's Elephant |

A shocked world was roused to the ghastliness of the Civil War in Nigeria, speechless at the tragic end of the passionate, volatile and highly gifted poet – one of the last century's finest, cut in the middle of the growth of the genius and power of his poetry, just one month after his thirty-seventh birthday. His friend, the poet Peter Thomas, was alone in his apartment in Salt Lake City, Michigan, where he had gone to teach at the university, when he heard that Christopher Okigbo had been killed near Nsukka, where they had met first and found a kinship through poetry. Peter Thomas phoned one of their mutual friends in New York, who confirmed to him Okigbo's death. There was a deep sadness in the wind, that snowy gray December evening which matched his mood. The Welsh poet looked down town to the neon sign atop Walker Bank, stunned, disbelieving, weeping. Suddenly he said aloud 'Oh, Chris, what a stupid way to go. Now I really am alone in all the world.'[5] And he wrote 'A Triptych of Memory (for Chris at Heavensgate).'

General Alex Madiebo summed up the impact of Okigbo's death in Biafra. The Biafran army commander declared in his memoir, *The Nigerian Revolution and the Biafran War.* 'The whole Army in general and the 53 Brigade in particular never completely got over his death for the rest of the war.'[6] Okigbo's death according to Ben Obumselu might have been a factor, which caused the major re-organization in the Biafran Army in the period. It was possibly remotely connected to the brief detention of Brigadier Hilary Njoku, the Biafran Military Commander, who was blamed for the failure of the operations in Biafra's northern sector where the poet died. The most important thing, however, was that in death Christopher Okigbo became a cult hero. His example, invoked in songs and heroic lyrics, inspired thousands of Biafran youths who identified with his 'martyrdom,' and were drawn to remarkable acts of heroism, fighting against that which led the poet to war in the first place: the decimation of a people in one of the greatest genocides of the twentieth century. The spirit of the Biafran struggle – a struggle which encompassed a people's attempt to protect their violated humanity – became synonymous with the life and times of Christopher Okigbo. Death redeemed Okigbo; it did not destroy him. The novelist Nkem Nwankwo observed eloquently that: '… in some unmarked grave in the Nsukka bush; the world's worst employee, worst husband and father, finally redeemed himself, was translated, like Palinurus, to immortality.'[7]

At Christopher Okigbo's funeral in Ojoto the background thunder of war was drawing closer to Idoto's habitation. The poet's father James Okoyeodu Okigbo had aged suddenly. He replayed in a symbolic sense, the tragic figure of Ezeulu the priest–patriarch of Umuaro, in Chinua Achebe's *Arrow of God* at the death of his favourite son, the tempestuous Obierika. James Okigbo never really recovered from his son's death. At Christopher's funeral, the old school master cut the figure of tragedy itself, walking about the compound listlessly, unable to come to terms with death, unable to reconcile his son's violent exit, 'eaten by the war.' His aunt Eunice, Okigbo's childhood nurse, was disconsolate. She broke intermittently into heart-rending dirges, often going to stand sadly before the poet's picture, which they just managed to find. Eunice loved Christopher so much that she had willed her house in Ahoada to him – her favourite of Anna's children. Pius Okigbo managed to keep a bold face and hide the deep pain of his private loss of a brother, a friend and a kindred spirit. Perhaps the one man who suffered the greatest grief was the poet's eldest brother, Lawrence. The war had brought them closer. They were beginning to achieve a greater understanding of each other at this stage of their lives. Lawrence, unused to having Christopher coming so close, was shattered when the news of his death was brought to him in that cable from the Government Lodge. He would never understand why his brother had to go at that stage. Only a few weeks before his death, Okigbo had rushed into his home in Enugu, had a hurried lunch, and left for the final time. This was the image that Lawrence retained: the hurrying shadow of his tempestuous younger brother – hurrying on to his death.

A few months after the poet's death, Lawrence's wife was delivered of a baby boy whom they named 'Christopher.' The strange thing, however, was that the little boy came with the same birthmarks on the neck and 'bullet marks' on the backside. So he was believed to be the poet re-incarnated. It was a belief more so sustained, because the two shared a strong physical and emotional resemblance. The Okigbos like most Igbo, although serious Roman Catholics, still held firmly to the belief of reincarnation present in *Odinala* – the Igbo belief system. Christopher Okigbo himself was convinced of his own reincarnation of his maternal grandfather – Ikejiofor – Priest of the Ajani shrine. There was a highly spiritual aspect to Okigbo's personality. The poet of *Labyrinths*, descendant of a lineage of priests in Ojoto, invoked the cult mystery of the water goddess around his poetic endeavour. But he was also fundamentally secular, a product of a hybrid imagination which combined both the dimensions of his secular humanism with the heritage of his traditional background and past. He lived, at least psychologically, as much in the dense mystery of that priesthood – of the prodigal priest-artist returning home through his timeless odyssey. The idea of his reincarnation replays itself in the unending cycle of life – the theme of self-renewal, of the eternal return of the seasons, as the basis of his poetry. With the birth of the child to Lawrence, it seemed that the cycle had truly perpetuated itself, and continued in 'a going and coming that goes on forever.'[8] Okigbo lived a life of contradictions, but he balanced his contradictions elegantly. He was almost always greatly misunderstood.

In his lifetime, Okigbo affected the image of the joyous epicurean. As Ben Obumselu said:

> Perhaps the reason why everybody liked Christopher was because he reduced life to laughter, to a great joke: he lifted the burdens of existence from many of us and carried it on own his shoulders. I mean, most of us took life too seriously: Christopher, in Ibadan, would dance always to the clatter of the typewriter as his typist typed along, just to make the man happy! He was quite unserious with life. And I also think we were unfair to him because we took him for granted, we failed to see that through his poetry, which was the thing that most mattered to him, Okigbo demanded understanding![9]

The essence of Okigbo's life was his poetry. He began to write it essentially to achieve a reconciliation with his own difficult past and stimulate some creative meaning from the complexity of his own colonial experience. Leslie Harriman said that his poetry was 'a furtherance of the passion of his life, which was to make other people happy. Christopher's career as poet began, I can say, simply to create laughter.'[10] Okigbo retained the passionate commitment of his friends. Torch Taire said that this was because he 'was absolutely committed and dedicated to friendship. Once he liked you, you could be sure he would do anything for you. In fact, anybody who truly knew Chris would accept that his friends were his life, closer to him than many of his relations. Once you were his friend, you were family.'[11] Okigbo had a pagan soul, and it was, like Virgil's Daphnis, more beautiful than was his poetry.

Christopher Okigbo's life can never be fully captured in a single narrative. He was far too fascinating an individual to fit into an easy mould. He retained, among his friends, a constant presence, undying because he was too real, and too vivid an individual to die. Once, in Professor James Ezeilo's home on the campus of the University of Nigeria, Nsukka, Okigbo had cropped up as the subject of discussion. Ezeilo suddenly began to hiccup. The hiccup persisted, and Ezeilo, declared: 'Oh yes, that is Chris. He must be having fun on me somewhere, now!'[12] The most memorable aspect about Okigbo's life is the impact he had on people with the exuberance and energy of his personality. Okigbo was known for acts of extreme generosity: he could go to dramatic lengths even at personal discomfort, to make people happy – to entertain.

Christopher Okigbo attracted friendship and loyalty with great ease, mostly because of his openness, and a temperament which demanded nothing of others, but an original life. An important description of Okigbo is contained in Nkem Nwankwo's assertion that:

> Chris's nature is such that he was incapable of bearing a grudge. He could be thick-skinned; incredibly callous; he could leave you in the lurch and calmly walk away while you cleaned the mess. His nature transcended duty, as well as morality; but he also allowed to others the same freedom from guilt or obligation as he took for himself. He was the least judgmental person you ever saw. His sunny disposition shone on everyone alike, friend or foe, as if enmity didn't matter, in fact as if he didn't know the word.[13]

An aspect of Okigbo's irreconcilable contradictions is reflected in his capacity to be at once capable of acts of selfish and emotional cruelty, and at the same time acts of extreme selflessness and kindness. He was amoral, yet extremely fascinated by the depth of individual moral character, humane and yet sometimes capable of callousness, dramatic and at once shy. He was possibly tortured by self doubt, and in many of the extreme actions for which he was noted – his bragging after sexual conquest, his competitiveness, his sense of the impresario – he was reflecting a deep fear, the need to be loved. He was a lonely person who, in the final analysis, found a voice to express his profound melancholy through poetry. He was bourgeois, bohemian and liberated; he expressed his disdain for form or convention, for the cant of Christian morality and freed himself from the repressions of his sexuality in childhood.

Okigbo admired brilliant and capable people. His own circle included some of the outstanding men of his generation, with whom he shared a lifetime in the search for true meaning. It was the great age of the intellectual aristocrat in modern Africa. An aristocracy fostered on a cult of individualism, of the libertine, and of excellence. Society could excuse them, because they were 'geniuses.' Africa was in the threshold of modern history in which those few elect – the equivalent of Dubois' 'talented tenth' – would be empowered to transform her, to lead her through the doorway of the century. Christopher Okigbo believed in the duties and obligations of the elect to his society. Except that his was tempered by a certain Whitmanesque exuberance which craved for a collective or shared experience, for a certain excitement and quest for friendship beyond the familiar barriers, across race, gender or social status. He was a citizen of the world with a global, cosmopolitan imagination. Yet his true friends were older people wizened by time. It is also without doubt that, through friendship, Okigbo tried to fill the gnawing void of his own inner conflicts, that part of his humanity that was utterly vulnerable. He suffered greatly from emotional insecurity and his brother Pius Okigbo, in a psychoanalytical way, suggested that might be the result of his mother Anna's death when Christopher was such a young boy – that death compounded the inner conflicts and melancholy of his childhood. Okigbo's loneliness was deep and private.

Nowhere better than in Okigbo's poetry, can we find him more alive. His death vexed the Kenyan scholar Ali Mazrui' so much, that he questioned and condemned the poet's choice of martyrdom, of his choice of death over art in his novel *The Trial of Christopher Okigbo*. Christopher Okigbo died the way he loved: with drama. Okigbo had discovered in the conflicts of a deeply experiential life his true vocation as a poet. He lived it and loved life to his death. He was without a care in the world. He expressed this carefreeness in his life in the way he lived: by scant regard for convention, by his relationship with his women, by his poetry, by his great echoing laughter, by the openness of his spirit, by the generosity of his soul, by his friendship, by the open doors of his house, by his extreme informality, by his Whitmanesque temperament and largeness which often proclaimed: 'I contain a multitude.' Even if his life was short, he produced enchanting poetry: dramatic and eventful, with tragic denouement. Christopher Okigbo's poetry is the result of the widest range of personal contacts, and experience – a vast knowledge of the world, ultimately affected by the humanistic education that he acquired. It is reflected in the universalism of this poetry, in its many cadenced appropriations. Okigbo was also a deeply observant poet, who utterly captured the profound, most essential impulses of life – from the transmutation of photosynthetic matter, to that inseparable union between body and spirit, which Anozie has described as the basis of Okigbo's neoplatonic poetics.

Okigbo's vast poetic universe is thus located in the context of his intriguing personal history as well as in all history collectively experienced, in life lived in a concise social context. Okigbo's poetry therefore can be explained as a man's apprehension of his life, of his universe, and of the social events which construct it: from the beginning till the end or as the poet puts it: 'from Dan to Beersheeba.'[14] Okigbo's poetry is passionate and autobiographical. It seeks to relate the most significant moments of an age, and voices the historical dilemma of his generation as few other voices have attempted in modern African literature. The range of influences which affected this poetry, from the biblical to traditional mysticism, from the classical to the modern, even the post-modern literary styles, is explored by Okigbo in the mannered tension of a keen and universal vision of art and life. Okigbo was incapable of accepting racism or ethnic boundaries, either in terms of the aesthetics of his poetry or in the context of the life he lived. Possible evidence of this was his preference to edit *Transition* rather than *Black Orpheus*.

Okigbo rejected such artificial boundaries to the capacity of human expressions of love, beauty and the fullness life. He rejected anything that limited his humanity. As he said in his letter to Sunday Anozie on 5 May 1966: 'I found the whole idea of a Negro Arts Festival based on color quite absurd. I did not enter any work for the competition, and was most surprised when I heard a prize had been awarded to *Limits*. I have written to reject it.'[15] Okigbo was not just being petulant, nor was he rejecting his Africanness. He was also as much protecting his own unique place, both as an individual and as an artist when he declared: 'There is no such thing as African writing. There is only good or bad writing!'[16] He was only emphasizing his universal humanity – much in the same way he reacted to Professor Philip Bordinat at the University Library at Nsukka. Christopher Okigbo had dramatized his disgust for racism in an extreme manner one evening in the company of some of his friends at Ibadan. Among them was Ignatius Atigbi, the West African Regional correspondent for Reuters. They had gone out in the company of three European women, one of whom was a teacher at Queen's School, Ede. One of the women made comments which Christopher Okigbo felt were intolerably racist. He excused himself and drove into the night: 'On his way he picked three prostitutes around Oke Padre who were sufficiently black.'[17] He came back to the Paradise Club, where his friends and the three European ladies were waiting for him and cheerfully announced to everybody: 'Gentlemen, these are our companies tonight. Take your pick!'[18] The ladies were horrified, and they protested. Okigbo's point was made.

So, what would lead Okigbo then to abandon his place as a chronicler to accepting a death fighting for his 'beleaguered people?'[19] What would force Okigbo, the nationalist and universalist, to throw his weight solidly behind the secessionist East?

When history reconciles these contradictions, then an understanding of Okigbo's actions will be revealed. Okigbo scholars may then also understand the poet's agony at the disintegration of Nigeria, whose independence, earlier in 1960, symbolized his own rebirth. The poet had clearly spent his life establishing friendship and other intimate relationships, and living within the experience of an organic society, in the Nigerian federation, and at the final separation as it seemed then, he was accepting a tragic and inevitable fact, albeit painfully. If we listen to Georgette Okigbo, who was one of the closest people to the poet during the war, Okigbo fought not for political considerations alone, but to guard against the siege upon the habitation of Idoto, and against the profanation of the citadel of knowledge which the university town Nsukka, 'where his poetry blossomed,'[20] symbolized. He often talked about the 'vandals at the gate … at the tower,'[21] a refrain, which Anoka remembers as part of a now lost poem. Like many intellectuals of his generation, there was a deep disappointment in the failure of Nigeria. When the time came, Okigbo saw only the extreme implications: the grey line between salvation and disintegration.

It has been suggested that he was quite naive and romantic in his idealism in the Biafran war. So, was he only dramatizing his own private fantasies? Did he go to the war front acting as García Lorca who had died during the Spanish Civil War? He was always fascinated by Lorca's prediction that he would die in the war and that his body would never be recovered. Mystery appealed intensely to Okigbo's imagination. On the other hand, did Okigbo go to the war in search of that intense experience, which fed the creative life of poets? He aspired to write his own 'Anabasis' – to sculpt his most ambitious poetic testament in that period, with the growth of a new voice, and its mantic chants. So perhaps he wanted the closest contact with pain and death, with the intense experience, which would transform his genius into new invocation. Unfortunately, Christopher Okigbo perished with his dreams. He had described his large prose work, *Pointed Arches* to Anozie as: '…neither fiction nor criticism nor Autobiography. It is an attempt to describe the growth of the creative impulse in me, an account of certain significant facts in my experience of life and letters that conspired to sharpen my imagination. It throws some light on certain apparently irreconcilable features of my work and life, and places them in a new perspective. I am hoping for publication by 1970.'[22] This manuscript was possibly eaten by termites at his abandoned home at the hill top, near the colliery mines, in Enugu. Okigbo was a consummate impresario who, before he was thirty-five, had already fashioned an autobiography for himself. He also fancied himself a good dresser, often in his time appearing in his white tuxedo and black bow tie, the appurtenances of his sigma-club years at the University College, Ibadan. Years later he would adopt khaki shorts and open-necked short-sleeved shirts in the free spirit of the Beatnik craze of the 1950s and 1960s. He became so comfortable in the casualness of his dressing, that he literally had no other dress code, from 1958, by which time he had dispensed with the formalism of the 'high societies' and the 'mad generation' and the 'sonorous arguments' of the top brass.

Okigbo's body was found and buried, as it is now clear, in an unmarked mass grave. Georgette Okigbo said: 'Chris's body was discovered and identified by Nigerian soldiers, and what I know is, it was buried somewhere, but not in Igboland. Christopher's body is lying somewhere else, possibly Kaduna.'[23] He would have loved that his body never be found, thus sustaining that mystique, the mystery of his own transfiguration. If he had a chance he would have pontificated and argued relentlessly on several reasons why his body must not be discovered. He would just as soon deprecate anyone, for daring to do that! That was Christopher Okigbo – a great mythmaker – whose life symbolized one man's constant attempt at experiencing life as poet, civil servant, businessman, school teacher, librarian, soldier, classic scholar, arms runner, cricketer, epicurean and, above all, as Idoto's reconciled prodigal. With his death, the poet became one of the most fascinating figures in the history of modern African literature. He personified the life of the intellectual aristocrat who preferred a commitment to justice and who offered himself in martyrdom, disdaining the secure existence of the intellectual observatory. He was the quintessential *'l'homme engagé'* – the intellectual man of action, one of the greatest figures of resistance in the modern era, product of the idealism of his generation – those born at the confluence of cultures, who tried to force change violently and failed. Christopher Ifekandu Okigbo is the poet of his generation against whom every other poet will be measured. Okigbo's place in the canon of modern twentieth-century poetry is summed up by Sunday Anozie:

> Nothing can be more tragic to the world of African poetry in English than the death of Christopher Okigbo, especially at a time when he was beginning to show maturity and coherence in his vision of art, life and society, and a greater sophistication in poetic form and phraseology. Nevertheless his output, so rich and severe within so short a life, is sure to place him among the best and the greatest of our time.[24]

*Path of Thunder*, his last poems written before the war, was published posthumously in *Black Orpheus* in February 1968, five months after the poet's death. It was startling. He had written with a deep and inspired urgency:

> The glimpse of a dream lies smouldering in a cave,
> together with the mortally wounded birds.
> Earth, unbind me; let me be the prodigal; let this be
> the ram's ultimate prayer to the tether... .[25]

The Earth took heed. The Republic of Biafra awarded him a posthumous order of merit and Chukwuemeka Odumegwu-Ojukwu, in honor to his personal friendship and admiration for the poet, named his own son born in that period, 'Okigbo.' So indeed, even though the star had departed, there would be generations after him in a 'going and coming that goes on forever...'[26] That was why Okigbo fought: his insistence that his lineage be not wiped from the earth; that the promise of cyclic return is maintained at the forge of life.

## NOTES

1  Interview with Georgette Okigbo, Ilupeju, Lagos, 1992.
2  Ibid.
3  Interview with Gaius Anoka, Owerri, 1992.
4  Interview with Georgette Okigbo.
5  Peter Thomas, Letter to the author, 1992.
6  Alex Madiebo, *The Nigerian Revolution and the Biafran War* (Enugu: Fourth Dimension, 1980).
7  Nkem Nwankwo, *Shadow of the Masquerade* (Nashville, TN: Niger House Publications, 1994).
8  Christopher Okigbo, 'Path of Thunder', *Labyrinths with Path of Thunder* (London: Heinemann, 1971) pp. 63–72.
9  Interview with Ben Obumselu, Lagos, 1994.
10  Interview with Leslie Harriman, Lagos, 1992.
11  Interview with Torch Taire, Lagos, 1994.

12  Interview with James Ezeilo, UNN, Nsukka, 1992.

13  Nkem Nwankwo, *Shadow of the Masquerade.*

14  Christopher Okigbo, *Distances, Labyrinths.*

15  Christopher Okigbo's letter to Sunday Anozie, 5 May 1966, quoted in *Creative Rhetoric* (New York: Africana Publishers, 1971).

16  Dennis Duerden, interview, 1963, with Christopher Okigbo, *African Writers Talking* (eds) Dennis Duerden and Cosmo Pieterse (London: Heinemann, 1972).

17  Interview with Ignatius Atigbi, Lagos, 1994.

18  Ibid.

19  Colin Legum, 'The Massacre of the Proud Ibos', *Observer*, London, 16 October 1966, p. 12.

20  Interview with Georgette Okigbo.

21  Interview with Gaius Anoka.

22  Christopher Okigbo's letter to Sunday Anozie.

23  Interview with Georgette Okigbo.

24  Interview with Sunday Anozie, Port Harcourt, 1993.

25  Christopher Okigbo, 'Elegy for Alto', *Path of Thunder.*

26  Ibid.

# Index

268

# Index

272